Metalwork

R. SANDHAM

Principal Lecturer in Charge of Metalwork, Loughborough College of Education,
Tutor in Metalwork, Loughborough College of Education Summer School,
Advisory Committee for Craftwork, Moderator for Craftwork (Metal),
and Assistant Examiner in Craftwork, Associated Examining Board

F. R. WILLMORE
D.P.L., D.L.C.Hons., M.C.C.Ed.

Senior Lecturer in Metalwork, Loughborough College of Education,
Examiner in Metalwork, City & Guilds of London Institute, South Western Examinations Board,
Assistant Examiner in Metalwork, Associated Examining Board

First published 1962
Reprinted 1963, 1964, 1966, 1967
Second edition 1971
Reprinted 1971, 1972, 1974

Published by Edward Arnold (Publishers) Ltd
25 Hill Street, London W1X 8LL

ISBN 0 7131 3246 9

Printed in Great Britain by
Fletcher & Son Ltd, Norwich

Preface to Second Edition

In this revised edition, Chapters 1 and 2 on the manufacture of Iron, Steel and Non-ferrous Metals and Alloys have been rewritten to bring them into line with current methods and Chapter 3 on Marking out, Measuring and Testing has had considerable alterations. All units and illustrations have been metricated. Chapter 11 on Lathework has been considerably revised particularly on the cutting of metric screwthreads. All reference to Imperial units has been removed from the text but some British Standard and appropriate conversion tables have been retained in the Appendices. All the examination questions have been extracted from more recent papers and some from CSE boards are included.

The first edition has been extremely well received and we feel has satisfied a real need in both secondary schools and colleges. The authors sincerely trust that this revised edition will continue to satisfy this need.

The authors wish to thank numerous engineering firms for the continued use of illustrations and for supplying new ones where necessary.

The examination questions are reproduced by kind permission of the GCE and CSE examining boards listed on page 247 for which the authors also express grateful thanks.

R.S.
F.R.W.

Preface to the First Edition

This work has been prepared to meet the needs of pupils working for O, and A, level General Certificate Examinations in Metalwork and Engineering Workshop Theory and Practice. It also covers the syllabus of the City and Guilds Handicraft Teachers Certificate (Metalwork) and is suitable for use by students in Training Colleges taking Metalwork as a main subject. Candidates preparing for the General Course in Engineering (Workshop Processes and Materials) and the early stages of the Mechanical Engineering Technicians course and practising teachers wishing to add Metalwork to their qualifications are amply catered for.

The authors are practical and experienced metalworkers and teachers. Both have industrial experience and have taught in Schools and both Technical and Training Colleges. Wherever possible, information and advice on how to do a job and why it is done in a particular way, and not merely what to do, have been incorporated. Sound traditional methods are emphasized, for the authors are firmly convinced that unless proper regard is given to fundamental principles in the early stages of metalwork teaching no scheme can be progressively successful. Expediency has no place in honest teaching.

Authorities generally agree that there is a need to improve the standards of practical craftsmanship. If this book in any way helps to rebuild the standards and enhance our national reputation as craftsmen, the authors will be well satisfied.

1962

R.S.
F.R.W.

ACKNOWLEDGEMENTS

The authors wish to take this opportunity of thanking the Principal of the Loughborough Training College for his encouragement during the preparation of this book.

They also wish to acknowledge the assistance of the numerous engineering firms who kindly supplied illustrations and blocks. These are individually acknowledged under the appropriate illustrations.

Finally, the General Certificate of Education Examination questions at the end of the book are reproduced by kind permission of the Examining Boards listed on page 247, to whom the authors express grateful acknowledgements.

Contents

Abbreviations

$$\begin{aligned}
\text{mm} &= \text{millimetre} \\
\text{cm} &= \text{centimetre} \\
\text{m} &= \text{metre} \\
\text{g} &= \text{gramme} \\
\text{kg} &= \text{kilogramme} \\
\text{cm}^3 &= \text{cubic centimetre} \\
\text{l} &= \text{litre} \\
\text{m/s} &= \text{metre per second} \\
\text{m/min} &= \text{metre per minute} \\
\text{rev/min} &= \text{revolution per minute} \\
°\text{C} &= \text{degree Celsius} \\
\text{dia} &= \text{diameter} \\
\text{t.p.i.} &= \text{threads per inch} \\
\text{s.w.g.} &= \text{standard wire gauge} \\
\text{H.S.S.} &= \text{High-speed Steel}
\end{aligned}$$

1 Iron and Steel

The discovery, manufacture and working of metals has been one of man's outstanding achievements and is possibly the largest single factor in his material well-being. Of the metals used by man, the most important are undoubtedly those of the *ferrous* group, i.e. those that consist largely of ferrite or iron. Such materials are of three basic forms, wrought iron, cast iron and steel. The manufacture of these materials has developed over a long period of history for, although the element iron is common and is widely distributed over the earth's crust, it occurs naturally in ores in combination with other elements together with earthy and unwanted material called *gangue*. It is the extraction of the iron from its ore and its manufacture into the various types of ferrous metal, each with its own distinctive properties, that has concerned man for so long and that is of fundamental interest to all metalworkers. It is important that a student of metalwork should know something of this development, together with the methods of manufacture, for when using metal in the workshop he is not manipulating just a raw material, but is working and shaping a substance developed as a result of much accumulated knowledge and hard work.

This development of iron and steel making depended in the first place on building a furnace that would produce the right conditions for the separation of the ore and produce a workable material. This occurred about 1000 B.C. and the method developed and spread from then until the year 1 B.C., this period being popularly known as the Early Iron Age. Objects of iron were made before this time, some of them dating back to before 3000 B.C.; but the metal was probably produced accidentally or was of meteoric origin. The type of iron first produced would be similar to wrought iron, for the hearths and furnaces of the time, which were used in the manufacture of copper and bronze, were not capable of melting the metal, but only of reducing it to a spongy mass in which particles of iron were mixed with slag. This material was extracted from the furnace hearth and repeatedly heated and hammered to weld the mass together and was then forged with increasing skill to produce ornaments, tools and weapons. As can be imagined, the product resulting from so crude a process was by no means consistent. If pure iron is left in a furnace at about 900°C and in contact with a substance rich in carbon, it will absorb some of the carbon and be turned into steel. This process is called *carburizing or cementation*. Occasionally the metal obtained would be of this form, i.e. of the type that we know as *carbon steel* and which, when heated and quenched, would produce a hard and brittle metal quite unlike the soft and pliable iron which would result from slightly different conditions. After years of practice and experience, steel of this type could at last be produced at will, and came into general use between the 7th and 10th centuries A.D., thus marking the second phase of development.

The next stage was not reached until during the Middle Ages when a tall chimney type furnace was developed which, using water driven bellows, was capable of reaching the high temperature necessary to melt the iron. The product of these furnaces was *pig iron* and, being fluid when tapped from the furnace, could be used for making iron castings. Wrought iron continued to be made in a hearth type furnace by the direct reduction of the purer types of iron ore, using a cold air blast and charcoal as fuel. The temperature raised by such means was thus insufficient to allow the iron to absorb carbon from the burning fuel.

During the 18th century great strides were made in improving these products, particularly with regard to the design of the furnaces, for until the middle of the 19th century cast iron, carbon steel and wrought iron were the only forms of ferrous metals known. In 1709 a method of smelting iron using coke as a fuel was developed at the Abraham Darby ironworks at Coalbrookdale. Charcoal, which was previously employed as the fuel for iron smelting, does not support a heavy load of ore and hence was a limiting factor in the size of furnace used. With coke available as a fuel, larger furnaces were built, culminating in the development of the blast furnace. At this time, cupolas using mechanical blowers were introduced for remelting and refining pig iron to improve the quality of the cast iron product. In 1730 a process for making carbon steel by melting pieces of carburized iron in a crucible was developed by Benjamin Huntsman. Being melted in a crucible and poured into moulds, the product of the Huntsman process was known as *cast steel*. The process depended on the construction of a furnace and crucible capable of withstanding temperatures above 1500°C. This achievement provided means of manufacturing steel for the cutting tools of the Industrial Revolution. Towards the end of the century, in 1784, Henry Cort developed a process for converting pig iron, from the blast furnace, into wrought iron. At one stage of the process the molten metal was manually manipulated in the furnace and the method of producing wrought iron by this means was known as the *puddling* process.

Apart from the discovery of the ore, possibly the most important phase in the whole history of iron and steel manufacture began with the invention of a method of producing a steel containing very little carbon. This occurred in 1856 when Sir Henry Bessemer discovered a way of converting pig iron into steel. With properties similar to wrought iron but being capable of controlled manufacture into a variety of bar, sheet, tube and other forms, this new type of steel, known as *mild steel*, rapidly came into quantity production. A second method of mild steel manufacture was developed by the brothers C. W. and F. Siemens in 1862. This was the *open-hearth* process. Only pig iron produced from the high grade low phosphoric ores could be used in these furnaces until, in 1876, Gilchrist and Thomas invented the Basic process of steel manufacture

2

which used the low grade pig iron of high phosphorous content obtained from most British ores.

More recent developments include the employment of electric furnaces to produce a whole range of alloy steels suited to specific purposes. The method of reducing low grade ores with a high silica content in the blast furnace is well established but a direct reduction method for high percentage iron ores, using hydrogen as a reducing agent, is frequently used. Oxygen also is being increasingly employed at all stages of steel production. Although the traditional Bessemer converters and open-hearth furnaces remain responsible for much of the steel output, improved techniques are achieving increased prominence. Improved basic converter methods involve the use of oxygen-enriched air or an oxygen-steam mixture, although high purity oxygen is used in some modern converters viz. LD, Kaldo, Rotor and Ajax. Oxygen is also blown onto the surface or is injected into molten pig iron as a pre-refining operation. Very large quantities of oxygen are required in these processes and special equipment known as *tonnage oxygen* plant is installed locally or the oxygen is piped to the steelworks.

Iron ore   Of the many types of iron ores found, those in which the element iron is present as an oxide, a carbonate or a sulphide are the more important, and of these, the group of iron oxide ores is the most widely used in iron and steel production. *Magnetite*, Fe_3O_4, or lodestone as it is sometimes called, has the highest iron content, and Swedish ore of this type may contain up to 70% iron. The great majority of the world's production of ferrous metal is from *haematite ore*, Fe_2O_3, small deposits of which occur in this country and in much larger quantitites in Spain and the American continent. A hydrated iron oxide, *limonite*, $2Fe_2O_3 3H_2O$, is found in the brown haematite ores of central Europe, Spain and Sweden. Lower grade ores which exist in this country as well as elsewhere contain an iron carbonate, $FeCO_3$, or *chalybite*. The average lower grade workable ores yield about 20 to 30% metal. *Iron pyrites*, FeS_2, an ore containing iron sulphide, is widely distributed but is not used in iron and steel production on account of its high sulphur content.

The form in which the ores exist also affects their use to man. Ores rich in iron occur in Australia, among other places, in a small granular form like sand that cannot easily be reduced. It also occurs in America as finely dispersed particles in very hard rock which makes extraction of the iron difficult. There are also large deposits of a workable ore in the Sahara desert which have not yet been tapped because of the inaccessibility of the field. The low grade ores, if occurring close to the surface and hence obtainable by quarrying, provide a more economical proposition of iron production than those of a richer nature which may exist deeper in the earth or at a distance from a coalfield. Furthermore other elements that may be present will have an effect on the suitability of an ore for iron production. The gangue can to a large extent be removed before

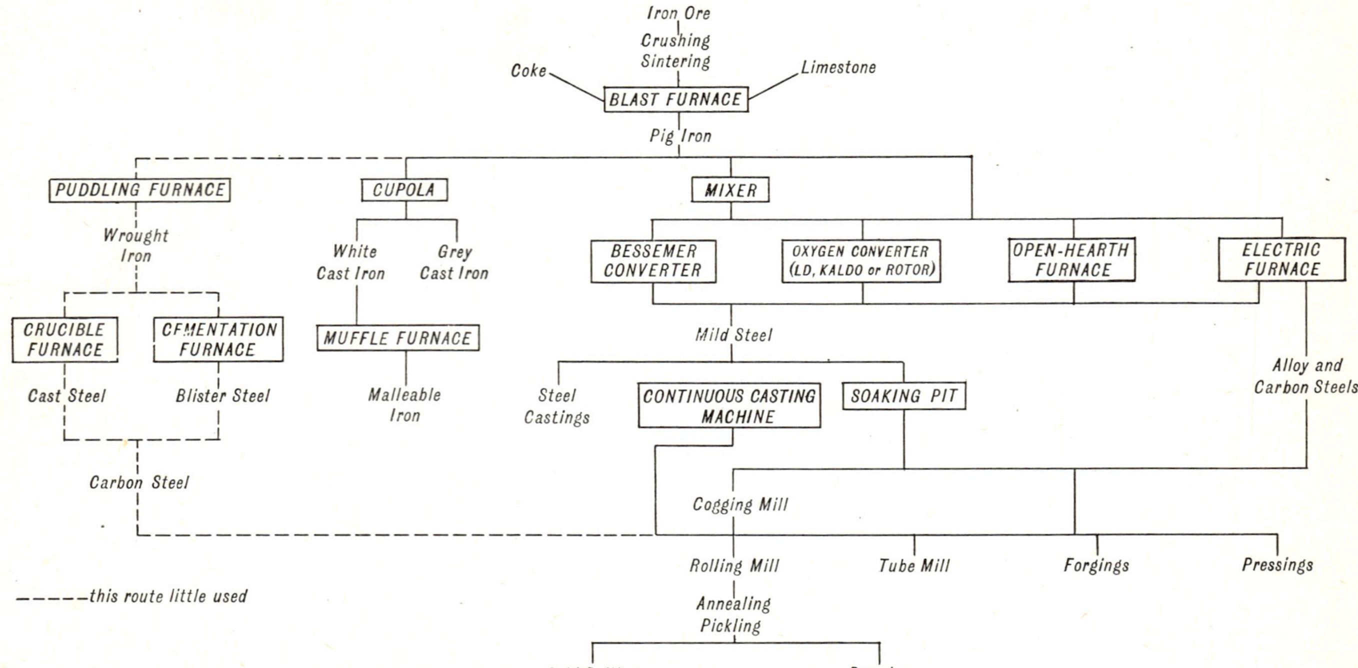

Fig. 1. Iron and steel production flow chart.

and during smelting but phosphorus and sulphur, which are present to a degree in all iron ores, are more difficult to eradicate.

Sintering   Before being fed into the blast furnace, iron ores are pre-treated to remove some of the unwanted solid matter, to drive off moisture and carbon dioxide and to produce pieces of ore of suitable size for smelting. The process by which this is achieved is called *sintering*. Ores containing magnetite may undergo preliminary separation by magnetism but the main sintering process consists of crushing, screening (sieving), mixing and roasting. During the process the ore travels by conveyor belt to areas where it is respectively sprayed with water, baked over gas jets and cooled by fans. The resulting compact mass is then broken into workable lumps and, at this stage, the lime flux needed in the blast furnace may be added.

The blast furnace   The ore is reduced and the iron extracted by *smelting* in a blast furnace. As indicated in the flow chart Fig. 1, this is the first stage of all iron and steel production. The blast furnace, Fig. 2, is a tall structure up to 30 m in height and with a hearth diameter of between 6 and 9 m. It consists of an outer shell of boiler plates lined on the inside with refractory fire bricks. The cylindrical hearth at the base is surmounted by two truncated cones which have

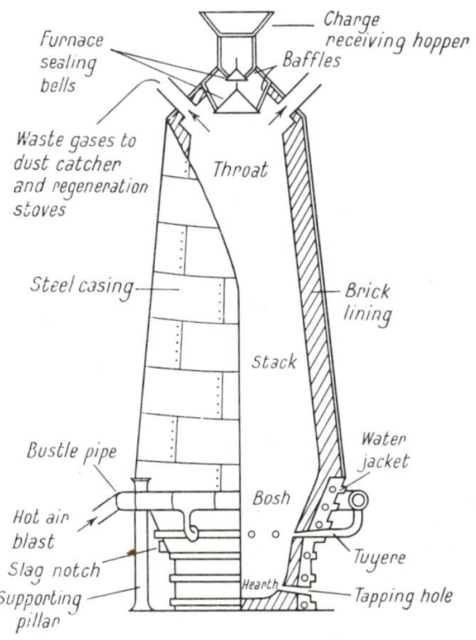

Fig. 2. Blast furnace.

the charging bells at the top and also the skip hoist by which the charge is fed. The charging bells, as well as distributing the charge, prevent the escape of gases, and hence heat, while successive charges are being fed. A feature of the modern blast furnace is that it can be used continuously for a number of years, in fact until the lining is burnt out, making the continuous production of pig iron possible. The waste gases are taken off in shafts to regeneration stoves where they are used to heat the blast. By introducing a heated blast at pressure the required temperature is attained. There are at least two regeneration stoves to each furnace, each containing a number of small brickwork flues. The bricks are heated by the hot exhaust gases and then the air blast is driven over them. The gas and air pass through the stoves in opposite directions and are frequently redirected to maintain the stove and furnace temperature. The hearth has at its base a tapping hole where the molten metal is run off, and at the top a slag hole through which the lighter slag is withdrawn. Around the lower cone is a circular bustle pipe carrying the air blast and from it a number of tuyeres through which the blast is introduced to the furnace. This lower portion of the furnace, which is subjected to the fiercest heat, is cooled by a water jacket fed by pipes encircling the hearth.

The charge which is fed to the furnace consists of iron ore, coke and limestone in proportions depending on the quality and composition of the ore. The greater the amount of gangue and impurities in the ore, the more coke will be required to heat it and the more limestone needed to form the slag. Before being fed to the furnace the large pieces of ore are crushed to a suitable size of about 100 mm cube and the smaller fine particles, or *fines* as they are called, are sintered. Furthermore to reduce the proportion of impurities, the lower grade ores undergo a process of *calcination* or roasting by which means some of the carbon, sulphur and water and other volatile material is driven off. Where ores are likely to vary in their composition, they are mixed in order to produce a consistent form of iron. The coke, as well as providing the fuel for maintaining the required heat, provides some of the carbon which assists the reducing action by combining with the oxygen in the iron oxide to form carbon monoxide gas. Coke is ideal for the purpose for it is strong enough to resist crushing by the weight of the charge above it, and being porous allows the blast to pass through. Coke is produced by raising special coking coal to a temperature of about 1300°C in closed chambers. The absence of air prevents the coal from burning and a hard, clean and porous fuel is left after the volatile materials have been driven off. It is important that the coal used should not have a high sulphur content as this element is picked up by the iron in the furnace and results in a poor quality material. Similarly a coke that produces a lot of ash could be troublesome and would absorb an undue amount of heat. The limestone acts as a flux and combines with the gangue, notably the silica, to form a liquid slag that floats on the top of the molten iron. It absorbs some of the impurities and prevents further oxidation.

The reduction begins to take place in the throat or upper portion of the furnace. The carbon monoxide gas rising from the lower layers of burning fuel reduces the ore to a porous mass. As the charge falls to a lower level it reaches a point where the temperature is sufficient to decompose the limestone, which then combines with gangue to form the slag. As the almost molten metal falls through the hottest part of the furnace it absorbs a part of the sulphur, any manganese and phosphorus that are present, and some carbon. The waste gases take away most of the carbon and oxygen released from the iron oxide, and the impurities are absorbed by the slag. The iron, now quite fluid, trickles to the hearth where from time to time it is led off by removing the clay stopper from the tapping hole. Prior to this the slag is run off through the slag notch. In some cases the molten metal is caused to flow along channels in sand to moulding beds where it solidifies into blocks called *pigs*. Hence the name pig iron. In the larger integrated iron and steel works it is run off into ladles and taken to receiving furnaces or mixers where it is stored at heat for the next process of conversion into steel or, more frequently, it is transferred in liquid form to the steel furnaces or converters. Recent developments in blast furnace operation involve the injection of oil, fine coal, oxygen or steam into the blast. The use of oil and fine coal can reduce the cost of production; oxygen increases the furnace temperature but requires the addition of steam to clean the melt.

The composition of pig iron varies within the following limits:

iron	88·7 to 97·6%	silicon 0·13 to 5·7%
carbon	2·3 to 5·5%	manganese 0·0 to 1·6%
phosphorus	0·0 to 1·7%	sulphur 0·0 to 0·9%

Furthermore the carbon may be present to a varying degree as graphite, free in the iron's structure or in a form in which it is combined with the iron, called *cementite*. Pig irons are normally classified into groups, according to the form of the carbon present, and range from a No. 1 or *grey iron*, in which nearly all the carbon is free, to a No. 6 or *white pig iron* having most of its carbon in the combined state. It is also divided into grades according to its phosphorus content, since when making steel, different processes are used for the low phosphorus or haematite irons and for the high phosphorus or basic types.

Cast iron　The refining of pig iron for making cast iron consists of the removal of some of the carbon and much of the phosphorus and is carried out in the foundry in a furnace known as a *cupola*, Fig. 143, Chapter 9. Similar in construction to a blast furnace, but on a smaller scale, the cupola is not worked continuously but is lit with a coke fire in the hearth, and pig iron, some scrap iron and a small amount of limestone are introduced in alternate layers. The proportion of pig and scrap depends on the type of cast iron required. Air, forced through tuyeres, causes the coke to burn and as the blast is gradually increased, the iron melts and falls to the base of the hearth. Oxygen is frequently injected along with the air causing a hotter melt and improved furnace efficiency. Following the removal of slag, the iron is run off into ladles and is then poured into moulds previously prepared to receive it.

The now much refined iron with a reduced carbon content of between 2·5 and 4% still contains the elements silicon, phosphorus, manganese and sulphur in varying proportions. Phosphorus, although difficult to remove, when present in small amounts causes the iron to be more fluid when molten and so is proportionately greater when castings of intricate shape are required. The presence of silicon gives a softer iron which is easy to machine and assists in producing a casting free from blow holes. An excess of sulphur makes casting difficult but tends to harden the iron, as does manganese, though small amounts of these two elements will combine to form manganese sulphide which reduces the hardening effect.

The form in which the carbon is present in iron determines the general classification into the grey and white cast irons. The type of casting produced depends on the grade of pig iron and scrap used, the ultimate silicon, content and on the rate of cooling. Grey cast iron has most of its carbon in the form of graphite, while in white cast iron most of the carbon is present in the form of an iron carbide, cementite, in which carbon is combined with iron. In both cases the carbon is free in the structure of the metal and is present in the form of flakes between the grains of iron. This gives cast iron a brittle nature but, as the grains are readily parted under the action of a cutting tool, it machines well. The machined surface of cast irons provides a good bearing surface for slow moving parts, as the small cavities left by the released carbon flakes assist in retaining a lubricant. Grey cast iron has a dark, rough appearance on its hard skin and is grey in colour on fracture. It is very fluid when molten and hence casts well. It is used for the general type of iron casting where great strength is not required except in compression.

In the general course of work it is suitable for exercises in turning, shaping, chipping, filing and scraping and is used in the craftroom for the bases of surface gauges, machine jacks, vices and the bodies of machine tools. When it is being machined, it is necessary to take a deep initial cut to remove the skin and so prevent excessive wear and damage to the cutting tool. When working by hand methods this skin should be removed with a cold chisel or treated by pickling in sulphuric acid, after which the metal can be filed with ease.

Cementite is a hard and brittle material and its presence in white cast iron produces a much harder and closer grained metal. It shows a whitish colour on fracture and is used for making higher grade castings where greater strength and resistance to shock loading is required. It is suitable for a further heat treatment process called *malleablizing*, by which its physical properties are greatly improved. It is rarely used in the craftroom though it has wide applications in industry.

Malleable cast iron The physical properties of cast iron, particularly with respect to its weak and brittle nature, can to a certain extent be improved by subjecting the finished castings to malleablizing.

Though not malleable in the accepted sense of the word, castings so treated are much stronger than the untreated iron. The process consists essentially of slightly reducing the carbon content and then dispersing the remaining carbon, now in the uncombined form, uniformly throughout the structure in minute particles. Hence thin sections of malleable castings consist of practically pure iron, as do the outer casings of heavier sections, the central core being very much refined. White cast irons with a comparatively high phosphorus and silicon content are suitable for malleablizing. They are packed into iron boxes containing an oxide of iron, usually haematite ore, and placed in a muffle furnace. The furnace is lit and maintained at a temperature of 900°C for a period of days and allowed to cool slowly over a few more days. During the process some of the carbon is oxidized and the castings are thoroughly annealed. This method, which is used extensively in this country, is known as the Whiteheart process as the fracture of iron so treated shows a greyish white. Another similar method by which a malleable iron, that has a much darker fracture is produced, is called the Blackheart process. It is common in the U.S.A. for it is more suited to the iron smelted from American ores. Because of their increased toughness and resistance to shock loads malleable castings can take the place of work that once required steel forgings or fabrications and, of course, complex shapes can be produced more cheaply by casting than by either of these methods. Malleable castings are therefore used for the bodies of horticultural and agricultural implements, machine handles and gear wheels and other parts of intricate shape which are likely to be subjected to heavy or rough usage.

Wrought iron The production of wrought iron today is very small compared with that of mild steel. However, being the purest of all the ferrous metals, reaching 99·9% in some cases, it possesses unique qualities and is still made by the puddling process in a few of the smaller ironworks. The process consists of removing most of the impurities remaining in pig iron after smelting and then combining the iron with some of the slag produced. This is done by heating the

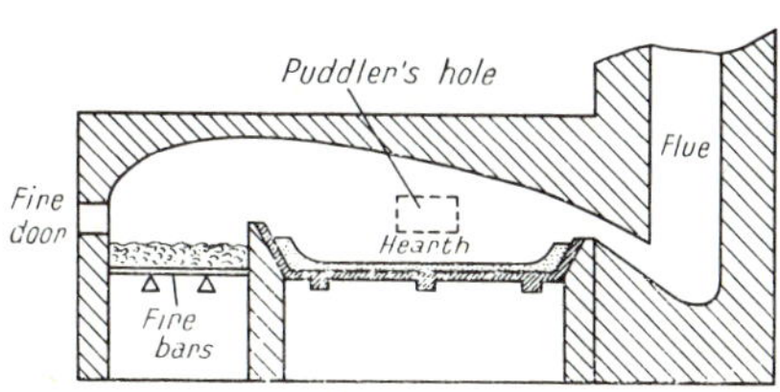

Fig. 3. Puddling furnace.

pig iron in a *reverberatory* type puddling furnace, Fig. 3, in contact with a substance rich in oxygen. The bed of the furnace is carried by a cast iron plate and the heat from the fire is carried over it by the draught and reflected to the metal in the hearth by the furnace roof. The draught is induced by a tall chimney and controlled by a damper. Pig iron is placed in the preheated hearth and the temperature increased until the iron is reduced to a molten state, the process being accelerated by agitating with a long bar called a puddling pole. As part of the carbon is oxidized and slag begins to form, millscale is added and the melt is briskly stirred by the puddler. Carbon monoxide gas rises, burns at the surface, and the melt appears to boil. As the formation of gas slackens, indicating that most of the carbon has been removed, the liquid becomes pasty and as much of the slag as possible is drawn off. The puddler then works the iron and remaining slag into balls or blooms of about 30 kg in weight which are then removed from the furnace and hammered or rolled into lengths of bar or strip. The hammering not only reduces the blooms to a convenient shape but also squeezes out some of the remaining slag. The little slag then left is drawn into long threads within the metal by the rolling. To disperse the slag even more evenly throughout the metal a number of bars are now wired together in a faggot, heated to a welding heat and re-rolled. The rolling at this heat fuses the bars together and the resulting bar contains a pronounced fibrous structure and has improved strength and malleability. The number of times the metal goes through this process of *faggoting*, heating and rolling determines the grade and quality of the iron.

Because of its fibrous nature and its ability to withstand shock, wrought iron may be safely used for sling hooks, shackles, couplings and haulage gear and lifting tackle of all types. Not only has it great resistance to fatigue but visible warning is given where fractures are likely to occur. It also has the ability to resist corrosion and is used for quality gates and railings and tubes for underground location. It can be worked when cold as well as when hot and machines easily. At elevated temperatures it does not immediately burn but becomes pasty and in that condition can be easily worked to shape on the anvil or welded by hammering alone. In the school workshop it is suitable for forgework exercises.

Mild steel   Steel is an alloy of iron and carbon in which all or part of the carbon, in the form of cementite, is chemically combined with ferrite to form a substance known as *pearlite*. Pearlite consists of fine threads of cementite layered with ferrite and, although cementite itself is hard and brittle, in this form it becomes comparatively soft yet retaining its strength. It is so called because when seen through a microscope it has the appearance of mother of pearl. Mild steel, containing as it does less than 0·3% carbon, has all its carbon in the form of pearlite, which is evenly distributed throughout the iron. It is a soft and ductile metal, easily cut by hand and machine tools, forges well and will fire weld. As such, mild steel is a general purpose engineering material and is the most widely used of all metals in the school workshop as well as in industry. It has numerous applications ranging from large girders for structural work to rivets and bolts, from ships' plates and car bodies to pipes, tubes and wire.

The conversion of pig iron to mild steel consists essentially of removing the remaining impurities and some of the carbon and leaving the remaining carbon in the form of pearlite. In practice, usually all the carbon is removed with the other elements, the required quantity then being put back into the molten metal. There are three basic methods of production: Bessemer and oxygen converters, the open-hearth process and electric-arc furnaces. In each case one of two processes is employed depending on the quality of the ore. An Acid process uses a furnace lining of silica bricks, and as only silicon, manganese and carbon are removed, it is restricted to high grade low phosphorus irons. In the Basic process the furnace linings are of crushed dolomite mixed with tar or magnesium limestone bricks and a slag is formed which will absorb sulphur and phosphorus also, and can thus convert pig iron that has been reduced from low grade ores with a high phosphorus content.

The Bessemer converter   The Bessemer process of converting pig iron to steel consists of introducing oxygen to the molten metal by blowing large amounts of air through it. This oxidizes away the carbon and impurities and the required quantity of carbon is then added to the charge. It is a cheap and rapid method,

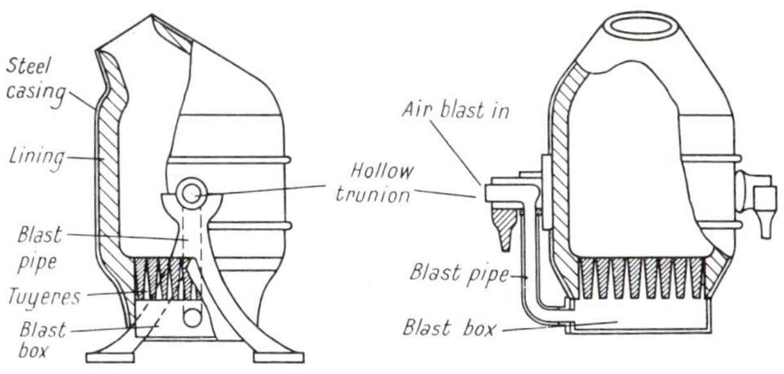

Fig. 4. Bessemer converter.

the whole process taking about 20 minutes, and with suitable furnace linings is used for the conversion of irons made from both low and high grade ores. The converter consists of a large container made of a steel shell lined with the refractory material, Fig. 4. The tuyeres at the base connect through a blast box to the air supply. The whole converter is pivoted at its centre and may be tilted while receiving its charge and again to discharge the metal. Bessemer converters are usually employed in integrated iron and steel works for they contain no means of heating the charge, the molten iron being brought from the blast furnace via mixers or storage furnaces where it is kept at heat until required. When poured into the tilted converter the metal does not reach the tuyere holes, and the blast is turned on before the converter is brought to its vertical position. The air pressure prevents the molten metal from running into the tuyeres and as the air passes through the metal the temperature rises as the impurities are burned away, the carbon is oxidized and the carbon monoxide burns at the converter mouth. During the first stage, known as the *boil*, violent agitation takes place in the metal, to be followed, in the Basic process, by a quiescent period when a dark brown smoke takes the place of the flame. This is known as the *after-blow* and marks the stage when the phosphorus is being removed. The blast is then turned off, the converter tilted to the horizontal position and samples of the metal are taken. The required amount of carbon in the form of spiegeleisen or ferro-manganese is added. This final stage of the process is known as the *kill* after which the molten steel is poured off into ladles.

Oxygen converters Oxygen converters are similar to the Bessemer converter but employ oxygen instead of air to bring about the chemical changes which turn iron into steel. In the Bessemer process it is the oxygen in the air that burns out the carbon and oxidizes the manganese, the silicon, and in the Basic process, the phosphorus. The use of pure oxygen accelerates the process and, due to the reduction of nitrogen in the refining gas some of which is absorbed by the metal, a superior ductile steel is produced.

There are three main oxygen steelmaking processes. In the first of these, the LD process—named after the initial letters of Linz and Donawitz, the Austrian towns where it was first developed—oxygen is injected at high speed onto the surface of the liquid iron, Fig. 5a. When the melt is of high-phosphorus iron, powdered lime is injected with the oxygen stream. In this case the blow is in two phases, the process being interrupted to remove the high-phosphorus-content slag which is a valuable fertilizer.

In the Kaldo process, oxygen is blown onto the surface of the molten iron in a converter vessel which rotates on an inclined axis, Fig. 5b. This process has greater flexibility in the range of steels that can be produced but is not as rapid as the LD method. The Rotor process is similar to the Kaldo but, in this case, oxygen is applied through two lances to the liquid metal while it is in a revolving horizontal vessel, Fig. 5c. One jet of oxygen is blown above the surface of the melt to effect combustion, whilst the second jet is blown below the surface to refine the metal of unwanted elements.

The open-hearth furnace Whereas in the basic Bessemer process the impurities in pig iron are oxidized away by making use of the oxygen in air, the open-hearth process employs an iron oxide combined with very high temperature (in the region of 1650°C) to perform the same function. Although taking longer than

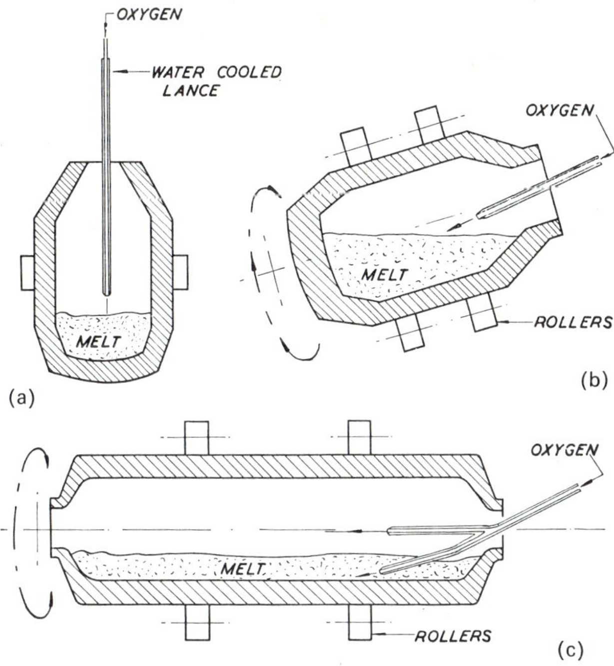

Fig. 5. Oxygen converters. (a) LD process   (b) Kaldo process
(c) Rotor process.

the Bessemer process—about 12 hours is required to convert a melt of 100 metric tonnes pig iron to steel—the open-hearth process has major advantages; thus a large proportion of the world's steel is produced by this method. Unlike the Bessemer process it can use a fair proportion of scrap steel in the melt, which, as well as the obvious advantage of conserving material, also assists in producing a more consistent and, in some cases, a better quality metal, because less carbon has to be removed. It is moreover more economical in the use of fuel, for the metal is heated in a closed chamber and the waste gases are used to heat the fuel gas and air instead of being blown into the atmosphere.

The traditional open-hearth method of steel production is also subject to modification where oxygen plant is available. One recent development (Ajax) employs long water-cooled retractable lances to direct and inject oxygen onto and into the molten metal.

The open-hearth furnace, Fig. 6, consists of a shallow hearth, in which the charge is placed, beneath a roof which directs the burning fuel to the metal. Hence the charge is heated in direct contact with the furnace flame. The high furnace temperature is attained by passing the fuel, in the form of producer gas, and air through regeneration chambers previously heated by the exhaust gases. When oil is used as a fuel it is slightly heated at the nozzle and injected under pressure. The fuel and air mix and burn above the charge, and as the direction of the fuel and waste gases through the regeneration chambers is frequently reversed, an ever increasing furnace temperature is reached. The regeneration

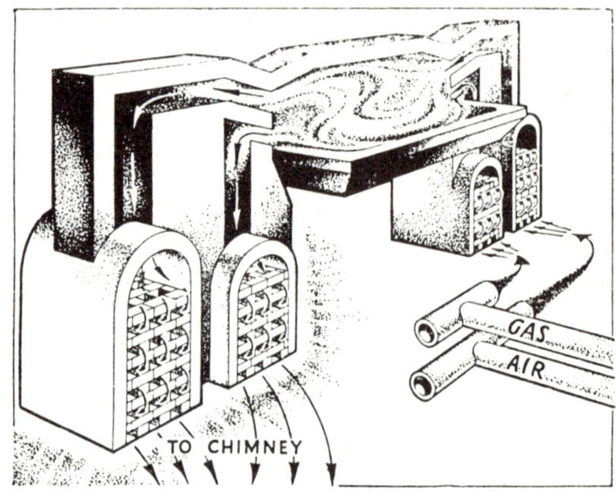

[*British Iron and Steel Federation.*

Fig. 6. Open-hearth furnace.

chambers consist of chequered brickwork providing a large surface area for the retention of heat. The charge of pig iron and scrap is fed to the hearth together with millscale and lime. A slag is therefore formed which absorbs the silicon, sulphur and phosphorus, the carbon being oxidized by the oxygen of the flame. Frequent samples are taken during the refining process and more lime and millscale added as required. Spiegeleisen or ferro-manganese is then added either to the melt in the furnace or as the metal enters the ladle, to bring the carbon content to the desired proportion. Alloying elements are also added when steels of a special composition are being produced. The molten steel is teemed or poured by tilting the furnace or removing a plug from the tapping hole.

Carbon steels The physical properties of mild steels are not much altered by simple heat treatment and hence cannot be used for cutting tools. As the carbon content of steel is increased, however, the metal becomes harder and is more greatly affected by heating and quenching. When the carbon content of steel approaches nearly 0·9%, pearlite saturation point is reached and as more carbon is added it remains in the steel as free cementite. The approximate compositions of the various grades of plain carbon steels are given in Fig. 7 together with their principal uses. Steels with above 0·9 % carbon therefore consist of pearlite plus cementite, and are of the type that may be hardened by heating and quenching. Such steels are classified as carbon tool steels.

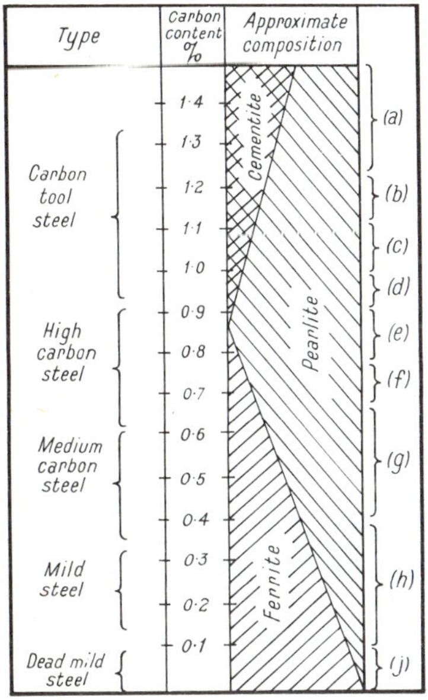

Characteristics and Uses

Difficult to forge. Can be hardened to high degree. Brittle and fractures under sudden shock and variations in pressure. Used for razors, wire drawing dies, files, etc.

Care needed in forging. Not weldable. Used for metal cutting tools.

Hard and fine-grained. Holds cutting edge. Used for drills, reamer, taps and woodworking tools, etc.

Easily forged. Used for chisels, punches, hot sets, springs, etc.

Hard, strong and tough. Resists sudden shocks. Used for forge tools, hammer heads, crowbars, etc.

Very tough. Withstands pressure. Used for press tools and dies, etc.

Heat treatment makes tough rather than hard. Used for heavy forgings, axles, set screws, steel rails, etc.

Cannot be hardened. Used for general engineering purposes, machine work and light forging. Easily forge welded.

Soft and ductile. Used for wire, boiler plates, etc.

Fig. 7. Grades of plain carbon steel.

The manufacture of these steels may be accomplished by a long established process of cementation, by which carbon is induced into wrought iron. The process is carried out in a natural draught furnace by packing bars of good quality iron into firebrick boxes and uniformly surrounding them with charcoal. At a heat of about 900°C, carbon monoxide gas from the charcoal enters the outside layers of the bars and permeates to the centre. The process takes a number of days, for in most cases a coal fire slowly brings the furnace to the required temperature. The bars are left to soak at heat and are not withdrawn until the furnace has cooled. Trial bars are withdrawn from time to time and tested for their carbon content, for the type of steel produced depends upon the time the bars are left in the furnace. Although the metal does not melt and the bars retain their original shape after treatment, the fibrous structure gives way to that of a granular and crystalline nature and the surface is broken in places, giving the resulting metal its name of *blister steel*. The surface of blister bars is more highly carburized than the central cores. One method of producing a more homogeneous material, though not used to a great extent today, is to bind a number of bars together, bring to a welding heat and hammer and roll to a single bar. This process may be repeated a number of times to produce higher quality steel. Bars obtained by this treatment are called *shear steel* and are suitable for such articles as scythes, shears and large knives.

The cementation method of producing blister and shear steel and also the crucible process for the production of cast steel, mentioned earlier in the chapter, have now both been superseded by the manufacture of carbon and tool steels in electric furnaces.

Steel with a carbon content above $1 \cdot 2\%$ is difficult to forge and readily burns at elevated temperatures. With about 1% carbon it will forge quite well and in the annealed state can be easily cut with hand and machine tools. In the school workshop it is employed in making scribers, punches, chisels, the blades of woodworking tools and screwdrivers, and all exercises involving hardening and tempering. Silver steel is a material of this type and, being manufactured in short lengths, accurately ground to size and annealed, it is suitable for making all cutting tools, particularly lathe tool bits for boring and screwcutting. Square bar and round rods are useful shapes to stock but as cast steel, in outward

Table 1. Workshop tests (iron and steel)

Metal	Test	Drop on anvil	Nick and hammer in vice	Grind on emery wheel
Cast iron	Grey	Dull note	Snaps easily. Coarse, dark fracture	Dark bushy stream with bright bursts
	White	Very dull note	Clean break. Finer white fracture	Dark red stream close to wheel with occasional bright bursts
Wrought iron		Dull metallic note	Bends well. Fibrous structure clearly seen	Fine stream of bright sparks
Mild steel		Medium pitched ring	Bends before breaking shows uniform grey lustre on fracture	Long white sparks in extended stream with primary bursts
Cast steel		High ringing note	Bends a little then breaks off. Silvery white fine crystalline fracture	Secondary white bursts from bushy bright stream
High-speed steel		Medium metallic ring	Resists blow then breaks cleanly. Very fine crystalline fracture	Dull red sparks close to wheel

appearance, is similar to black mild steel bar, they should be stored separately and painted a distinguishing colour. Bars of octagonal cross-section are useful for chisels and the shape makes them readily recognizable. Workshop tests for determining the various types of ferrous metals are given in Table 1.

Electric furnaces   Almost all the carbon and alloy tool steel produced today is carried out in electric furnaces; increasingly these furnaces are also being employed to make common steels. There are two types of electric furnaces—the 'carbon arc' and the 'high frequency induction' furnaces, Fig. 8. Both types of furnace can be temperature controlled to a fine degree and the metal melted in them is free from the effects of the oxidizing atmosphere given off by the burning fuel of a gas or coke-fired furnace.

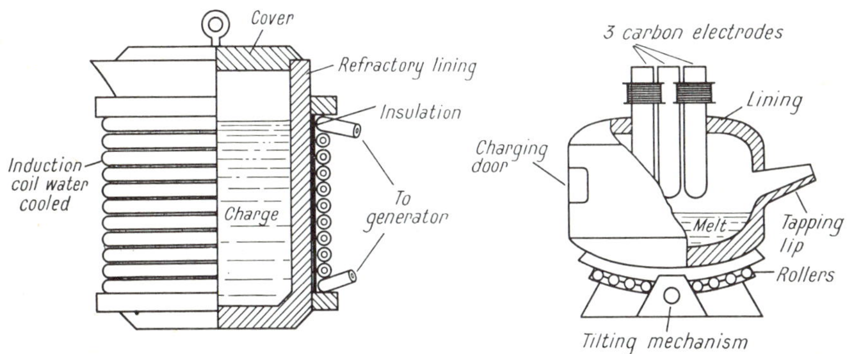

Fig. 8. High-frequency induction furnace and electric arc furnace.

In the electric arc furnace heat is generated, as in electric welding, by a spark passing between electrodes. The carbon electrodes of the furnace, of which there are usually three, are lowered to the charge in the furnace hearth and the arc is struck. The electrodes are automatically controlled to maintain the correct gap as the charge melts. When tool steels are being produced in the electric arc furnace, the metal fed in is either scrap of known carbon content or good quality open-hearth steel. The process for making mild steels is similar to that of the open-hearth process; in this instance the furnace may be lined for either the Acid or the Basic process.

High frequency induction furnaces operate on the heating effect of an electric current which is induced in the metal from a surrounding coil through which an alternating current is passed. The charge is placed in a form of crucible of heat resisting and insulating material which is surrounded by the water-cooled induction coil. In some types of induction furnaces, further laminations of special alloy steel carry the portion of the magnetic field, not passing through the metal, to a central core at the base. Not only can high temperatures be obtained in this way but the degree of heat can be very accurately controlled. Furthermore an automatic stirring action is caused by the electrodynamic forces set up within the molten charge. This ensures a uniformity of composition in the resulting metal and brings all parts of the melt in contact with the slag, thus absorbing any impurities.

Vacuum melting and casting The elimination of hydrogen and other gases in the production of high quality steels may be accomplished by casting or by both melting and casting in a vacuum. In one method employed, the metal is poured into a mould placed in a vacuum chamber. Alternatively, a pre-heated ladle is placed inside an evacuated tank and steel from another ladle is poured into it through the vacuum. The whole process of melting, adding alloying elements and pouring into moulds may be carried out by remote control in a single vacuum chamber. However, sometimes two chambers are used, one or both being evacuated.

Alloy steels The addition of various alloying elements in different proportions to the melt of an electric furnace enables a wide range of steels with specific properties to be produced. These alloy steels include the high-speed tool steels and the stainless steels, as well as special corrosion, wear and heat resisting alloys. These special alloys are necessary because of the increasing demands of the engineering, chemical and power generation industries. The toughest of the high-speed steels consists of 14% tungsten with a small amount of chromium alloyed with a 0·69% carbon steel. This steel is used in the manufacture of various small tools for cutting mild steel and non-ferrous metals. The addition of about 5% cobalt produces a hard alloy suitable for making tool bits for cutting cast iron and high tensile steels. Press tools for cold working metal usually contain chromium and molybdenum; the addition of vanadium makes an alloy steel suitable for hot working. Tools and dies for working plastic materials frequently contain nickel as an alloying element while the corrosion resisting 'stainless' steels contain up to 20% chromium with varying percentages of carbon and nickel. The effects of the more common alloying elements are shown in Table 2.

High-speed steels and stainless steels may be worked by machine and hand tools. They can be forged and welded using appropriate techniques but the removal of the oxide formed during heating necessitates special treatment. As high-speed steels undergo a secondary hardening process rather than a tempering process, temperature controlled furnaces and quenching baths are required.

Finishing processes The molten metal from the steel furnace is teemed (poured) into moulds to form steel castings called *ingots*, or it may pass direct into a casting machine to produce *billets*, which are slabs or bars of metal, by a continuous

Table 2. Principal alloying elements in steel

Element	Effects	Principal uses
Phosphorus	Promotes cold shortness. Small amounts give increased strength and resistance to corrosion	Usually unwanted though difficult to eradicate
Sulphur	Promotes hot shortness. Weakens steel by making brittle	Assists machinability and free-cutting
Nickel	Increases hardness and strength Refined structure. Resists fatigue and corrosion. Lowers critical point. Little expansion when heated	Measuring tapes, railway points and crossings, engine valves and turbine blades. Element in Invar
Molybdenum	Increases elasticity, strength at high temperatures and machinability	Parts aero-engines
Chromium	Resists wear and corrosion. Increases hardness and toughness	Stainless steel. Cutting and crushing tools. 4% in H.S.S. Acid containers
Vanadium	Toughens and strengthens steel. Fatigue and wear resistant	Crank shafts. 2·5% in H.S.S.
Manganese	Air hardening. Non-magnetic. Increases strength and wear resistance	Conveyors, gears
Tungsten	Resists corrosion and effects of acid. Gives hardness and strength at high temperatures	Main ingredient (14%) in H.S.S. Cutting tools. Engine valves
Cobalt	Increases hardness, strength and retains magnetism. Non-corrodible. Enhances red hardness	Permanent magnets. Cutting tools. 1% in H.S.S.
Titanium	Promotes sound homogeneous metal	Small tools. Spanners. Keys and wrenches

casting process. When poured into moulds the metal is fed from the base of the ladle to the base of the mould. Pouring in this way prevents slag inclusion, avoids danger from splashing and produces castings free from flaws. When the outer layers of the ingot have solidified, although the central core may still be in a liquid state, it is lifted from the mould and taken to a *soaking pit*. This is a form of underground oven where ingots are stored at a uniform temperature until required for the final shaping process.

From the soaking pit some of the ingots go to the hammers and presses for forging into a diverse range of articles from marine crankshafts to car axles. Those that are to be formed to the standard shaped sections of bars, rods, sheets, wires, channels, tubes, etc., are taken first to the cogging mill, where the red hot ingot is formed into a more manageable size, called a *bloom*, by squeezing between rollers. As the bloom is passed forwards and backwards the rollers are brought closer together and the bar turned 90° at each pass. At this stage, the ends of the bloom formed from the impure ends of the ingot are sheared off and returned to the furnace as scrap. Further squeezing between shaped rollers forms the blooms into billets and then into bars of the various cross-sections. The cylindrical rollers of the slabbing mill produce plates, sheets and strip metal. Finally the sections are either cut into lengths or, as in the case of strip and some small diameter rod, are wound into coils. Metal finished in this way has a scale of oxide on its surface and is known as black bar or sheet. Mild steel so produced is used for general purposes and as an alternative to wrought iron for forgework.

The stages of teeming and making ingots can be eliminated by first feeding the molten metal to a reservoir and then to a water-cooled mould where the exterior surface of the metal is solidified but the core remains molten. On its way to the rolling mills it is further cooled by water sprays and reaches each stage of the required metal finishing process at the correct temperature.

Steel may be brought more accurately to size and its surface finish improved by cold rolling or drawing. Known as bright drawn steel, it is to be preferred for craftroom purposes. This type includes a special free cutting steel, containing a small amount of sulphur or lead, for machine work. Before being cold rolled, the black bar is pickled in dilute sulphuric acid, washed and then oiled, and is passed again through rollers similar to those used in the previous processes. The sheets and bars are then heat treated to relieve the internal stresses set up by the rolling and a final light rolling is given to increase the surface finish. Bright drawn steel bars are first rolled nearly to size and then pulled through a die having a hole of the shape of the cross-section of the required bar. Wires are drawn through successively smaller holes in a draw plate. Dies and draw plates are of a hard alloy steel or metal carbide and in some cases have a reducing bush of diamond. Drawing work-hardens the metal and it must be annealed both between successive draws and at the end of the process. To prevent oxidation of the surface, the heating is carried out in a furnace from which air is excluded by pumping in another gas or by packing the steel in carbon-rich granules in steel boxes. Metal finished in this way has a bright and oxide-free surface, and is usually true to shape and size within 0·025 mm. Furthermore, steel produced by cold rolling and drawing in conjunction with suitable heat treatment, is more homogeneous and has improved physical and mechanical properties.

Pipes are formed from strip by rolling to shape and butt welding the seam, and seamless tubes by first piercing the end of an annealed bar and then squeezing the metal over a mandrel while revolving it between angular rollers.

2 The Non-ferrous Metals and their Alloys

The non-ferrous metals, that is, those that do not contain iron, comprise the second major group of metals. They include a wide range of materials possessing very different properties but unlike the ferrous metals none are subject to corrosion by rusting. Few have commercial applications in their pure state but, when mixed with other metals, they can be made to provide alloys with desired properties and characteristics. A brief description of the common non-ferrous metals is given together with the methods of extraction and production. This is followed by lists of the more frequently used alloys tabulating their average compositions and some of their specific properties and uses.

Aluminium In appearance aluminium is a white metal, light in weight with specific gravity 2·7; it is soft and in its pure form its tensile strength is too low for most engineering purposes. It is highly malleable and ductile and can be beaten into very thin sheet or drawn into fine wire. It melts easily (about 660°C), and is easily formed into machine parts by casting. Because of its high resistance to corrosion it is used extensively for domestic articles such as food containers

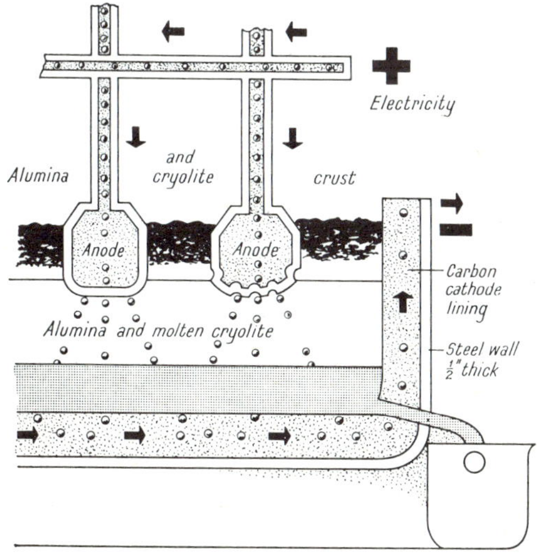

Fig. 9. Aluminium furnace.

and spun utensils. Owing to the insolubility of its oxide it cannot be soldered in the usual way, but considerable strides have been made in recent years and it may now be joined quite readily by hard solders (see Chapter 4). Aluminium foil is used for sealing milk bottles and as a wrapping for confectionery. Powdered aluminium is used as a base for aluminium paint to give protection against atmospheric conditions. Aluminium has many wider applications and much more commercial value when alloyed with copper, zinc and silicon.

Most aluminium is prepared from its ore by an electrolytic process. The crude ore *bauxite* is found extensively in many parts of the world, the largest production being in North America. The purified alumina (aluminium oxide) is dissolved in a bath of fused cryolite (double fluoride of sodium and aluminium), and fluorspar (calcium fluoride), contained in an iron vessel and kept molten by an electric current, Fig. 9. Carbon rods act as the anode, which may be moved up or down as required, and the iron vessel forms the cathode. The temperature of the bath is kept above $900°C$ by a current of 10 000 amperes supplied at a low voltage. The alumina is decomposed into aluminium and oxygen, the liberated oxygen combines with the carbon of the anode, forming carbon dioxide, and escapes through a hole in the furnace lid, leaving the aluminium to settle to the bottom.

Copper Easily distinguished because of its red colour, copper is a very malleable and ductile metal, an excellent conductor of heat and electricity, and is also highly resistant to corrosion by liquids. When exposed to the atmosphere it quickly loses its bright appearance and eventually turns green; this is due to the formation of copper carbonate or *verdigris* which protects the metal from further oxidation. Copper is used extensively for making wire, cable and parts of electrical machines where current has to be conducted. Soldering iron bits are made of copper and at one time so were the better domestic utensils. Copper may be cast but its mechanical properties are greatly improved by rolling and forging. In the school workshop copper is available in sheet, tube, wire, rod and bar and is readily joined by both hard and soft soldering. It 'work-hardens' when beaten or drawn but is easily annealed by heating to a dull red and quenching in water or allowing to cool in air. Subsequent pickling in heated dilute sulphuric acid will dissolve the black oxide that forms on the surface of the metal during heating.

Copper ores are very widespread with major deposits in Western America, Canada and central and southern Africa. It is also found in Europe, Asia and the far east. Copper in its pure state is found to a small extent, mainly in the Lake Superior deposits in the U.S.A. but most is extracted from sulphide or oxidized ores. The main sulphide ores are chalcopyrite containing about 34% copper, and bornite which contains 55% metal. Malachite and Cuprite with about 55% and 88% copper respectively, constitute the main oxidized ores. These ores are extracted both by mining and quarrying. They are crushed and sieved to remove worthless matter and then ground into fine particles in water and separated by flotation. The raw concentrates are next smelted in a reverberatory furnace, Fig. 10, and most of the remaining impurities are removed from the resulting matter in a converter similar to the Bessemer converter used in steel production. Further refining takes place in a second reverberatory furnace or, when very pure metal is required, by an electrolytic process.

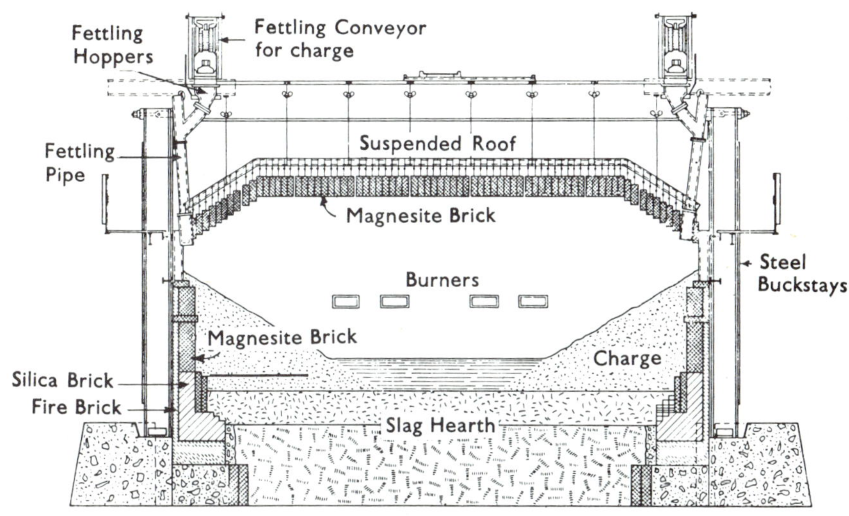

[*Copper Development Association.*

Fig. 10. Cross-section of copper smelting furnace.

Lead Lead is the heaviest of the common metals and has a specific gravity of 11·3. It is plastic and malleable and may be 'cold-rolled' into thin sheets. In colour it is a bluish grey and has a dull lustre but upon exposure to the atmosphere becomes a dull grey. It is not affected by water or acids and is used for roof coverings, water pipes and as containers for acids. Because of its low melting point (330°C) lead sheets are readily joined by burning, using a blowpipe. It is also alloyed with tin to make solders and bearing metals. Lead oxides are much used as a base for lead paint.

Lead is obtained from a lead ore, mostly galena, by sintering and then reduction in a blast furnace. The ore is first crushed to a coarse powder and then separated from impurities by a froth flotation process. Sintering or roasting removes sulphur and produces lumps of sinter which are then reduced in a blast furnace. As lead and zinc ores frequently occur together, much lead is now produced by a process that deals with the combined ores simultaneously, Fig. 12.

Tin   Tin is silvery white in colour with a yellowish tinge and has a crystalline structure; it is ductile and may be rolled into tinfoil but it is not strong. If a thin bar of tin is bent a distinct sound called 'tin cry' can be heard; this is due to the deformation of the crystalline structure. The purer the tin the louder is this cry. The greatest use for tin in its pure form is for the coating of thin steel sheets to give tinplate but it is also often used for alloying with other metals. A small proportion of tin added to a melt of cast iron simplifies the casting procedure and produces a more uniform metal with a high hardness. Tin is the main constituent of *Pewter* from which ornaments and articles of domestic tableware are made. A modern tarnish resistant pewter alloy contains an average composition of 91% tin, 7·5% antimony and 1·5% copper.

[*Courtesy Malayan Information Agency.*
Fig. 11. Tin streaming.

Malaysia is the premier producer of tin and contributes annually about one third of the world supply. Most of the tin deposits are alluvial and water is the principle mining agent. Powerful jets of water force out the tin-bearing material and water is used to wash the tin ore free; this process is called *tin streaming*, Fig. 11. The ore is then reduced to powder by crushing and again washed and sieved. Next it is calcined or roasted in a reverberatory furnace to get rid of the sulphur and to convert any arsenic present into oxide. The ore is again washed, mixed with slaked lime and powdered anthracite and then smelted in a reverberatory furnace. When completely fused the mass is stirred and more flux added. After further heating and stirring the tin is run off into moulds. At this stage it is called 'crude tin' and has to be refined. This is done by melting on the sloping bed of a reverberatory furnace. The purest tin, being most fusible, melts first and is run off. The purified metal is again melted and stirred and impurities, in the form of slag skimmed off. The longer this latter process is continued the purer the tin will be, but there is a considerable loss of metal in the slag.

Zinc Zinc is a bluish-white metal with a high lustre which tarnishes little when exposed to the atmosphere. In its pure state it is malleable but becomes brittle when heated. At 200°C it is sufficiently brittle for it to be powdered. Zinc is available as rolled sheet, in which form it is used—particularly on the continent —for roofing and other building features; it also forms the casings of dry-cell electric batteries. Zinc is extensively used as a protective coating for steel and as such, is widely used in the building and engineering industries. Steel may be given a protective zinc coating in a number of ways. When applied in the molten state it is called *galvanizing* and high-speed continuous galvanizing is often the final stage in modern strip steel production. When zinc is deposited electrically the process is called *sherardizing*. Zinc may also be sprayed on to a prepared steel surface or applied as a constituent of paint. Pressure die castings of zinc and zinc alloys are commonly used for parts of cars and domestic appliances. When alloyed with copper to make brass, zinc then forms part of a material with a very wide range of applications.

Deposits of ores containing zinc are widely distributed throughout the world, with the largest known deposits in North America, Australia and the U.S.S.R. Zinc is mainly obtained from lead-bearing sulphide ores. The most common of these is *blende* or *sphalerite*, though *marmatite*, which contains iron, is also an important source. Before the metal can be extracted the zinc ores have to be concentrated and separated from the worthless gangue materials. Two methods are used: the first, a wet gravity method takes advantage of the differences in density between the mineral particles and the gangue; the second, a flotation process, depends mainly on the reluctance of water to wet the mineral sulphide particles. The zinc sulphide concentrates are then roasted or 'sintered' to form the crude oxide. During this process, which may be carried out on a hearth or 'flash roaster', sulphur dioxide is evolved and used for making sulphuric acid. Thus nearly all zinc producers are acid manufacturers and also often make superphosphate fertilizers.

A standard method of zinc extraction consists of roasting at about 1100°C, the ore, together with anthracite, in banks of small horizontal fireclay retorts. Zinc, which forms as a vapour, is collected as liquid metal outside the furnace. More recently a method of extracting zinc by smelting has been developed. A blast furnace, Fig. 12, is fed with a pre-heated mixture of roasted zinc concentrates and coke and supplied with hot air blasts. Zinc vapour is removed in a stream of gas containing carbon dioxide and carbon monoxide and is then condensed by contact with a spray of molten lead. The lead circulates continuously through a heat exchanger and a separating chamber where the molten zinc settles out and can be run off at a purity of 98·8%. Lead and zinc concentrates can be smelted simultaneously if roasted mixed lead-zinc concentrates are fed in; by this method low-grade concentrates can also be treated.

An electrolytic process accounts for about half the zinc now made. Roasted concentrates are dissolved in sulphuric acid and, after intensive purification of

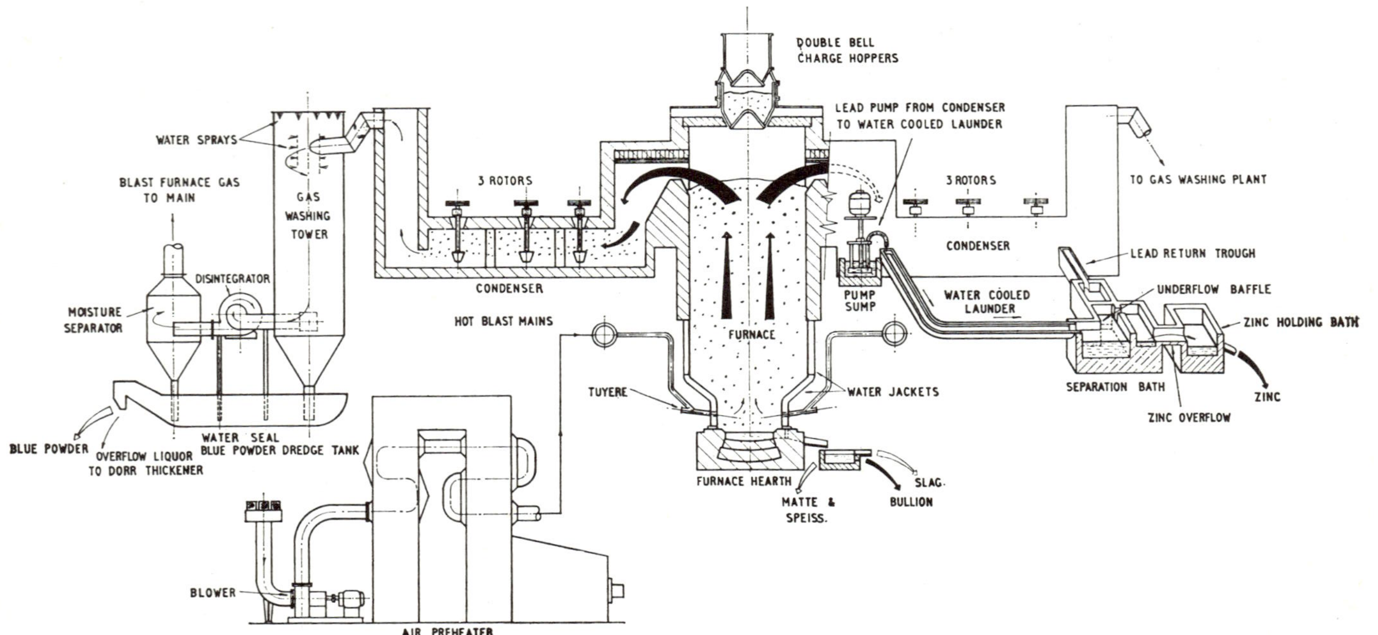

Fig. 12. Zinc production.

[*Imperial Smelting Processes Ltd.*

the solution, including treatment with zinc dust to precipitate nobler metals, zinc is deposited electrolytically on aluminium sheets, from which it is stripped off, melted and cast into slabs; the acid is simultaneously regenerated and used repeatedly. The purity of the metal so formed is greater than 99·95% and can be maintained above 99·99% when desired.

A further process, operated in America and Germany on a limited scale, involves a vertical retort in which a mixture of crude oxide and coke is heated internally by the passage of a heavy electric current through the charge. In this electro-thermal refining process, the zinc vapour which is formed may be either mixed with air to form zinc oxide, or be condensed as metal.

Alloys An alloy is a mixture of two or more metals in varying proportions. One purpose of alloying is to improve fusibility, the melting point of the alloy in most cases being lower than any of its constituents. Alloys too are usually harder and tougher, they give cleaner castings, tenacity and elasticity are improved, the colour is changed and they possess all the properties characteristic of a metal. When making an alloy, first fuse the metal with the highest melting point and if there are several constituent metals proceed in order and add the one with the lowest melting point last. The molten metal must be constantly stirred or the heavier metals will sink to the bottom and the alloy will not be homogeneous. Some form of cover should be used to prevent oxidation.

Non-ferrous alloys are numerous and vary greatly with respect to their properties and uses. They are produced to a consistently high standard and within the limits laid down by the British Standards Institution.* As such they are more properly identified by their BSI specification number but may be classified into groups according to their main constituents; they are also frequently known by their common or traditional names. The various groups of non-ferrous alloys are briefly explained in the following sections and the average compositions and properties and uses are tabulated.

Effects of Alloying

Tin Always increases the hardness and whitens the alloy.
Zinc Increases the fusibility, but does not decrease the hardness, unless used in very large percentages. It increases the malleability when the alloy is cold, but decreases it when hot; thus brass high in zinc cannot be forged at red heat.
Lead When used in small quantities increases the ductility of brass, thus making it more suitable for bending, bossing, repoussé work, etc., but if added in large percentages it tends to make the brass very short and brittle.
Bismuth Lowers the melting-point of nearly all alloys, but tends to cause brittleness.

* British Standards Institution, 101–113 Pentonville Rd., London, N.1.

Phosphorus Causes great fluidity, thus enabling sound, clean castings to be obtained.
Nickel Hardens alloys, and gives good wearing properties.
Antimony Imparts a hardness to alloys, and has the remarkable property of expanding slightly on cooling.

Alloys containing mercury are termed amalgams; those containing two metals are known as 'binary' alloys; and those containing three as 'ternary' alloys. The expression 'ternary' alloy is sometimes used loosely to indicate an alloy containing tin.

Aluminium alloys The addition of copper strengthens and hardens aluminium. An addition of up to 8% copper increases the tensile strength and a further increase of up to 12% improves the machining properties. The addition of zinc also has the effect of hardening aluminium but if the addition is above 13% then the alloy becomes 'hot-short' and is not suitable for castings. The addition of

Table 3. Aluminium alloys—average compositions percent

Name	Properties and/or uses	Cu	Si	Mg	Mn	Ni	Al
Casting alloy LM2	Pressure die castings	1·5	10				rem.*
Casting alloy LM4	General purpose alloy for sand and gravity die castings	3	5				rem.
Casting alloy LM6	Easily cast into thin or complex shapes		12				rem.
Wrought alloy N4	Ductile when annealed—work hardens. Pressings, containers and welded structures. Fabrications			2·25			rem.
Wrought alloy H12	General purpose high strength alloy. Aircraft structures and stressed components	2·25	1	1		1	rem.
Aluminium bronze	A strong, malleable and ductile alloy	90					rem.
Duralumin	Strong. Machines well. Age hardens. Light weight fabrications	4	0·4	0·5			rem.
Y alloy	Maintains strength at high temperatures. I.C.E. pistons. Light weight forgings	4			1·5	2	rem.

* Remainder

$2\frac{1}{2}$ to 3% copper reduces the tendency to hot-shortness. The casting alloys possess little or no copper but instead contain varying amounts of silicon according to their required strength/fluidity ratio.

Copper-tin Alloys Copper-tin alloys are called bronzes and their manufacture dates back to the time when primitive cutting tools, weapons and vessels were made from bronze. Throughout the ages bronze has remained a popular metal for statues and architectural fittings, because its ease of casting, resistance to corrosion and the attractive patina that is acquired through weathering, make it most suitable for out-door use. The addition of a small amount of phosphorus produces a copper-tin alloy known as *phosphor bronze* which has been used extensively for solid bearings in machine tools and engines. Gunmetal, as originally used for cannon, and bell-metal, used for casting bells, also come into this category.

Table 4. Copper-tin alloys—average compositions percent

Name	Properties and/or uses	Sn	Mz	Pb	Zn	Cu
Casting bronze	Age hardens. Castings and statuary	5	1			rem.
Phosphor bronze	Bearings and gearwheels	3–7		0·1		rem.
Gunmetal	High-speed solid bearings. Pumps, valves and statuary	3–10		1–4	2	rem.
Bell-metal	Hard, Sonorous. Used for bell castings	20				rem.

Copper-zinc alloys These are generally classified as brasses but the proportions of the constituents produce widely varying properties. When the proportion of zinc is small the cold-working and machining properties are improved. With a slightly increased zinc content the brass becomes more suitable for hot-working. Equal parts of copper and zinc give a low melting point alloy which is used as spelter. Brass is available in four tempers, previously known as soft, half-hard, hard and spring-hard, they are now denoted by the ISO* symbols: M = as manufactured; O = fully annealed; T (followed by another letter) = a specific heat-treatment; and H (followed by a number) = a specific degree of work hardness. Brasses containing up to 37% zinc are most suitable for cold-working and may be pressed, rolled and drawn. Those containing between 40 and 44% zinc are best suited for hot-working, and are used for hot pressings and stampings. If much bending of brass is to be attempted then it is essential to know just what its composition is or results can be most frustrating. If varying qualities

* International Standards Organization.

are ordered then they must be carefully marked and stored separately. Gilding metal which contains 80 to 90% copper is used very extensively for beaten metalwork. To improve the machining qualities of brass an addition of 2 to 3·5% lead is included, but has the tendency to make the metal 'hot-short'. Brass is produced in the form of strip, bar, tube and sheet and also as castings, extrusions and stampings.

Table 5. Copper-zinc alloys (brasses)—average compositions percent

Name	Properties and/or uses	Zn	Al	Pb	Ni	Cu
Alpha brass	Coldworking—rolling, pressing, drawing	28–37				rem.
Alpha beta brass	Casting, hot pressing, extruding	40–45				rem.
60/40 brass	General purpose brass. Simple forming and fabrication	40				rem.
Cartridge brass	Maximum ductility. Deep drawing	30				rem.
Naval brass	Hot working. Resists corrosion by sea water	37				rem.
Free-cutting brass	Electrical and mechanical components	40		3		rem.
Aluminium brass	Increases strength. High tensile brass	30	2			rem.
Gilding metal	Excellent coldworking properties. Rich colour. Jewellery and ornamental metalwork	10–20				rem.
Nickel silver	Corrosion and tarnish resistant. Tableware. Electrical components	13–27			10–30	rem.
German silver	Cheap jewellery and cutlery	25			15	rem.

Tin-lead alloys These alloys produce the soft solders and pewter. The alloys are harder than lead, their melting points being lower than the separate constituents and falling as the proportion of tin rises. Pewter is very malleable and ductile and is readily beaten into shapes for measures and tankards; it may also be cast. Type metal used in printing and the white metals used for machine bearings may also be classified under this heading.

Table 6. Tin-lead alloys—average compositions percent

Name	Properties and/or uses	Sn	Pb	Sb	Bi
Fine solder	Very low melting point	66·6	33·3		
Tinman's solder	Soldering tinplate	50	50		
Plumber's solder	Wiping pipe joints	33·3	66·6		
Pewter	Tarnish resistant. Tableware, ornaments	80	20		
Type metal	Expands on cooling. Printer's typeface	5	80	15	
White metal	Machine bearings	6	76	18	
Fusible alloy (Rose's metal)	Melts below water boiling point (For fusible plugs)	25	25		50

Zinc-based alloys A wide variety of small fittings and components for motor vehicles, domestic and commercial apparatus etc. are manufactured by machine die casting methods in zinc-based alloys. Intricately shaped articles to a high degree of accuracy are produced rapidly and cheaply by these means. Alloys suitable for bearings also fall within this class, while new zinc-based alloys suited to more sophisticated forming techniques are now being developed.

Table 7. Zinc-based alloys—average compositions percent

Name	Properties and/or uses	Al	Cu	Mg	Zn
Alzen 305	Bearing metal	30	5		rem.
Zinc die casting alloy	Permanent mould castings	4	1	0·04	rem.
Superplastic alloy	Vacuum forming	22			rem.

3 Marking-out, Measuring and Testing

The accurate marking-out of work is fundamental to all metalworking processes and the methods employed are common to all branches of the craft. Measuring and testing are carried out both during the manufacture of an article and in its final checking. The tools and instruments used in these processes constitute a most important part of the metalworker's equipment and a knowledge of the techniques by which they are used is most necessary. Although more advanced work is often brought to its final shape and size with machine tools, in conjunction with measuring instruments alone, work is still frequently marked out as a guide during machining operations. Furthermore, working to a line with hand tools forms an important part in training. Many of the simple marking-out and testing tools can be made in the workshop.

Preparation of surfaces for marking-out Lines scribed on the surface of the softer non-ferrous metals are clearly visible, and a scriber will trace a line on the surface oxide of cold-rolled sheet and bar steel that can readily be seen. On the rough surface of cast iron and the smooth surface of bright drawn steel, however, some form of coating is required to give emphasis to the marked out lines. Castings that will not be subjected to a lot of handling can be coated with chalk in the areas where they are to be marked out; otherwise a white wash or white matt lead paint is used. Bright steel should be given a fine coat of copper by applying copper sulphate solution, or treated with a proprietary brand of marking fluid. Copper sulphate solution is prepared by dissolving the crystals in water and, being non-acid, will not cause undue corrosion. A good substitute for a marking blue can readily be made in the workshop by colouring a thin shellac polish with a soluble dye such as gentian violet. In the application of these solutions the surface of the metal must be free from grease and the work should first be cleaned with emery cloth.

Scribers The scriber, Fig. 13, having a hard and sharp tool steel tip, will scratch a fine line on metal that can be readily seen against the surface oxide or applied coating. There are many patterns of scribers and making this simple tool is a good exercise. In the choice of scribers for practical instruction, they should in the first place be of a safe design. The bent end of a double-ended scriber enables it to be used in places inaccessible to a straight scriber, but this is not frequently needed and a single-ended type is therefore more suitable initially. A square or hexagonal head to the shank will prevent the scriber from rolling from the bench and provides a place for the number of the tool kit to which it belongs, or for the owner's initials. The head however must be kept small and not invite the use of a hammer. A well finished and pleasantly shaped tool will not tend to become lost by being swept away with swarf or scrap metal and, as well as being easily identifiable, will last longer and produce better work than an inferior one. The point of the scriber should be sharpened by holding it at an angle to the vertical, introducing it to the face of the wheel, and rotating. This will result in a stronger point. For marking out tin plate a scriber of brass is used to prevent rusting; it can also be used on finished work when it is important not to scratch the surface.

The straight edge of a good steel rule is sufficiently accurate for the marking out of straight lines and the preliminary testing of the straight edges of work, and a 300 mm rule will be found most suitable.

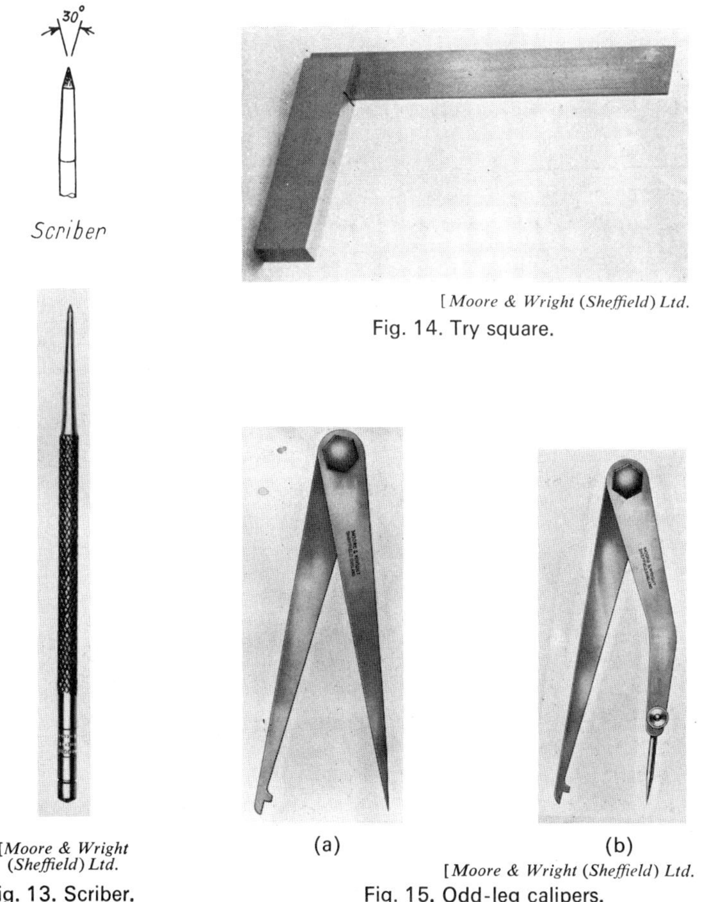

[*Moore & Wright (Sheffield) Ltd.*

Fig. 14. Try square.

[*Moore & Wright
(Sheffield) Ltd.*

Fig. 13. Scriber.

(a)

(b)

[*Moore & Wright (Sheffield) Ltd.*

Fig. 15. Odd-leg calipers.

Try squares   The try square, Fig. 14, is used for setting out lines at right-angles to an edge or face, and for the testing or 'trying' of edges and surfaces at 90° to each other. It is thus an important instrument and must be used and treated with care to preserve its accuracy. Various qualities of engineers' squares are available and sizes vary according to the work. A good quality square with a case hardened stock and a 125 mm hardened and tempered blade, of workshop grade, will be found to be suitable. Larger and smaller squares should be kept for the occasions when a 125 mm square is inadequate, and one of these could very well be of the inspection grade and used to check the workshop squares.

In use, the stock of the try square is held firmly against the edge of the work by the thumb, and the blade pressed against the face side or edge of the work, by the fingers of the same hand. As with the rule, the scriber is first placed on a point through which the line will pass and the blade positioned against it. Errors will not occur if this procedure is followed, for the blade of a try square, being of heavier gauge than that of a rule, demands greater care with regard to the angle of inclination at which the scriber is held.

Odd-leg calipers   Sometimes known as 'hermaphrodite' or 'jenny' calipers, odd-leg calipers are used in basic marking-out processes for scribing a line parallel to an edge, and to locate the centre of a circular bar or disc. Generally of the firm joint pattern, two types are available. The simple type (Fig. 15a) in which the scribing leg is made of a toolsteel and hardened and tempered, is perhaps the more suitable to begin with, but sharpening the point reduces the length of the leg and the efficiency of the tool. The type consisting of two case hardened mild steel legs (Fig. 15b) and with a separate scriber point, though less easy to maintain, will have a longer life.

In setting firm joint calipers of any sort, the approximate setting is first done by hand, and the final adjustment made by holding the joint between finger and thumb and tapping one leg on the bench to reduce the distance, and by tapping the joint on the back of the vice to open the legs slightly. Measurements are taken from the end of the rule as with outside calipers, Fig. 17b. To find the centre of a parallel bar, the odd-legs are first set to the approximate mid-distance, and a short line scribed from each side of the work in turn. The error in the preliminary setting is then easily seen and, after appropriate tapping of the leg, the process is repeated until the two lines are coincident. Similarly the centre of a disc may be found by setting to the near radius dimension, and at least three arcs made with the gauging leg over the side of the disc. The centre can then be judged as midway between the scribed arcs, or their points of intersection.

Centre and dot punches   Although most metalworking components and parts are finished to size by reference to a gauge or measuring instrument, there are occasions in bench fitting, especially during basic processes when the marked-out line is the only guide to the final shape and size. When filing or removing metal down to a scribed line, with the aim of working to the centre of that line, the line itself becomes difficult to see and hence requires further emphasizing. A light centre punch with a point angle of 60° is used for this purpose. A row of very fine dot punch indentations is made along the line about a quarter of an inch apart. When finished to size the work will then show a row of semi-circular marks around its periphery and small vee grooves along its edge. These are finally removed completely along with the sharp edge of the work. Dot punches, Fig. 16a, are also used to locate the centre of circles, radii and arcs, in order to

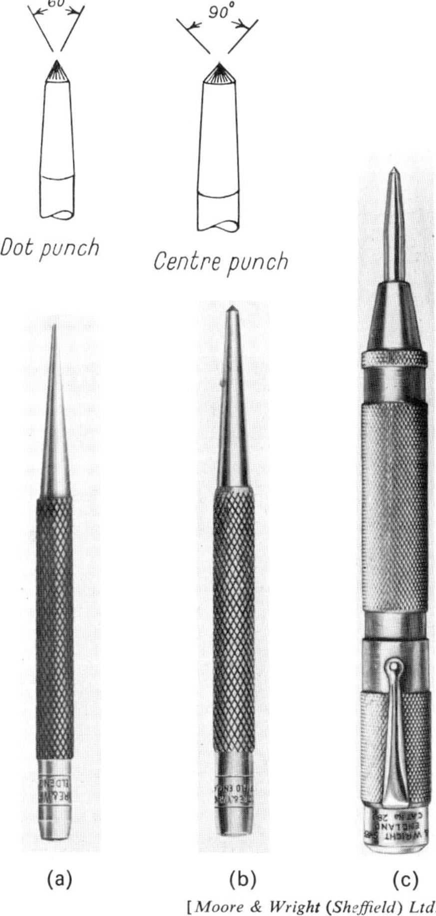

[*Moore & Wright (Sheffield) Ltd.*

Fig. 16. Centre and dot punches.

provide a firm anchor for the stationary leg of dividers. Similar indentations made around centre punched hole locations give an indication of the accuracy of drilling operations, enabling their correction before the drill has reached its full diameter. The dot punching of large work is facilitated by the use of an automatic centre punch, Fig. 16c. The pressure of the blow can be varied and dots of the required size produced accurately and at speed.

A heavier punch is required for setting the position of the holes to be drilled, for, in order to prevent the drill wandering when being introduced to the work, an indentation must be provided the upper diameter of which is larger than the web of the drill being used. This centre punch, Fig. 16b, therefore has a point angle of 90° and is made from heavier bar than the dot punch. The accurate drilling of a hole depends almost entirely on the positioning of the centre punch mark and great care should be taken in its marking-out. The location is shown by the intersection of two scribed lines at 90° to each other. The punch is held with the third finger near the point of the punch and placed on the intersecting lines, while being held at an angle to the vertical, in order that both the point of the punch and the position of the mark can be seen. The punch is then brought to the vertical and a light blow given with the hammer. If, on inspection, the mark is seen to be correctly placed a sharper blow is then given to enlarge the mark. If however it is slightly off its position it can be 'pulled over' by inclining the punch and applying light taps with the hammer while bringing the punch to the vertical.

Dividers The universal tool for the marking-out of circles, radii and arcs, and for the transference of measurements from rule to work, is a pair of dividers, Fig. 17a. Having two similar legs of hardened steel, with a scriber point to each of them, they may be of the firm joint or spring adjustable types. Spring dividers are to be preferred for small work, as fine adjustment by screw and nut can readily be made, and when held and used correctly there is little danger of the legs moving under pressure. When set to the required distance, the dividers are placed in the palm of the hand and the thumb brought over between the legs to assist the spring in keeping them apart. The making of a true and clearly defined circle is further facilitated by the rotation of the work as well as the dividers. Measurements are taken from the centre of the rule with both of the legs located against an engraved line. Wherever possible dimensions should be transferred to the work in this way in order to avoid errors of parallax that may result when measurements are made direct from the rule.

The length of the leg determines the size of dividers. The 125 mm size is comfortable to handle and will accommodate the usual range of work. To avoid wear on the screw, the legs should be pressed together when making a preliminary setting. The provision of a split quick-action nut assists the prevention of wear and speeds the setting. As with the whole range of marking-out and testing instruments, the care of the tool should include an occasional oiling.

36

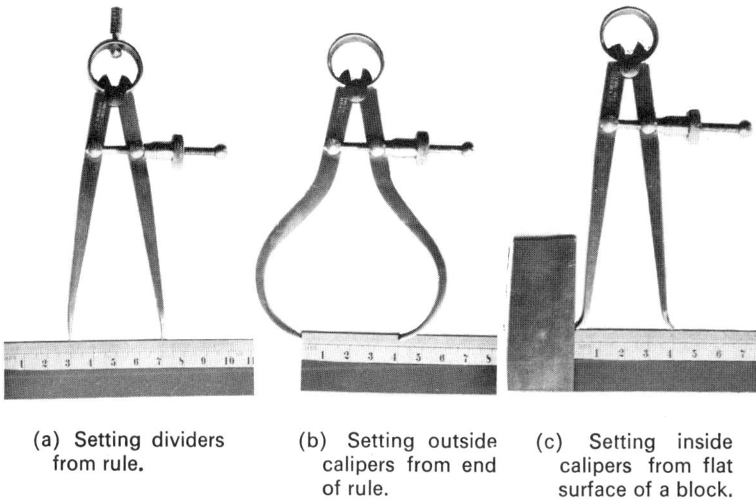

(a) Setting dividers from rule.

(b) Setting outside calipers from end of rule.

(c) Setting inside calipers from flat surface of a block.

Fig. 17. Setting dividers and calipers.

Trammels Dividers become less accurate and more difficult to use as the radius of the arc being scribed gets larger. This is due to the decreasing angle between the legs and the work, which makes one leg tend to slip from its locating dot punched indentation, and the other present the side rather than the point of the leg to the work. Trammels provide a convenient method of marking out the larger circles and radii. These consist of two scriber points which may be moved laterally and locked in position, on an interchangeable beam or arm, Fig. 18. The points are vertical in all positions, and the beam may be extended, or a larger one used. Trammels may be obtained (or made) with a fine adjustment screw to one of the legs and with a chuck that will take a pencil lead as well as a

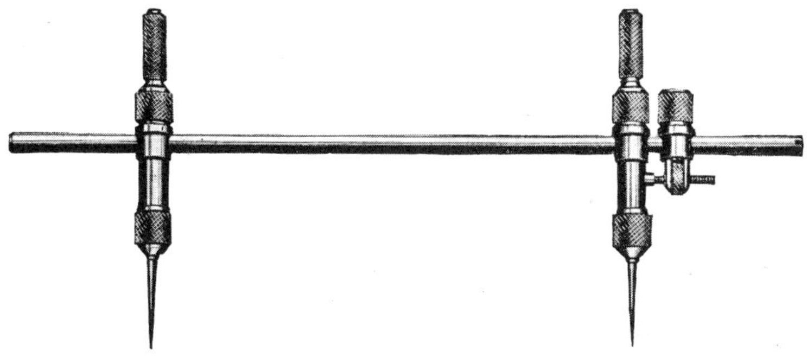

[*Buck & Hickman Ltd.*

Fig. 18. Trammel.

hardened scriber point. They are therefore useful for marking out tinplate and are an additional drawing aid for large work.

Combination set   The combination set of instruments provides a useful range of basic marking-out, measuring and testing tools. It consists of a protractor head, square head and centre head, together with a rule which is interchangeable and can be located in any of the three heads; it can be used for a great variety of operations (Fig. 19).

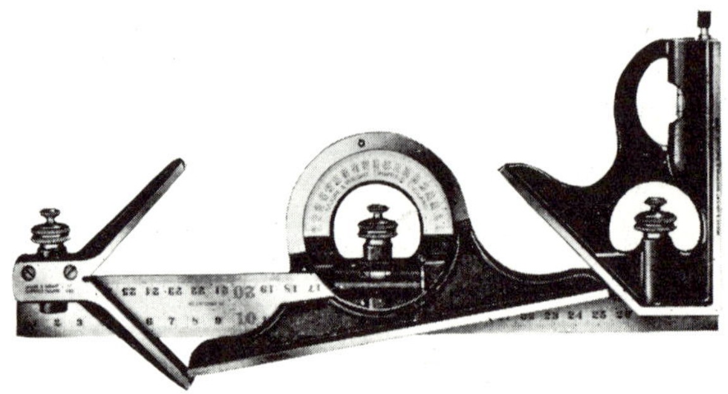

[*Moore & Wright (Sheffield) Ltd.*

Fig. 19. Combination set.

When the rule is placed in the protractor head, all the work of which a bevel gauge is capable can be accomplished, with the additional advantage of the direct reading of the angle. The head also contains a spirit level which enables it to be used for the checking of any face at an angle to the horizontal and for the setting-up of work on the surface table or machine.

The rule, when used in conjunction with the square head, enables angles of 90° and 45° to be marked out and tested with accuracy, and its incorporated level facilitates the setting-up of work to these angles to the horizontal and the vertical planes. This application also provides a convenient rule holder on the marking-out table and a depth gauge with a variety of uses. A small scriber is attached and a spring clip supplied enabling the head, with the rule locked in position, to stand firmly on the surface plate when setting the surface gauge from it.

The centre head is more limited in its scope but it does provide a useful tool in the setting-up of circular work and, as well as its primary function as a centre square, it is an accurate gauge of the 90° angle, and of the 45° angle when fitted with the rule.

Surface plate and surface table   In the workshop measurements must often be transferred to the work from a true and flat surface or plane of reference. This plane of reference is provided by the surface plate or, for larger work, by the surface table. The surface plate consists of an iron casting with an upper surface of proved flatness supported by a ribbed undercarriage to prevent distortion, Fig. 20. The three bearing points on which it stands provide a tripod base, enabling the plate to stand firmly on an uneven bench top and thus preventing the surface from being subjected to undue stress. Two carrying handles are usually provided, together with a cover which should remain in place whenever the plate is not in use. Because of their high degree of accuracy and the laborious methods by which they are produced, surface plates are expensive pieces of equipment and must be kept clean, protected from damage and lightly oiled after use. These plates are used for marking-out and testing only; no other work must be done upon them.

[T. S. Harrison & Sons Ltd.

Fig. 20. Surface plates.

The surface gauge and scribing block   From the plane of reference provided by the surface plate, measurements are transferred to the work by means of a surface gauge or a scribing block. Scribing blocks of various types have means whereby a scriber point may be positioned at the required height above the surface of the plate and a line scribed on the work at exactly this distance. The surface gauge is similar in function and in appearance but it has additional advantages. It is provided with a means of fine adjustment of the scriber, it has dowel pins through the base for locating against the edges of the plate or machine slide, and has a cut away portion in the base block which enables the pillar to be rocked and to be set at an angle.

In use the scriber point is set at the required height against a rule held vertically above the plate. The rule may be held by the hand against an angle plate or vee-block, in a rule holder designed for the purpose, or in the square head of the combination set, Fig. 21a. The block is then moved over the surface of the plate and the scriber point touches against the work which in turn is held still on the plate. Although one end of the scriber is bent to facilitate working near the surface of the plate, in practice the transference of small dimensions by this means proves difficult. Small scribing blocks can readily be made in the workshop for this purpose or the work can be raised on to inverted vee-blocks or parallel bars, and measurements taken from a higher level.

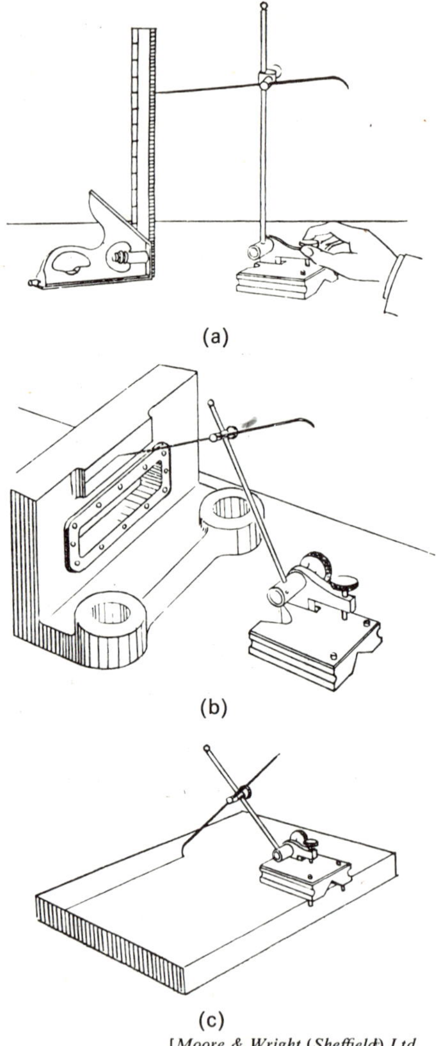

(a)

(b)

(c)

[*Moore & Wright (Sheffield) Ltd.*

Fig. 21. Use of surface gauge.

As well as its function as a marking-out tool, the surface gauge is used to test the height or size of work by comparison with work or blocks of known size, or of one part of a piece of work with another part of the same piece. Such a test is that of the parallelism of a bar. The curved end of the scriber is adjusted to just contact the upper surface of one end of the work and then, by moving the point over other portions of the bar, variations in size can be felt.

Feeler gauges Tests with the surface gauge will indicate variations in size, but to measure the small discrepancies, feeler gauges can be used. Consisting of a number of blades of varying thinness, feeler gauges are available in sets. A small set of Metric sizes with a range of from 0·03 mm to 1 mm is usually adequate, for such a set will enable measurements to limits of 0·01 mm to be gauged. The number of hundredths of a millimetre thickness is printed on each leaf. Care must be taken to ensure that the delicate blades do not become bent or damaged.

Vee-blocks Circular work and round bars can be conveniently held in vee-blocks while being marked out or tested. Usually made of cast iron (though some smaller ones are of case hardened mild steel), vee-blocks are manufactured in pairs, Fig. 22. Both blocks of the pair are given identical numbers and should be kept and used together on occasions when more than a single block is required. Grooves along the sides of the smaller blocks are provided for the use of clamps which hold the work firmly in position when marking out, testing and machining.

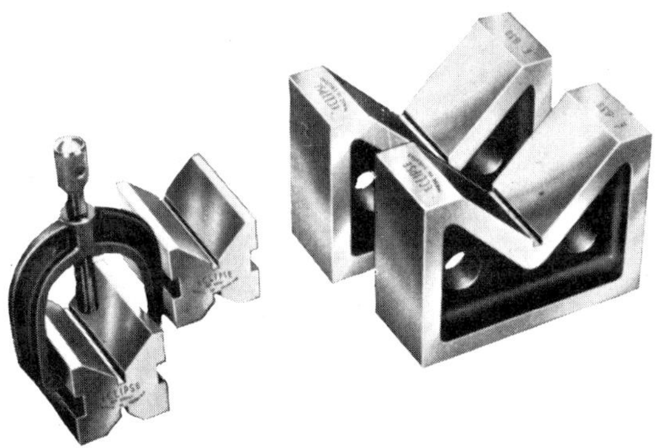

[*James Neill & Co. (Sheffield) Ltd.*

Fig. 22. Vee-blocks.

Angle plates Irregular work and some larger work that cannot be readily supported by blocks and bars, will need to be bolted to an angle plate for marking-out as well as for machining. Angle plates, consisting of simple castings machined on two faces at 90° to each other, are provided with holes and slots in various positions in which to put holding-down bolts. Plates are also machined on their ends to enable marking-out to be done from both the horizontal and vertical planes, while the box angle plate permits the accurate location of work in many positions and increases its adaptability and usefulness, Fig. 23. Angular

41

work, or work requiring lines at an angle to a surface to be marked upon it, can be clamped to an adjustable swivel angle plate. Although not used much in instructional marking-out and measuring work in the metalwork room, a selection of the smaller plates should be available, for they have wider applications in machine work to be described later.

Webbed end   Box

[James Neill & Co. (Sheffield) Ltd.

Fig. 23. Angle plates.

Calipers The measurement and gauging of the diameters of circular bars (and some other work) calls for an instrument that will straddle the work and enable the size to be compared with the scale of a rule or with pieces of known dimensions. For the preliminary testing of such work, calipers are used. These may be suited to either outside or inside dimensions and be of the firm joint or spring adjustable types. The methods of adjustment are similar to those of the odd-leg calipers and, as with dividers, the spring type are to be preferred.

The setting of outside calipers is done from the end of the rule, while inside calipers should be set by placing one leg and the rule against a flat surface, Fig. 17. In both cases, care must be taken to ensure that both contacting points of the legs are at the same distance from the edge of the rule. Inside calipers can also be set between the anvil and spindle faces of the micrometer, and outside calipers from built-up measuring blocks. With practice, a high sense of feel can be developed and great accuracy attained. A good exercise to show this 'feel' of calipers, in the early stages of a course, is the filing of a parallel strip of metal, and its testing with a straight edge and calipers. With the strip held on a flat surface and the calipers resting lightly in the hand, they should be able to be drawn evenly along the work. Any variation in width can readily be felt.

Vernier scale A further range of measuring instruments incorporating vernier scales enable measurements to be taken to a greater degree of accuracy than is possible by the direct reading of an engraved scale. A small sliding scale (the vernier scale) is attached to the jaw or arm of the instrument, Fig. 24, and, moving against the main scale, makes possible the accurate division of the main scale graduations. The number of divisions on the vernier scale corresponds to the fraction into which it is desired to divide one division of the main scale and is engraved over a distance equal to one division less than a similar number of graduations on the main scale.

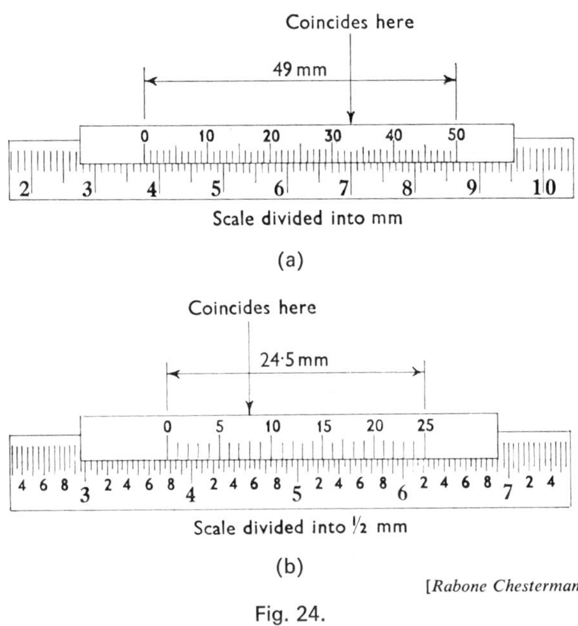

[*Rabone Chesterman.*

Fig. 24.

The principle of the metric vernier range of instruments may be seen in Fig. 24. In Fig. 24a the main scale has 1 mm divisions and the vernier scale is divided into 50 parts over a length of 49 mm. Each division on the vernier scale therefore will be $\frac{49}{50}$ mm or 0·980 mm and the difference between a main scale division and a vernier division will be 1 mm $-$ 0·980 $=$ 0·02 mm (1/50 mm). The main scale reading to the left of the zero on the vernier indicates the number of whole millimetres and the line on the vernier which coincides with a line on the main scale indicates the number of additional 1/50 mm (0·02 mm). In the illustration the reading is 37·66 mm (37 mm on the main scale plus 33/50 mm (0·66 mm) on the vernier scale).

In Fig. 24b, the main scale has $\frac{1}{2}$ mm divisions but, to facilitate reading, the vernier is arranged to be read on alternate lines on the main scale. The vernier scale is divided into 25 parts over a length of 24·5 mm hence each division will be $\frac{24·5}{25}$ mm or 0·980 mm. The difference between a single vernier division and two main scale divisions will therefore be 1 mm $-$ 0·980 $=$ 0·02 mm. When reading the instrument, first note the distance to the left of the vernier zero to

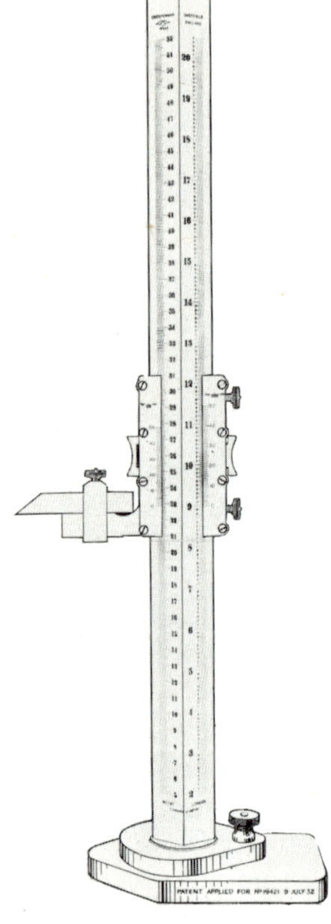

Fig. 25(a). Vernier height gauge.

[*Rabone Chesterman.*

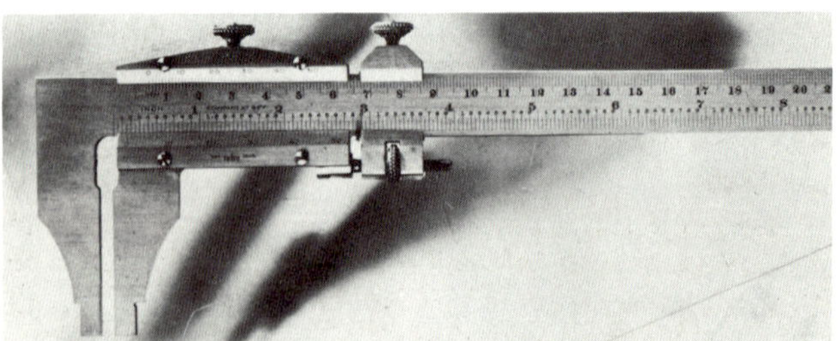

Fig. 25(b). Vernier calipers.

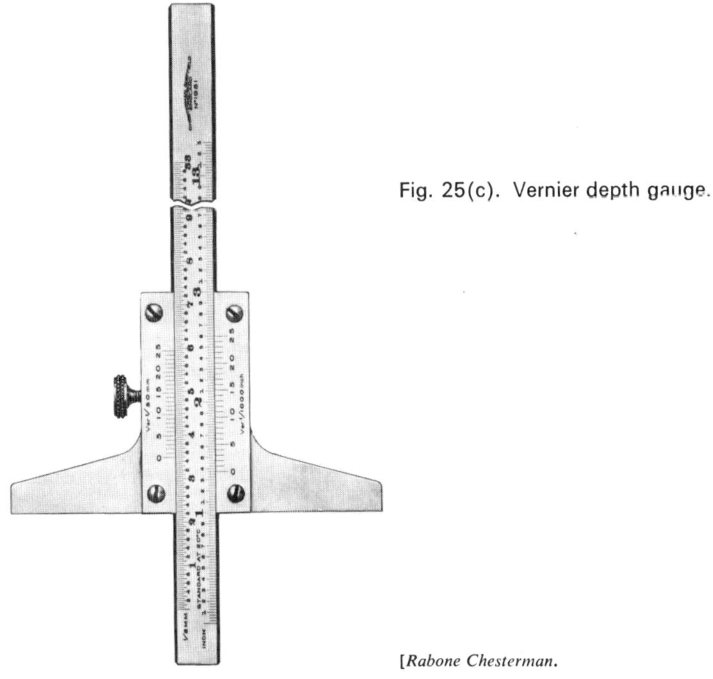

Fig. 25(c). Vernier depth gauge.

[*Rabone Chesterman.*]

the nearest ½ mm and then add the vernier reading In the illustration the reading is again 37·66 mm (37·5 mm on the main scale plus 8/50 mm (0·16 mm) on the vernier).

In reading vernier instruments, therefore, a direct reading is taken from the position of the vernier zero mark, and then the amount by which the zero mark has passed the main scale mark is shown by the vernier mark, which coincides with a line on the main scale. It will be seen that the vernier line which coincides with a main scale line is more easily identified by observing the lines immediately to the left and to the right. The adjacent vernier line to the left is slightly to the right of a main scale line and that on the right side is slightly to the left.

The *height gauge* is normally used on machine slides and the surface plate. It consists of a heavy base supporting the column on which the main scale is engraved. The pattern illustrated, Fig. 25a, has a screw for fine adjustment, and the operating screw is engaged and disengaged for rapid setting by a nut at the back of the movable head. The means of fine adjustment on *vernier calipers*, Fig. 25b, is by a knurled nut, screw and clamp, positioned behind the sliding frame carrying the vernier scale. The sliding jaw is first approximately positioned by hand after releasing the two clamping screws. The screw on the clamp is then tightened and fine adjustment made by means of the nut. Finally the jaw is clamped to the beam. Internal measurements can also be made with the vernier calipers, but the thickness of the jaw ends (size varies with different models but is engraved on the jaws) must be added to the reading taken from the scale. Similarly the thickness of the arm must be added to the reading when using the scriber point on the height gauge illustrated. In a similar way the depths of holes, recesses and shoulders may be accurately measured by means of the *vernier depth gauge*, Fig. 25c.

Vernier protractor   The vernier scale, when adapted to an instrument of angular measurement, enables measurements to be made to within 5 minutes of arc. In the vernier protractor, the main scale is divided into degrees round the circumference of a complete circle, Fig. 26. The vernier scale is attached to the inner

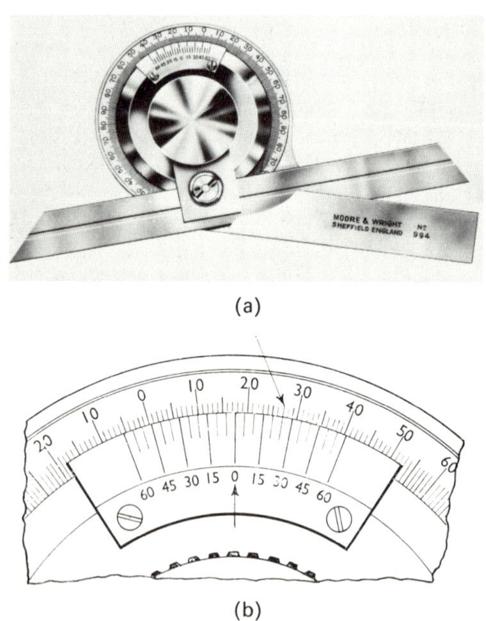

(a)

(b)

[*Moore & Wright (Sheffield) Ltd.*

Fig. 26. (a) Vernier protractor and (b) reading.

disc which carries the rotating arm and is divided into twelve divisions each representing 5 minutes. Two vernier scales are provided, one to the right and the other to the left of the zero mark. When taking readings in a clockwise direction the scale to the right of the mark is used; the left hand scale is used when setting in the other direction. In reading the protractor, the number of full degrees to the right or left (as the case may be) of the zero mark is first noted, and then the number of minutes, as indicated by the vernier scale, is added to it. For example, in Fig. 26b the number of degrees to the left of the scale is 17, to which 25 minutes are to be added, making a total reading of 17 degrees and 25 minutes. Because both sides of the stock and blade are used for a variety of applications, great care must be taken to ensure that the *angle required* is set off, or read, and not its supplement or complement. Until one has become skilled in its use it is better to note the zero mark on the vernier scale each time, count the angle through which the zero on the scale rotates, and then add on the minutes, still traversing the eye in the same direction.

Micrometer calipers   As shown in Fig. 27, the micrometer caliper consists of a rigid frame and carries at one end a hardened and optically flat anvil face. The micrometer head is attached to the other, the spindle of which has a correspondingly accurate face. When these faces are brought together, the thimble scale zero mark will be in line with the datum line of the main scale, and the end of the thimble will register with the zero mark of the main scale. It is the distance between these faces that is measured. The micrometer illustrated will measure from zero to 25 mm; larger dimensions are catered for by micrometer calipers reading between 25 and 50 mm; 50 and 75 mm and so on.

From Fig. 27 it will be seen that a nut (6) is located at the end of a hollow sleeve (4), which has a datum line running parallel to its axis. To avoid confusion when reading the thimble, the traverse lines are set on both sides of the datum line at a distance of 1 mm apart. The screw which passes through the nut and sleeve carries the spindle at one end and, at the other end, a cap to which the thimble is fixed. The thimble is bevelled at its lower end and is divided into 50 equal divisions round the circumference of the bevel. A single complete

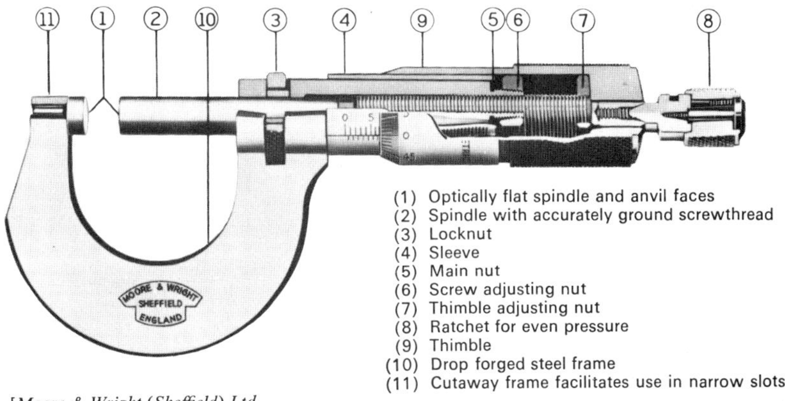

(1) Optically flat spindle and anvil faces
(2) Spindle with accurately ground screwthread
(3) Locknut
(4) Sleeve
(5) Main nut
(6) Screw adjusting nut
(7) Thimble adjusting nut
(8) Ratchet for even pressure
(9) Thimble
(10) Drop forged steel frame
(11) Cutaway frame facilitates use in narrow slots.

[*Moore & Wright (Sheffield) Ltd.*

Fig. 27. Micrometer calipers.

revolution of the thimble will therefore move its end, and the face of the spindle by a distance equal to 0·5 mm. A rotation of 1/50th of a revolution, readily seen by the passage of the thimble scale past the datum line of the main scale, will cause the spindle to move 1/50th of 0·5 mm or 1/100th mm, or 0·01 mm.

Micrometer scales The principle of the micrometer scale, which is used in a wide range of precision measuring instruments, is the fine linear traverse made possible by the action of an accurate screw through a correspondingly precise nut. In metric instruments the screw is given a thread with a pitch of 0·5 mm so that a complete revolution of the screw will cause it to move laterally 0·5 mm. Metric micrometers are usually designed to measure a total distance of 25 mm, larger dimensions being catered for by separate attachments or different frames to which the instrument is attached. In reading the micrometer scale the position of the end of the thimble is first noted in relation to the main scale, and the number of mm's and half mm's read off. The number of 1/100ths mm is then seen by the number on the thimble scale which is coincident with the datum line of the main scale. To obtain the micrometer reading add these together. For example consider Fig. 28a.

Complete spaces above datum line is 4	= 4·00 mm
Additional space visible below datum line is 1	= 0·50 mm
Addition of line on thimble coinciding with datum line is 17	= 0·17 mm

Reading = 4·67 mm

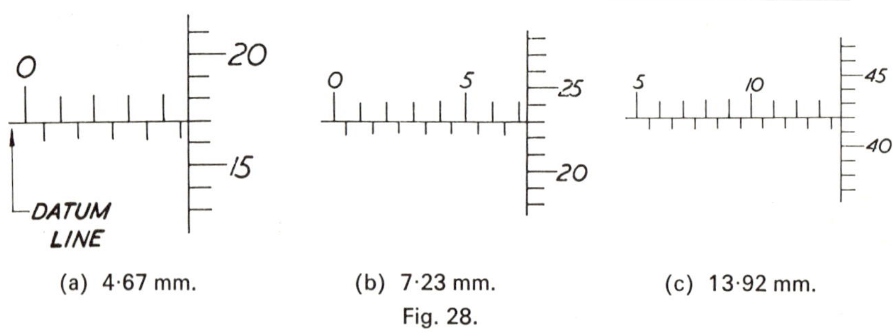

(a) 4·67 mm.   (b) 7·23 mm.   (c) 13·92 mm.

Fig. 28.

e.g. Fig. 28b

Complete spaces above datum line is 7	= 7·00 mm
Additional space visible below datum line is nil	
Addition of line on thimble coinciding with datum line is 23	= 0·23 mm

Reading = 7·23 mm

e.g. Fig. 28c

Complete spaces above datum line is 13	= 13·00 mm
Additional space visible below datum line is 1	= 0·50 mm
Addition of line on thimble coinciding with datum line is 42 =	0·42 mm

Reading = 13·92 mm

A vernier scale is engraved on the barrel of some micrometers enabling accurate readings to be made to within 0·002 mm (two thousandths of a milli-metre). Micrometers with vernier scales are read in the same way as the plain micrometers and the vernier reading as shown by the coincident lines, is added to it. E.g. in Fig. 29,

No. mm (below the datum line)	= 8·000
No. of additional $\frac{1}{2}$ mm (above the line)	= 0·500
No. of 1/100 mm (on thimble scale)	= 0·000
No. of 1/1000 mm (coincident vernier line) =	0·006

Reading = 8·506 mm

Further features of the micrometer caliper are the clamp ring by which the spindle can be locked in position, and the ratchet by which an even pressure can be obtained by different operators. These two features are of little practical value in the metalwork room. The clamp ring, which turns the instrument into a set gauge, is of use only when batches of similar work are being inspected; its use can cause damage to the instrument if the inexperienced attempt to force it over oversize work or rotate the thimble with the spindle clamped. The ratchet is an attempt to eliminate the human error in quantity production; students should try to get the 'feel' of the micrometer and not to rely on the ratchet.

Correct handling of the instrument is important to preserve its accuracy. The 0–25 mm micrometer is normally held in the palm of the hand with the little finger through the frame and the thimble rotated by the thumb and forefinger. Larger micrometers will of necessity have to be held with both hands but they must always be treated with the respect due to expensive and precise instruments and they should never be subjected to the slightest strain. Micrometers should be checked periodically, the 0–25 mm micrometer caliper by cleaning the faces, bringing them together and noting the alignment of the scales. Larger mi-crometers are checked over slip gauges or the standard roller or bar gauge sup-plied with the instrument. With the spindle in a free position it should also be tested for endplay indicating wear in the nut. If errors are detected, they can be corrected by removing the thimble by unwinding it to the extreme (and this is the only occasion when the spindle should be withdrawn) and tightening the nut slightly by screwing the collar further along the taper on the split nut. On reassembly, the alignment of the zero mark in relation to the datum line should again be checked. If incorrect, this fault can be corrected by rotating the barrel with the small 'C' spanner provided, thus making the two lines coincident. With care, such faults will rarely occur and a micrometer should not be tampered with unless its condition so warrants it.

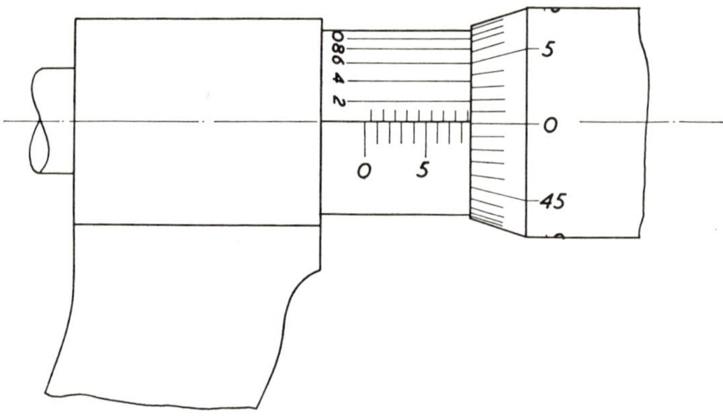

Fig. 29. Micrometer vernier.

Depth micrometers are used for measuring the depth of holes, slots or recesses and, on occasions, the distances between two parallel faces. The depth micrometer has a micrometer head mounted on a flat base, Fig. 30a. It can be tested on a flat surface or against a slip gauge and adjusted in the same way as the micrometer heads of other instruments. It will be seen from Fig. 30a that the top cap may be unscrewed and the capacity of the micrometer increased by inserting longer rods. The total capacity of a depth micrometer may range from zero to 300 mm. It must also be observed that a reading is taken from right to left and not from left to right as with micrometers designed for external measurements. The depth micrometer reading shown in Fig. 30b is thus 17 mm plus 0·22 mm = 17·22 mm.

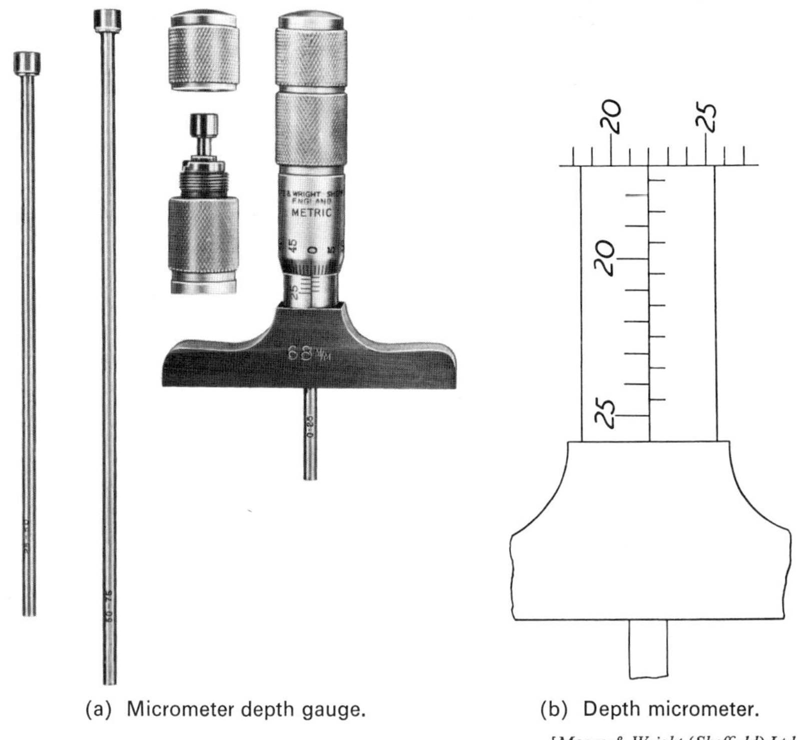

(a) Micrometer depth gauge.

(b) Depth micrometer.

[*Moore & Wright (Sheffield) Ltd.*

Fig. 30.

Standard test gauges

Radius gauges   Radius gauges, Fig. 31b, are used to check small radii and fillets, both internal and external. Supplied in sets of sizes, varying by 0·25 mm from 0·75 mm to 5 mm, numerous applications will be found for their use in the workshop.

Screw pitch gauge   To check the pitch of a screw thread when a matching nut is required, or to check the correct setting of a lathe after a first light cut has been taken when screwcutting, screw pitch gauges are used, Fig. 31a. They are useful also for the gauging of the radii at the crest and trough of vee-threads.

Thread angle gauge   When shaping a tool with which to cut a screw thread of a standard form, a thread angle gauge is used, Fig. 31c. As can be seen, various parts of the gauge are suited to the different thread forms and by its use screw-cutting tools are also set up on the lathe.

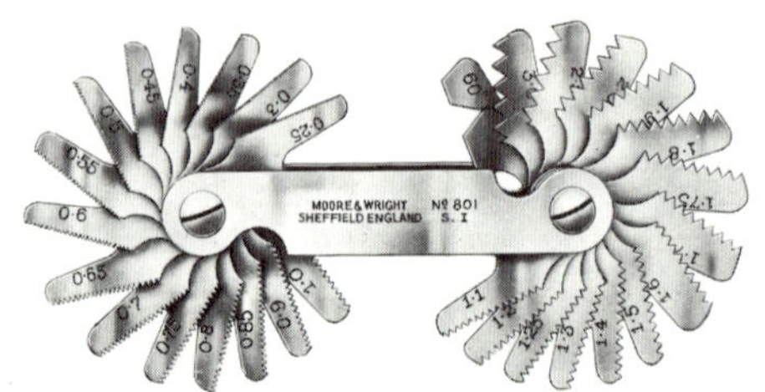

(a) Screw pitch gauge.

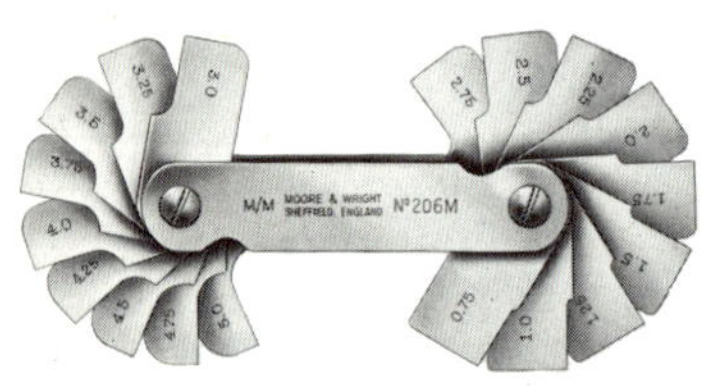

(b) Radius gauge.

(c) Thread angle gauge.

[Moore & Wright (Sheffield) Ltd.

Fig. 31. Standard gauges.

4 Benchwork

The metalwork bench   Normally in a school workshop there is sufficient bench space provided so that each member of the class may have a vice of his own. To quote *Metalwork in Secondary Schools**, 'A vice and the common hand tools are provided for each boy at his bench, which he also regards as a base where he plans whatever work he may do at fixed equipment in other parts of the workshop'.

A solid, rigid bench is essential if accurate work is to be done. Metalwork benches do not need metal tops, which are noisy and unpleasant to work on. They are usually made of wood and this absorbs the metallic noises of the workshop. Angle-iron edging let in flush with the top can be fitted with advantage, especially if the tops are of soft wood. Vices should not be fitted opposite each other and should be as nearly over a leg as possible. The height of a bench is important—between 750 mm and 850 mm is convenient. When the vice is fitted, the top of the vice should be level with the worker's elbow, so that when filing the forearm is level. When a number of vices are fitted along one side of a bench, they should be so arranged that all the back jaws are in line to accommodate long work. A perpendicular dropped from the back jaw should just clear the front of the bench top.

Leg vice   This is an older form of vice and is now used mainly for forge work, chipping, cold-bending or other forms of heavy work. It is a strong vice and will

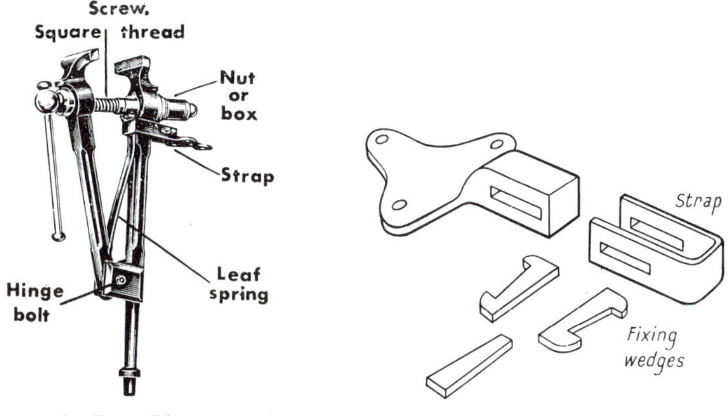

[*William Allday & Co. Ltd.*
Fig. 32. Leg vice.

Fig. 33. Leg vice securing device.

* *Metalwork in Secondary Schools*, H.M. Stationery Office.

stand up to hard usage. It consists of a long leg which may be fastened to the bottom of the bench or let into a socket grouted into the floor. A shorter leg is hinged to the longer one by a bolt, and a square-threaded screw working into a long turned nut tightens the vice. It is held in the open position by a strong leaf spring. The longer leg is fastened to the bench top by a strap which is keyed to the leg, Fig. 33. The leg vice is usually made of wrought iron or mild steel and has cast steel jaw pieces. The big disadvantage of the leg vice is that, as the front jaw moves in an arc of a circle, there is only one position in which the jaw faces are parallel, consequently it is difficult to grip work level. This disadvantage led to the design of the engineers' parallel vice.

Engineer's parallel vice is usually of cast iron but can be obtained in steel. Hammering on the sliding jaw of a cast iron vice must never be permitted or it may lead to a breakage. The size of a vice is according to the width of the jaw.

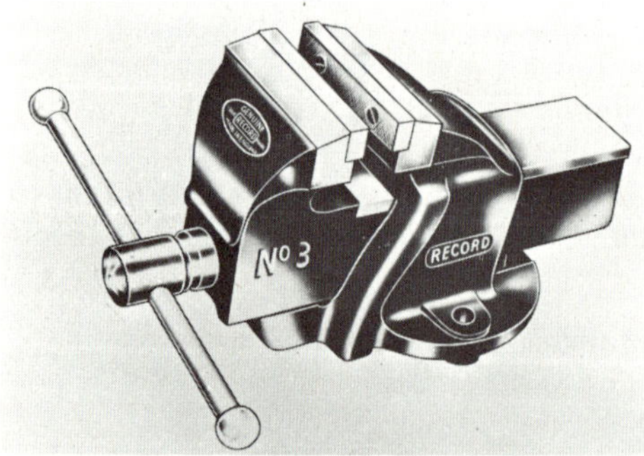

[*C. & J. Hampton Ltd.*

Fig. 34.

Fitted to each jaw is a cast steel face piece; this is normally serrated to improve the grip but may be smooth. If vices with smooth jaw pieces are installed in a workshop there should also be heavier vices with serrated jaws. The back cheek carrying the fixed jaw is of saddle form and allows the stem of the front cheek to slide through. The stem is of channel form and houses the screw which is shouldered and pinned to the front of the moving cheek. The screw may turn in a solid nut or in a half nut if the vice is fitted with an instantaneous grip (Figs. 35 and 36). If this arrangement is fitted the jaws can be moved quickly either in or out by operating the small spring-loaded lever which lowers the nut out of contact with the screw. The nut may be re-engaged at any point along the screw. This instantaneous grip arrangement adds considerably to the cost of a vice and is only worth while fitting where time is important. Some teachers fit rubber rings under the shoulders of the tommy bar; this reduces the noise in the

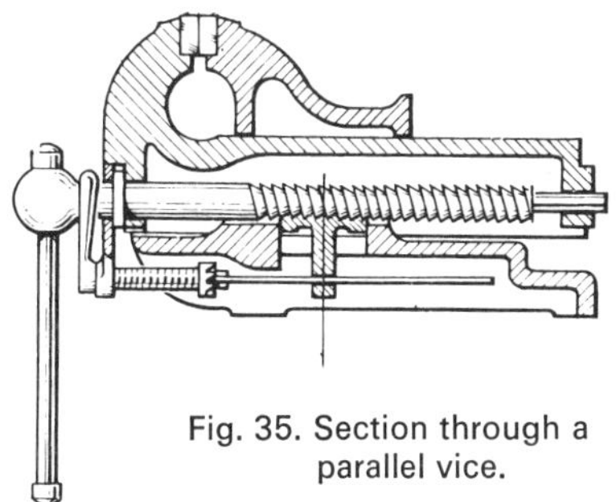

Fig. 35. Section through a parallel vice.

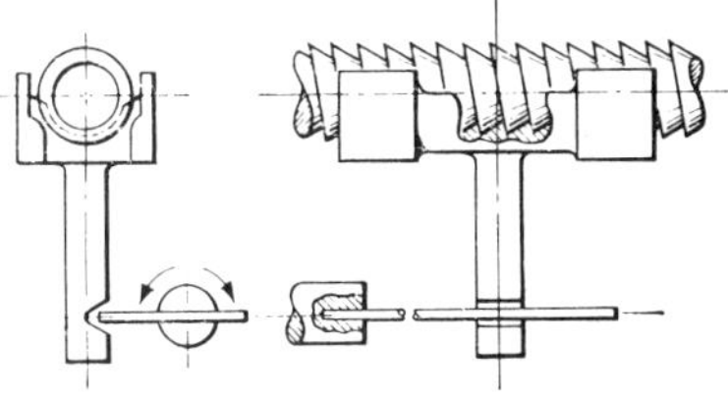

Fig. 36. Nut of an instantaneous grip vice.

shop a little and also prevents pinching of the flesh between the thumb and first finger of the user.

Vices must be fixed firmly to the bench top; bolts are to be preferred to coach screws, and must be level. Vices should be removed periodically and thoroughly cleaned and oiled and should be left loose when not in use.

Vice clamps Whilst the serrated jaws improve the grip on the work they also mark it; this can be avoided by putting vice clamps over the jaws. One commercial form, made from fibre, is illustrated but they may also be made from tinplate, lead, copper, brass or aluminium. Tinplate clamps must be fitted carefully to prevent cutting the hands. Lead clamps may be cast in the shop and melted and recast when worn. Brass, copper and aluminium are expensive but the latter may be melted and used in castings.

The clamp illustrated in Fig. 38 will be found most useful for holding screw threads; the spring clip at the end is fitted before the holes are drilled and tapped.

Hand vices, Fig. 39, are useful tools for holding small parts which cannot be conveniently held in the larger parallel vice. One of these hand vices should be housed conveniently near each drilling machine for holding small work and, particularly, thin sheet metal which must never be held in the hands.

[*C. & J. Hampton Ltd.*

Fig. 37. Vice clamps.

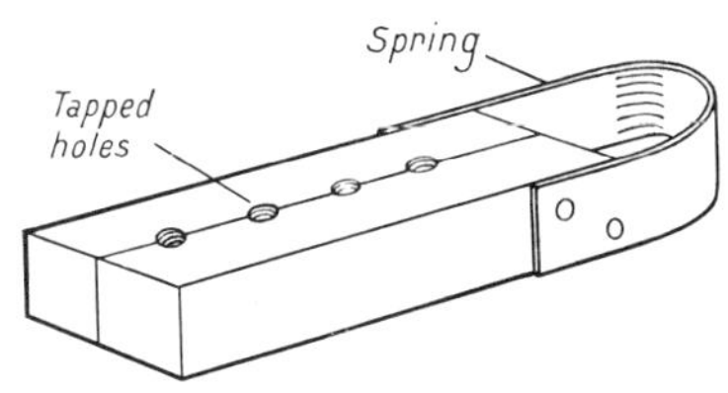

Fig. 38. Clamp for screw threads.

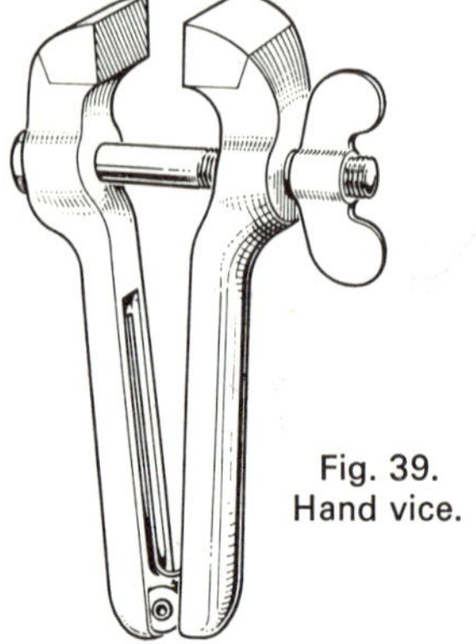

Fig. 39.
Hand vice.

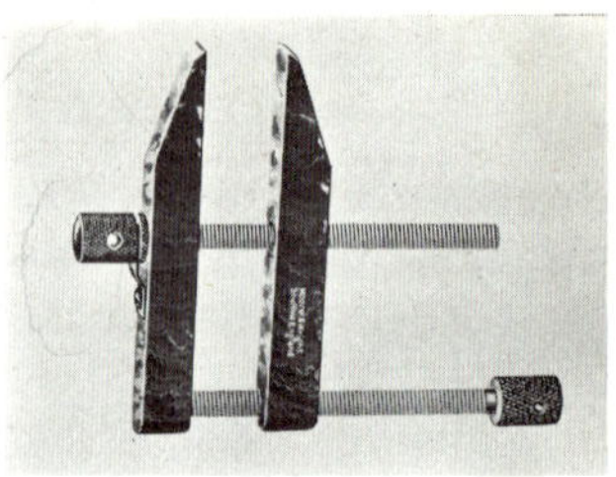

[*Moore & Wright (Sheffield) Ltd.*]
Fig. 40. Toolmakers' clamp.

Instrument vices enable small work to be held in almost any position or at any angle. *Pin vices* and *pin tongs* are used for handling work too small to hold in the fingers.

Toolmakers' clamp　This is used for holding together pieces of metal whilst marking out, drilling or cutting to shape, Fig. 40. The jaws should be kept as nearly parallel as possible, the final pressure and leverage being obtained by tightening the screw nearest the end. It is made of mild steel, case hardened, and is obtainable in a large range of sizes. Always use it within its capacity and do not strain it. Once the screws are bent they are difficult to use and become a source of annoyance.

Saws

Hacksaws　The hacksaw, Fig. 41, is used by the fitter to cut metal to shape before finishing off by filing, its use being limited to straight line cuts. The blade is held in tension in a frame such as the one illustrated. The blade is fitted with the teeth *pointing forward* so that it cuts on the forward stroke. All hacksaw frames are so made that the blade may be turned at right-angles for the convenience of making deep cuts. The width of the piece being cut is limited to the depth of the frame.

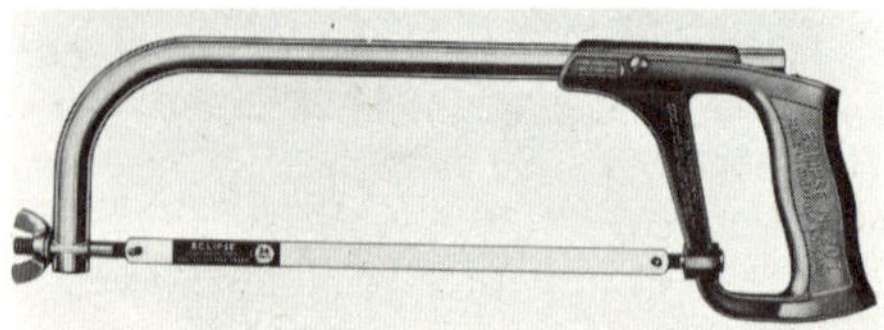

Fig. 41. Hacksaw.

Hacksaw blades are available in lengths of 250, 300, and 350 mm. They are made from cast or high-speed steel and may be all-hard or flexible. Schools normally use flexible blades as the all-hard blades snap very easily. The most economical proposition would be the high-speed-steel flexible blade.

Careful selection of blades must be made to suit the job in hand. When ordering blades, the following information must be given: length, number of teeth per 25 mm, depth of blade, usually 13 mm, gauge, usually 0·65 mm, and the temper, flexible or 'all-hard'. For some purposes, such as slotting a screw head, the hacksaw is too thin, For these jobs an assortment of slotting blades is available.

Hacksaw blades for hand use are available with 14, 18, 24 and 32 teeth per 25 mm. Each tooth size is designed for cutting particular types and sizes of materials, as follows:

---

14   Large solid sections of soft materials such as mild steel, aluminium, brass and copper

        THE MOST SUITABLE FOR GENERAL USE

18   Small solid sections of soft materials such as mild steel, aluminium, brass and copper
Large solid sections of hard materials such as alloy steel, heat treated steel and stainless steel
Heavy angles and cast iron

24   Small solid sections of hard materials such as alloy steel, heat treated steel and stainless steel
Sections between 3 mm and 6 mm thick such as heavy tubing and sheets, and medium angles

32   Sections less than 3 mm thick, such as thin tubing and sheets, and light angles

---

The tooth sizes selected must be such that at least three consecutive teeth will always be in contact with the material being cut.

Using the hacksaw   The correct grip and stance is essential, the latter being much the same as for filing. The hacksaw is held by both hands, one at each end of the frame. The index finger of the hand on the handle is held alongside the frame to control direction. The metal to be cut must be held securely. If it is in a vice, the line of the cut should be as close to the vice as practicable and, unless for some very good reason to the contrary, should also be vertical. Use the full length of the blade and not the middle four inches, because if not used to capacity the newer part of the blade with full set on the teeth will later jam and break. A 250 mm blade is a good average size and will do most work in school. The hacksaw must always be kept moving in a straight line; if it moves sideways at all, again the blade is liable to break. Start the blade lightly and make a nick with the corner of a file if starting seems difficult. Speed of cut should be regulated to about fifty strokes per minute, resisting the tendency to go too fast. When cutting cast steel reduce the speed by a half. Never use a hacksaw to cut through

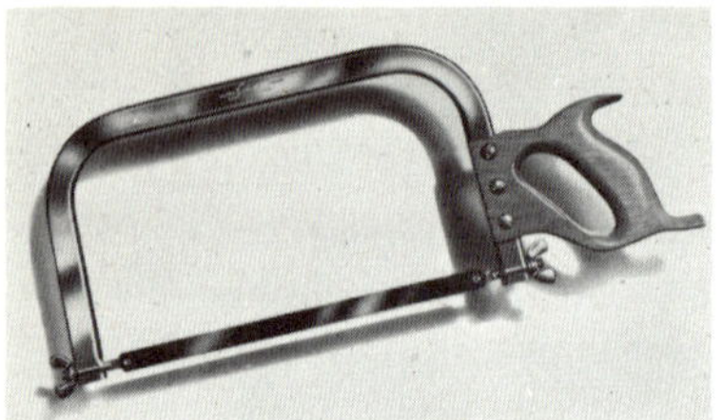

Fig. 42. Girder saw.

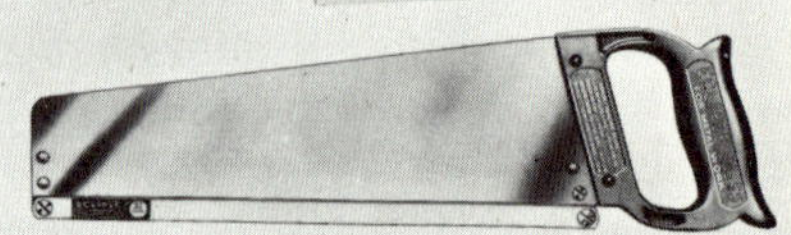

Fig. 43. Sheet saw.

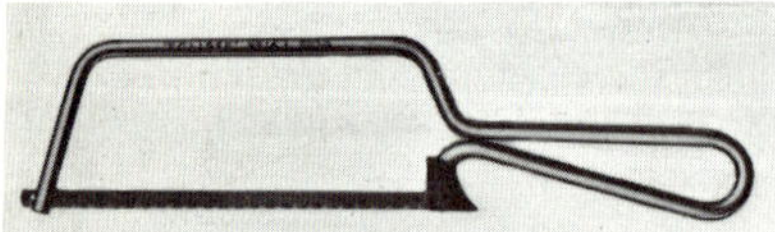

Fig. 44. Junior saw.

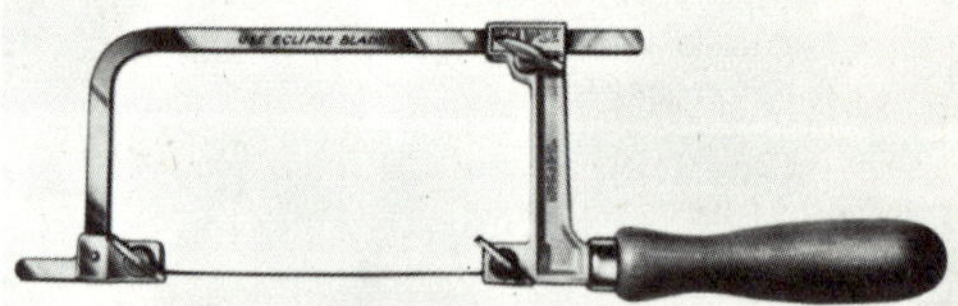

Fig. 45. Piercing saw.

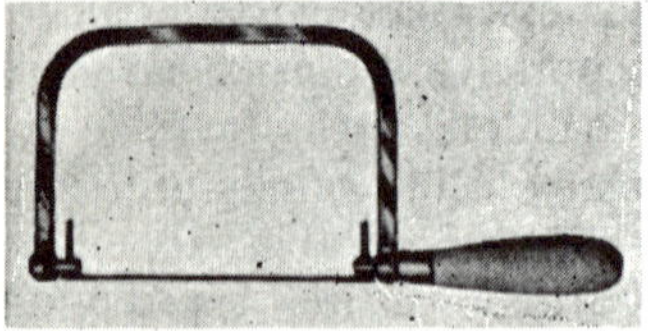

Fig. 46. Coping saw.

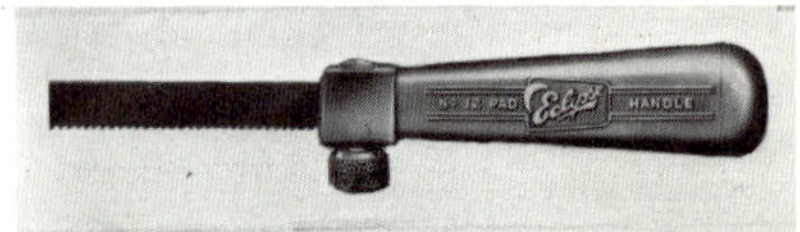

Fig. 47. Pad handle.

[James Neill & Co. (Sheffield) Ltd.

cast steel bar; keep an old square file, nick round the bar and then break off. Should a blade break part way through a cut do not insert the new blade in the old cut but turn the job round and start afresh. Avoid too much pressure on the blade and erratic use, and practice long steady strokes of an even pace. Do not cut across the edge of thin material, cramp it down flat and approach at a shallow

58

angle so that the teeth of the blade are in contact with as much metal as possible. If thin sheet gets between the teeth they will break off. If the tension in the blade is insufficient it is liable to twist and break and difficulty will be found in trying to keep the cut on a straight line.

Girder saws   Illustrated, Fig. 42, is a girder saw frame which is very useful for deeper saw cuts; the depth under the frame is about 250 mm. One of these in a metalwork shop would be quite sufficient.

Sheet saws   As the name suggests, this tool, Fig. 43, is for cutting large sheets, and again the standard size of hacksaw blade is used.

Junior saws   This saw, Fig. 44, is very useful for small work; the blade is held under tension by the natural spring in the frame.

Piercing saws   As mentioned earlier, the hacksaw is limited to cutting along straight lines. There is a choice of saws available for cutting out curved work. Illustrated in Fig. 45 is a piercing saw, with an adjustable frame, which is most useful as, even if a blade is broken, the broken piece if of reasonable length can still be used. The piercing saw however is limited to cutting in the plane of the frame only.

Coping saws   The two ends of *coping saws*, Fig. 46, may be turned at an angle to the frame, so adding to their versatility, but care must be taken not to twist the blade.

Another tool for curved work, although not strictly speaking a saw, is the *tension file*. It is a thin round flexible file and is held by clips in the standard hacksaw frame.

An odd *pad handle*, Fig. 47, is most useful in the workshop as pieces of broken blade may be used in it.

Guillotine   Almost all workshops have a guillotine, Fig. 48, for cutting sheet metal. This must be sited carefully so that large sheets may be cut on it and it is usually fixed on to a solid, heavy bench or a stool. If carelessly fitted the leverage of the machine when in use can lift the top off a bench. A guillotine is useful but can be a very crude tool, doing one job and making several more. If metal is cut carelessly, it becomes very twisted, and is most difficult to flatten without damage. It is better to purchase metal in strips of the width required and cut to length in a power saw. Most guillotines have provision for cropping round bar, which is again a crude business as it mutilates the end. It is quicker and better to saw to length using a hacksaw, or junior saw on smaller sizes. A guillotine should always be used within its capacity and immobilized when not in use. The handle must be bolted or locked in the upright or horizontal position, depending upon the situation, for safety.

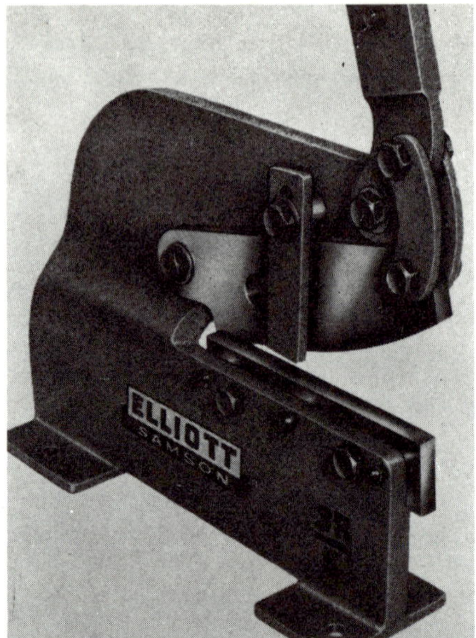

[*B. Elliott & Co. Ltd.*

Fig. 48. Guillotine.

Engineer's ball pein hammer   Of the many different shaped hammer heads this is perhaps the most common, Fig. 49. Hammer heads are made from cast steel shaped to suit the work on which they are to be used and are graded by the weight of the head. Common weights in the workshop are 225 g, 340 g and 450 g, heavier hammers being used for forge work. The shafts are made from hickory or ash and carefully fitted and wedged. If a shaft has to be replaced, great care must be taken to get the centre line of the shaft and the hammer head in line. The hammer shaft should be gripped towards the end and not under the head, and the weight of the blow may be regulated by swinging from the wrist or elbow or shoulder. The blow must always be flat and the edge of the face must never be allowed to come into contact with the work or marks will be made which will be difficult to remove; also the hammer head is liable to chip and will subsequently do even more damage.

Copper hammers, Fig. 50, are most useful for delivering a blow where it is essential that the work should not be bruised or damaged, and are specially useful for tapping a machine vice into position or bedding work on to parallels. They are most effective if used with a slack wrist and allowed to drop on to the work.

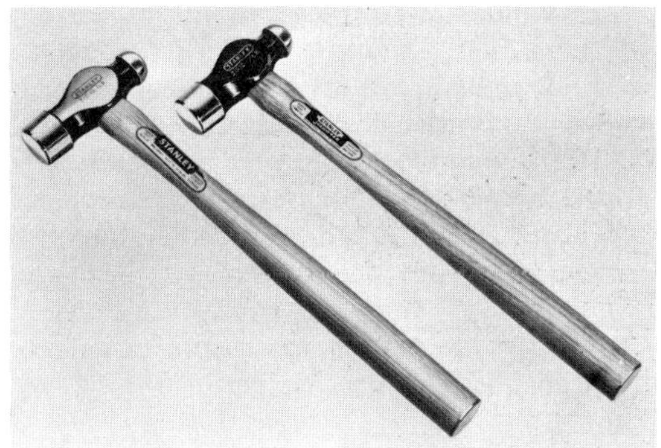

[*Stanley Works (Gt. Britain) Ltd.*

Fig. 49. Engineer's ball pein hammers.

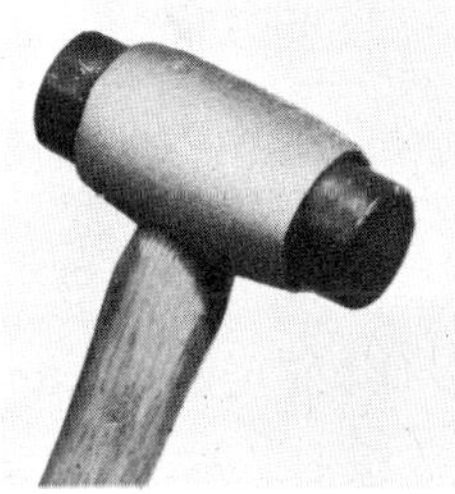

[*F. J. Edwards Ltd.*

Fig. 50. Copper hammer.

Chisels These are usually forged from octagonal or hexagonal cast steel, hardened and tempered, and vary in length and shape according to their particular purpose, Fig. 51. The commonest form of chisel is the engineer's flat cold chisel, so called because it is used to cut cold metal. The forging angle is about 15° to 20°, but the cutting angle will vary with the metal to be cut, usually between 40° and 70°. The cutting edge is ground to a slight radius, and not straight, to reduce the possibility of the corners breaking off. The more acute angle is

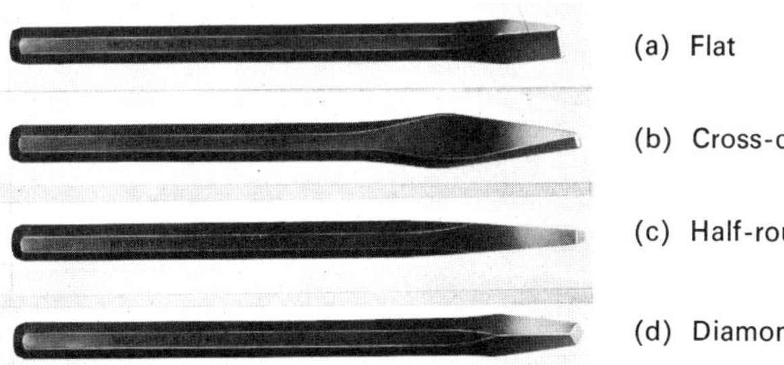

[*Moore & Wright (Sheffield) Ltd.*

Fig. 51. Chisels.

for the softer metals, and the harder the metal the more obtuse the angle. Only the cutting edge is hardened and tempered, the head is left soft so that hammer faces are not damaged. Being soft the head is liable to spread and mushroom; this spreading must from time to time be ground off, because if a glancing blow is struck the pieces will be broken off and can be dangerous. The flat chisel is used to cut sheet metal either held vertically in the vice or horizontally on a

61

chipping block. It is also used for trimming and fettling castings and getting at and into places inaccessible to machine tools. Chisels may be regarded as rather crude tools and in inexperienced hands can create a lot of extra work; edges are left jagged and jobs in sheet metal become twisted. However, they have a place in the school metalwork shop and can be most useful in reducing the work of the hacksaw. Hacksaw blades are easily broken and are expensive to replace.

Cross-cut chisel, Fig. 51b. This is not used a lot in these days of shaping and milling machines. It has a narrow cutting edge and is used for cutting slots, channels and keyways.

Half round or round nose chisels, Fig. 51c, are particularly useful for cutting oil grooves in bearings and bushes or for drawing over the centres of holes which have run off during drilling.

Diamond pointed chisels, Fig. 51d, have much the same purpose as the round nose chisel and are also used for cutting cast iron pipes to length.

Files The file, Fig. 52, is one of the fundamental metalwork tools and is required for almost all jobs. It is made of cast steel, the blade being hardened and tempered, but the tang is left soft. Files are classified by their length, section and cut.

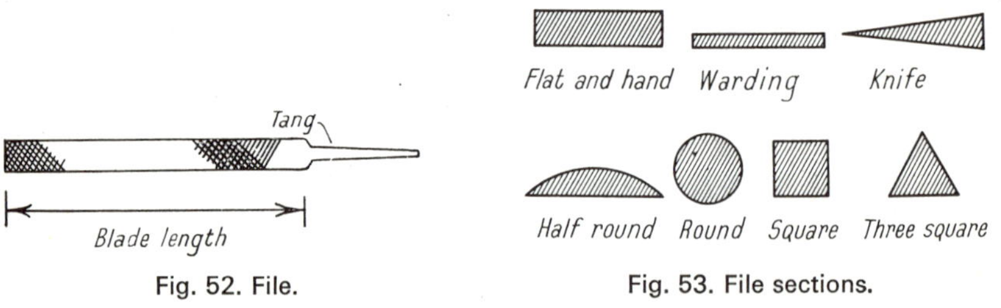

Fig. 52. File.   Fig. 53. File sections.

Length This is measured along the blade only and does not include the tang. Files may be obtained in lengths from 75 mm to 500 mm, but 150 mm, 200 mm and 250 mm files will do most school jobs, with a few smaller files kept apart for special work.

Section Files are available in a large number of sectional forms all designed to fulfil a definite purpose, Fig. 53.

Flat files are rectangular in section but taper in width and are cut on both edges. They are frequently confused with *hand flat* files, also rectangular in section but parallel in width with only one edge cut. The uncut edge is called the *safe edge* and is most useful for working in square corners when only one face has to be cut.

Half round In section this is a segment of a circle and tapers in width and thickness towards the end. The taper in the thickness is on the curved and not the flat face. They are most useful files for concave curves but must be used with a sweeping movement from side to side. Better results will be obtained when finishing if the file is turned over and the flat side presented to the work, Fig. 54.

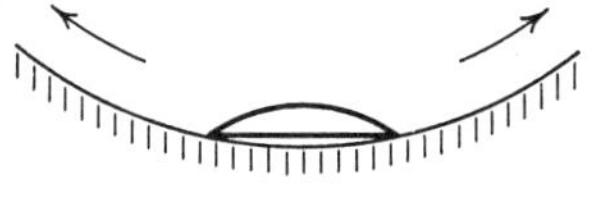

Fig. 54.

Square As the name implies, the section is square, sides are parallel for two-thirds of the length tapering towards the end. Square files parallel over the full length can be obtained and are called 'parallel squares'.

Round The section is circular and, as with the square, is tapered for the end third. These files may be obtained parallel, when they are known as 'parallel rounds'. The smaller sized taper rounds are called 'rat tailed files'.

Three square In section an equilateral triangle tapering as square and round but may be obtained parallel. They are particularly useful for getting into and producing clean corners.

Warding file Similar in section to the flat file but much thinner, this file is parallel in thickness and most useful for cutting out narrow slots, as in keys, to fit the wards of a lock.

Curved tooth files Obtainable from different makers under different names such as 'Dreadnought', 'Millicut', etc., these files, Fig. 55, are cut as shown and are particularly useful on soft metals such as aluminium, copper and fibrous materials which will seriously clog and pin a file.

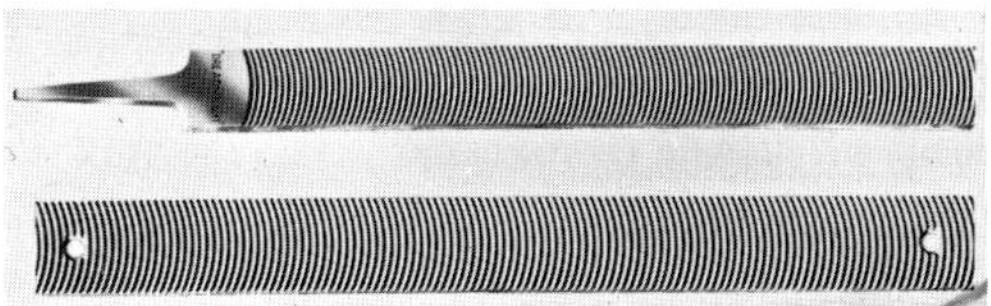

[*Firth Brown Tools Ltd.*

Fig. 55. Curved tooth files, flat tanged and plain flexible.

Manufacturers produce a special file, suitably cut, for each metal but as it would be impossible in a school workshop to keep them separate a compromise has to be aimed at.

Cut As the name suggests this refers to the fineness or coarseness of the teeth, Fig. 56. There are five main cuts, Dead Smooth, Smooth, Second Cut, Bastard and Rough. It must be appreciated however that the coarseness varies in the same cut with the size of the file, Fig. 57; the smaller the file the finer the teeth.

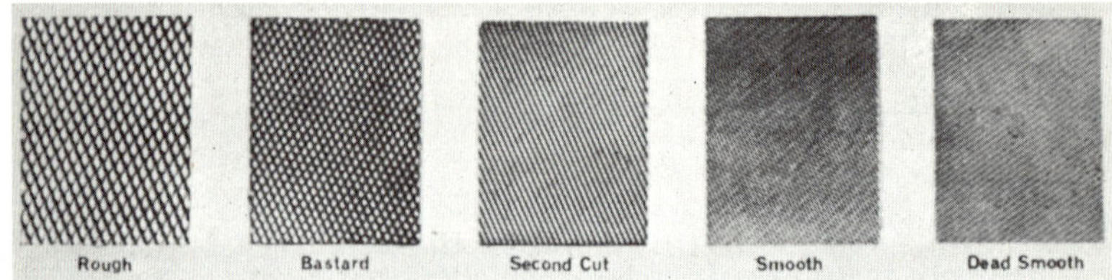

[English Steel Corporation Ltd.

Fig. 56. Cuts.

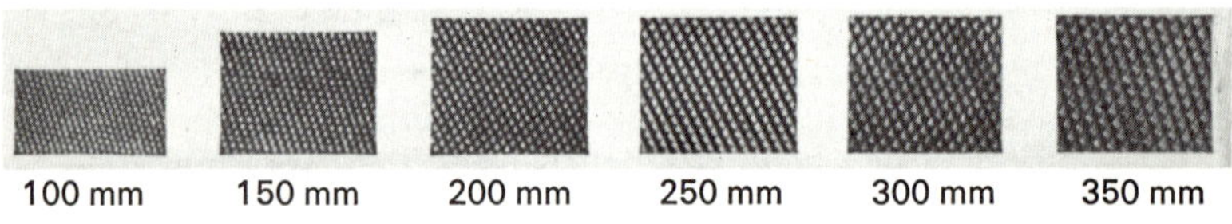

[Nicholson File Co.

Fig. 57. Coarseness range.

Files may have single or double cut teeth; the angle of the single cut is about 55° and the double cut about 85°.

These angles vary with the material and purpose for which the file is intended. *Needle or Swiss files*, Fig. 58. These are intended for fine work and must be used with great care as they snap very easily. They do not require handles, the ends being knurled to give a grip.

Illustrated in Fig. 59 is a type of file which is favoured by agricultural engineers. Instead of the normal tang it has a rounded handle which permits it to be carried safely in an overall pocket and has a hole by which it can be hung. It is available in single and double cuts and has one safe edge. It could be a very useful file in schools, since there is no handle to split and no dangerous sharp tang.

File handles are usually of wood, ash or beech, with a ferrule to prevent splitting. Handles need to be fitted carefully, as if knocked on too hard they will split and are dangerous to use. If the hole is too small it must be drilled out to suit the tang to be fitted. It is most important that the file should fit the handle straight with its axis or it will be difficult to use accurately. Files must never be used without handles, which are available from 75 to 150 mm long by 12 mm.

Filing   Filing is an art and one that is not very easily acquired. There are however a number of fundamentals which if observed will help considerably. First the work must be held firmly in the vice with a minimum amount of metal projecting and the edge or surface to be filed must be horizontal. The file handle is grasped in the right hand, as shown in Fig. 60, with the end of the handle in the palm of the hand and the thumb on top. The left hand is used to apply pressure

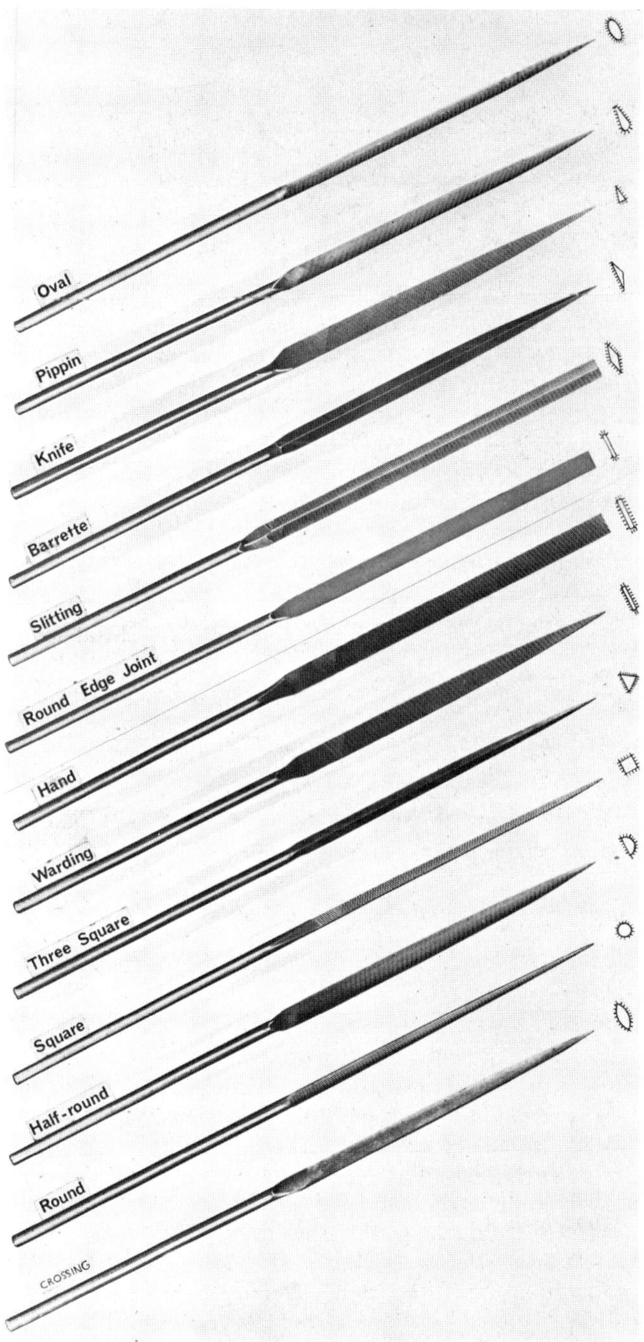

[*Firth Brown Tools Ltd.*

Fig. 58. Needle files.

Fig. 59. Handy file.

at the end of the file blade and may assume one of three main positions. For heavy work it will be as in Fig. 60, for medium work as in Fig. 61, and for light and very careful, accurate filing as in Fig. 62. Stance and balance and the preservation of the balance as the weight is transferred from right foot to left are most important. The feet should assume a position to the left of the vice similar to the one shown in Fig. 63, but of course the natural splay of the feet must be taken into consideration when checking this. The stroke is made with the right arm moving from the shoulder, the right elbow being kept close in to the body and the forearm kept horizontal. As the stroke proceeds the body

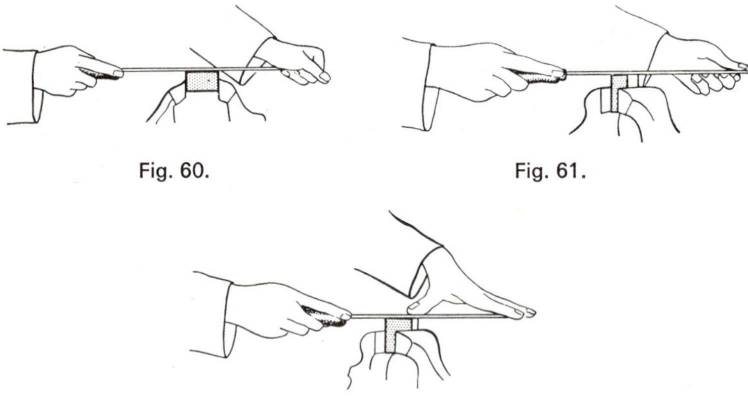

Fig. 60.

Fig. 61.

Fig. 62.

sways a little and the weight is transferred to the left foot, the body provides the weight of the stroke, the right hand the direction. When cross filing over a length of material the file moves from left to right at the same time as across; this is illustrated in Fig. 64. The file, on its cutting stroke, should always be travelling away from the body with a free unrestricted movement. If it is desired to file from right to left, then a fresh stance must be taken as in Fig. 65 and not merely the direction of the arms altered. The aim should be to keep the file horizontal throughout the stroke, which should be slow and steady and as long as the file will permit. The correct speed is about 50 to 60 strokes per minute,

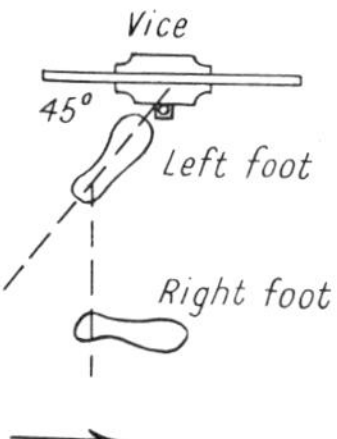

Fig. 63. Position of feet for cross-filing.

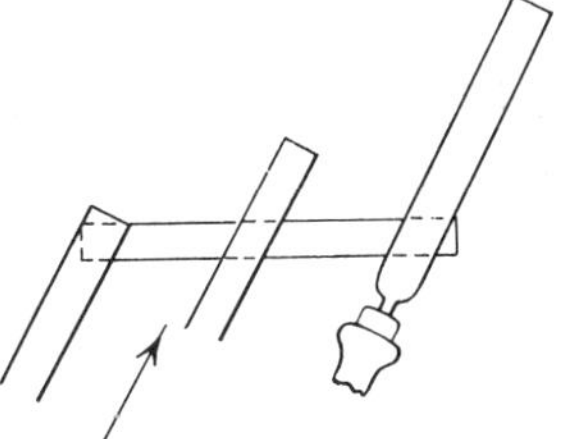

Fig. 64. Path of file when cross-filing left to right.

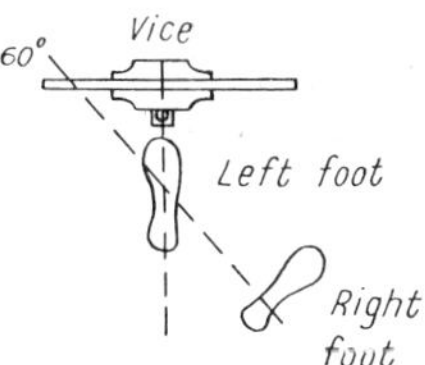

Fig. 65. Position of feet for cross-filing right to left.

reduced to about half this rate for cast steel. Of course, until correct balance and transfer of weight is mastered, there will be a tendency to produce a rounded surface. Pressure is applied on the forward stroke only, the file being allowed to slide back over the surface on the return stroke. Files are not perfectly flat but slightly convex over their length and this assists in producing a flat surface. Checks must be made as the filing proceeds to see if the surface is flat and square. The job is usually held up to the light against a straight edge or try square and the high spots are revealed. Which files are used will of course depend upon the amount of metal to be removed, but it is usual to start with the larger, coarser files and work through to the smaller, finer ones depending upon the quality of surface required. If the work has been correctly marked out and dot punched on the line, filing is continued until the punch marks break out on the edge being filed.

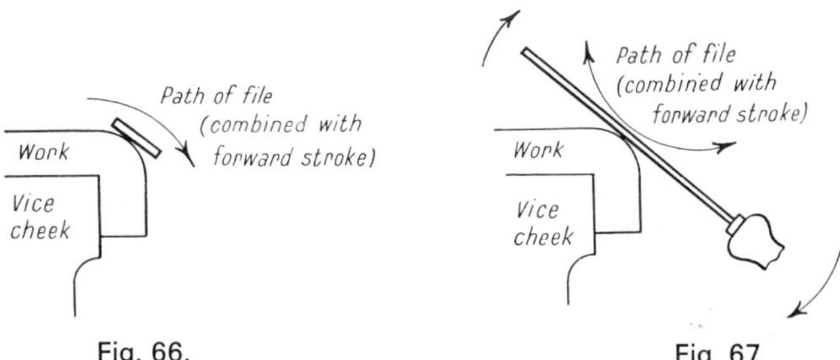

Fig. 66.

Fig. 67.

When filing curved surfaces, rough to shape with a coarse file, but in order to obtain a smooth curve rotate the file by a turn of the right wrist. The file must be kept horizontal throughout the stroke against the tendency for the left hand to get too low. The work must be fixed so as to overhang the vice, otherwise the file will come into contact with the corner of the hardened vice cheek and damage the file, Fig. 66. In order to produce such a curved surface some workers operate the file in line with the vice jaws and not across them. If this is done the file must be rocked, as shown in Fig. 67, in the opposite direction to the curve of the job. This method is quite effective on broader edges but at what stage to introduce it needs consideration. It will of course be realized that all that has so far been written refers to the right-handed worker. For the left-handed worker the fundamentals still apply, positions are merely reversed.

Drawfiling This is done to finish off an edge or a surface and to remove the marks made by the previous cross filing. The file, usually a smooth one, is held at right-angles to the work and moved forwards and backwards over the surface. This movement gives a series of finer scratches to the surface, all in one direction. As the drawfiling process removes very little metal it should be used for finishing only. It will generally be found that the best and sharpest part of the file is that near the tang; use this for drawfiling. To complete the surface emery cloth is laid along the file and used with the same motion. The grip of the file is important when drawfiling. The index fingers should be on top of the file and if possible over the surface to be filed. This keeps the file flat and prevents it rocking (see Fig. 68).

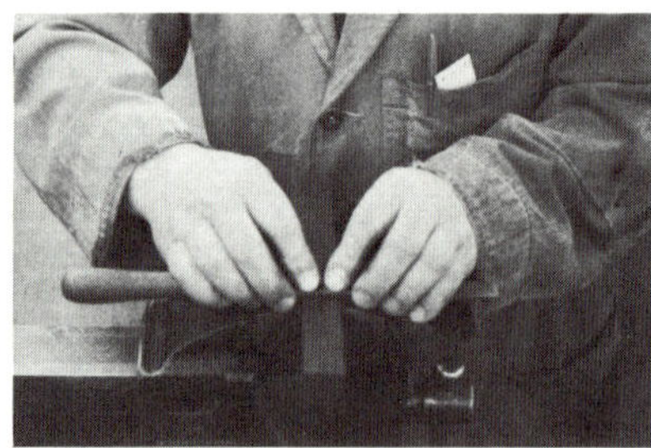

Fig. 68. Drawfiling. (Note index fingers on top of file over work.)

When filing a surface, greasy and perspiring hands should not be rubbed over it or it will be slightly oxidized, and the file will slip for several strokes before biting.

It was said above that in the drawfiling process the marks produced are in one direction only, thus giving a smoother finish. This principle can be applied to cross filing on surfaces that are not too wide. Practice gripping the file as in Fig. 62 and keep the file moving in one direction only along the length of the job. If this method is adopted a smoother and flatter finish will be obtained much more quickly. This is followed by drawfiling, also in the same direction.

Holding flat pieces to be filed The holding of thin flat pieces of metal so that the surfaces may be filed can be a problem. A good method is to put the metal on a flat block of wood and prevent it sliding and turning by knocking in pins at strategic points. The *plate vice* is perhaps the best method, but these are rarely used.

Care of files Files are expensive and not easily replaced; they must therefore be treated with care in order to prolong their effective life. Remember to lay them down carefully on the bench top side by side, ready to hand and not in a heap rubbing together. They should never be used on hardened steel and the speed of the stroke must be reduced when working on hard material. So far as possible avoid use on the skin of iron castings, but where this has to be done first chamfer the edge so that a minimum of contact is made with the hard surface. Arrange work in the vice so that contact with the hard jaw piece is avoided. New files should be first used on brass and when they are no longer effective transferred to use on steel. Files used on steel will not subsequently cut brass. In order to keep them separate paint the tang or handle yellow. When stored, files should be kept separately in trays or racks and not be allowed to rub together. Files should not be scrapped too readily, they may be sharpened and finally recut; this service is well worth while. They may also be ground to make scrapers or, if annealed and then suitably hardened and tempered, they may be made into hand turning or wood turning tools. This heat treatment is important; if used in their hard state they may break and cause serious injury to the user.

[*Nicholson File Co.*
Fig. 69. File card.

Pinning When a file becomes clogged with small particles of metal it is said to be *pinned*. If these pins are not removed they make deep scratches in the surface being filed and cause a lot of extra work. The softer the metal being filed the more easily does the file become pinned. To reduce this tendency, first select the correct file for the metal and as an additional precaution rub it with chalk. Frequent brushing in line with the teeth is a help when filing metals liable to cause pinning, but when pins really get wedged it may be necessary to use a file card, Fig. 69, or remove each pin separately using a thin piece of brass. Some craftsmen do not like using a file card because the steel bristles damage the teeth of the file.
Emery cloth To give a really smooth finish to a metal surface it is usual to finish with emery cloth. This is available, in various grades and qualities, in sheets or in rolls. If bought in sheets it is usual to tear off strips and lay these along the file. If wrapped round the file the cloth backing cracks up and the

emery cloth does not last so long. The better quality emery cloths have superior cloth backing which lengthen the life. Emery cloth must be used on a flat stick or dead smooth file but never on the finger.

Scraping A selection of scrapers is shown in Fig. 70. The flat one is for use on flat surfaces and the half round and three square for use on bearings. Scraping has to a large extent been superseded by grinding and very little work today is hand scraped; it is too slow and much too expensive. The object of scraping is

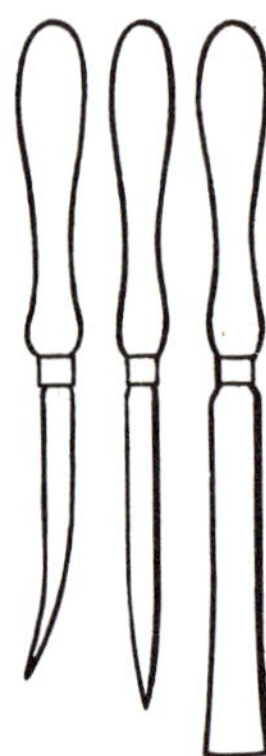

Fig. 70. Scrapers.

to produce flat, true surfaces and it is generally confined to cast iron machine slides and parts which have to work together. To test the surface for flatness a surface plate is used and, depending upon the size of the job, it may be rubbed on the plate or the plate rubbed over the job. The surface of the plate is carefully covered with a thin, even layer of engineers' blue. The job, which has been machined flat on a shaper, miller or planer, is rubbed on the blued plate which marks the high spots. These high spots are scraped off at an angle of about 45° to the centre line of the job. The work surface is wiped clean, the blue on the surface plate is spread carefully with the fingers, and the process repeated. This

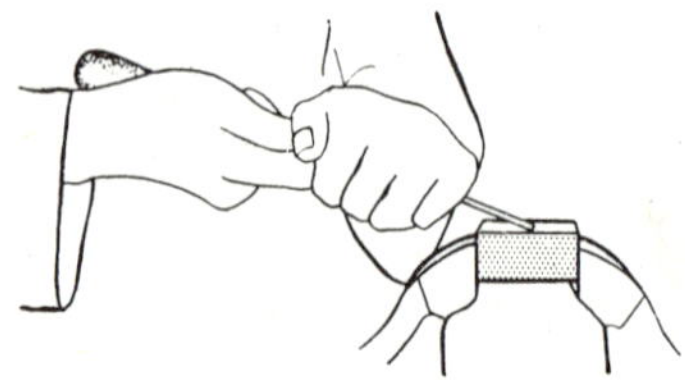

Fig. 71. Holding the scraper.

time the high spots are scraped off working at an angle of 90° to the first scraping. This procedure is continued until about a 75 or 80% coverage of blue evenly distributed over the surface is obtained; the other 20% of the area being slightly lower acts as a reservoir for lubricant. If two working surfaces were 100% flat they would wring together and stick. Scrapers may be bought, or made from old files, which should be kept as hard as possible and given very little temper. After grinding, the cutting edge should be carefully finished off with an oilstone. The cutting edge of flat scrapers should be slightly rounded so that small areas may be picked out for scraping. The correct method of holding the scraper is shown in Fig. 71 and the angle at which it is held is adjusted until the scraper cuts efficiently.

Reamers and reaming When it is required to produce a hole smoother and more accurate in size than can be obtained by drilling, a reamer, Fig. 72, is used. Reamers may be for hand use in a tap wrench or have taper shanks for use in machines, such as the tailstock of a lathe. The flutes of hand reamers are usually straight and those for machine reamers have a left hand spiral. Holes which are to be reamed must be drilled or bored to within 0·05 mm or 0·1 mm of the finished size. If too much metal is left for the reamer to remove, excessive wear will be caused and the reamer will very soon be under size and of no further use. To produce the hole for reaming, number or letter drills must be used; if suitable ones are not available, then the hole, if large enough, may be bored. Adjustable or expanding reamers, Fig. 73, are another solution. They can be reduced in size until they just fit the drilled hole and then enlarged by easy stages until the required size is obtained. This may be checked by a plug gauge or the part which is to fit the hole. This can be a laborious business but with a little patience excellent fits can be obtained. Reamers are limited to following the drilled hole and will not correct any errors in position or direction.

Taps and tapping Taps are used for cutting internal threads, as in a nut, Figs. 74 and 76. Generally they are made and sold in sets of three—taper, second and plug—and are used in that order. Before tapping, a suitable hole must be drilled a little larger than the core diameter of the tap.

Tables of tapping sizes are given (see pp. 237–241).

Taps are made from hardened and tempered cast steel and, in the smaller sizes, are extremely brittle and easily broken. For initial tapping exercises, taps of not less than, say, 8 mm should be used. It is also good practice, where the nature of the work permits, to drill a hole slightly larger than the given tapping size and to accept a shallower thread.

Having drilled the hole, select a tap wrench, Fig. 75, that will not give too much leverage and tighten it on the taper tap so that it will not come loose when in use. Attempts to tighten the wrench with the tap in the hole will almost certainly result in a broken tap. Enter the tap in the hole and turn forward and

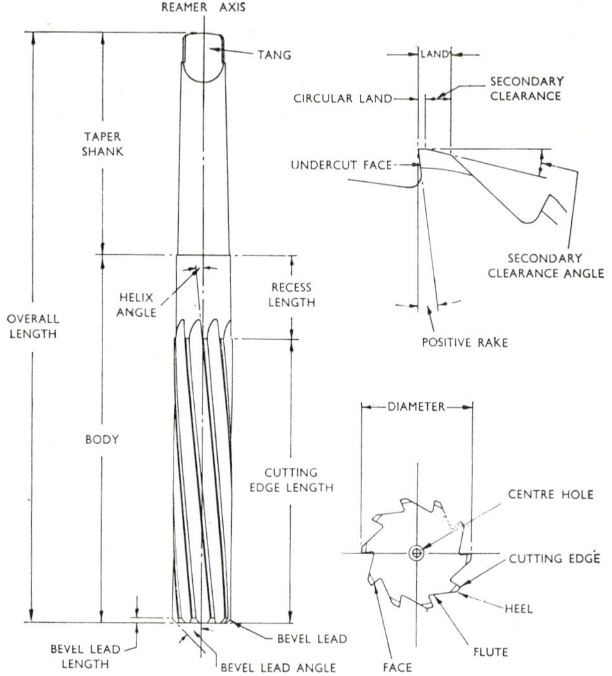

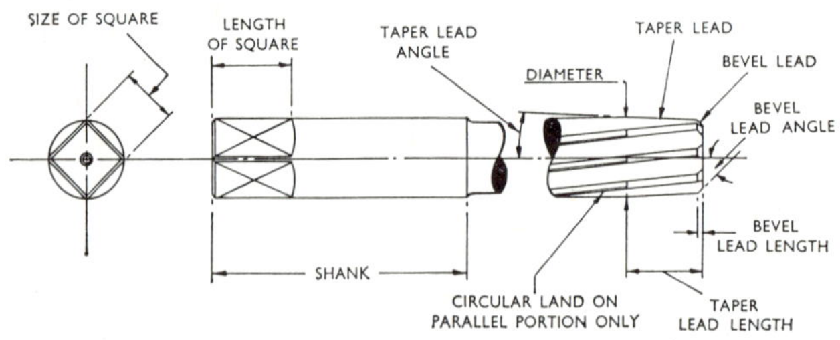

[Sheffield Twist Drill and Steel Co. Ltd.

Fig. 72. Reamer.

[Buck & Hickman Ltd.

Fig. 73. Adjustable reamer.

backward, taking great care to keep the tap square to the face and in line with the drilled hole. If the surface is not large enough to test this squareness with a try square, get the assistance of another boy to sight the tap from the side; the operator himself can sight from the front. The backward turn is to break the cuttings and ease the next forward turn. All material except cast iron and brass require the use of a cutting oil. Lubricating oil eases the process but does not assist the cutting action. The value of the use of cutting oils and pastes has to be experienced to be appreciated.

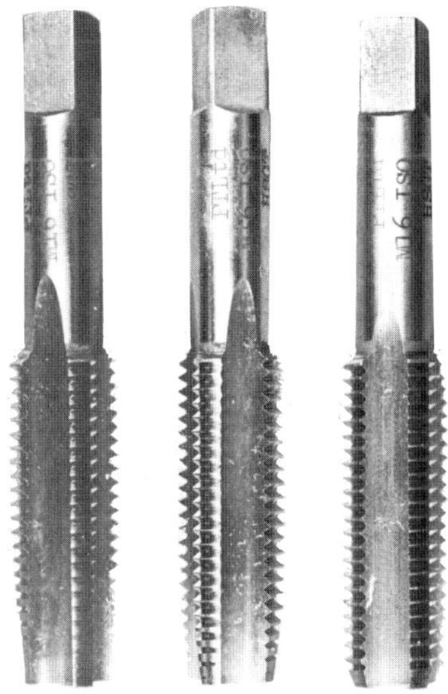

[Precision Tools Ltd. Birmingham.

Fig. 74. Set of taps.   Fig. 75. Tap wrench.

If the hole to be tapped is a through hole, the taper tap may be screwed straight through and the second and plug taps will not be required. If the through hole is a long one, however, then difficulty may be found in screwing the taper tap straight through, because the tap will tend to jam; if the screwing is persisted in, the tap will break. As soon as the taper tap begins to jam, remove it and use the second tap, and when that one tightens use the plug tap. Repeat the use of taper, second, plug taps until completion. If this procedure is adopted, tapping will be made easier and the danger of breakage considerably reduced. The same procedure is adopted with blind holes, great care being taken not to screw the tap hard against the bottom or again it will be broken. Before the tapping of a blind hole can be completed, it may be necessary to clean out the swarf from the hole several times, and at the same time wipe the tap clean. Short blind holes present further difficulties. To start and finish a thread in a short distance requires great care, since it may not be possible to use the taper tap at all, as this will merely ream out the hole. Starting with the second tap is of course more difficult, especially to start it square. To get over this, the job should be left *in situ* after drilling and the tap fitted into the drill chuck, carefully pulling the drill spindle forward and backward. If the shank of the tap is too large for the chuck, then a centre can be fitted and its point entered in the centre hole of the tap. Large

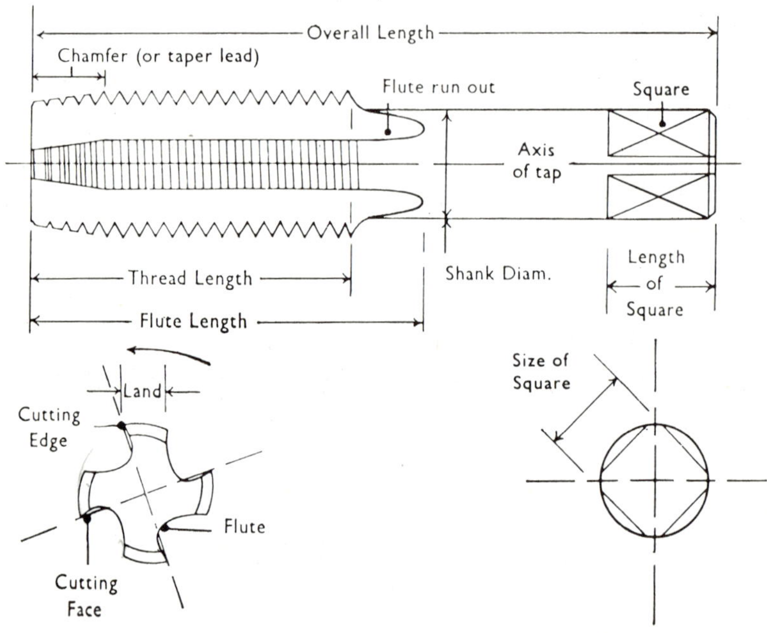

[*Easterbrook, Allcard & Co. Ltd.*

Fig. 76. Section of tap.

taps should always have centre holes at the shank end for this reason, and also when being used on the lathe. Always preserve an even torque or twisting force, and a better 'feel' can be obtained with small taps if the job as well as the tap and wrench is held in the hands.

Broken taps Taps broken into tapping holes can be a problem and are most difficult to remove. Tap extractors are available and are effective on large sizes. It is sometimes possible to break out the tap with a small chisel or punch or even screw it backwards out of the hole. On some occasions the broken piece may be driven out from the other side, especially if it is the end of a taper tap. Depending upon the job, it may be possible to soften the tap by heating with a fine blowpipe flame and then carefully redrilling. If, however, the tap is broken in cast iron, great care will have to be taken with the heating, as local heat may crack the casting. On many occasions the best and quickest way out is to scrap the job and start again.

Stocks and dies External screwthreads are cut by dies, the die being held for turning by means of a stock. These stocks and dies take various forms, some of which arc shown in Fig. 77. The dies are made of hardened and tempered cast steel and the stock of mild steel. The circular split pattern permits only a little adjustment, but the split or loose dies have much more adjustment and for that reason are easier to use. They may be opened sufficiently to fit right over the bar and tightened on to it, thus making a square start easier. Some stocks incorporate a guide, which also helps in getting a square start, but sometimes the guide gets in the way when working a full thread down to a shoulder. A slightly tapered end also helps in getting a square start, but the taper must be true and is best cut

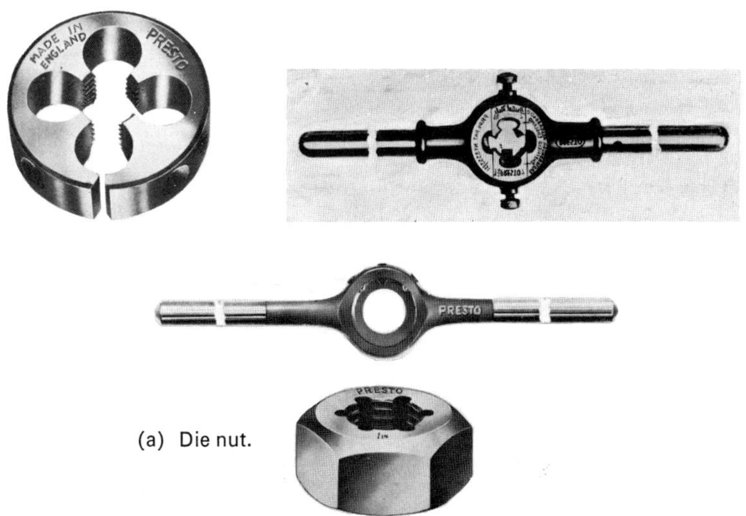

(a) Die nut.

[*Easterbrook, Allcard & Co Ltd.*

Fig. 77. Stocks and dies.

on a lathe. If a true start is not made the die, being narrow, weaves its way down the bar and a *drunken thread* results. All dies have a wider side, the threads being chamfered to make starting easier. The wider side is usually the named side but this is not always the case.

In effect, the die is a nut with cut-away portions providing the cutting edges. It is used like the tap with a forward and backward movement which must be steady and even and not jerky. If force is applied suddenly the die will be broken or at least some of its teeth broken off. If teeth are broken off at the starting edge of the die it becomes almost impossible to start it square. When cutting an external thread and also tapping a hole to fit, the hole should be tapped first and should provide the standard. As the die is adjustable it is started fully open and then gradually reduced until the thread is a good fit in the nut. The die must never be tightened on the work but must be removed, tightened and started again; otherwise it is liable to seize and strip the thread A cutting oil or paste should be used as for tapping. Die nuts, Fig. 77a, are not used for cutting threads but for finishing off a thread to size or for correcting a bruised thread in places where it would be impossible to get a stock and die. The die nut is manipulated by means of a spanner.

If dies are intended for cutting threads on brass they must not be used on steel or they will cease to be effective on brass and prevent a clean, sharp thread being obtained.

Cutting large threads by hand is hard and tedious work, so whenever possible such threads should be struck on a lathe and then finished off with a die. Very accurate threads must be cut on a lathe. Most threads are right-hand, but left-hand ones are cut for special purposes. Left-hand taps and dies may be obtained to special order.

Standard screwthreads

ISO Metric screwthreads* are a range of threads that have been internationally agreed upon and are approved by the British Standards Institution. They will eventually supersede all other standard screwthreads. ISO Metric threads may be of either Coarse or Fine pitch. These are tabulated in Appendix 1. The ISO Metric Coarse range of threads covers most of the work undertaken in industrial and school workshops and, as such, is called 'ISO Metric'. This range is designated by the thread diameter in mm followed by the letter M (e.g. 3 M, 6 M); the ISO Metric Fine screwthreads, which are only used for special applications, carry an additional letter F (e.g. 5 MF, 7 MF).

ISO Unified threads are also recognized by the British Standards Institution and, like the ISO Metric threads, have ranges of both coarse and fine pitches. Unified threads are based on Imperial dimensions and are designated by a fraction of an inch followed by UNF (Unified Fine) or UNC (Unified Coarse) e.g. $\frac{1}{4}$ UNF, $\frac{3}{8}$ UNC (Appendix 1).

Old British Standard screwthreads BSW (British Standard Whitworth), BSF (British Standard Fine) and BA (British Association) have been superseded by the ISO Metric and ISO Unified threads. However, as many of these threads exist at this time, details of the standards are given in Appendix 3. Also tabulated in Appendix 3 are other Old British Standard threads for specialized work, viz. ME (Model Engineer's) and BSB (British Standard Brass).

* International Standard Organization.

Thread forms   The basic form of the ISO screwthreads, both Metric and Unified, is shown in Fig. 78a. Other thread forms such as the *square, acme* and *buttress* shown in Fig. 78b, c and d, are cut by machine and are used on machine tools, vices, cramps and the like.

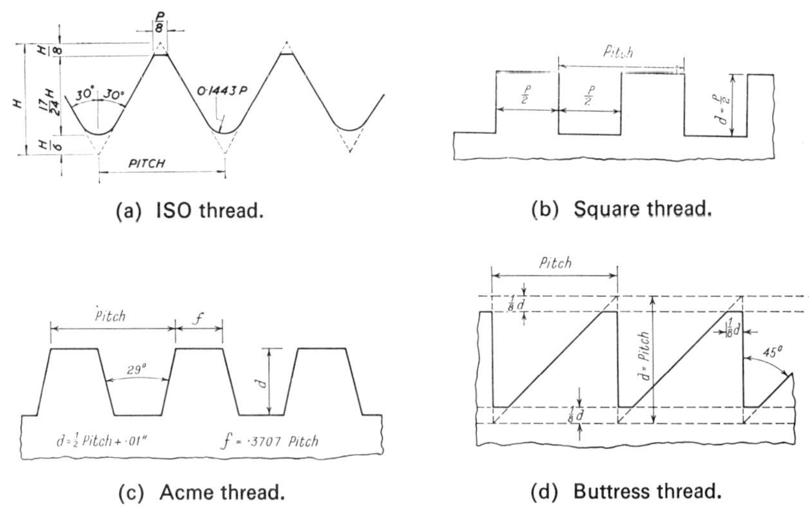

(a) ISO thread.

(b) Square thread.

(c) Acme thread.

(d) Buttress thread.

Fig. 78. Screwthread forms.

Riveting   Rivets are used to join together metal parts or plates, and may be arranged so that the joint is a permanent one or, if a single rivet is used, it may act as a hinge or pivot. As a method of permanently joining metals it has been superseded, for many applications, by spot and seam welding but still has a place in the handicraft workshop. Rivets are classified by the shape of the head, their length and diameter. The common head shapes are shown in Fig. 79— *snap, pan, countersunk* and *conical*—the situation and type of work deciding what form the head must take. Rivets are made in most metals and it is usual to have the rivets and the parts to be joined of the same material.

Parts which are to be joined by a number of rivets should be clamped and drilled together and all rivets inserted before any riveting is done, or it might be more convenient to complete one rivet to fix the joint and then drill and rivet the rest. If the latter procedure is adopted swarf from the drilling may get between the parts and prevent a tight, close joint being made.

Avoid leaving too much tail to rivet over; it will depend upon the rivet snap being used, but $1\frac{1}{2} \times$ dia is usually about right. Rivets must never be cut to length by cutting pliers; always saw off and file square. If an attempt is made to hammer the tail of a rivet as left from cutters it will most certainly bend and cause a lot of unnecessary trouble. The head of the rivet must be firmly supported and the tail pulled through by using the rivet set. Two or three sharp blows with the flat of the hammer will spread the rivet and fill the hole and then, using the ball pein end, roughly form the head and finish off with the rivet snap, Fig. 80. The support will depend upon the shape of the head. Snap heads must

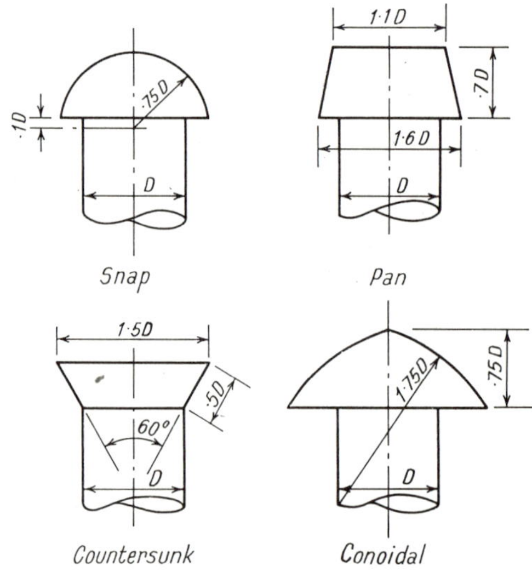

Fig. 79. Forms of rivet heads.

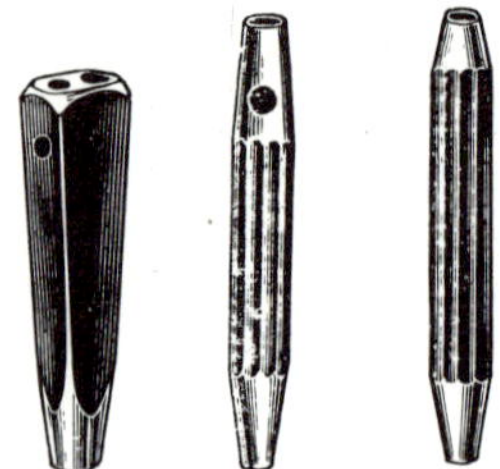

[*William Allday & Co. Ltd.*

Fig. 80. Rivet sets.

be supported in an appropriately shaped *dolly*, flat and countersunk heads on a solid bench block. If too much tail is left the rivet bends, parts get out of line and it is most difficult to correct. If the tail is too short, then of course the dolly will have little or no effect. When joining by countersunk rivets, where the surplus is to be filed off so that the head does not show, it is good practice to put a spot of oil in the countersink before riveting. Do not use too much or the hammer may slip and cause damage, and if possible the rivet should be of the same material as the metal being joined. If bright drawn steel is to be riveted it is made much more amenable if it is first annealed.

If a rivet being used as a pivot becomes too tight it may be slackened off by holding the head over a hole of the same size and smartly tapping the head on the other side. Before doing this arrange the joint so that it is in its tightest position.

Rivets may be removed by chipping or filing off the head and then punching out the rest or, if the head is countersunk, by carefully drilling out the head portion and again using the drift. To remove the head by filing is kinder and will cause less damage and bruising. In industry, large rivets are worked hot and when cooling pull the parts together and form a good tight joint. A riveted joint may break down in several ways. If the rivet is too small in diameter it may shear or if the rivets are placed too close together or too near an edge the metal will split.

Rivet and joint proportions Forms of riveted joints are illustrated in Fig. 81. A general formula for determining the diameter of rivets is:

$$D = 1 \cdot 2 \sqrt{t},$$
$$\text{when } D = \text{diameter of rivet},$$
$$t = \text{thickness of plate}.$$

Another formula for the diameter of rivets, and formulae for the distance between the centres of the rivets, or, as it is termed, the 'pitch', together with the necessary overlap, are:

$$t = \text{thickness of plates}$$
$$d = \text{diameter of rivet} = t + 8\,\text{mm}$$
$$p = \text{pitch} = 1 \cdot 6t + 32\,\text{mm}$$
$$l = \text{lap of plates} = 3t + 30\,\text{mm}$$

Riveted joints which are to be made steam- or water-tight are finally caulked. The tool is rather like a blunt chisel and is used in the manner shown to seal the edges of the plates, Fig. 82.

Brazing Brazing is a form of hard soldering and is a method of joining metals by means of a fusible alloy known as *spelter*. Brazing is employed when it is necessary to have a joint stronger than could be obtained by soft soldering; a well brazed joint is as strong as if the job were in solid metal. A single riveted joint is only 55% as strong as solid metal and a treble riveted joint 80%. As with soft soldering, an alloy of the spelter and the metal being joined is formed at the joint. Spelter is an alloy of copper and zinc in various proportions, the larger the amount of zinc the lower the melting point. Equal parts of copper and zinc melt at 870°C, two parts zinc to one of copper at 795°C, and four parts

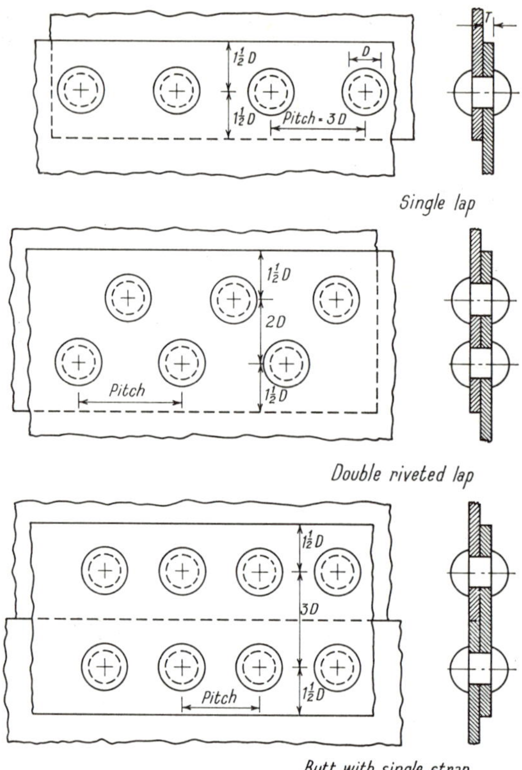

Fig. 81. Rivet placings and spacings.

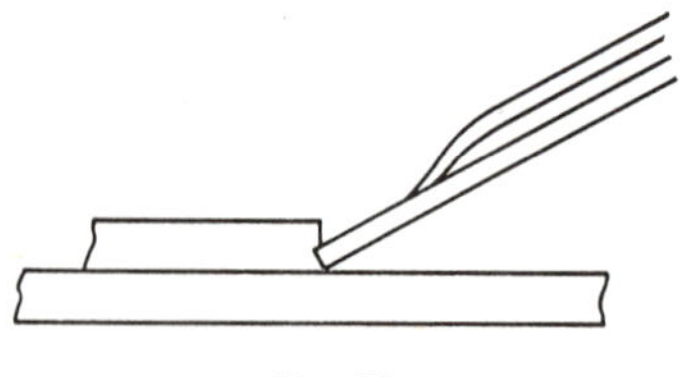

Fig. 82.

zinc to one of copper at 705°C. For ease of use employ a spelter with a low melting point, and always make sure that it will melt before starting the job. If brass is to be joined it is much safer to use silver solder. Spelter is obtainable in powder, granulated, ribbon, or stick form. When used in powder and granulated form it is usual to mix it with the flux.

The operation of brazing is usually performed in a brazing hearth, which may have a fixed or revolving pan, Fig. 83. The heat to melt the spelter is provided by a coal gas and air flame mixed in a blowpipe, Fig. 84, the air pressure being obtained by treadle operated double-acting bellows, Fig. 85, or an electrically-driven fan. Experienced craftsmen prefer the treadle operated bellows as this gives greater control of the flame. The pan of the brazing hearth must be lined with firebrick and a bed made of small coke or asbestos cubes, the latter being preferable as they provide a cleaner bed. A plentiful supply of firebricks should be available adjacent to the hearth to pack round work to be brazed. It is one

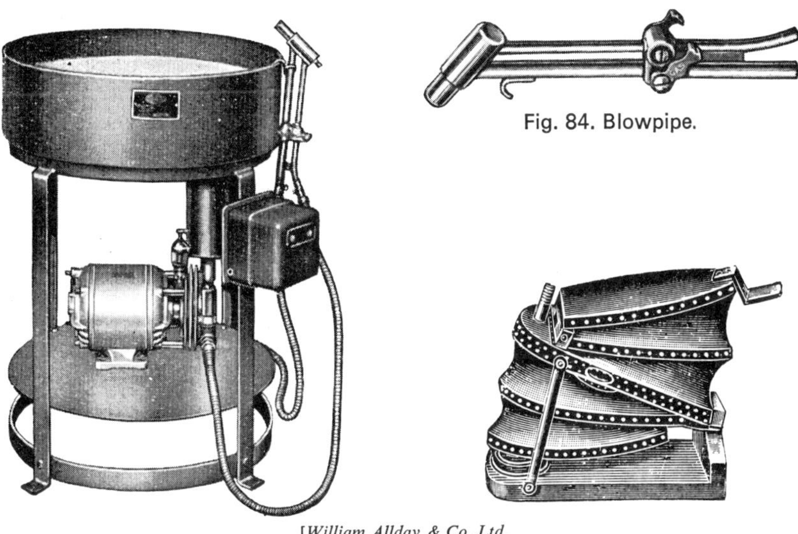

Fig. 84. Blowpipe.

[*William Allday & Co. Ltd.*

Fig. 83. Brazing hearth.

Fig. 85. Standard double blast foot bellows.

of the essentials when brazing to arrange the job so that the flame can be played directly on to the joint and to see that it is well packed round with firebricks to conserve the heat. If a good oven is made for the job it will get up to brazing heat much more quickly; it is a common fault of the inexperienced to try to braze before the job is hot enough. The heat to melt the spelter must come from the job and not the flame. Also make sure that the job is so arranged that the spelter may be applied easily and that when molten it runs into and not away from the joint. The joint must also be accessible to the *tickler*. This is merely a length of 3 mm round mild steel thinned or pointed at one end and with a ring at the other for hanging up.

The tickler is used to apply flux during the brazing process and to move around globules of spelter into all parts of the joint. The common flux for brazing is *borax* but it has disadvantages. The function of the flux is to protect the cleaned surfaces and to dissolve any oxide which may form. Borax does this admirably but vitrifies on cooling and is most difficult to remove.

Perhaps the easiest way to tackle the job is first of all, to pickle it in an acid bath and then scrape off with the end of an old file kept specially for the purpose. If a pickle bath is used, then it must be kept for that purpose alone and not confused with the one used for non-ferrous metals. If screwed or threaded parts are brazed and the thread becomes loaded with borax, on no account must the die be used to remove it, as the die will then be ruined. There are a number of proprietary brands of fluxes for brazing which work quite as efficiently as borax but which do not vitrify to anything like the same extent.

The job to be brazed must first of all be filed clean where it is to be joined and then covered immediately with a paste made of the flux and water. If the joint has been machined or threaded this should have been done dry as cutting oils and pastes will be difficult to remove. If necessary secure the job with iron binding wire or fix together with clamps, Fig. 86. If the nature of the job is such that

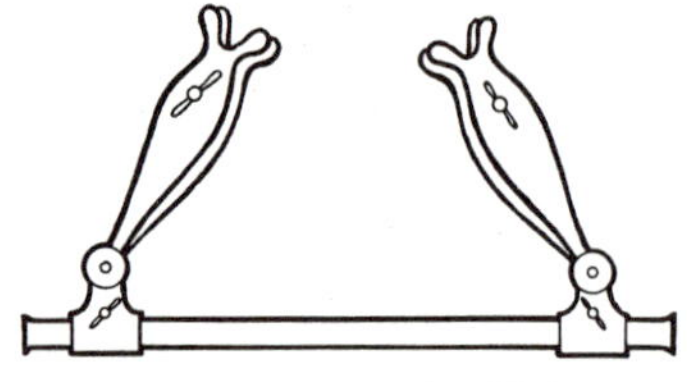

[*Buck & Hickman Ltd.*

Fig. 86. Pipe jointing clamps.

expanding air will force the job apart, file flats or drill holes to allow the air to escape. Any joints made which are to be subsequently brazed should be easy but not slack. Bed the job in the hearth and apply heat, slowly at first or the flux will bubble and blow out. As soon as the flux is molten increase the heat until the job is at a bright yellow-red heat. As the job is heating up, keep the tickler loaded with flux working around the joint; it must not be allowed to get dry or it will oxidize. Once the operation is started the flame must not be withdrawn or again oxidation will take place and the job will have to be filed clean again before it can be successfully brazed. Should the job be of two parts, very unequal in size, the flame must be so arranged as to bring both parts to brazing heat at the same time. Again it is a fault of the inexperienced to apply the spelter too early, in which case it will settle in blobs around the joint and is most difficult to remelt and persuade to flow. Before applying the spelter warm it and dip in the flux. It will be found that flux adheres to warm spelter but not to cold.

If the joint is clean and fluxed and at the correct heat, the spelter will melt and run easily, so take care not to apply too much, or the surplus may have to be removed. Do not disturb the joint until it is at black heat and then do not quench but allow it to cool slowly. If soft soldering is done on a brazing hearth great care must be taken not to leave any in the hearth. When working in non-ferrous metals or silver, the soft solder may be picked up, thus causing a black stain which burns into and pits the surface of the metal. If the pitting becomes sufficiently deep the job may have to be scrapped.

Joining aluminium Considerable strides have been made in recent years in methods of joining aluminium. Almost all firms who supply brazing and welding rods and fluxes now produce hard solders and fluxes for joining aluminium. With a little practice these may be used in the school workshop and give highly satisfactory results. A great danger in these processes is of course that the aluminium itself may melt, because the melting point of the solder is very little below that of the aluminium. It is a wise precaution to rub hard soap on the aluminium near the joint, and when this turns black the melting point of the aluminium is approaching.

Care is required in the use of the flux, as it goes moist when exposed to the air. Remove from the tin as much as is required for the job and then close tightly, because if the tin is left open for any length of time the contents will be ruined. Flux removal after the soldering operation is most important; if it is not completely removed it will attack and corrode the metal. In addition to solder for aluminium, a metal for filling blow holes or repairing defects in aluminium castings can also be obtained. Complete instructions for the use of these solders and fillers are supplied by the makers, and they may be melted by the torch flame usually available in the school workshop.

5 Sheet Metalwork

This branch of metalwork demands a knowledge of geometrical drawing and developments, cutting out, bending, joining, soft soldering, silver soldering and brazing. It involves the use of tinplate, brass, copper, sheet iron, aluminium and galvanized iron. In schools, we are concerned mostly with the first of these, the tinplate.

Manufacture of tinplate Tinplate is sheet steel with a coating of tin on both sides. It is manufactured in varying thicknesses, the common range being from 0·15 mm up to and including 0·49 mm in increments of 0·01 mm. Tinplate sheets are available in a wide variety of sizes from about 450 mm square to 800 mm × 1 m. When required for large-scale production it is produced in coils of up to 500 mm wide and weighing up to 150 kg. The thickness of the tin coating also varies but is usually less than 0·0025 mm. Tinplate is normally measured by the weight of tin per plate area and is either defined as 'grammes per square metre' or by a coating code number which also indicates the method of manufacture. The tin coating may be applied to the base sheet by hot dipping in molten tin or by electroplating using a tin-bearing electrolyte.

Hot dip tinning From the rolling mill the sheets are cut into commercial sizes and pickled in hydrochloric or dilute sulphuric acid and scrubbed with steel wire brushes to remove the oxide. The cleaning processes make the sheets rather brittle and they have to be annealed in a muffle furnace, care being taken to keep them in a neutral atmosphere to prevent further oxidation. The next stage is to temper them slightly to give the plates that springy property associated with tinplate. Finally, before being taken to the tinning bath, the plates are again dipped in acid and scoured with sand. In the tinning room are vats of boiling grease and vats of tin of various qualities. The plates are first placed in the grease vat, coated with grease and then transferred to the vat of coarse tin where they get a first coating, and then to the vat containing finer tin for another coat. When removed the plates are brushed with a hemp pad, dipped in a vat of very fine tin and finally again in a grease vat. After this they are passed through rollers to remove the surplus tin and allowed to cool. Having cooled, any grease left on the plates is removed by drawing them through sawdust and they are finally polished on a woollen covered bench top, by means of a wool pad. The steel base may also be handled in the form of continuous strip but this process accounts for only a small proportion of the total output.

Electrolytic tinning   This is a continuous strip process and follows naturally the process of continuous strip manufacture of the base steel strip. The tinned steel strip may be sheared to sheet before dispatch but may also be supplied in coil. The electrolytic process permits more accurate control of uniformity and thickness of coating and different thicknesses of coating on each surface of the strip are possible. Coating thicknesses are from 0·0004 to 0·0015 mm. The three most important electrolytes used in tinplate production are based on stannous sulphate, alkaline stannates and stannous halides. For satisfactory adhesion of the tin the plate must first be cleaned; this is also an electrolytic process. The cleaning agent usually contains sodium hydroxide and alkaline phosphates or silicates and is used at a temperature of 80°C. The strip then passes into rinsing and scrubbing plant to remove all traces of detergent and is next pickled. For this process the electrolyte is usually sulphuric acid 5 10% concentration. After again rinsing and scrubbing the strip passes to the plating bath. Here the electrolyte is a solution of stannous tin in phenolsulphonic acid at a temperature of 40–50°C, the anodes are of pure tin. Finally the strip is treated with cotton-seed oil, this prevents chafing of the surfaces and assists separation by the user.

Care of tinplate   If first-class work is to be produced the tinplate used must be of good quality. Having bought a good quality tinplate then do look after it, try and preserve the excellent finish provided by the manufacturers. At one time tinplate came in boxes interleaved with tissue paper but alas those days have gone. The aim should be to prevent the surface getting scratched, thus removing the tin coating. Take out a sheet from the stock and use this until finished, do not be putting it backwards and forwards into stock or the next sheet will become so badly scratched as to make it unusable. Poorer quality tinplate does not take a curved bend freely but tends to bend in a series of short flats leaving a lined appearance. To overcome this the plate which is to be given a curved bend should be run through the tin rolls, first one side up and then the other; this is said to break the grain.

When marking out on tin use a brass scriber or a sharp pencil and cut exactly on the line first time. Should it be necessary to file it, put it down flat on a clean bench top, its edge just overlapping, and file carefully with a smooth file. Avoid hitting it; move it around by hand as much as possible on clean polished stakes. Never hammer tinplate but use mallets or suitably shaped pieces of hardwood. Tinwork stakes must be kept for tinwork and no hammers used on them, they should be oiled and kept covered when not in use.

The cut edges of tinplate should be coated with solder and not left raw or they will start to rust. As cut edges are usually at joints this is quite easily arranged. If too much solder is used on a joint do not file it off or the steel plate will be revealed and again corrosion will commence. Get a hot clean soldering iron, run it slowly over the joint and have an assistant to wipe it quickly with a clean rag to remove the surplus solder.

Arrange the work when soldering so that the solder runs into and not away from the joint and also arrange it so that the step in the joint is a ledge on to which the soldering iron is rested. If joints are clean and fluxed and the iron is clean, hot and tinned, no difficulty should be experienced. The tendency for beginners is to move the iron too quickly; the metal being joined must be brought to a temperature slightly above the melting point of solder, which is between 140°C and 160°C, depending upon quality of the alloy. The joint will be heated more quickly if, instead of using the extreme point of the iron, the full edge of the square point is drawn along the joint. Take full advantage of the size of the copper bit, heat the whole of it, not just the point being used. Joints which are to be soldered must be well fitting as solder will not fill large gaps. There must be clearance to allow the solder to penetrate and to be drawn in by capillary force as the solder wets the metal. Metals such as tinplate and tinned surfaces need slightly less clearance than untinned surfaces. A clearance of about 0·07 mm to 0·12 mm is adequate for most circumstances.

The size of bit is important and must bear relation to the size of job being done. If heated in a tinman's stove it may be a good idea to have two bits, one to be heating whilst the other is being used. An electric iron has the advantage that it remains hot. If the job is too large for an iron, then a blowpipe or small gas jet, Fig. 87 may have to be used. For all soldering work at school use blow-pipe solder rather than stick, to avoid getting too much solder on the job, or better still melt a stick into a thin groove to make thinner sticks or wires. Do not beat out the solder until flat and then cut off thin lengths as this method makes the solder greasy and dirty. Wire solders are available, they melt quickly and being uniform in section it is easier to collect just the right amount for a joint.

[*Buck & Hickman Ltd.*

Fig. 87. 'Davi-jet' burner.

In use, of course, the tinplate loses its lustre but it may finally be polished by washing in hot water and rubbing with clean sawdust or polishing with *venetian lime.*

Just how the marking out on the tinplate is done will depend upon the nature of the job. If it is straightforward rectangular or compass-curved work, it can be drawn straight on to the plate, but if the shape has to be developed it will have to be drawn out on paper, cut out carefully and the cut-out shape pasted on to the plate, care being taken not to distort the shape during pasting. If the shape is such that it may easily be distorted then cut out a rectangle of paper surrounding the shape required and paste this on. Satisfactory tinplate work demands extreme accuracy and where parts have to fit the thickness of the metal must be taken into consideration.

Solder paste This consists of pure tin or solder with a high tin content in powder form suspended in flux. The parts to be soldered are cleaned, painted with solder paste, put together and then heated to the usual soldering temperature. With care in application a good joint is obtained, with the further advantage that it does not show any solder. Craftsmen tend to regard its use as bordering upon sharp practice and avoiding the issue of acquiring basic skills, but it has its uses and applications.

Solder powder This consists of powdered tin or solder mixed with its own weight of some powdered flux such as sal ammoniac. The surfaces to be joined are cleaned, one surface is covered with the powder and the other one clamped to it and heat applied.

Tinman's snips Tinplate may be cut on a small guillotine or by tinman's snips. If a guillotine is used, it is better to reserve one for tinplate, kept sharp and set carefully. Tinman's snips, Figs. 88, 89, 90, are available in a variety of shapes and sizes, and are measured by their overall length. They should not meet at the handle end, since if held close in to the body to get extra power and purchase, when they eventually break through they will pinch the flesh as the ends meet.

[F. J. Edwards Ltd.

Fig. 88.

[F. J. Edwards Ltd.

Fig. 89.

[F. J. Edwards Ltd.

Fig. 90.

Folding bars Angular bends are made by means of folding bars, Fig. 91, and it may be necessary when using them to adjust the position of the bending line to allow for the thickness of the metal. Illustrated is a folding bar, Fig. 92, which is easier to handle than the sprung commercial type. It is also an advantage to have one edge rounded, since this is a great help when making the initial bend for a wired edge. For bends which have to be taken beyond 90° a hatched stake is used.

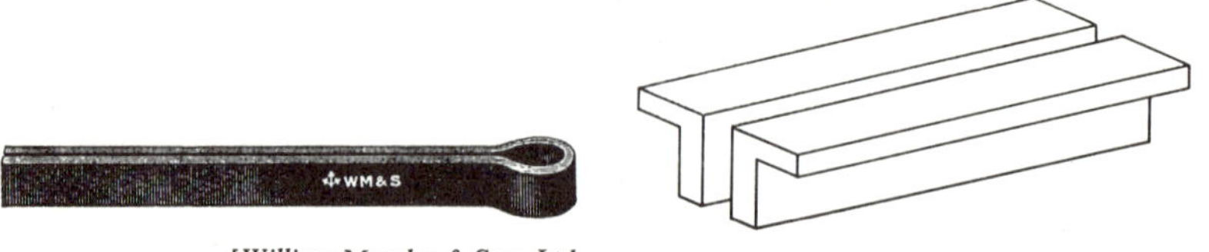

[*William Marples & Sons Ltd.*

Fig. 91. Tinman's folding bar.

Fig. 92. Folding bar.

Tinman's stakes   These are sold by weight and are held in sockets in a low stake bench. It is bad practice to hold them in a vice as the shanks become mutilated by the serrated jaws of the vice. All working faces and edges should be highly polished and kept covered when not in use. Their uses are as follows:
The hatchet stake, Fig. 93, is used for preparing edges for seaming and wiring.
Tinman's anvil, Fig. 94, has a highly polished flat surface and may be used for straightening and planishing, and throwing up square bends.
Round bottom stake, Fig. 95, for squaring up edges and setting up the bottom of cylindrical work.
Half moon stake, Fig. 96, for throwing up edges of curved work and for preliminary stages of wiring curved edges.
Bick iron, Fig. 98, for forming taper handles, spouts and tubular work in general. The narrow flat anvil end is very useful on rectangular work.
Funnel stake, Fig. 97, for larger conical and cylindrical work.
Creasing iron, Fig. 99. The grooves are of various sizes and are used for making beaded and wired edges and cylindrical tubes.

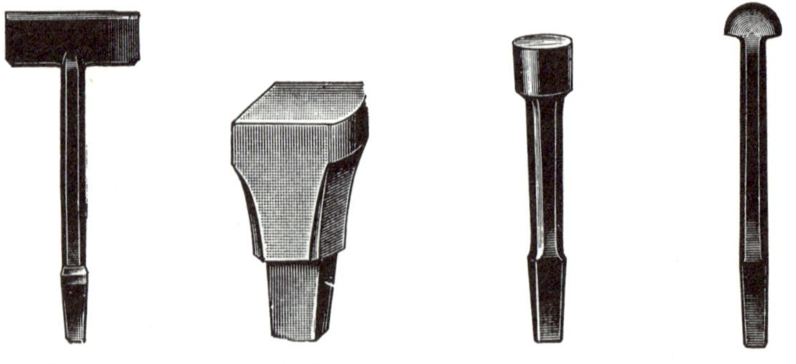

Fig. 93. Hatchet
stake.

Fig. 94. Tinman's
anvil.

Fig. 95. Round
bottom stake.

Fig. 96. Half-moon
stake.

[*William Allday & Co. Ltd.*

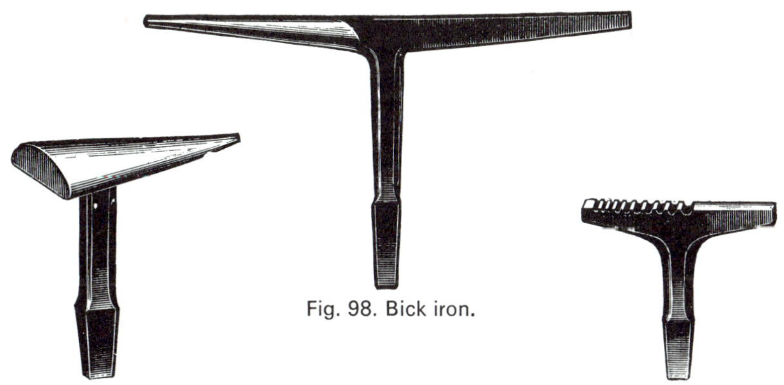

Fig. 98. Bick iron.

Fig. 97. Funnel stake.

[William Allday & Co. Ltd.

Fig. 99. Creasing iron.

Other stakes are extinguisher, grooving, side, square pan, ball-headed, etc.; sizes and weignts may be found by consulting a manufacturer's catalogue.

Other tinwork tools are:

Creasing hammer, Fig. 100. This has thin rounded edges and is useful in the preliminary stages of a wired edge.

Pein or *paning hammer*, Fig. 101, has a thin acute pein and is used where edges of the metal have to be tucked close to the main body as in wired edges.

[William Marples & Sons Ltd.

Fig. 100. Creasing
hammer.

Fig. 101. Paning
hammer.

[William Allday & Co. Ltd.

Fig. 102. Groove punch.

[F. J. Edwards Ltd.

Fig. 103.

Groove punches or *seam sets*, Fig. 102. The grooves are round or rectangular for setting wired edges and folded seam joints.
Boxwood or *hardwood mallets*, Fig. 103. The size is taken as the diameter of the head and is used for flattening and bending tinplate over the various shaped stakes.

Soldering irons, Fig. 104   The heads of soldering irons are made of copper because this metal is a good conductor of heat. There are two main shapes, *straight* and *hatchet*, and these are obtainable in a wide range of weights, the larger and heavier ones retaining their heat longer than smaller ones. The size of iron

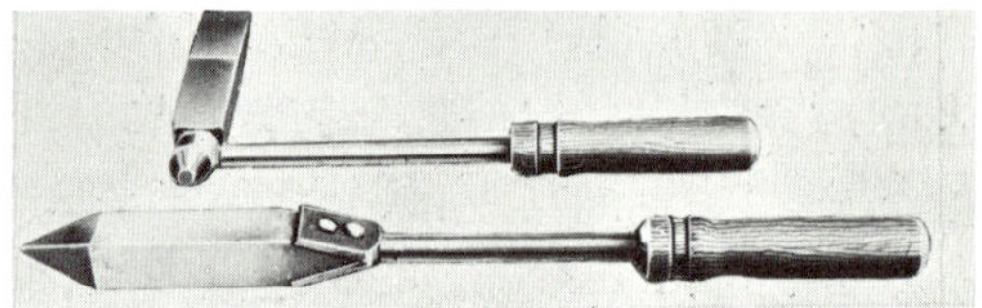

[F. J. Edwards Ltd.

Fig. 104. Soldering iron.

chosen must of course bear relation to the job in hand but must not be too heavy and clumsy, especially for boys' use. Copper unfortunately oxidizes rapidly when heated and it is, therefore, necessary to coat the tip of the iron with a layer of solder before use, in order to prevent oxidation. This is known as 'tinning' the iron and once done the iron will remain clean and free from oxide for a long time provided it is not overheated or burnt in the stove. Immediately after each reheating the iron should be fluxed and given a fresh coating of solder.

To tin a copper bit, first heat in the stove and, when a green flame appears, remove, rest the stem on the edge of the bench top and quickly file clean with a file kept on the soldering bench for the purpose. Remove as little metal as possible with the file, a couple of rubs on each face should be sufficient. The fluxing and tinning is best done in a small hole in a sal ammoniac block which is filled with solder, the bit being held vertically in the hole. To try and flux one face at a time is too slow as the exposed faces oxidize. Do not dip the iron into paste, or the paste melts and becomes unsuitable for use. Dipping in acid, though very effective, makes a lot of dirt; a vapour is produced which settles on all the tools in the vicinity, condenses and makes them greasy.

Tinman's stove   Two types of soldering stove are illustrated, Figs. 105 and 106; the simple one is quite adequate for most school use. When the iron is being heated and the green flame appears, the iron should be withdrawn and rested on the edge of the stove so that the tip is adjacent to and not in the flame. Some stoves have an automatic cut-off, Fig. 107; withdrawing the iron lowers the gas

Fig. 106. Soldering stove.

Fig. 105. Unlined soldering
iron heater.

William Allday & Co. Ltd.

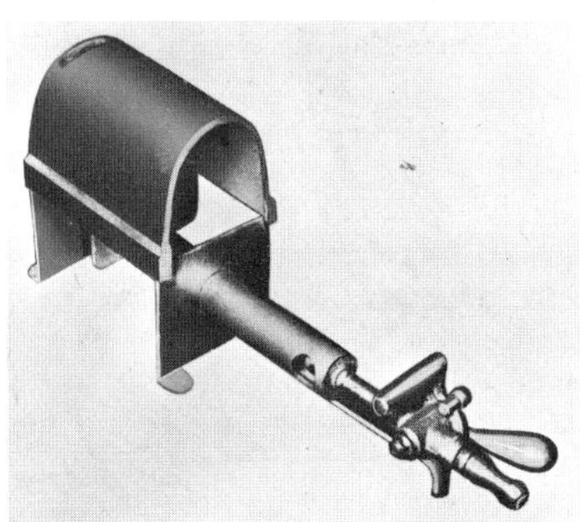

[F. J. Edwards Ltd.

Fig. 107. Soldering iron heater with
automatic cut-off.

[William Allday & Co. Ltd.

Fig. 108. Combined soldering
iron heater and lead pot.

flame and saves fuel. Illustrated also is a heater with a lead pot, Fig. 108, which is very useful for filling pipes with lead prior to bending. Care must be taken of course to preheat any tubes to be filled. A pot filled with solder is also useful for tinning small articles and to assist with larger soldering jobs. The metal is quite readily removed when cold but to avoid confusion scratch an S for solder or L for lead on the top surface just before it solidifies.

The soldering bench   The top of the soldering bench must be considered. If the top is of wood then the stove must rest on an asbestos mat. Ideally the whole bench top should be covered with soft asbestos secured neatly in position with aluminium angle round the edges. Hard asbestos is dangerous as this 'shales' and flies when heated. Metal tops too are undesirable and may be dangerous, but if there is no alternative then the job must be placed on an asbestos mat or piece of wood to prevent heat being conducted away. Acids corrode a metal top, and get under the skin, and if heated expansion causes the metal to fly. A vice is useful on a soldering bench but again if work is held in it for soldering some form of heat insulation must be provided. This is best done by providing a piece of wood shaped to hold the job for soldering and gripping this in the vice.

Fluxes   These are used to assist the solder to flow and to reduce any oxide present or protect the joint from any further oxidation. Fluxes which reduce the oxide are known as *active fluxes* and are acids, and any residue must be carefully washed off with hot water. They must never be used on electrical work. The protecting fluxes are *passive* and usually take the form of a paste or grease; joints must be clean before the paste is applied. Some of these fluxes may be made up in the school workshop, but all are available commercially under various trade names.

Hydrochloric acid is used when soldering zinc and galvanized iron.

Tallow is used by plumbers when soldering lead.

Sal ammoniac in powder form is used for iron and copper.

Gallipoli oil or Venice turpentine is used for soldering alloys of low melting points such as Britannia metal and pewter.

Resin, in powder form, has a wide variety of applications and as it does not cause corrosion it is most useful for electrical work.

Zinc chloride may be used on tinplate, brass and copper.

Preparation of zinc chloride   This is perhaps the most common flux to be found in a workshop and is more familiarly known as 'killed spirits'. It is made by dissolving zinc in hydrochloric acid or spirits of salts. The preparation should be done in a lead or earthenware pot and preferably in a fume cupboard as the vapour given off is most offensive. Scraps of zinc are added to the acid causing effervescence; zinc continues to be added until effervescence ceases. The scum which forms on top is removed by pouring through a filter paper. For general use add about 50% water, and use a stronger solution for copper. If the acid

92

has not been properly killed black streaks will appear on the soldered joint; to avoid this, use rather more zinc than is strictly necessary.

Tinwork joints, Fig. 109, are briefly described below.
Lap seam, a simple convenient joint but not very strong.
Countersunk lap seam, similar to the lap seam but with one edge set down so as to present an unbroken surface on one side. The crease also gives stiffness to the joint.

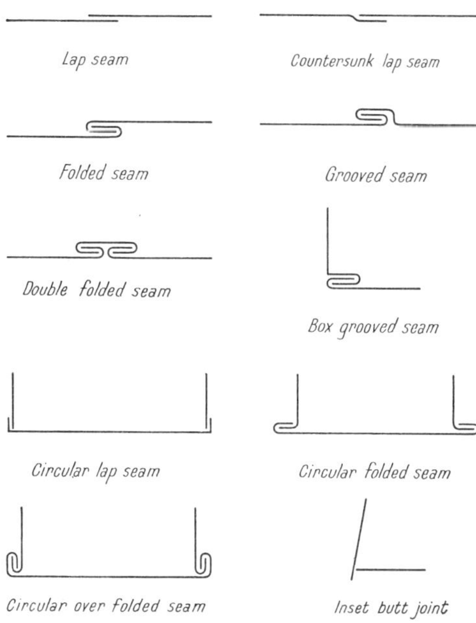

Fig. 109. Tinwork joints.

Folded seam   The edges of the joint are bent over on the hatchet stake or folding machine and closed over a piece of metal of the same thickness, hooked together and flattened with a mallet. When used on a continuous piece, the bends must be made in opposite directions.

Grooved seam, similar to the folded seam but in addition is set down by means of a seam set, care being taken not to damage the tin either side of the seam. This joint presents an unbroken surface on one side. Before this joint is made a suitable seam set must be obtained and measured; if the initial bends are too large the set will inevitably cause damage.

Double folded seam, a stronger joint than the folded or grooved seam and is usually used on thicker plate.

Box grooved seam or cash box joint, is used for joining plates at corners, the knock-up is inside the box and the outside of the corner is flush.
Circular lap seam or 'snuffed-on' bottom, for the bottoms of cylindrical vessels.
Circular folded seam or 'panned-down' bottom, also for cylindrical vessels.
Circular over folded seam or 'knocked-up' bottom   An extension of the previous joint and if well made is quite water-tight without soldering.
Inset butt joint, used for bottoms of conical work, the corners being filled with a fillet of solder.

When making rectangular boxes with simple lap joints, the joints should be arranged on the outside, as they look much neater. If clean right-angle bends are required in thicker sheet they must be grooved on the inside, as shown in Fig. 117a. Flux the groove before bending.

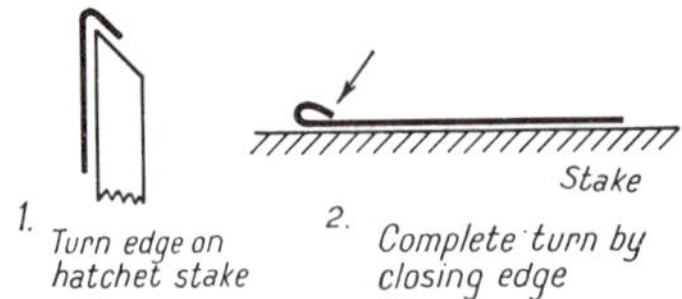

Fig. 110. Beaded edge.

Avoid leaving the edges of tin raw or as cut; the simplest treatment is to bend over a small amount as shown, Fig. 110, to give a beaded edge. The amount bent over will depend upon the size of the job in hand. The bend is usually made over a hatchet stake and completed by means of a mallet on any suitable flat stake.

A better and stronger treatment is to wire the edge and again the diameter of wire used will depend upon the size of the job. To wire the edge, first bend over an amount equal to $2\frac{1}{2}$ times the diameter of the wire, using a hatchet stake or, as suggested previously, using a folding bar with a rounded edge. Tap the turnover with a mallet until it is parallel, tuck in the wire and complete the turnover using a paning hammer, Fig. 111. The edge may be completed in a

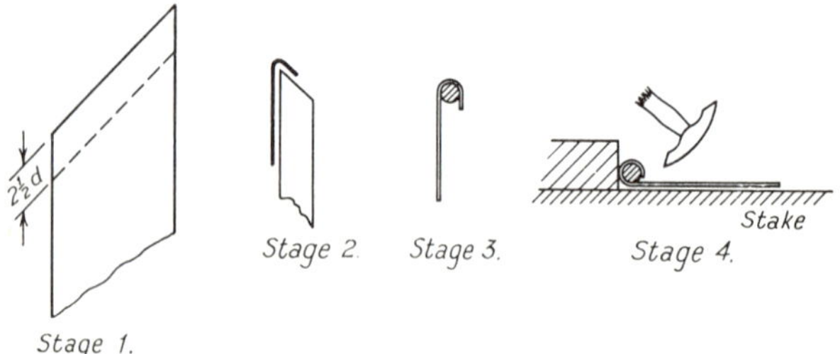

Fig. 111. Wired edge.

suitable groove in the creasing iron. It is better to allow too little rather than too much for wiring; if too much is allowed the excess is most difficult to get rid of. Rectangular boxes are wired after the box has been thrown up and its seams soldered. The allowance for wiring is cut through before bending and the wire is left exposed at the corners. Cylindrical work which is to have a wired edge is usually wired in the flat and then bent to its circular form. If it is wired after shaping, the joint in the wire may be arranged in some place other than at the joint in the work. For wiring jobs in tinplate use tinned iron wire rather than galvanized; if any soldering is involved this will simplify the work considerably. The raw edges of tinplate on folded and wired edges are better soldered to prevent corrosion.

Sweating   This is a term applied to the joining of parts that have been tinned. The tinned parts are held together and heated until the solder melts and the pressure is maintained until the solder solidifies.

Other sheet metals   *Galvanized iron* is stronger and thicker than tinplate and is used for outdoor work. It is sheet steel with a coating of molten zinc. Smaller parts which have an electrically deposited coating of zinc are said to be Sherardized. Galvanized iron may be soft soldered if hydrochloric acid is used as a flux and the point of the copper bit is frequently rubbed on a sal ammoniac block.
Terne plate is sheet steel with a coating of tin lead alloy which has a preponderance of lead.
Copper vessels which have been tinned make excellent cooking utensils, especially where a quick heat is required. The tin is not easily dissolved by vegetable or meat juices.
Aluminium sheet of suitable thickness may be joined in the same way as tinplate and unless required to hold liquid need not be soldered. Aluminium of course may be joined by hard soldering, referred to earlier.

Aluminium which is to be used out of doors should be *anodized* to resist oxidation.

6 Beaten Metalwork

The shaping of sheet metal by beating with a mallet or hammer is one of the oldest of the metalworking crafts, the methods of working and the processes having changed little with time. As well as being a traditional craft, this branch of metalwork gives much scope for creative work and provides a very satisfying activity. An understanding of the nature of metals, their capabilities and limitations, results from the practice of such work and, by the consideration of both functional form and decoration much can be learnt about the true nature of design.

The properties that are exploited in beaten work are the malleability, ductility and, to a lesser extent, fusibility of the material. Copper, which is very soft and most amenable to shaping by beating, is often used in the early stages, though gilding metal is the common material for school beaten metalwork. Other brasses are in most cases too hard for general work though, where colour is important, soft annealed sheet brass may be used for shallow work. Pewter and Britannia metal have little application in the school craftroom, and silver, which is possibly the most rewarding of all metals to shape in this way, is in most cases too expensive. Aluminium is suitable for the smaller introductory jobs, but as it is less easily annealed and soldered it is usually reserved for the more simple one-piece articles.

Tools and equipment   Much of the equipment and many of the tools used are similar to those in general use in the workshop and the few that are peculiar to beaten work can in many cases be made in the craftroom. The first requisite is a solid wooden block for hollowing. A portion of a tree trunk to stand upon the floor is ideal for this purpose though smaller blocks to suit the vices may be used, Fig. 114a. Elm is often used, though most hard woods will do. The blocks are shaped so that malleting takes place on the end grain. A raising stake and a selection of the standard shape planishing stakes are necessary, Fig. 112. Smaller stakes and those for special purposes are made as required. The quality of the work produced depends very much on the condition of the stake surfaces. They must be free from marks and scratches, well polished and should be covered when not in use. When in use they are held in metal sockets in a stake bench or in the vice, and the smaller stake heads in a metalworker's horse, Fig. 112. The basic hammer shapes are shown in Fig. 113; others that are required may be forged from cast steel.

An acid bath for cleaning and pickling work after heating must be provided. If the acid bath is fitted with a lid that is hinged at the front, protection against splashing is afforded. If a hot pickle bath is installed it should be placed in a fume cupboard fitted with an extractor fan. Acid baths should be positioned near the sink and running water.

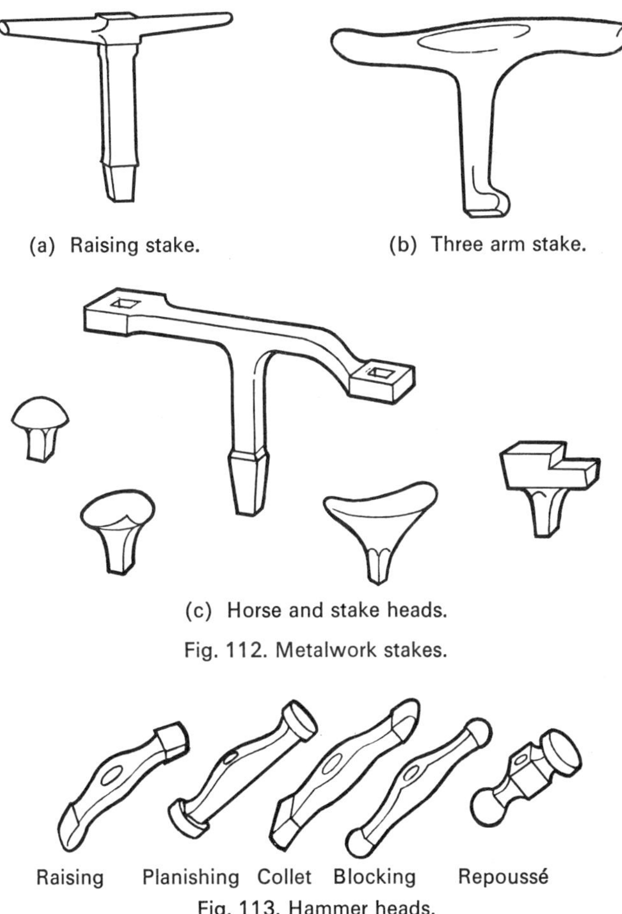

(a) Raising stake.   (b) Three arm stake.

(c) Horse and stake heads.

Fig. 112. Metalwork stakes.

Fig. 113. Hammer heads.

Hollowing Hollowing is a method of shaping shallow dishes and bowls by beating sheet metal on a wooden block or sandbag with a round-ended mallet or hammer, Fig. 114b. When a hammer is used, the process is often called blocking. It is also a preliminary operation in the production of taller forms by raising. The metal is tilted away from the block and struck on the near side, working in circles from the outside to the centre. The blows are aimed at a point a little

97

away from the point of contact between block and metal and must be evenly spaced and of equal force. The beating of circular forms at all stages is assisted if rows of concentric circles are described on the disc with pencil compasses and a radial line drawn to indicate the starting point. Waves and crinkles that are formed towards the edges are hammered out as they appear.

As the metal becomes work-hardened through repeated beating, it must be frequently annealed. Care must be taken to heat uniformly to avoid uneven expansion as the work is brought to a dull red heat. The method of cooling does not affect the resulting soft nature of non-ferrous metals but uneven quenching could affect the shape. Hence work should be allowed to cool in air. The oxide

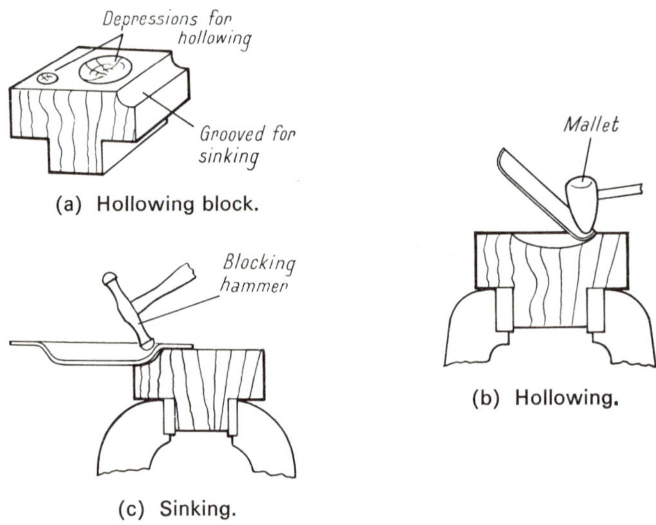

Fig. 114. Hollowing and sinking.

and impurities that form on the surface of the heated metal are then removed by pickling in an acid solution. Dilute sulphuric acid of one part in ten of water is used after annealing. The action takes place more quickly if the pickle is heated, and a hot pickle bath can be used with advantage, particularly to remove the borax flux after soldering. Hot work should not be introduced to a cold bath as the surface of the work may become pitted and there is a personal danger from splashing. Nickel or other non-ferrous tongs should be used to insert work to the bath, as the presence of iron in the pickle will cause contamination of the surface of other metals. If this occurs work should be dipped in dilute nitric acid. After pickling, the work is well washed under running water, further cleaned with pummice powder and then dried in sawdust. If this procedure is not carried out after each heating, oxide will be hammered into the metal and a good finish and polish will not ultimately be achieved.

Sinking Sinking is a process similar to hollowing in which the centre of a disc is sunk, leaving a margin which becomes a flat rim in the final shape, Fig. 114c. The disc is held horizontally on a shaped block of wood and the metal sunk with a mallet or blocking hammer. Pins positioned on the flat surface of the block can assist a beginner to gauge the depth of the border. At intervals the tray or dish is inverted on a surface plate and the rim flatted with a block of wood and a hammer. The base is also trued in the same way.

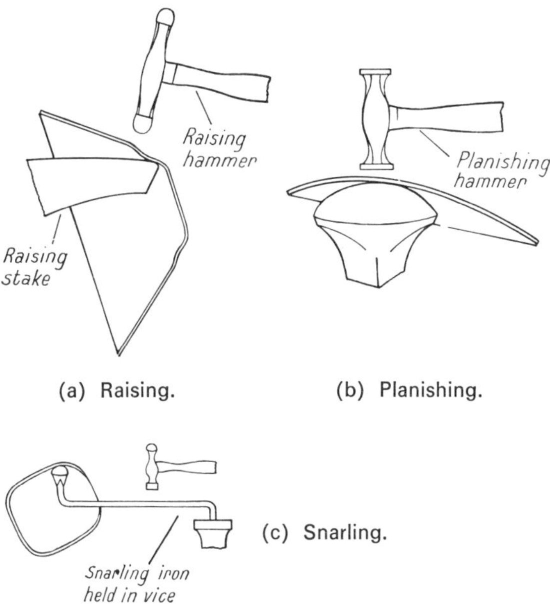

(a) Raising.   (b) Planishing.

(c) Snarling.

Fig. 115. Metal beating operations.

Raising Shallow forms only may be accomplished by hollowing and sinking, the deeper and taller shapes being formed by raising. In raising, the disc of metal is hammered on the outside while resting on the edge of a suitable stake, Fig. 115a. Work is raised from the centre to the outside, the blows falling in concentric circles as with hollowing. With the work tilted slightly from the body of the stake, the hammer strikes the metal a little in advance of the stake edge, the work being held firmly in the left hand. Blows should be of sufficient force to carry the metal touched by the hammer face down to the top of the stake but not heavy enough to trap and thin it. Raising, when correctly done, has a distinctive sound, the dull note first emitted blends with a ring as the metal cotacts the stake. The disc is turned a little, the next blow struck and the process continued until a definite ridge is formed around the work. Further rows of blows are then made at a distance of slightly less than the width of the raising hammer face. Each course of raising should decrease the diameter and increase the depth by up to 10 mm. When approaching the outside edge or rim of an article care must be taken to prevent folding the metal. Waves that occur are removed by striking blows at the front of the wave formations and working towards the edge. The work is then trued up and will require annealing before further raising is attempted. Shallow forms may be raised with a boxwood mallet over a mushroom stake.

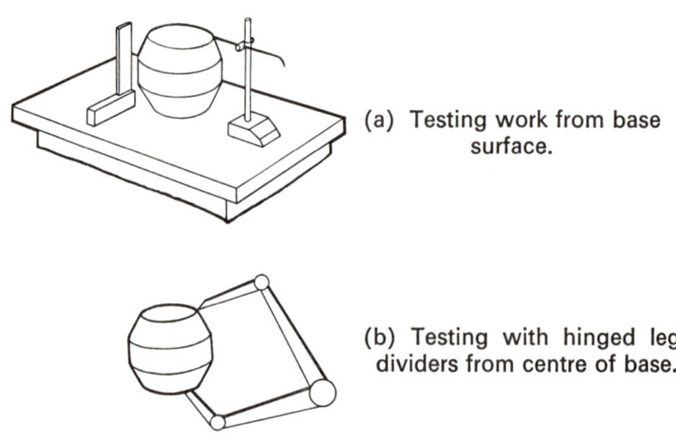

(a) Testing work from base surface.

(b) Testing with hinged leg dividers from centre of base.

Fig. 116. Testing work.

Incorrect raising may cause work to flare out at the top. If this occurs an extra course should be started where the flaring begins. The sides of the work should be almost straight after work has been raised, and if a curved shape is eventually required a series of straight steps should first be formed to approximate to the final shape. This assists in the testing of the accuracy of the shaping operation and in correcting any faults. The flats are then *snarled* or planished true to shape. Work is tested on a surface plate with a try square and scribing block, and with dividers as shown in Fig. 116. Work that leans to one side can sometimes be corrected by reversing the direction of rotation while raising or extra hammering may be needed on one side only.

Caulking Caulking consists of thickening the edge of sheet metal by hammering directly on the edge with a raising hammer. It gives greater strength to the rims of raised work and is often required before seaming. Work is caulked before annealing to prevent buckling. Flat sheets are held in folding bars and other shapes supported on a sandbag.

Snarling   Tall raised forms and those with narrow necks often require hammering on the inside to stretch the metal, fill out a hollow or true up the shape. Such operations may be accomplished by the use of a *snarling iron*, Fig. 115c. With the work positioned on the iron head, the arm is struck with a hammer and the head rebounds against the inside of the rotated work.

Planishing   Having formed a shape by hollowing, sinking or raising, the surface is trued and all marks of the previous working removed by planishing. A flat or very slightly domed hammer is used and the work is trapped between the stake and hammer face as each blow is struck, Fig. 115b. The ringing sound emitted is quite different from that of the other metal beating operations. The selection of the correct stake and hammer is of great importance, for the shape of the work is not materially altered apart from the removal of ridges, lines and other imperfections of the surface. The portion of the stake used approximates to the portion of the work under the hammer face and, as with other metal beating operations, the hammer falls in the same place on the stake and the work is rotated beneath it. Collet hammers are used to planish concave curves. The hammer blows must overlap and the whole surface be covered with hammer marks of equal size. Planishing is not primarily a form of decoration though the facets produced are allowed to remain on some articles. Work requiring a smooth surface has the planishing marks buffed out. Planishing starts at the centre of an article and proceeds to the outside for, as the metal is hardened, the article is pulled true and the final form set.

Seamed and box work   A further range of articles may be made by developing the shape as for sheet metalwork. Butt joints are invariably used and are silver soldered. Joints are prepared by filing or scraping and, when a lid of the same shape as the base is required, the box is first made complete and the parts sawn apart, Fig. 117. Hinges are made by first creasing a strip and then drawing it through a draw-plate to form a tube or *chenier*, Fig. 117c. The short lengths are then positioned on a shaped strip with the chenier joint in contact with the metal, Fig. 117d. Tall conical and cylindrical forms are developed in this way, the joint is soldered and shaping and planishing are then carried out. Irregular shapes such as narrow spouts and hollow handles are developed and seamed.

Soldering and jointing   Hard soldering is used almost exclusively in the jointing of articles in this type of work and consists of melting an alloy and fusing the joint at a temperature above red heat. Brazing applies to the process using various alloys of copper and zinc and is often used as the first of a series of joints, as the spelter melts at approximately 875°C. Alloys containing a proportion of silver are used within the range 600°C to 800°C and are graded *easy*, *hard* and *enamelling*. When these are employed the process is called *silver soldering*. The best grades, with about four parts silver to one of copper and zinc, are used in the silversmith's trade on solid silver work. There are many other trade alloys using some silver. They are cheaper to buy, often slightly yellow in colour and are classified as common solders. Soft lead solders are not normally employed on work in this class as articles on which they are used cannot then be annealed, pickled or plated. They are useful however for final joints

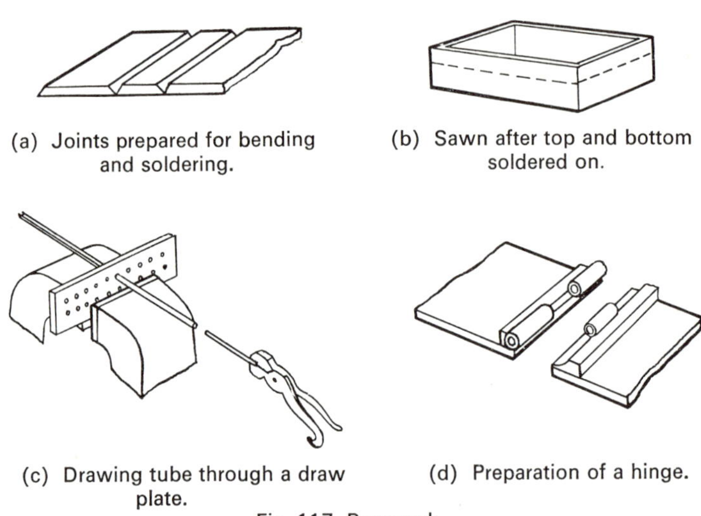

(a) Joints prepared for bending and soldering.

(b) Sawn after top and bottom soldered on.

(c) Drawing tube through a draw plate.

(d) Preparation of a hinge.

Fig. 117. Box work.

when it is important not to anneal the work. Soft soldering should be restricted to a special soldering bench since lead solder left on the hearth will stain and may cause holes to be burned in non-ferrous metals that are subsequently heated upon it.

The main obstacle to hard soldering is the oxide which forms on the surface of heated metal and prevents the solder running along the joint. This can be prevented by the application of borax as a flux. It is applied before heating by mixing a powder with water or forming a paste with a borax cone on a slate. The joint itself must be a good fit and clean before attempting to solder, and the portions held together by a soft iron binding wire, clips made from split cotter pins, or stitches, Fig. 118. In some complicated joints, the previously soldered joints may be protected by the application of jeweller's rouge or loam mixed with water. When heating for soldering, the whole work must be heated first to prevent loss of heat from the joint. Move the flame off the work occasionally to see the colour, and bring both sides of the joint to the same temperature. Solder will flow towards the hottest point and the flame may be used to flush the solder along the joint. A thin steel wire dipped in the flux may also be used to assist the flow. Solder may be applied as *paillons* (small pieces) or in a strip held in tongs. After soldering, allow the work to cool slowly to prevent the joints cracking due to uneven contraction, and remove wires before pickling.

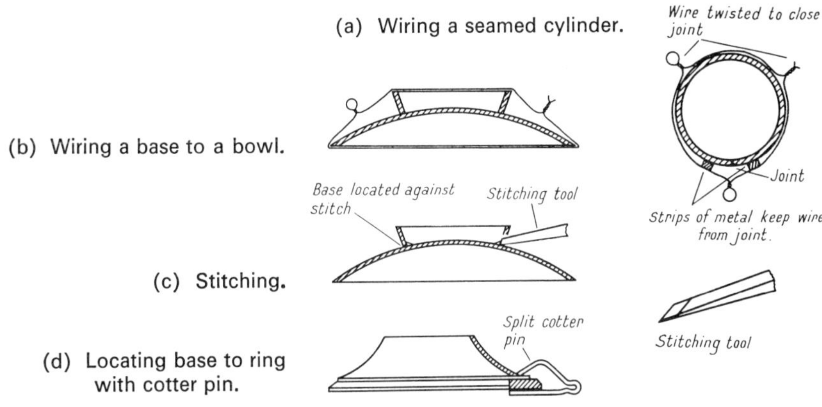

Fig. 118. Locating work for soldering.

The rims and edges of work may be strengthened by the application of wires. Such wires are often used to decorate the article. Half round and rectangular wires may be filed and round wires twisted, or plaited and then flattened by hammering or passing between metal rolls. Wires are brought to shape and size by drawing through suitably shaped holes in draw-plates. They must of course be frequently annealed during the process and when heated they should be coiled to ensure that they are brought to an even temperature throughout.

Etching   Etching forms a simple and effective method of decorating the surface of beaten work. The surface to be treated is first coated with an acid-resisting ground; the portions to be etched are then removed and an acid applied. The most convenient way to proceed is to trace or sketch the design on the work and coat it with a transparent ground made of white wax and gum mastic. The outline is then scratched away with a scriber or tool made for the purpose. A solution of equal parts nitric acid and water is suitable for etching brass and copper, a weak solution of hydrochloric acid is used for aluminium. When sufficient depth has been acquired the work is removed from the acid and washed under running water. The wax is then removed by heat or turpentine.

Repoussé   A great variety of decorative forms may be applied to work by embossing portions of the surface and relieving others by the use of punches and a light hammer. Such work is generally known as *repoussé* though it is often referred to as 'chased work'. Light gauge metal may be punched if laid on lead or a wooden block coated with pitch. Heavier sheet should be embedded in pitch in a tray or a hemispherical bowl which, if placed on a circular ring, makes for convenient working at all angles. The pitch is prepared by mixing plaster of Paris with heated Swedish pitch in equal parts. A little tallow is added to make the mixture less brittle. The back of the work is lightly oiled before bedding to the heated surface of the pitch, to aid its eventual cleaning on removal. Bowls and hollow forms are filled with pitch, a metal bar being placed in the centre to facilitate holding in the vice.

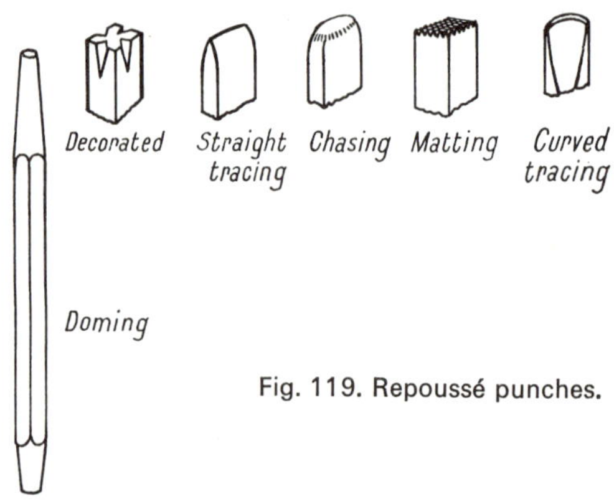

Fig. 119. Repoussé punches.

Simple decorative features may be accomplished by the use of shaped punches alone or by the use of a tracing punch, Fig. 119. More involved designs are first scribed on the work and the outline traced. The work is then inverted on the pitch and the design embossed from the back by the use of suitable punches to form the necessary relief. It is then once more positioned with its face uppermost and the design sharpened and the surface finished with chasing punches. The background is then sometimes treated with a matting tool to give emphasis to the embossed form. Many varying shaped tools will be required and these are made to suit as the work proceeds. Cast steel is used, the surface given a smooth finish and polish, and the tool hardened and tempered. The flutes on bowls and other articles are prepared in this way by using a range of tracing and chasing tools. The final chasing of repoussé work corresponds to the planishing of hollowed and raised forms.

7 Forgework

Blacksmith's hearth   Illustrated in Fig. 120 is a blacksmith's hearth. As a means of heating metal it is slow, uneconomic and in this technological age unscientific, but it is the traditional method and for that reason alone justifies a place in the school metalwork shop.

Forgework demands a high degree of skill and coordination but if correctly and progressively approached very satisfactory results can be achieved. A hearth made from mild steel needs to have a firebrick lining or the fire will in time burn its way through the plates. If made of cast iron this brick lining will not be

Fig. 120. Blacksmith's hearth.

necessary. On top of the bricks, or iron in the cast iron forge, put a layer of builder's sand with a depression at the end of the tuyere. On the top of the sand put riddled blacksmith's breeze, with an additional supply at the back of the hearth where it can be warming prior to being raked on to the fire. This warming is important as cold or damp coke will split and fly dangerously if put straight on to a hot fire. Clinker formation is unavoidable and it is important that this should be removed when the fire is cool. If attempts are made to remove it when hot it will inevitably break up and spread all over the hearth. Usually the hearth will cool down sufficiently in the lunch break to permit the clinker to be removed in one piece. Lift it clear with a poker and remove by means of tongs. A gas poker is very convenient for lighting the fire but it must be placed a little above the blast hole and certainly not below it. If possible a supply of best washed blacksmith's coke breeze should be obtained; the ordinary domestic supplies of coke are quite unsuitable. The hearth should have an adequate chimney with an extraction fan if possible to carry away fumes, particularly from wet coke. If the hearth has a wet tuyere then the water trough at the back must be regularly inspected to see that it is kept full. A water tap over the tank is most convenient. Another water tank must be provided, to be hung or stood in front of the hearth, which is used for quenching metal and cooling off tools. On most hearths the

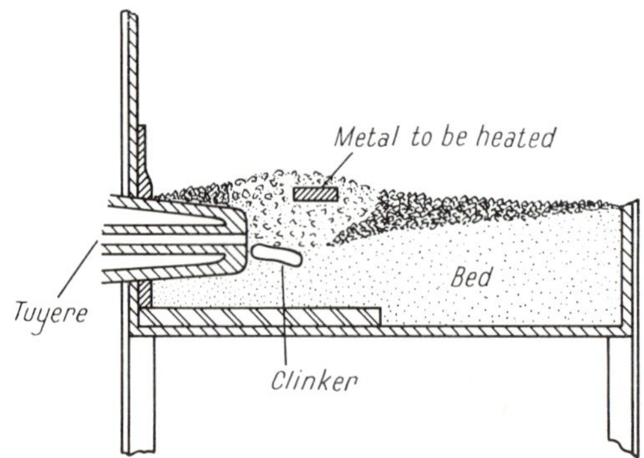

[*After Fig. 28 of 'The Blacksmith's Craft', Council for Small Industries in Rural Areas.*

Fig. 121.

blast is provided by an electrically driven blower, the amount of air being regulated by a rheostat and a mechanical sliding shutter. To prevent damage to the tuyere through being repeatedly knocked by heavy bars, it is advisable to paint a line on the operator's side of the hearth to mark the extent of the projection of the tuyere. Another method is to push down into the edge of the hearth on the operator's side a piece of, say, 3 mm metal projecting out from the back cheek as far as the extent of the tuyere and standing about 150 mm proud of the hearth.

The placing of the metal to be heated in the fire is important, Fig. 121; it should not be dug in below the most effective part of the fire.* The blacksmith's hearth is best situated in a dark part of the workshop to enable the heat of the metal to be judged more accurately. The floor around the forge is better if made of sand or dirt rather than concrete, which will shale and fly if hot metal is placed on it; a sand tray must then be provided as a receptacle for hot metal. Another advantage of a dirt floor is that the shock of hammer blows will be absorbed, they will be more effective, and the anvil will not bounce.

* See the Council for Small Industries in Rural Areas publication *The Blacksmith's Craft.*

The anvil Illustrated in Fig. 122 is a London pattern anvil. Anvils are graded by weight, an average weight being about 50 kg. The sizes of the various named parts are clearly set out for each weight in manufacturers' catalogues. The body of the anvil is usually made of wrought iron with a face of cast steel welded to it. The quality and finish of this face should be carefully preserved, any cutting or chiselling being done on the table. The *bick* has varying shapes and contours

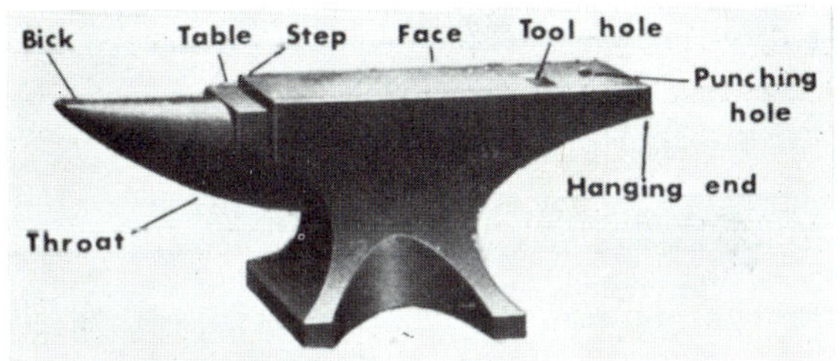

[*William Allday & Co. Ltd.*

Fig. 122. Anvil and stand.

and it is a matter of practice to know where to put the metal to produce the shape required. Hardies, bottom swages and fullers are made to fit the hole in the anvil. The anvil is best set up on the trunk of an elm, to give the anvil 'life' rather than bounce as with a cast iron stand. Arrange the working height carefully; a low anvil can be back-breaking to work at.

Swage block Fig. 123 shows a typical swage block, complete in its stand. As with anvils, swage blocks are sold by weight. A block 300 mm × 300 mm × 100 mm weighs 50 kg, the stand to match, 75 kg. It is a rectangular block with varying sizes of vee and half round notches on its edges and round, square and rectangular holes through its face. The swage block may be regarded as a special form of anvil; it may be turned to any required position. The holes in the face may be used for punching and bending, and the grooves on its edges for accommodating work of various sections.

[*William Allday & Co. Ltd.*

Fig. 123. Swage block
and stand.

Fig. 124. Floor
mandrel.

Leg vice (see Fig. 32, p. 53)   A strong, substantial vice is necessary for forge-work and is usually a leg vice fixed to a wooden bench or to a mobile vice bench. When fixed to a wooden bench the leg is let into a steel socket grouted into the concrete floor. If an engineers' vice is provided it must be of steel, and not cast iron, and preferably with a quick release device.

Floor mandrel   Fig. 124 shows the very useful floor mandrel—a hollow cast iron cone available in varying heights and weights. It is used for finishing off and rounding up rings and hoops. When used to bend around, precautions are necessary to avoid twisting the work, as with the bick of the anvil.

Small tool rack   Fig. 125 shows a rack for tongs, top and bottom swages and fullers, hammers and all small tools. Never rack tongs which are hot or whose jaws are wet with oil from quenching.

Fig. 125. Rack for small tools.

Tongs   A selection of tongs is shown in Fig. 126, each taking its name from the shape and purpose of its mouth. A few notes on the correct selection and care in use of tongs follow later in the chapter.

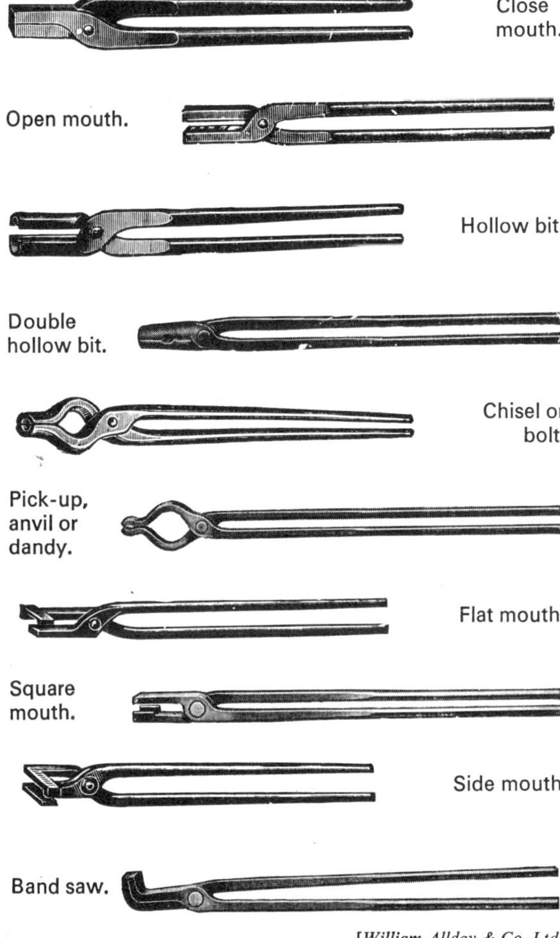

Fig. 126. Tongs.

Chisels   There are two main kinds for hot and cold use. Hot chisels are thinner and cut more easily into the hot metal and they are also longer so that the smith can keep his hand at a comfortable distance from the hot metal. When in use the hot chisel must be quenched frequently or its temper will be destroyed.

Sets (Fig. 127)   Again there are two main kinds for hot and cold use and both are used in conjunction with the sledge hammer. Like the chisel, the hot set is thinner and may be hafted or rodded.

William Allday & Co. Ltd.

Fig. 127. Sets.

Hardies (Fig. 128) do the same work as chisels but are made to fit into the square hole in the anvil. There is usually one for hot, and another for cold use.

Punches and drifts (Fig. 129) are made in various shapes for making holes in hot metal; they must be long enough to be used with reasonable comfort, or they may be rodded.

[*William Allday & Co. Ltd.*

Fig. 128. Hardie.

[*William Allday & Co. Ltd.*

Fig. 129. Taper rod punch.

Swages (Fig. 130) are supplied in pairs, top and bottom, and are available in sizes from 6 mm to 65 mm, measured across the diameter of the curve. The bottom one fits the hardie hole and the top one is usually rodded and is struck by the sledge hammer. Between them the work is brought down to size and given a good cylindrical finish. The blacksmith turns the work between the swages as the top one is being struck.

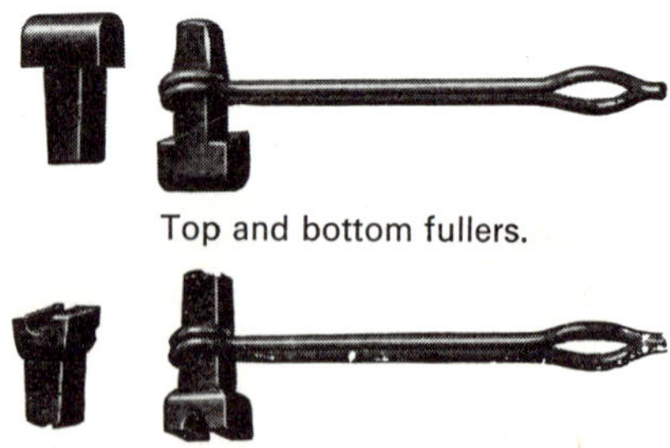

[*William Allday & Co. Ltd.*

Fig. 130. Fullers and swages.

Flatters and set hammers (Fig. 131) are used in conjunction with a sledge hammer for finishing off and flattening work which has been reduced by fullering.

Saddles (Fig. 132) are used to finish off sections after splitting as, for example, with a toasting fork, the distance apart of the prongs is too small to use the end of the anvil. They may be made in varying heights and from different sections according to the kind of work. They may be made quite quickly by bending a piece of flat steel to a shallow channel shape and then welding on the inside a piece of square bar which will fit the hardie hole.

[*William Allday & Co. Ltd.*

Fig. 131. Flatter and set hammer.

In the course of time a blacksmith accumulates a lot of tools made for particular jobs, these should be kept for their specific purpose and new tools made, rather than alter a tool to suit. This of course applies to all crafts; expediency is not a good motto for craftsmen.

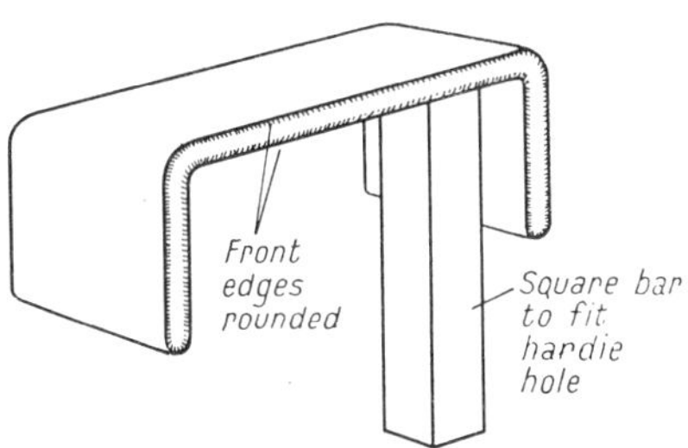

Fig. 132. Saddle.

The fire Successful forgework depends first on a good clean fire, and this necessitates constant attention. The size and intensity of the fire must be adjusted to suit the particular job in hand. The size of the hollow in the sand bed at the end of the tuyere limits this somewhat, but if too much coke is put on the fire will spread. It can be kept in bounds by damping with water from a swab or a ladle.

A common fault is to have too much draught, which of course increases the amount of oxygen; this combines with the fuel, burning it out too quickly. The fire then becomes hollow, the blast plays directly onto the metal increasing oxidation perhaps to the point of burning the metal. The smith calls this oxidizing fire a 'thin fire'. Another objection to too much blast is that it encourages the formation of clinker. An experienced smith after each time he rakes coke on to the fire, pats it down with the rake to reduce any tendency to hollow; he thus keeps a close fire. Coke must never be shovelled onto the fire or dirt from the bed will be included and increase the tendency to form clinker. New coke which is added to the hearth must not be brought straight from the bin but must first be riddled. Briefly then it should be the aim to keep as small and as slow a fire as is necessary for the job in hand and to keep it close and compact. It will be appreciated that smaller fuel helps considerably.

A certain amount of scale is always produced and a wire brush should be kept to hand and the metal quickly brushed before hammering. The face of the anvil must also be kept free of scale by brushing or wiping over after each period of use, preferably as soon as the metal has been resettled in the fire. On no account must scale be hammered into the metal.

Working heats for different metals and purposes* Judging the correct heat can only come with practice and varies from hearth to hearth and with the situation of the hearth. Metals appear hotter in darker situations, and it is quite impossible to judge accurately in the direct glare of the sun's rays. Again it must be appreciated that the time taken to attain these heats will vary with the section of the metal and, if a particular job has varying sections, even greater care and skill will be necessary. It is a common fault with the inexperienced to try and work with the metal too cold or to go on working after the heat has been lost. Black mild steel is better than wrought iron for early work, as wrought iron, if worked too cold, splits and shreds. An ideal material for school work is a soft iron, that is, a mild steel containing very little carbon, phosphorus and sulphur. A high sulphur content causes 'hot shortness', meaning brittle when in the red hot state. Phosphorus has the opposite effect making steel 'cold short', meaning a tendency to break when cold. The usual supplies of black mild steel vary considerably in quality; some of it is very poor indeed and behaves discouragingly.†

Fig. 133.

Forgework consists of heating metals until almost plastic and then manipulating them by hammering. Most forgework is done in black mild steel, or

* All the various heats, and the processes carried out at these heats, are set out in Chapter 4 of *The Blacksmith's Craft* and are not repeated here.

† By consulting B.S. 970 it will be found that steels E.N.2, E.N.2.A and E.N.2.A/1 would be ideal for forgework but to find a source of supply is most difficult.

wrought iron if it is for outdoor use, as it contains less carbon and does not corrode so much as mild steel. Forgings are usually tougher and stronger than castings, and the mechanical properties are better, as the grain structure follows the shape of the forging, Fig. 133, and is not interrupted by changes of section.

Forgework practice   Always try to complete a job in as few heats as possible, because if metal is kept at forging temperatures for an excessive time *grain growth* will occur and the quality of the steel deteriorates.

The anvil should be as close to the hearth as convenient so that no time or heat is lost. The bick, Fig. 134, should be on the left of the smith. If very long work is being handled it may be necessary to move the anvil further away to accommodate this length. All tools required for a particular job should be ready and immediately to hand. The stance of the smith is important if he is to get the most out of his effort; the right foot should be up to or underneath the hanging end of the anvil and the right shoulder over the job. Nothing looks more amateurish than to see someone working at an anvil with the work and the hammer at arms length.

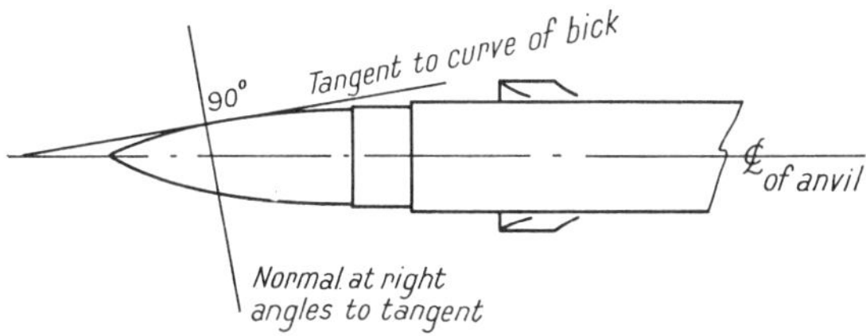

Fig. 134.

Lightweight tongs of about 900 g should be used in school work, and they should be of the box type to avoid the danger of metal flying out when turned edgeways on. (Standard tongs are about 1350 g to 1800 g and heavy tongs weigh between 2 and 3 kg.) Tongs must fit the metal to be forged and the smith's first operation is to do this by heating the mouth of the tongs, gripping the metal and then tapping the jaws to fit on the anvil. The tongs are then quenched. It must be appreciated that only slight adjustments should be made in this way, and indeed only small adjustments are necessary provided the correct tongs have been selected. Tongs should be quenched periodically for comfortable handling and to prevent their getting too hot and losing their shape. The use of rings on the reins of tongs relieves the need to grip them and makes it easier to lift and manipulate the work.

A good leather apron should be worn for forgework, both for keeping clothes clean and for safety. Always wear it the same side out, or in a short time it will not be fit to wear at all.

In addition to providing suitable tongs, hammers should be provided whose weight takes into account the strength of the boys who are to use them. For schoolwork a hammer of 450 g or 675 g is usually heavy enough, older students may use a 900 g hammer and, occasionally, a 2 kg sledge hammer. When working in pairs on heavier work, and with a 3 kg sledge, special care is needed for safe working. Beware of mushrooming on the heads of sets, swages and fullers, etc. If a mushroomed tool is hit a glancing blow with a 3 kg sledge the broken splinter of steel could fly a long way and penetrate deeply into flesh.

It is sometimes difficult to decide how much metal will be required for a job, especially where there is any considerable change of section. Make a quick calculation of the volume of the finished job and then by taking the same volume of stock the problem will be solved. The length of material required for curved work can be quickly arrived at by laying a length of soft iron wire along the curve on the drawing.

To keep curves in one plane is often a problem too. If the simple precaution is taken to hold the metal normal to the curve of the beak of the anvil there is no problem at all. Do not hold the metal at right-angles to the centre line of the anvil or a twist will be inevitable. Also, if a constant regular curve is required then the bar to be bent must have an even heat, otherwise the bar will bend most where it is hottest. If a bar is not required to be bent in a particular place, but it is impossible to avoid getting it hot in the forge fire, then quench quickly by immersing in the bosh or by pouring water on from a ladle. Immediately before another heat is taken tap the metal into the required plane. If this is not done the metal will get further and further away from the shape required and more and more difficult to correct. If a number of similar bends are required then the heat must in each case be the same; hotter metal gives a quick bend, cooler metal a slow bend. For a job of this kind the smith must make a mental picture of the colour of the heat and be able to repeat it. If a sharp bend is required in a particular place it may be necessary to mark it with a centre punch; also, chalk marks put on when the metal is cold are still visible when the metal is hot.

Generally speaking, too much energy is put into forgework, resulting in damage and bruising of the metal. A lot of work can be done by pulling and pushing rather than by hitting. If a number of curved bends of the same size are required, set a couple of short round bars upright in a vice, the distance between them being as the size of the metal to be bent. If suitable horns to fit the hardie hole in the anvil are available, these will do just as well. Heat the metal, drop in between the rods and pull to the shape required. If the bend must be in a particular place, put marks on the rod in the vice and follow the procedure shown in Fig. 135. For right-angle and curved bends in thin rod, heat, place the rod over the anvil, and using the head of the hammer push the rod over; a minimum of hammer taps will complete the shape. Avoid hammering at the bend or trapping metal between hammer and anvil. If the metal is struck as shown in Fig. 136 results

114

will be much more effective. To get the metal back in the fire in the right position, it helps to mark with metalworkers' chalk as shown in Fig. 137, and when replacing the metal the chalk mark must line up with the edge of the hearth.

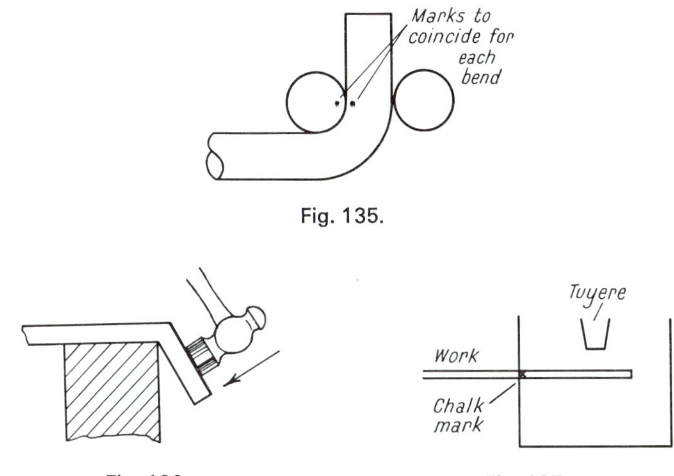

Fig. 135.

Fig. 136.

Fig. 137.

Basic forgework operations

Drawing down   A typical example is making a point on the end of a bar; as the section is reduced the length will be increased. This operation is done at a near welding heat and the metal is held at a suitable angle to the face of the anvil. This angle depends upon the sharpness of the point required. Position the metal on the far side of the anvil as shown in Fig. 138. If the end of the metal is in the

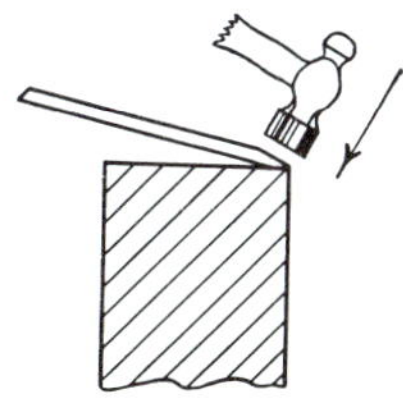

Fig. 138.

centre of the anvil the hammer will slide off and hit the anvil, damaging its surface. If it is a heavy piece of metal that has to be drawn down, then preliminary hammering is better done over the bick of the anvil, as this has a fullering action. The work will need to be finished off on the face of the anvil. For very heavy work a fuller and the bick of the anvil will produce quicker results. If a round point is required, first draw down square, then to octagonal, and then to round; if drawing down to round is attempted straight away the metal will hollow on the end or *Pipe*.

Spreading   This is much the same as drawing down except that more hammering is done on two opposite faces and the metal is allowed to spread. The spread can be controlled by hammering the other two faces or edges.

Upsetting or jumping-up   In this operation the cross-section of a bar is increased in size and the length shortened. This is not an easy operation and it is perhaps better, where possible, to start with large section bar and draw down. The metal must be at a near welding heat at the point to be upset and, depending upon length, may be bounced on a block let into the floor or on the anvil or held on the anvil and hit with a hammer. Upsetting on the end of a bar is easier than at a point along its length. Wherever possible use as long a length as can be handled and bounce on the floor block to let the weight of the metal do the work. To heat at a point along the bar the arrangement shown in Fig. 137 is most useful. When jumping up, the bar is liable to bend, and must be straightened out before proceeding to the next heat. If the shape is allowed to get out of hand it can be very difficult to get back. To confine the heat to the part required it may be necessary to quench by pouring on water from a ladle.

Bending   Small section black mild steel may be bent cold but much bruising may result. Take a bright red heat and bend as shown in Fig. 136 or over the bick if a radius is required. As mentioned previously, when bending over the bick the metal must be held normal to the curve and not at right-angles to the anvil.

Hot and cold cutting   This may be done over the hardie or by means of sets. Do not confuse hot and cold sets, because if the cold set is used on hot metal its temper will be drawn.

Cold cutting   Thin section bar is cut over the hardie. Do not cut through, but nick opposite sides and then snap off by hammering on the far side of the anvil. If nicked too deep over the hardie its edge may be damaged by contact with the hammer. The cutting of heavier section is a two-handed job involving the use of a cold set and a sledge hammer.

Hot cutting   For this, take a bright red heat and repeat as for cold cutting, using the hot sets or hot chisels. If for any reason cutting is done right through a piece of metal, the operation must be done on the table and not on the face of the anvil.

Twisting   Twisting of metal bars is used as a decorative feature in iron work, and is quite simple to do if tackled correctly; it is also quite effective. A square bar twisted is more rigid than the same size bar left square; the effective distance across the diagonal is the same in all directions. The complete twist must be done at one heat, which must be uniform over the length to be twisted, otherwise an uneven twist will result. The hotter the metal the quicker will be the twist, and the cooler the metal the slower the twist. Care must be taken when making the twist to keep the metal straight, as subsequent straightening can be difficult. The inexperienced must use a double-handed wrench, since a single-handed one will most certainly result in a bent bar. If a number of identical twists are required, then a sleeve must be made from a suitable piece of tubing of a length equal to the length of the twist required. The tubing must be a slack fit on the bar or it may stick when the twist is completed. For identical twists the heat in every case must be the same and the wrench must be marked with a piece of chalk so that the operator will know when a complete twist has been made. Twists are not necessarily full turns, they may be $\frac{1}{4}$, $\frac{1}{2}$ or $\frac{3}{4}$ turns; they are not limited to square bars but may be in flat bars or bars forged to some particular section. Interesting results can be obtained by fullering or cutting grooves on the faces before twisting or by twisting a combination of bars welded at their ends.

Punching and drifting   As mentioned previously, forgings are stronger than shapes formed by other means because the grain structure follows the shape of the forging. The punching of holes is one way of ensuring this grain flow. To punch a hole, the metal must be at near welding heat and the punch is driven quickly through until stopped by the thin piece on the underside which, being chilled by the anvil, stops the punch. When turned over, the position of this thin cold piece is easily seen, as it appears darker than the surrounding metal. The punch is held against the dark patch and knocked through to complete the punching. Round holes are first punched with a thin oval punch; this ensures that the walls around the hole are kept at a maximum thickness. Oval and round punches may be used separately or round punches may be made oval at their ends. *Drifting* is the opening out of holes previously punched. The end of the punch must be kept cool by quenching quickly each time it is removed from the metal.

Fullering   Fullers are used in pairs, top and bottom, the bottom one fitting into the hardie hole of the anvil. They are graded in size and are measured by the diameter of the curve. They are used for making shoulders before drawing down or for assisting in the preliminary stages of drawing down. The action of fullering is to change the direction of the fibres of the metal without severing them.

Welding* Fire welding in a blacksmith's hearth is a difficult operation and requires much practice in order to recognize the correct welding heat for the particular metal being used. It is essential that the operator should know his fire and that it should be clean and free from clinker. The whole operation must be done quickly before the heat is lost or before oxide has a chance to form. A thin oxidizing fire is no use for welding as the oxidized faces will not weld. Neither must the fire be too quick or the metal will not be at welding heat all the way through. The simplest weld for a beginner is the *faggot weld* where the metal is bent over on itself to increase thickness; it is much easier than having to handle two separate pieces. When separate pieces are to be welded the surfaces to be joined should be downwards in the fire, and it is a wise precaution to mark the faces which are to be on top when the weld is made with a liberal chalk mark. It is most difficult to recognize which face is which when the metal is at welding heat. Wrought iron is much easier to weld than mild steel, the latter being made easier if fluxes are used. Two very good fluxes are Laffite Welding Plate and a powder marketed by The Amalgam Co. of Sheffield.

* For a full and detailed description of the welding process readers cannot do better than refer to the publications of the Council for Small Industries in Rural Areas. Their descriptions and illustrations for the making of scrolls, water leaves and all other forgework operations are excellent and worth studying in detail.

8 Heat-treatment

The facilities available for heat treatment will, in many metalwork rooms, be restricted to the forge fire and the open flame of a gas blow torch, and as in forgework will demand an estimation of temperature by observation. In this respect an early appreciation of comparative temperatures, and the workshop methods of judging them, is necessary. Fig. 139 lists some of the more common heat treatment processes alongside the approximate temperature at which they take place and shows the visual changes in steel by which the temperatures may be judged. The heat treatment hearth, furnace or forge is positioned in a darker area of the room where changes in colour are more readily seen and whenever possible the processes are carried out in daylight rather than under an artificial light which has an effect on the colour observed.

Annealing   Possibly the first occasion when the need to change the state of a piece of metal arises is when it has become hard after working. Most metals work-harden under the compression strains of hammering, rolling, drawing and repeated bending and may be brought to a softer and more manageable state by annealing. Copper and its alloys may be annealed by bringing to a dull red heat and quenching in water, or allowing to cool in air. Aluminium also is annealed by a similar process, though it is heated to a much lower temperature, for it melts before reaching a visible heat.

Structure of steel   It is however with steel that most of the heat treatment processes will be carried out. The various grades of steel can, by the appropriate treatment, be made to cover the whole range of metallic properties from the very soft and ductile to the very hard and brittle. The degree to which these properties can be obtained in any one piece of steel will depend on the amount of carbon present. As we saw in Chapter 1, the carbon present in steel is in chemical combination with some of the ferrite and is in the form of cementite. When the carbon content of a normalized steel is just below 0.9%, the cementite and ferrite together form a substance known as *pearlite*. At percentages below this figure the steel consists of pearlite and ferrite, while if the carbon content is above 0.9% it will consist of pearlite and cementite in varying proportions. These substances are only detected under great magnification and the different grades of steel look very much alike.

When steel is heated the form of these carbon combinations is altered. The change begins at a temperature called the *lower critical point* and is completed at a temperature known as the *upper critical point*. The difference between the

Heat treatment processes and melting points of metals

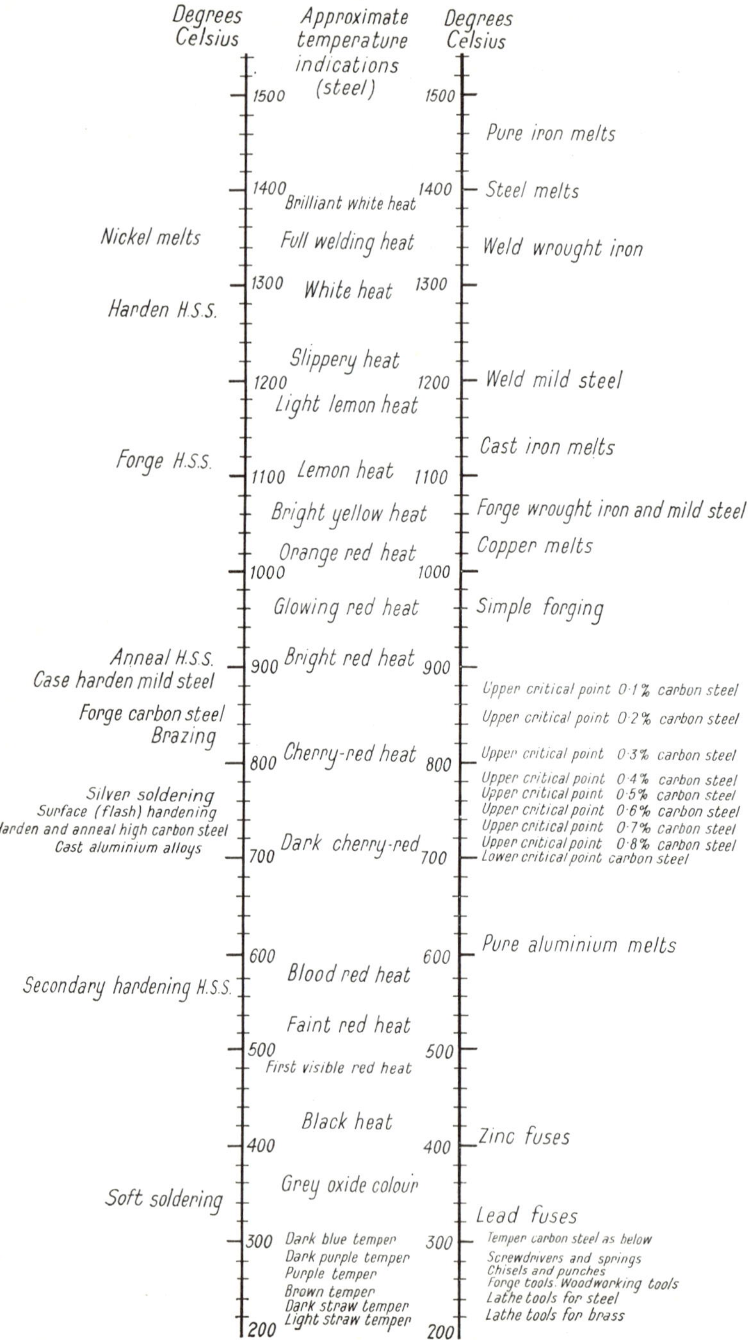

Fig. 139.

two temperatures constitutes the *critical range* of the steel. At temperatures above that of the upper critical point, the carbon combination is of a form called *austenite*, Fig. 140, the transformation taking place during the passage through the critical range. The lower critical point is approximately the same (about 700°C) for all types of steel. A steel with a carbon content of just below 0·9%, i.e., containing 100% pearlite, has no critical range, its upper and lower critical points being at the same temperature. As indicated in Fig. 141, the range increases as the carbon content decreases from this figure, and as the upper critical

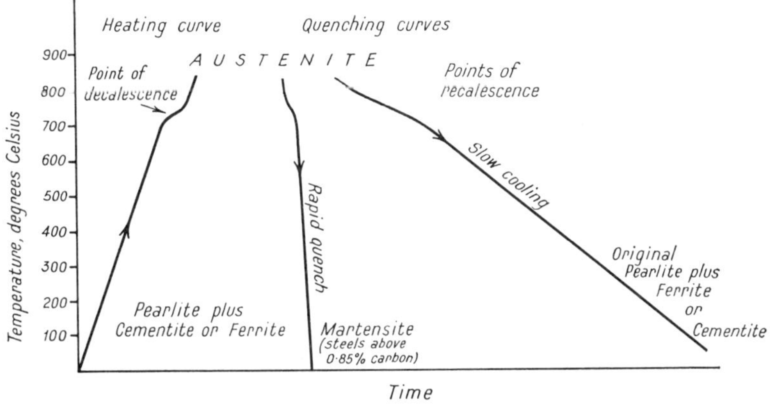

Fig. 140. Arrest points on heating and quenching curves.

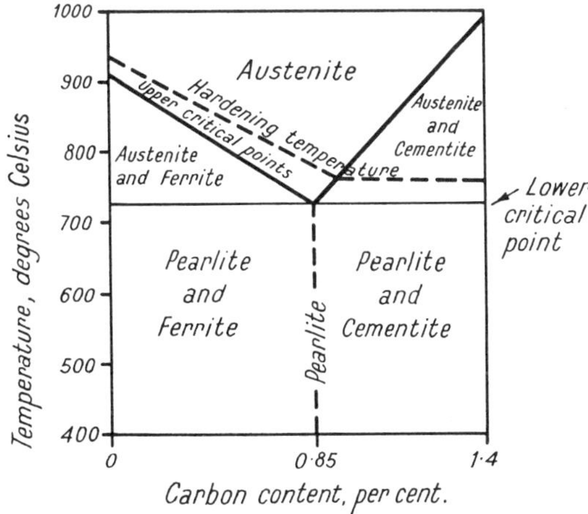

Fig. 141. Carbon steel hardening temperature and critical range.

point of the very low carbon steels approaches 900°C. The critical range also increases as the carbon content rises above 0·9%, but, as these steels rapidly deteriorate when heated to the higher temperatures, the lower critical point only is considered for heat treatment purposes.

The changes taking place in a steel as the temperature is increased are accompanied by an arrest in the rate of temperature rise at a point called the *point of decalescence*. A similar check in the rate of cooling occurs at the point of recalescence, Fig. 140. Furthermore, as the temperature of a piece of steel rises, internal stresses are relieved, the grain becomes smaller and its structure is refined. The maximum grain refinement takes place within the critical range. If the temperature is further increased, grain growth occurs and the structure coarsens once more. The method of annealing steel therefore is to raise its temperature until all the changes are complete, i.e. to the upper critical point; austenite is then formed and the grain is small. It is then allowed to cool slowly in order that the austenite may be converted to its stable form of refined pearlite plus ferrite or cementite. In practice the work is raised to a dull red heat, maintained at that temperature for a short time to ensure an even distribution of heat, and then allowed to cool in the embers of a dying fire or in the shut down furnace. Care must be taken not to overheat the steel as this creates a coarse grained material. In the later stages of the cooling, the work may be buried in sand or a material that will retain the heat, if it is inconvenient to leave it in the furnace or fire.

Such treatment is required by steels that have become work-hardened by manipulation in the cold state or have been hardened by previous heat treatment, before they can be machined or cut with hand tools. It is also necessary to anneal work after it has been forged, to relieve the uneven stresses set up by the prolonged heating and hammer blows of varying force on different parts of the work. Steels also attain a certain degree of work-hardness and lack of uniformity of structure, through processes concerned with their manufacture. Therefore, before dispatch, they undergo a form of heat treatment similar to that of annealing, and most steel will be delivered to the metalwork room in a state in which it can be easily worked. When the steel is softened and the grain structure refined the process is called *normalizing* and gives steel its 'normal tensile strength' and not maximum softness as does annealing. The heating of the steel is as for annealing, but once the required temperature is reached the work is removed from its source of heat and is allowed to cool in still air. It is generally the lower carbon steels that are normalized, the medium and high carbon steels should be fully annealed. The occasional hard spots found in some black steel bar may be removed by normalizing the steel in the workshop.

Hardening   If steel is suddenly quenched from a temperature above its point of decalescence, the austenite, instead of being transformed back to the original composition of the steel, undergoes a transformation to a hard and brittle sub-

122

stance, known as *martensite*, as it passes rapidly through the critical range to the point of recalescence. The resulting steel will then have these qualities depending on the amount of carbon present. This is the process of hardening. To attain maximum hardness, together with the smallest grain size, the steel must be heated uniformly to just above the upper critical point for steels with less than 9% carbon, and to just over 700°C for those with more than this figure, and suddenly quenched. All the austenite is then transformed to martensite. If the quenching is less fierce, or is delayed to a point at the lower end of the critical range, the complete transformation to martensite does not take place. Less hard combinations of carbon and ferrite are formed, called primary *trootsite* and primary *sorbite*. These substances, being present to a varying degree with martensite and pearlite, give a tough quality to the steel.

The degree of hardness attained will depend on the amount of carbon present in the steel as well as on the form in which it is trapped on quenching. The full hardening effects are only noticed in steels with a carbon content of above about 0·8%, and such steels are known as high carbon or plain carbon tool steels. Below 0·4% carbon content no noticeable change takes place on heating and quenching. These are the mild steels and they cannot be hardened in this way. Between the two are the medium carbon steels which will attain a degree of toughness rather than hardness.

The effects of heating high carbon steel to varying temperatures and then quenching are best demonstrated in the workshop by preparing a short bar of the metal with small filed grooves or saw cuts about 10 mm apart. The bar is then heated on the forge fire, or with a brazing torch, until one end of the bar becomes white hot and begins to disintegrate, while the other end is allowed to reach only a black heat. The bar is then suddenly quenched in cold water, taken to the vice and pieces broken from the bar from the overheated end. The first fracture will show the deleterious effects of overheating, for layers of oxide will have penetrated the metal, making it obviously quite useless. The adjacent portions can be seen to be weak because of their enlarged grain structure. Next, the cleanly broken, brittle, yet correctly hardened steel with a fine grain will be observed. The following sections will afford greater resistance to the hammer blows while at the insufficiently heated end the steel will bend, indicating that no change has taken place.

The comparative degree of hardness attained at the various stages can then be roughly ascertained by attempting to mark the surface with the corner of an old file, the resistance to the file lessening from the steel heated to above its critical range to that where the lower critical point was not reached.

The hardness of steel is normally tested by measuring the amount of penetration of a small hardened steel ball, pyramid, or a diamond under a given load. The amount of penetration determines its relative hardness denoted by a number on a fixed scale. Such methods are beyond the scope of the average metalwork room.

Heating work   The manner in which work is heated also has a marked effect on its resulting qualities. When heated on the forge the metal must be laid in the top of the fire and away from the air blast. As the temperature varies in different parts of the fire the work must be turned frequently and withdrawn when judging its temperature. If a blow torch is used, the air blast must not impinge upon the steel or excessive oxide and eventual burning will result. A neutral or reducing flame is employed. It is also important to prepare the hearth to suit the job before heating commences. Firebricks should be arranged to reflect the heat on to the work, which should be raised from the base brick and supported on asbestos cubes. If work is laid flat on a firebrick, the brick also must be

[*Kasenit Ltd.*

Fig. 142. Bench type muffle furnace.

brought to the temperature of the work, before an even heat is reached. The time taken in doing this will cause excessive oxide formation on the surface of the metal. The work must also be supported in a way that will cause it to suffer no distortion when heated. Thin work is placed on a sheet of metal and heated from below. Some work is best heated in a steel tube. Do not direct heat at the sharp cutting edges of tools; heat the larger masses first and allow the more delicate parts to be heated by conduction. When removing work from the source of heat use heated tongs, as cold tongs will take the heat from the area in contact with them. Work can be protected from scale formation by applying to the surface a solution of boracic acid, silica paint or a patent non-scaling powder, but in most cases if the work is brought rapidly to heat oxide will be kept to a minimum.

The prolonged heating of steel in an open atmosphere also causes some decarburization of the surface. Liquid bath furnaces, by preventing contact with air altogether, eliminate the loss of carbon and scale and oxides are not formed. Salt bath furnaces are used in a medium temperature range to about 900°C and, as an even distribution of heat is ensured, they are used for parts having uneven masses, and particularly for wire rod. Other furnaces used for heat treatment may be fired by gas, oil or electricity and be of the natural or forced draught types. A simple *muffle furnace*, Fig. 142, gives an even distribution of heat and, as the flames do not come in contact with the work, a minimum of oxide is formed. A controlled reducing atmosphere inside the furnace, aided by a gas screen which forms across the doorway, prevents the infiltration of cold air and protects the work. Operating at temperatures between 650°C and 1000°C, natural draught furnaces enable the whole range of heat treatment processes to be carried out on the plain carbon steels.

Although, to obtain a uniform structure throughout, all parts should be brought to the same temperature, some small tools will require different sections at various grades of hardness and toughness. Punches and chisels, for example, require a hard cutting tip, a body that is tough and resilient, and a head that is best left soft. In the heat treatment of such work only the tip is heated to hardening temperature, the other portions being raised to a temperature which will give the desired properties to the steel when quenched.

Quenching Quenching suddenly in cold water will cause steels to attain maximum hardness, though a more fierce quenching medium is obtained by using brine of 10% sodium chloride solution. Caustic soda in similar proportions has the same effect and is less corrosive. As however the surface of the steel will cool first and the centre at a slower rate, there is danger of warping and cracking caused by the contraction of the core and outer layers at different stages. Also, as the recalescent point is reached on cooling an expansion takes place in the metal, and if this occurs to the central portion of a piece of metal when the surface has cooled and set, great internal stresses are set up within the metal. These effects can be eliminated to some extent by the method of introducing work to the quenching media. Long tools are dipped in a vertical position, the cutting edge first. Thin strips are introduced on their edge rather than on a side. The thicker parts of work of uneven section are also made to enter the cooling liquid before the less heavy sections. When work is plunged into cold water a steam blanket forms around it preventing complete contact with the liquid. To ensure rapid cooling, therefore, the work is moved about in the quenching media, usually in a circular or figure eight motion and not too violently or a surface may lose contact with the media in its wake.

The employment of a quenching media other than water or brine can assist in giving the type of cooling required and help to prevent distortion and cracking of the work. Where the surface finish is important and where maximum hardness is not required, work may be quenched in oil. A number of quenching oils are available and may be of the mineral, fatty or vegetable types.

Such oils should have a high flash point and *whale oil* is suitable in this respect. When quenching in oil, the whole of the heated portion of the work must be immersed, for there is danger of firing the oil. Quenching in such media gives little danger of cracking or distortion but they are not fierce enough for metal cutting tools of plain carbon steel. A method suitable for workshop use is to quench first in water to bring the temperature rapidly to below the point of recalescence (this is indicated by the cessation of hissing) and then transferring to oil for the final quench.

Tempering Work so heated and quenched is hard and will withstand abrasion when cutting metal, but it is brittle and will break under load. By reducing the hardness slightly, a more elastic material is produced, yet one that will still maintain a cutting edge. The process by which this is achieved is called tempering. It is accomplished by heating the work to a much lower temperature than that employed in hardening, and again quenching. Such reheating causes the breakdown of the martensite, in which the carbide is in a plate-like form, to that of the granular form of trootsite and sorbite. The final constituents of a tempered steel are very similar to those that have undergone a delayed quenching from the lower end of the critical range. The structure is therefore termed secondary trootsite or secondary sorbite. Tempering is used, as the required structure and properties are more easily obtained by this means. The heat to which work is raised is between 230°C and 300°C and will depend upon the use to which the tool will be put. A turning tool, for example, which will be subjected to a steady uniform pressure, can be left harder than a chisel which will receive intermittent blows and a screwdriver which will not be required to cut but to withstand torque stresses.

In the workshop, tempering temperatures are judged by the colour of the oxide that forms on the surface of steel during heating. If bright steel is gradually heated it will first assume a pale straw tint, changing to a darker brown and then, through shades of purple, to a dark and finally a light blue. As the temperature rises so the brittleness and hardness will be reduced, and the steel can be withdrawn from the source of heat and quenched at a predetermined stage. Quenching after tempering can quite safely be done in cold water. When judging temperatures in this way the work must be clean, for oil on the surface will affect the oxide colours. Heating must be uniform and thorough, for it is possible to heat the surface only, which will show the oxide colours, leaving the centre of the steel cold. Small tools, and those that have a single cutting edge, are heated away from the tip and the colours allowed to run along the bar. Not only is adequate heating ensured by this method, but colours spread over wider bands and a larger area is brought to the required state. The work is quenched the moment the desired colour reaches the tip. Work that requires an even temper throughout is best heated on a plate or in a tube. As the oxide colours are but a rough indication of surface temperature a further method is to immerse the work in heated sand. Tempering baths in which a liquid is heated are also used. Up to 250°C, an oil of high flash point is suitable, while above this temperature fusible salts may be employed. Alloys of tin and lead enable the range of temperatures to be accurately attained, by varying the percentages of the molten metals, in a fused metal bath.

A method of hardening and tempering small single point cutting tools in one operation is to heat the tool for 25 mm–50 mm at its cutting edge to the hardening temperature and then quench the tip only in water. On removal sufficient heat is retained in the body of the tool to temper the point. The tip is then cleaned with an abrasive stone and fully quenched when the desired colour reaches the tip. On the initial quench the work must be moved slightly up and down in the water to prevent cracking, which may occur at the water line if the steel is moved only in the horizontal plane.

It is often required to heat treat steel to give a tough quality rather than hardness; to give greater tensile strength rather than resistance to wear. Such treatment is termed *toughening* and is accomplished by quenching at a temperature below the critical range and in a less fierce quenching medium. Steel of a medium carbon content would be used, there being insuffixient cementite present to allow a fully hardened condition to be attained. The heat treatment of springs comes in this class, where the steel must be hard enough to enable it to return to its original shape, yet must be flexible. Springs are tempered to the full blue colour. It is important to heat uniformly and evenly throughout and is best done in a controlled furnace. If attempted in the workshop, springs should be heated on a plate or in a tube. A method of heat treating small springs is to harden and quench in the normal way and then to dip in oil. The spring is then indirectly heated until the oil ignites and again is quenched.

Case-hardening   Steels that do not contain sufficient carbon to enable them to be hardened by heating and quenching, i.e. the mild steels, may be given a hard skin or case by heating in contact with a substance rich in carbon. Such case-hardened steels are not suitable for cutting tools but are used where the surface only is subjected to wear and where a soft core, able to withstand sudden shocks, is desired. In the metalwork room such articles as spanners, the locating faces of tap wrenches and tool holders, etc., will be case-hardened, as will gauges, vee-blocks, parallel bars and test equipment generally, if facilities exist for grinding after heat treatment. Mild steels of between 0·15% and 0·2% carbon are the most suitable for this treatment. The process consists of first carburizing the surface of the work by packing it in cast iron boxes in a case-hardening compound and bringing to a red heat. Carburizing compounds may be of ferro-cyanide or products of wood charcoal, bone or leather. Proprietary brands of compound are available that are non-poisonous and free from fumes when heated. They are hence the more suitable for school use. The separate articles are given at least 25 mm of compound on all sides and are packed firmly so that they do not collapse and bend when heated The boxes have an airtight lid and are sealed with fireclay. At a temperature above the critical point steel becomes porous to CO_2 gas and absorbs carbon from the compound, which penetrates to a depth depending on the time the work is kept at heat in contact with it. A carburized case of about 0·8 mm is attained in approximately four hours at 850°C, and deeper cases take proportionately longer. It is usual to leave work, which will later be ground, about 0·3 mm to 0·4 mm oversize, and this must be taken into account when deciding upon the depth of case required.

On removal from the furnace and the box, the steel consists of an outer case of high carbon steel, with the carbon content gradually decreasing towards the central core. The core, however, will have developed a coarse grain structure due to its prolonged heating. The next stage in case-hardening is therefore to refine the core. This is done by heating to about 900°C and quenching in oil. The work is then again heated to about 760°C to refine the case, the grain of which became enlarged during the previous heating. Quenching from this temperature finally hardens the case. The soft core renders tempering unnecessary, although thin sections, which have possibly been hardened right through, should again be heated and quenched at 200°C. Portions of case-hardened work such as screw threads, which are required to be left soft, are copper plated or coated with a clay or stopping-off compound before treatment. Parts on which further machining is to be done are left oversize and the carburized layer ground away after treatment.

The surface of mild steel is also carburized in a liquid bath furnace containing a compound of cyanide. Being of a poisonous and dangerous nature, it is not a method suitable for schools although it is widely used in industry. If attempted, certain precautions should be taken. The work must be perfectly dry before entering the bath and should be preheated on the top of the furnace. Protective clothing must be worn against dangers of spitting when quenching, and the work well washed in clean hot water after treatment. The furnace must, of course, also be fitted with an extractor fan, to remove the poisonous fumes.

Small articles of mild steel may be given a thin hard case by surface or open-hearth carburizing. The work is brought to a dull red heat, dipped in the hardening compound, reheated and quenched. A case of a few hundredths of a millimetre deep may be obtained in this way, though repeated applications will produce a thicker skin. Some of the prepared compounds can be applied by mixing with water to a paste, and on occasions it may be found advantageous to pack the work in a steel box or tray made for the purpose. Hardening of the case is effected by scraping away the congealed compound, reheating and quenching. No core refinement is necessary, for grain growth does not occur at the lower temperatures at which these compounds are absorbed.

When work of this nature is being done, care must be taken to ensure that no compound falls on the hearth, or later work to be heated will acquire hard spots and may be spoilt. A special container or tray filled with broken firebricks or coke is used to prevent hearth contamination.

Alloy and tool steels   Most of the heat treatment operations performed in the workshop will be restricted to the plain carbon steels, but if lathe and shaping machine tools are made, the hardening of high-speed alloy tool steels may be necessary. The heat treatment of these differs from that of the plain carbon steels and, because of the great variety of this type of material, treatment should be given to the maker's specifications. Instructions should be obtained from the manufacturer when tool steels are ordered. Generally, alloy tool steels are hardened by heating to between 1100°C and 1300°C and quenching in oil or a blast of cold dry air. They are never quenched in water. As this class of tool steel maintains its hardness and cutting edge at a red heat, they are not tempered. It is found, however, that by bringing to a temperature within the range 400°C to 600°C and quenching, the hardness is increased. This process is called *secondary hardening*. Although it is possible to heat treat high-speed and alloy tool steels on the forge fire, the process demands some skill and is better accomplished in a special furnace. High-speed steel furnaces consist of two chambers. The upper chamber is for preheating the steel to about 850°C, for alloy tool steels must be brought slowly to a red heat the conductivity of the metal being poor. Work is then transferred to the lower chamber where it is brought rapidly to its hardening temperature. No soaking time is allowed. High-speed steel is annealed by heating to 850°C, maintaining at that temperature for a time, and then allowing to cool slowly in the furnace.

9 Foundry work

Foundry work is a branch of engineering in which metal is reduced to a fluid state by means of heat and is then poured into moulds to form castings. The cavities in the sand moulds are formed by means of *patterns*.

The metal to be used for castings usually arrives at the foundry in the form of *ingots* although some scrap metal is quite often used in addition. Ingots of cast iron are reduced to a molten state in a *cupola* and the non-ferrous metals and alloys in some form of crucible furnace.

The cupola As may be seen from Fig. 143, the cupola is a cylindrical metal structure lined with firebrick. On the underside are doors through which work-men may gain access for repairing the refractory lining when necessary. Project-ing from the side, at the bottom of the cupola, is the *tapping spout* and on the

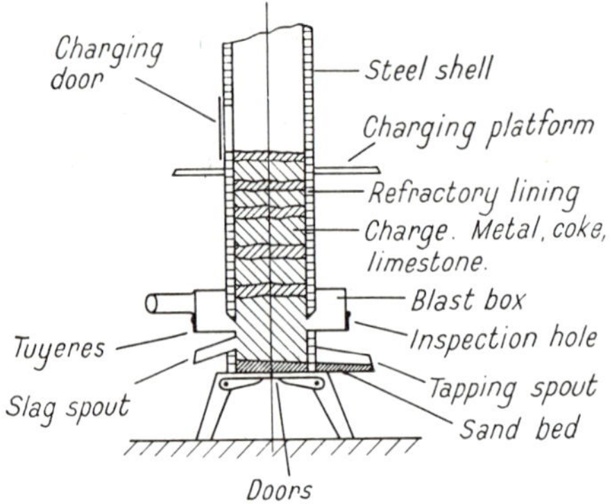

Fig. 143. Cupola.

opposite side, but a little higher, is the *slag spout*. Above the slag spout is an inspection hole and just above that, wrapping itself completely round the cupola, is the *blast box* which is connected to some form of blower. From the blast box to the inside of the cupola are a number of *tuyeres* through which the blast enters to assist in the combustion and reduce the metal to a molten state. It is now modern practice to introduce extra pure oxygen through special additional tuyeres placed below the blast box. The advantage of this is that combustion is much more rapid near the hearth and the depth of the zone of combustion is less than with the air alone. Practical advantages are, that hotter metal is

130

obtained, less coke is required, and a metal with a higher carbon content is obtained; this is because the higher temperature causes more carbon to go into solution from the coke. Around the cupola at a height of about 3·5 to 6 m, depending upon capacity, is a charging platform and at a convenient height above this is a charging door. When the doors at the bottom of the cupola have been closed the floor is made up with burnt sand; this floor slopes towards the tapping spout. On the top of the sand is placed wood and then coke to a level just above the top of the tuyeres. The wood is then lit and the natural draught due to the height of the cupola draws the fire and the coke ignites. When the coke is thoroughly ignited charges of metal, coke and limestone are put in, repeating in that order until the level of the charging door is reached. At this stage the blast is started and molten metal will begin to form and collect at the bottom on the sand bed. As mentioned previously, the metal charge consists of pig iron and cast iron scrap with the addition sometimes of steel scrap. Coke is used because it keeps a more open fire and does not solidify under the weight of the metal charge; limestone is used as a flux. When sufficient metal has been melted, as observed through the inspection hole, slag is run off by unplugging the slag spout and then the molten metal is run off at the tapping spout. From the tapping spout the metal is run into ladles and from the ladle is poured into the moulds. According to the size of the castings being produced the ladle may be carried by crane or handled manually. In its passage through the cupola the metal picks up carbon and sulphur from the coke but loses some silicon. The amount of sulphur will depend upon the quality of the coke. The addition of steel scrap reduces the carbon content, and these additions must be carefully calculated to produce the grade of iron required. A cupola is kept in operation for a period of about 12 hours after which it is closed down, cleaned out, and the refractory lining repaired where necessary. Depending upon the size of the foundry several cupolas are installed, used and repaired in rotation.

Crucible furnace   The non-ferrous metals and alloys are melted in some form of crucible furnace which may be fired by coke, gas, or oil. According to the amount of work being done these crucible furnaces will house batteries of crucibles which are made of *plumbago*. The charge is introduced to the crucible in the form of broken ingot, scrap castings, or runners and risers from previous castings. As the metal melts the crucible is lifted out and the metal may be poured into a ladle, or for small castings, carried direct to the mould.

A casting is produced by pouring molten metal into a mould, made of metal or sand, in which there is a cavity of the shape required. Metal moulds are used in increasing numbers for making small castings in large quantities. They are used mostly for the production of *die castings* in zinc and aluminium alloys.

In sand castings the cavity is obtained by means of a wooden or metal pattern of the desired shape. In simple castings the wooden pattern is exactly the same as the desired casting plus contraction and machining allowances.

Green sand moulding Green sand moulding is so called not because of the colour of the sand but because damp sand is used. The simplest sand mould is merely a depression formed in a level bed of sand into which molten metal is poured and allowed to cool. Most sand moulds are made in two parts, the damp moulding sand being rammed around the pattern; suitable moulding boxes or *flasks* are used for holding or handling the mould. Moulding boxes may be of wood, steel, or cast iron, the two parts, top and bottom, being called the *cope* and *drag*. These two parts are accurately located or registered by means of lugs or pins. Wooden flasks are made with different size pins so that the boxes cannot be assembled together the wrong way round. If the flask is in more than two parts the in-between parts are called *cheeks*. For dry sand moulding the flasks

[*Sterling Foundry Specialties Ltd.*

Fig. 144.

[*Sterling Foundry Specialties Ltd.*

Fig. 145.

must be of metal in order to withstand the heat applied when drying the mould. Heavy cast iron flasks for large moulds are fitted with *loops* or *trunnions* so that they may be lifted by means of cranes. Larger flasks from say 600 mm square and upwards have crossbars in the cope to assist in carrying and holding the sand. Smaller flasks used in schools may also have them as well as narrow strips of wood or grooves on the inner sides of the flasks.

Moulding sand The quality and condition of the sand is an important factor for successful foundry work.

Moulding sand must possess three properties:

1. *Refractoriness* to withstand heat.
2. *Permeability* to allow escape of gases.
3. *Sufficient bond* to hold the shape of the mould.

Refractoriness is increased if the sand has a high silica content. Silica fuses at a high temperature, well above that of the molten metal. Other less desirable substances to be found in sand are lime, limestone, magnesium, iron oxide, soda and potash. These substances reduce the melting point of the clay and silica when mixed with them. Lime is the least desirable as it has the greatest effect in reducing the melting point. The less there are of these substances the less the sand will fuse and stick to the castings.

The bonding property or cohesiveness is imparted to moulding sand by the presence of clay; between 3% and 6% is a desirable quantity. This may be present in the sand as dug—it is then called a natural moulding sand—or it may be produced synthetically by adding sufficient colloidal clay to washed sand, according to the cohesiveness required. Water content also has a marked influence on cohesiveness; more water helps to bind the sand together but reduces permeability. Moist sand will give sharper, cleaner and better defined moulds; if the sand is too dry, definition will be lost, corners will break away under the flow of metal, or the mould may collapse completely. If this happens after the mould is finally put together the casting will be completely spoiled. Theoretically the moisture content should be about 8%, but the moulder needs a more practical guide. To test for moisture content, take a handful of sand and squeeze and break carefully; the edges of the break should remain firm and not crumble. Another test is to add moisture until the sand holds together when squeezed in the hand; it should break up if thrown back on to the moulding bench. Over-dampness is most dangerous, as molten metal poured into a damp mould is liable to spurt back up the runner; moreover the pourer should always stand well clear of the runner. If a number of boxes are being poured, retreat from the completed ones rather than approach them to get at the rest. Too much moisture also makes an excess of steam in the mould, blow holes will be formed, and gases will be trapped because of the impermeable condition of the sand, giving hollows or a porous texture to the surface of the casting. With repeated use the sand will become dry and have to be moistened. This is done by sprinkling on water and thoroughly mixing with a spade. Small quantities of sand kept in a bin should have a damp sack placed over them after each period of use to keep them in condition.

Use of sand   To start the process, turn over the drag on to the moulding board, place the pattern inside, sprinkle with parting powder and cover with a layer of riddled facing sand. Add moulding sand and ram until the drag is filled, and finally strickle off flat. Turn over the drag, fit the cope, add the other half of the pattern if it is a split one, and dust again with parting powder. Position sprue pins for runner and riser, cover with facing sand, ram and strickle flat. Remove the sprue pins, separate the boxes and cut suitable gates and vents.

Parting powder or dust or sand (it may be known by any of these three names) is very fine sand or dust or burnt clay or French chalk. Proprietary brands of powder may be obtained but the essential characteristic is that they must contain no bond. Their function is to prevent the surfaces of the high bond moulding sands from sticking together or from sticking to the pattern. Moulding sands should not stick to the surfaces of the pattern if they have been adequately filled, and the pattern polished and varnished. The quality of the finish on the pattern is reflected in the finish obtained on the casting. Parting powders are dusted over the surfaces of the sand from a cotton bag.

Facing sand   Another factor towards improving the quality of finish on castings is the quality of the sand in contact with the pattern. If a good finish is required, facing sand must be used and the immediate layers of moulding sand must be riddled on to the pattern. The fineness of the riddle depends upon the quality of work required, and the thickness of the layer of riddled sand depends upon the size and weight of the job. The facing sand forms a thin coating which is slow to melt and therefore does not stick to the casting. Also, a film of gas is formed between the sand and the metal, again preventing the metal from burning into the sand. Facing sand also separates more easily when cold. The usual method of applying the facing sand is to sprinkle or brush it on to the mould when the pattern has been withdrawn. Graphite is also used for iron castings for finishing, and—for aluminium—proprietary brands of mould coats may be sprayed on to the moulds.

Ramming   Rammers, Fig. 146, are used for evenly and quickly packing the sand into the flasks. They usually have a peen and a butt end; the *peen end* is wedge-shaped and the *butt end* has a flat face and is round in section. The

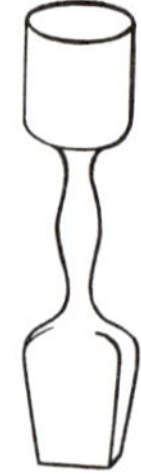

Fig. 146. Rammer.

majority of the ramming must be done with the peen end, the butt end being used only to flatten off the surface before strickling. If the butt end is used inside the flask, the surface of the sand is made too flat and the next layer will not key to it, and is liable to fall out when the box is lifted. The ability to ram correctly comes with practice; ramming too hard reduces the permeability, air and gases are trapped and blow holes result. On the other hand, ramming too soft gives a weak mould and the flow of metal is liable to break it down, giving sand inclusions and sand holes. The drag needs to be stronger, having more weight to carry, and must therefore be rammed harder than the cope. As the jointing surfaces are subject to more wear and tear they also need to be rammed more firmly. The feel of a properly rammed mould comes only with experience.

Gating   This operation is the forming of openings or channels by which the molten metal enters the mould cavity. The placing of sprue pins for runners and risers is important and a matter of experience and depends upon the shape of

134

the casting. The aim should be to position the gates where the natural flow of the metal will fill the mould quickly, and at a uniform temperature, so that all the casting can cool off at the same rate. Unequal rates of cooling will result in cracks. The size of the sprue pin also needs consideration; the whole gate should never be heavier than the part of the casting to which it is attached. One function of the gate is to feed the shrinking casting. If the gate is too large and heavy it acts in reverse and, in shrinking, draws from the casting. If other considerations allow, select a point on the casting where the gate can be broken off and cleaned up with least trouble. Care must be taken if gates are broken off, and not cut off, to get the break in the gate and not in the casting.

Runners and risers   These are formed by placing a tapered cylindrical piece of wood or sprue pin in the cope and ramming sand around them. Pouring basins should be cut in the sand before sprue pins are removed. When pouring, the object is to keep the pouring basin full of metal so that impurities float on top and do not enter the mould. The gate at the bottom of the runner should be cut deeper than the channel to the casting, in order to receive the force of the first fall of metal and prevent turbulence in the casting. Gates must be kept absolutely free from loose sand, otherwise it will wash into the mould.

Risers have a similar function to runners but in addition they indicate to the pourer when the mould is full and also act as a vent. Both runners and risers may be topped up with molten metal in order to assist the feeding of the casting. The shape of the top of the runner and riser is a good indication of what is happening inside the mould, especially when casting aluminium where a lot of shrinkage takes place. Risers should be placed on the highest part of the casting in the mould.

Venting   The object of venting is to release gases from the mould which are formed when the metal is poured. There is first of all the air filling the mould cavity before pouring and the steam formed by the hot metal as it makes contact with the damp sand. There are also gases formed by the burning of facing sand, mould coats, core binders, etc. It is most important that these gases be removed as quickly and completely as possible through vent holes and risers, otherwise they are forced back into the mould making it bubble or blow. Also they may blow metal out through the runners and risers or form blow holes within the metal, usually near the surface. Unfortunately such blow holes are not discovered until the metal is machined and may lead to the casting being scrapped; if they are not found by machining they may cause serious structural weakness. The natural porosity of the sand is not sufficient to get rid of the gases and in any case this depends upon the tightness of the ramming. Ventilation is assisted by making *vent holes*, by driving a thin pointed rod into the sand from the outside whilst the pattern is still in place. Penetration by the wire is stopped, say, about half an inch short of the pattern and the amount of the venting depends upon the size and weight of the casting. The heavier the casting and the longer the cooling time the more numerous must be the vents. Small moulds may be vented by making fine scratches, from the points where gas is likely to be trapped, towards the outside of the flasks. It is a simple matter to work out the flow of metal and decide where gas is going to get trapped and where venting is necessary.

Cores   Cores are used to form holes, cavities or pockets in castings which would be difficult or impossible to make in green moulding sand. They are held in position by the two halves of the mould itself or by means of *chaplets*. Cores are made from core sand mixed with a suitable binder and pressed or rammed into appropriately shaped core boxes. They are then baked in an oven until hard and dry and are then strong and easily handled. Cores with oil binders are dried in a temperature of about 200°C. Core sands are almost pure silica obtained from ocean or lake beaches; the bond, usually linseed oil provides the binder. Cores must be refractory to withstand the heat of the metal, and the sand must hold together when damp and be sufficiently strong to hold its shape until dried. Cores must also be sufficiently permeable to allow gases to pass through them. Obviously gases escape in all directions, some through the core, and to facilitate this large cores are made with holes through the centre. When moulding such cores, provision must be made for vents to be taken from the ends of these holes When cores are symmetrical, they may be made in halves, the two parts being held together by their prints in the mould. If this procedure is adopted only half a core box need be made.

The nature of core binders must be such that they are not driven off by the heat of the metal before the casting solidifies. The bond should be such that it is destroyed gradually with the cooling casting, and eventually completely destroyed, so as to facilitate removal after the casting has been knocked out of the sand. A number of natural and synthetic core binders are used in industry, their aim being to speed up the hardening process. For schools, raw linseed oil is recommended, the baking being done over a gas flame or in a simple oven of mild steel plate placed over the lower portion of a simple soldering stove. The simplest form of core is the plain cylinder and this may be bought in convenient diameters ready-made at almost any foundry. The more complicated cores must be made in suitably hollowed wooden boxes and can involve a lot of work. They may also be made in plaster of Paris in a wooden box, especially if the shape is such that it may readily be strickled. It may occasionally be more convenient to make the core in pieces and join together rather than make intricately shaped boxes. The deciding factor may be the number of castings required. Bear in mind that round core may be bought and, within limits, quite readily sawn and filed to shape.

Plate moulding   This is a method used when large quantities of small simple castings are required. It is almost always used in conjunction with moulding machines. The patterns are usually of metal and are in two halves on opposite sides of a central board, Fig. 147. It is important that this central board must register accurately with the cope and the drag, so that when removed the moulds in the two flasks are exactly opposite. One side of the pattern is moulded in the drag, turned over, and the cope side moulded. The boxes are then separated, the board with its patterns removed, and when the flasks are assembled the mould is completed. The runners are usually on the top side of the plate only.

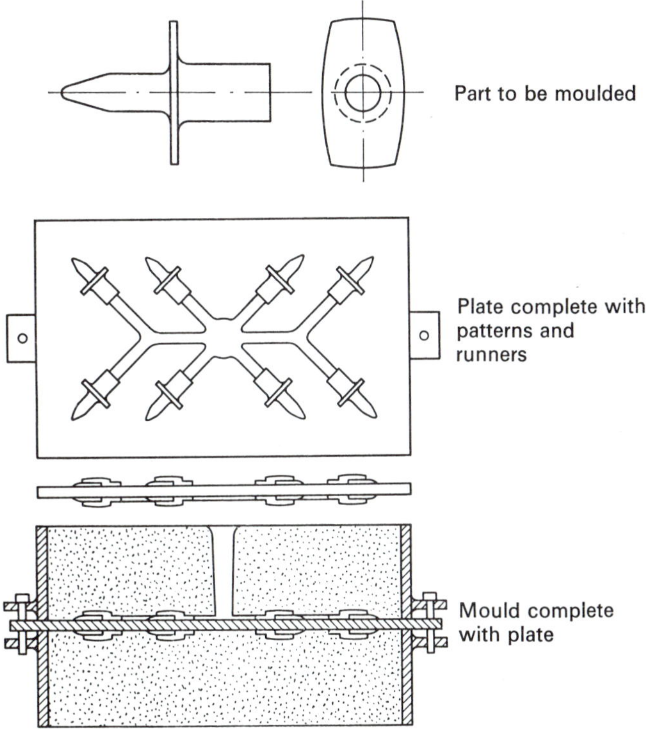

Fig. 147. Plate moulding.

Die casting This process is again for large quantity production. Factors to be considered when deciding its use are: the time required to make sand moulds compared with the cost of metal dies; the expected life of such dies; and whether or not cores are involved. The life of cores is usually much shorter than that of dies.

There are two main types of die casting, *gravity* and *pressure*.

In the gravity method, the molten metal is poured into dies, which may be of cast iron or steel. In principle and appearance they are much the same as sand moulds, but for convenience the joint is usually vertical and not horizontal. Runners, risers and vents must be arranged in much the same way as for sand moulding, but the dies must be preheated to receive the metal. Depending upon the speed of the complete operation, the heat from the previous casting should be sufficient to preheat for the next. Metal moulds need to be treated with a refractory wash to prevent contamination by iron pick-up.

Pressure die casting is very similar to the gravity process, the difference being that the metal is forced or pressed into the dies. The pressure may be supplied by compressed air or hydraulically. In a fully automatic die casting machine, the metal is injected, the die opens after a suitable pause for solidification, the casting is ejected and the die closes again ready for the next charge. Pressure die castings are better in several respects than those produced by the gravity method. They are usually more accurate so that subsequent machining time is reduced or in many cases dispensed with altogether. Thinner, less heavy and consequently cheaper castings are produced, finish is better and mechanical properties are superior.

Temperature control   The importance of accurate temperature control in melting aluminium is most important. Most faults in defective castings can be traced to too high a melting temperature. The instrument used to measure the temperature of the molten metal is called a *pyrometer*, and the type most commonly used is one incorporating a thermo-electric device. It consists of a thermocouple, that is, two wires of different compositions welded together at one end. It is

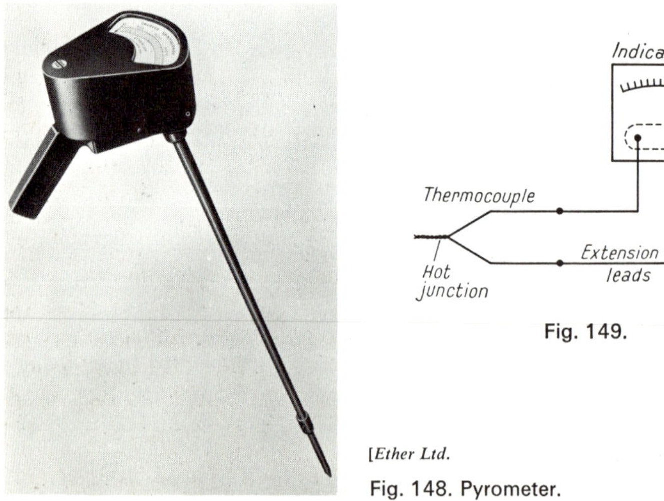

Fig. 149.

[*Ether Ltd.*

Fig. 148. Pyrometer.

connected at the other end by suitable leads to the measuring instrument—a galvanometer calibrated in degrees of temperature. When the welded ends of the thermocouple are plunged into the molten metal, an electromotive force is set up causing deflection of the galvanometer needle. The amount of deflection depends upon the difference in temperature between the welded ends in the molten metal and the other ends connected to the galvanometer. The most convenient pyrometers are portable and may be taken to any point in the foundry, but they are more liable to damage and should therefore be handled with care.

Patterns We saw at the beginning of the chapter that the cavities in the sand moulds are formed by means of patterns. Patterns are usually made of wood, and because of this have a limited life; if a long life is required for the pattern, it is better made from aluminium alloy, which when polished will give much cleaner castings. When making a wooden pattern for the purpose of moulding an aluminium alloy pattern, an allowance for the double shrinkage must be included. Metal patterns are very useful in school, as they are less liable to damage when ramming the mould than wooden patterns. It is most desirable, however, at some stage to design a job, make your own patterns and work the job through to completion.

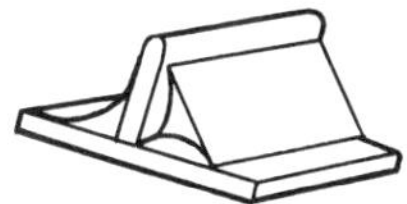

[*Buck & Hickman Ltd.*

Fig. 150. Leather fillet.

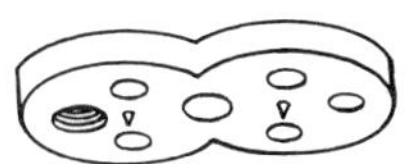

[*Buck & Hickman Ltd.*

Fig. 151. Rapping plate.

When making patterns there are certain fundamentals to be observed. The first is that they must have *draft* or taper to facilitate the removal from the mould. If too much taper is given it may make the casting difficult to hold for subsequent machining operations. According to the type of metal, allowance for contraction must also be made, and this is most easily taken care of by using a contraction rule. This rule is, of course, longer than the standard one. Within the limits imposed by the job, aim at an even thickness of metal and avoid sudden changes of section. There must be no sharp corners, and all curves and fillets should be generous. Leather fillet may be purchased to fit into corners, but plastic wood and plasters also give satisfactory results. If there are any large bosses for holes these must be cored or the unequal rates of shrinkage will result in cracks or hollowing. Having covered the essential dimensions and requirements, aim to give the pattern a pleasing shape and appearance. Any time spent in finishing the pattern is time well spent; it is easier to finish the pattern well than to spend time later trying to get a finish on the casting. Fill the pattern well, and rub down before painting and between each coat of paint; the finished pattern will then slide easily from the mould. If the casting is later to be machined, consideration must be given to this at the pattern making stage; for example, how is the machining to be done and how is the casting to be held? It may be necessary in some cases to cast on extra lugs to facilitate the machining process.

When a pattern will be wanted for some time to come, its life will be lengthened by the addition of a *rapping plate*; the continuous spiking of patterns does a lot of damage. A rapping plate is a metal plate let in flush and screwed to the pattern. It has plain holes for inserting a rapping bar and a screwed hole for fixing the draw screw. The simplest form of pattern is called a *flat-back*; this is plain on

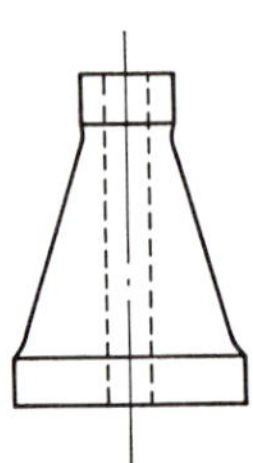

Fig. 152. Machine jack body.

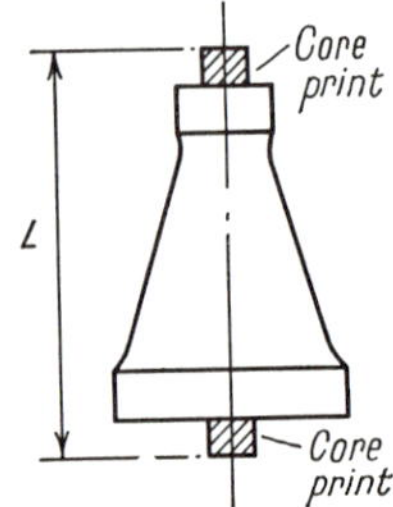

Fig. 153. Pattern for machine jack body with core prints.

one face and moulded in one flask only, and makes a suitable starting point for beginners. If the shape of a pattern is such that it needs to be moulded in both flasks, then wherever possible use *split patterns*; they are considerably easier to handle and the necessity for making an 'odd side' box is avoided. Split patterns must be carefully dowelled together so that both halves register perfectly.

When patterns are made for use by an outside foundry, certain colour standards have to be observed, and these are specified in British Standard 467. The colours indicate to the moulder what subsequent treatment the casting is to have; he can then arrange the pattern in the mould so that the better

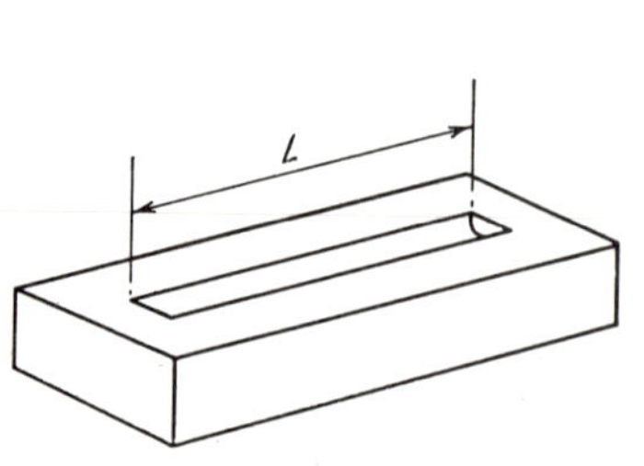

Fig. 154. Half core box.

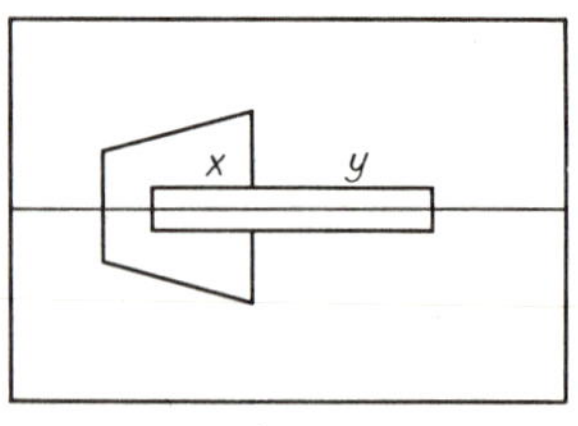

x. Stopped core
y. Length of core counter balancing x.

Fig. 155.

metal will finish where it is most wanted. The simplest colour arrangement is red or orange for parts to be left as cast, yellow where machining is to be done, and black for core prints. If a cored hole is to be machined, the ends of the print are painted black and the periphery black with yellow stripes.

The pattern may be such a shape that sand will stand proud of the drag or hang from the cope, and it may not be then possible to get a parting line of sand level with the flask. This will be dealt with in greater detail later.

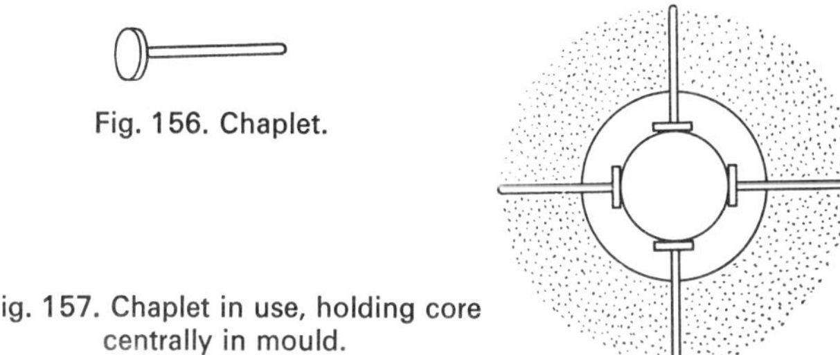

Fig. 156. Chaplet.

Fig. 157. Chaplet in use, holding core centrally in mould.

The body of a small machine jack is illustrated in Fig. 152, and is to be cast with a cylindrical hole through its centre, requiring the use of a simple cylindrical core. The pattern will be made to the shape of the casting plus allowances for contraction and machining and the addition of the core prints shown. Suitable core for this simple job may be bought at any foundry, or made in a core box, or rammed into a piece of metal tubing of the right size. If a core box is made, then the core can be made in two halves and held together by the print impressions

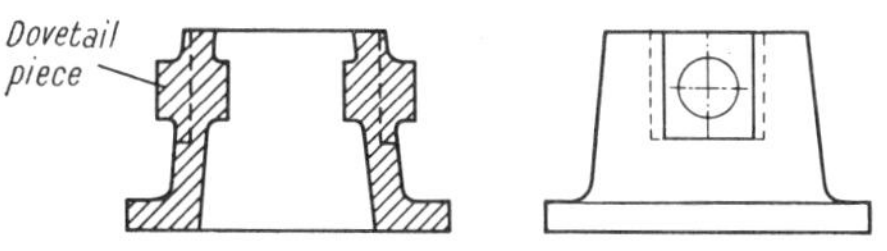

Fig. 158. Casting with internal and external bosses.

Fig. 159. Dove-tail piece for pattern.

in the mould. Only the half core box shown needs to be made. On those occasions when the core does not extend all the way through a casting, arrangements must be made to locate the core centrally and prevent it being moved by the weight and wash of the metal. One method is to make the single core print sufficiently large so as to counterbalance the weight of the portion lying in the mould. Another method is by using *chaplets*. The most common form of chaplet is a nail bedded into the mould, its head supporting the core. The material from which the chaplet is made will depend upon the material being cast.

Loose pieces are incorporated in patterns in situations where it would not be possible to withdraw the pattern without damaging the mould. Fig. 158 shows such a casting where loose pieces would be necessary in the pattern and the core box. These loose pieces are usually dovetailed to the main body of the pattern; the dovetail must slide easily. The core box is simply a hollow box of the right size, care having been taken to include the prints top and bottom. The two loose cylindrical pieces are located by a metal rod or piece of dowel passing through their centre and right through the box. The box is rammed with the loose pieces in position, the rod is withdrawn and the box carefully lifted off the core sand. The loose pieces will remain in the sand and are readily removed sideways by a wood screw or metal pricker, their imprint being left in the core sand.

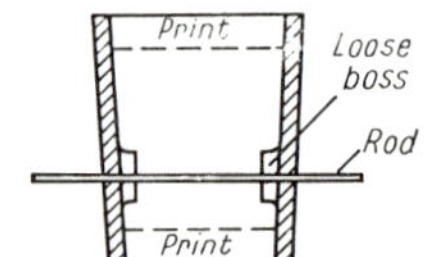

Fig. 161. Core box, loose bosses and metal rod or dowel.

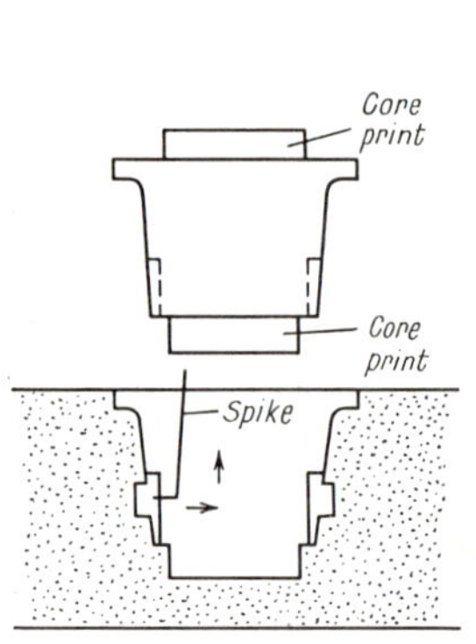

Fig. 160. Removing dovetail piece from the mould.

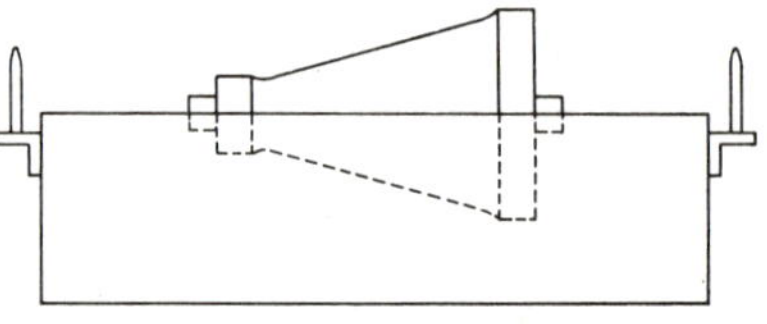

Fig. 162. Odd-side box.

Odd-side boxes   If the pattern is not a simple flat-back, that is, its widest part is not on a face, then the procedure is slightly different. An 'odd side' box has to be made. The body of the machine jack is a case in point. The procedure is to take the cope and, with the locating pins upwards, ram with moulding sand. Next, cut out sand to house the pattern to half its depth, ram carefully round and strickle flat as shown. Next fit the drag, sprinkle with parting powder, ram and strickle flat. Remove the drag carefully and turn over. Then knock out the sand in the cope and, with the pattern in position in the drag, replace the empty cope, sprinkle with parting powder, position sprue pins and proceed in the usual manner. A skilled moulder could probably manage without making the odd side but generally speaking more satisfactory results will be obtained by having one. If a large number of castings are required from such a pattern the advantages of a split pattern will be appreciated. Another method is to mix a binder with the sand for the odd side, allow it to harden, and use as long as it will last; an additional half flask will be required for this. Where convenient the odd side may be made in plaster of Paris or of wood.

Green sand cores Where a hollow casting is required, and the hollow is sufficiently large, the green sand core formed by the pattern will provide the required hollow. The casting shown is a case in point. If this procedure is to be adopted, the taper on the inside of the pattern must be more generous and greater care must be taken when rapping. If rapping is excessive then the centre core of green sand will be broken off. To reduce this danger, wire or nails may be used to strengthen the core and its attachment to the main mould when the box is being

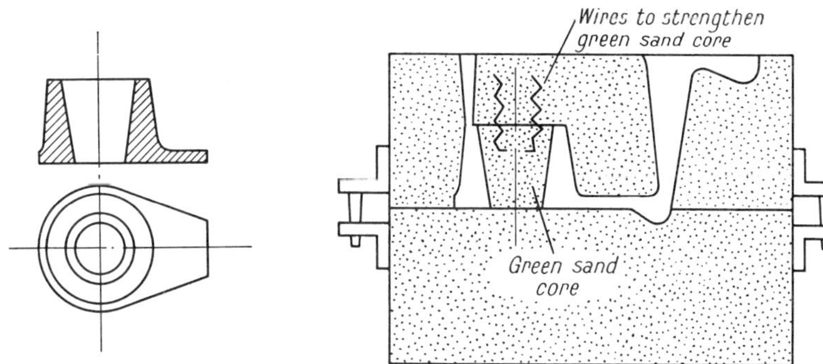

Fig. 163. Pattern of casting suitable for green sand core.

Fig. 164. Section through mould showing green sand core.

rammed. It is much safer if it can be arranged to have the green sand core standing rather than hanging, but there will be occasions when it will have to hang.

In all moulds where sand is enclosed by the pattern great care must be taken when rapping not to break the included sand from the main mould.

The moulding process for a simple 'flat-back' pattern The pattern, a wooden one, is for a simple aluminium alloy face plate suitable for a woodwork lathe.
Process (Fig. 165) Select suitable flasks, allowing about 25 mm minimum of space between any part of the pattern and the flask. Turn over the drag and put on the moulding bench or turn-over board; if the bench top is flat a board is not necessary.

(a) Place the pattern in position bearing in mind the placing of sprue pins later. Sift a little parting powder over the pattern. Riddle a covering of sand over the pattern. Add unsifted sand and pack with the peen ended ram.

(b) Complete the packing with the butt ram, and strickle flat using a rigid straight edge. Turn over the drag.

(c) Fit the cope, sprinkle with parting powder and position the sprue pins. Riddle a layer of sand over the pattern, add unsifted sand and pack with the peen ended ram.

Complete the packing, finish off with a butt ram and strickle flat. If venting in addition to the riser is necessary, provide this by using a venting rod.

(*d*) Cut the pouring basin with the spoon tool, rap and remove sprue pins. Run the fingers round the top of the sprue holes to remove any sharp edges; if this is not done they will be washed off by the molten metal and will appear as sand inclusions. Separate the flasks, putting the cope down carefully.

(*e*) Cut channels from the pattern to the sprue holes using the gate knife; the bottom of the runner should be deeper than the channel.

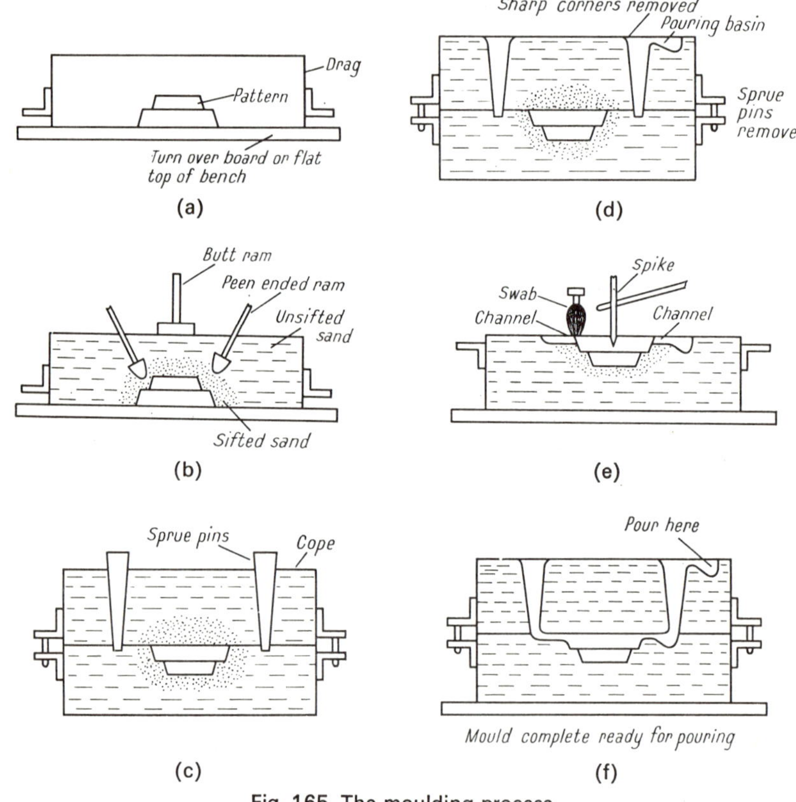

Fig. 165. The moulding process.

Moisten the sand round the edges of the pattern, using a swab or soft brush, taking care not to make the sand too wet.

Drive a sharp spike into the pattern, rap sideways in all directions and lift carefully.

Run a finger through the channels to remove sharp edges. Make any slight repairs necessary, using the appropriate tool, and blow out any loose sand very carefully with bellows.

Spray with mould coat if required.

(*f*) Replace the cope and cover the sprue holes until such time as the mould is poured.

Making a mould using a split pattern   The split pattern illustrated in Fig. 166 is for the foot of a shooting stick. Using the half pattern without the dowels, proceed exactly as for the flat-back until the stage where the cope is fitted. Fit the cope, position the half pattern with the dowels over the half in the drag, sprinkle with parting powder, position the sprue pins and proceed exactly as for the simple flat-back.

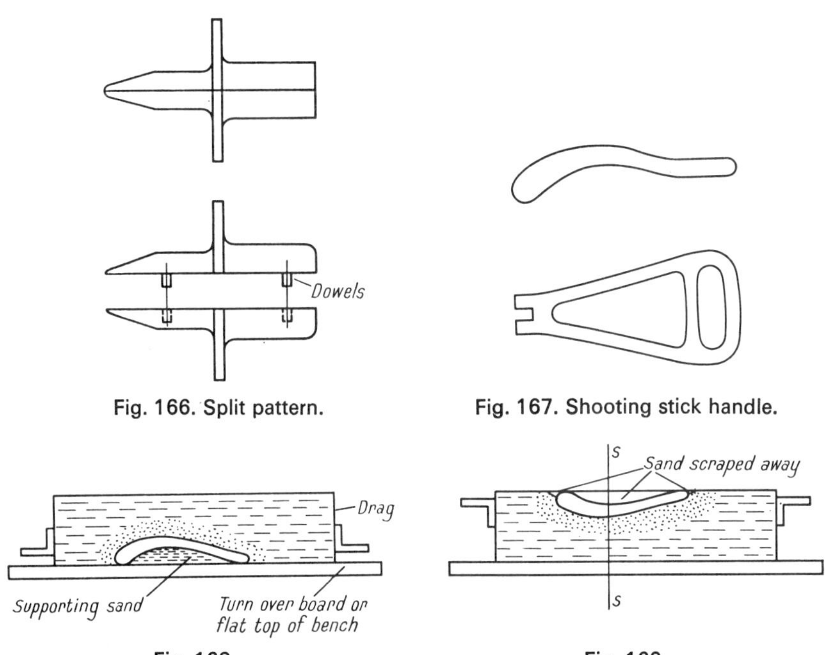

Fig. 166. Split pattern.   Fig. 167. Shooting stick handle.

Fig. 168.   Fig. 169.

It must not be assumed that all patterns will split exactly on the parting line of the flasks; it is sometimes necessary to have an uneven parting line. The pattern of the shooting stick handle illustrates such a case. To mould this pattern the procedure is as follows:

Place the pattern in the drag on the bench top or moulding board as shown in Fig. 168 but support the underside with sand. Sprinkle with parting powder and complete ramming of the drag as before. Turn over the drag and scrape the sand away carefully to reveal the pattern. This is done over the area of the pattern only and not over the complete area of the box. A section SS across the drag would appear as in Fig. 170, the sand from the pattern level sloping gently to that at box level. Fit the cope, sprinkle with parting powder, position the sprue pins and complete the ramming. When the cope is lifted the sand to fill the hollow in the drag will hang as shown in Fig. 171.

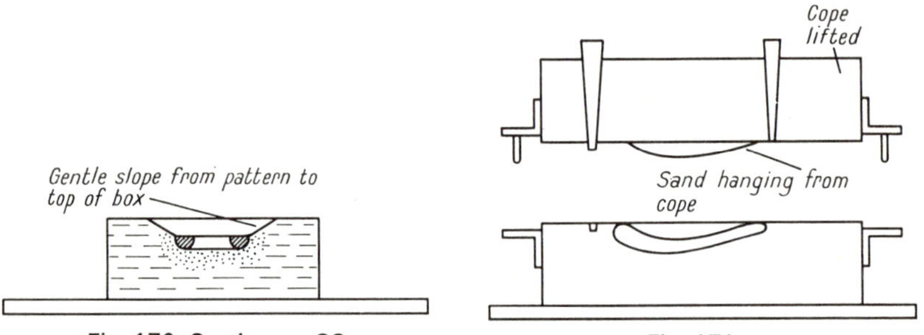

Fig. 170. Section on SS.   Fig. 171.

Moulding tools   All the trowels, slicks, corner slicks, etc., are used for finishing off and touching up the mould after the pattern has been withdrawn. The appropriate tools are also used for cutting the pouring basin and the channel from the bottom of the runner and riser to the pattern, Fig. 172.

Trowels   The illustration shows an English trowel, which is convenient for working up into a square corner, and a taper trowel, which is more useful for working along the curved edges of a pattern. Trowels are measured by the length and width of the blade.

Slicks are used for repairing and slicking small surfaces. They are named according to the shape of the blade and measured at the widest part of the blade. Fig. 172 shows a Heart and Square.

Lifters and cleaners are used to clean and finish the bottom and sides of deep narrow openings.

Gate knife is for cutting the channel from the mould to the bottom of the runner or riser.

Spoon tool is convenient for cutting the pouring basin.

Corner slicks are, as the shape implies, for finishing off fillets and corners of moulds.

Draw spike   This is a spike for knocking into the wooden pattern in order to withdraw it.

Draw screw is for the same purpose as the draw spike; the end is threaded to screw into the rapping plate.

Swab   This is a soft-pointed brush for moistening the edges of the mould before lifting the pattern. The angle at which it is held will decide the area to be covered. Care must be taken not to get the sand too damp.

Bellows are used for blowing out loose sand from the completed mould; they must be used gently, too vigorous use will damage the mould.

146

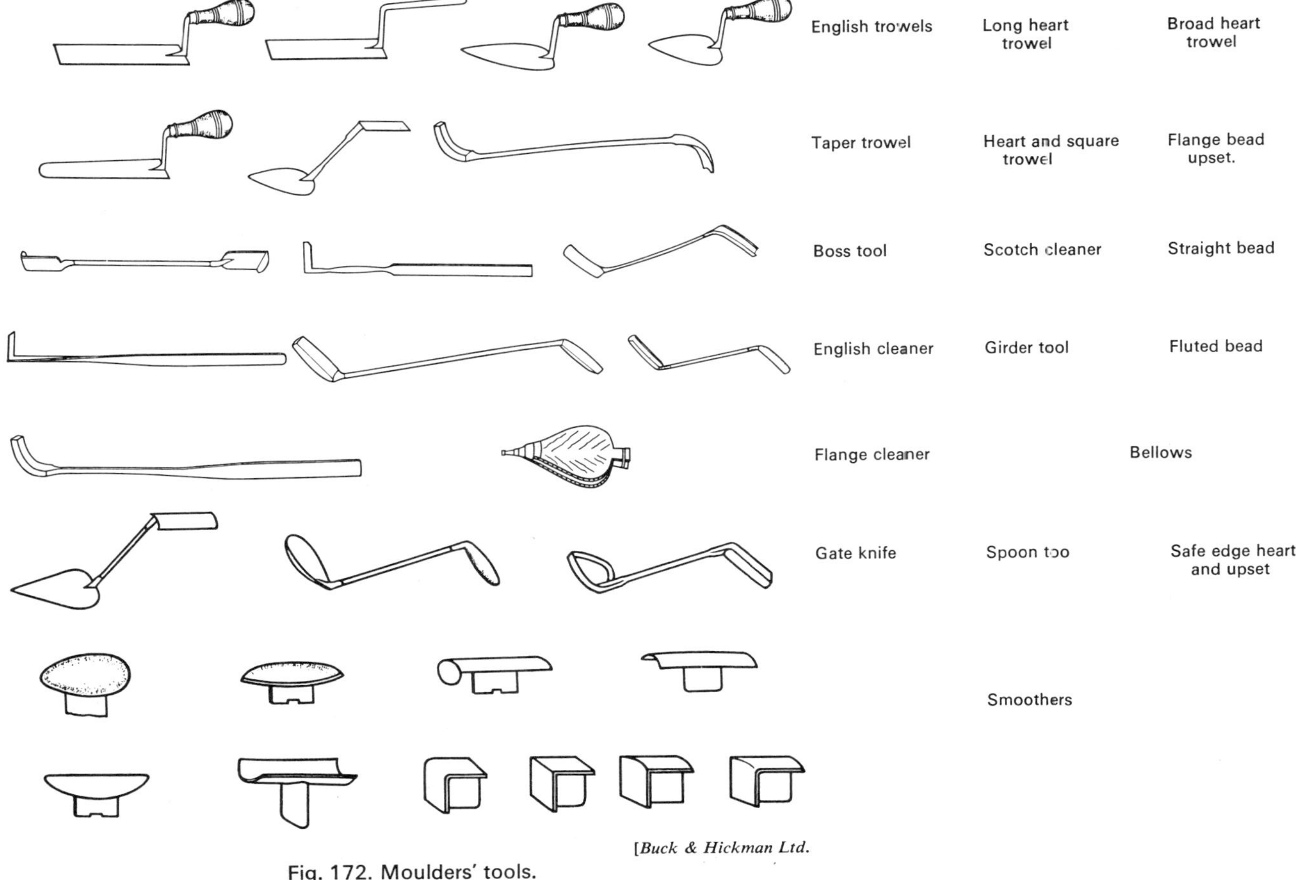

Fig. 172. Moulders' tools.

10 Drilling

Hand drills   The *hand drill* illustrated in Fig. 173 is used for light hand operations and drilling in situ; it has a capacity up to 5 mm diameter.

The *breast drill*, Fig. 174, is used for heavier hand operations and has a
capacity up to about 13 mm diameter.

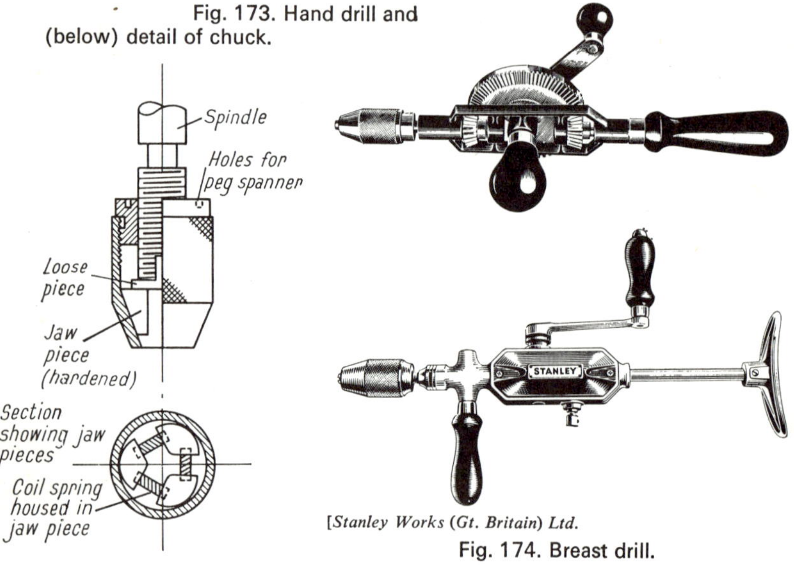

[*Stanley Works (Gt. Britain) Ltd.*
Fig. 174. Breast drill.

Electric hand and pistol drills, Fig. 175, come in various sizes and capacities and
are used for drilling holes in situ. The larger type may be held in a stand for use
as a 'sensitive drill'. It is convenient to have a power plug hanging over work
benches for connecting pistol drills.

Drilling machines   The *bench drilling machine* has a capacity up to 10 mm or
13 mm diameter, and may or may not be fitted with an intermediate table.

The *pillar drill*, Fig. 176, is similar to the bench drill but has a longer column
and stands on the floor; it also has an intermediate table. The capacity of pillar
drills is usually 13 mm or 20 mm, the spindle having a taper socket to accommodate taper shank drills. For industrial purposes pillar drills may have several

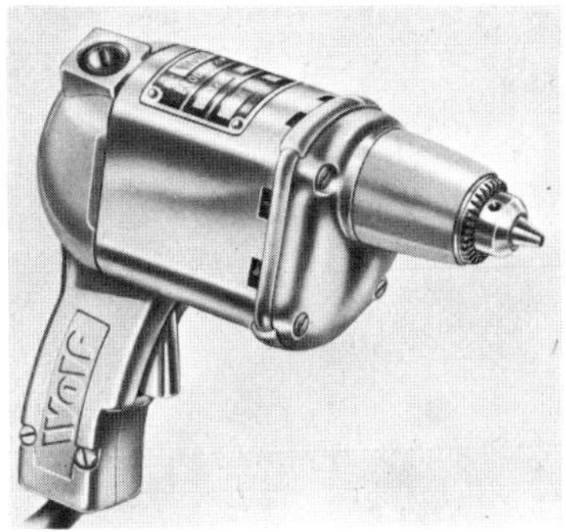

Fig. 175. Electric hand and pistol drills.

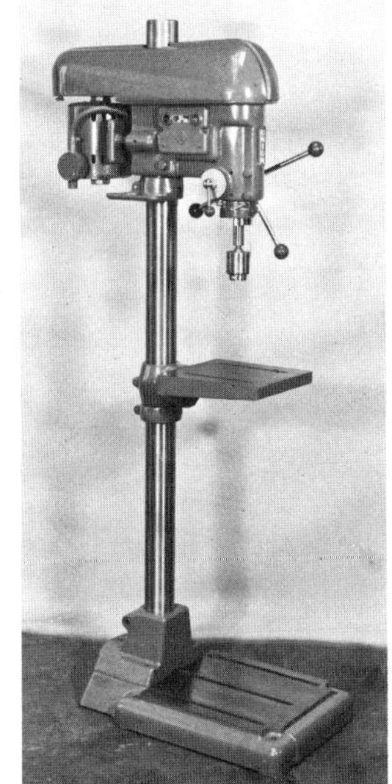

Fig. 176. Pillar drill.

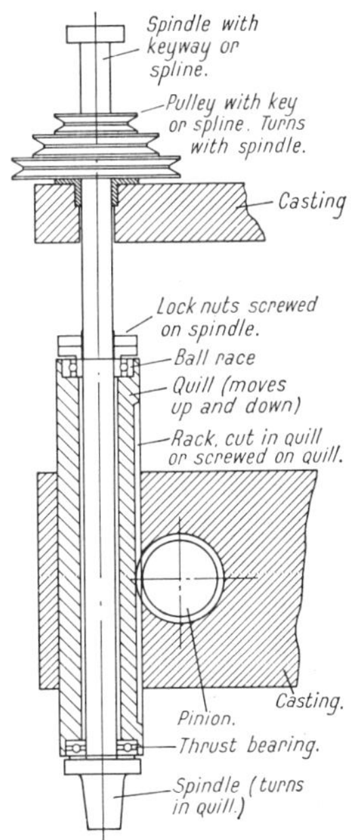

Fig. 177. Section of drill spindle.

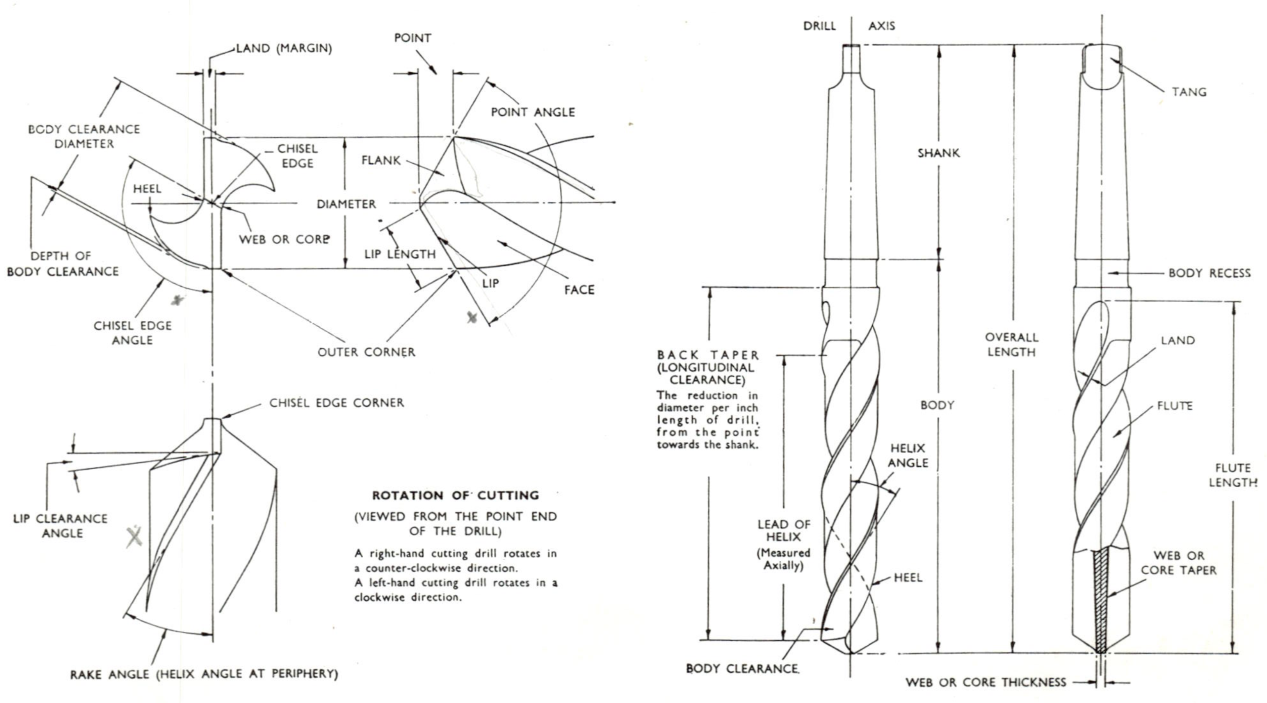

Fig. 178.

[*Sheffield Twist Drill & Steel Co. Ltd.*

spindles all operating over the same table; they are then called multiple drills. Bench and pillar drills are known as 'sensitive drills' because they are sensitive to hand pressure applied at the simple lever. The pressure is usually counterbalanced by a weight in the supporting column. Some pillar drills also have power operated feeds. Care must be taken not to allow the table of a pillar drill to fall to the bottom of the column. This can happen when adjusting its height and if the table falls rapidly its supporting casting will be broken. Some manufacturers now fit a sleeve clamp just below the table, but if this is not provided fit an old piece of vee belting at the foot of the column so that if the table does fall it will not be broken. On some drills provision is made for raising and lowering the whole head casting on the column. Stringent precautions are then necessary, such as replacing hand levers by nuts and bolts and fitting a sleeve on the column immediately below the head. If the head were allowed to fall a serious accident could occur.

Radial drills are used for much heavier work. Castings may be bolted to the block or to the machine bed. The spindle is carried on a saddle which may be traversed along the radial arm; this in turn may be rotated and moved up and down the main column. The drill spindle may be fixed in any desired position within the range of the machine. Some radial drills have more than one bed; this allows other castings to be set up while one is being drilled, so that the drill never stands idle.

Twist drills   For engineering purposes almost all drilling is done by twist drills with parallel or taper shanks, Fig. 178. Smaller drills usually have parallel shanks and those above 13 mm have taper shanks. Small drills break easily, and with taper shanks would be most uneconomic in schools, since the taper shank type is expensive. Drills may be made of carbon or high-speed steel. Small drills of carbon steel do not snap so easily and cost less; if used at correct speeds they will last just as long as high-speed drills. Table 9 gives details of recommended speeds for high-speed twist drills; carbon steel drills should be run at about half the speed of high-speed drills. Jobbers' drills are also useful for school work; they are shorter than standard and therefore less liable to break. Some manufacturers have a stub drill range; these are even shorter. Drills are obtainable in millimetre sizes from 0·3 mm to 100 mm.

Twist drills are available with quick and slow helices to suit the metal being drilled. The slowness or quickness of the helix decides the rake of the drill and those follow the same principles as lathe tools for the same materials. The resemblance of a drill to a lathe tool can be seen in the drawing, Fig. 179. A B being equivalent to the top rake on a lathe tool. Quick-helix drills, Fig. 180, are for use on aluminium, copper and other soft metals, the slow helix, Fig. 182, is for brass, phosphor bronze and gun metal. It is most dangerous to use a quick-helix drill on brass, it will most certainly grab into the job, and unless the job is securely fixed it will be thrown off the machine table. If a slow-helix drill is not available, grind back the two cutting edges, Fig. 181, on a normal drill; it can then be used quite safely.

Special drills with a slow helix and a front angle of 60 to 70 degrees are used for drilling thermo-setting plastics (Bakelite, Vulcanite, Ebonite etc., i.e. plastic materials which cannot be cut with a knife). These drills reduce the end pressure, or thrust, and minimize the break-away of the material on the underside as the drill breaks through. The thermo-plastics (Polystyrene, Perspex, Cellulose, Acetate etc.) are distinguished from the thermo-setting group in that they may be cut with a knife. These materials are best drilled with quick-helix drills which have an included point angle of 140°. Thermo-plastics have low thermal conductivity and soften at a low temperature. There is therefore danger of the material melting if correct operating conditions are not observed.

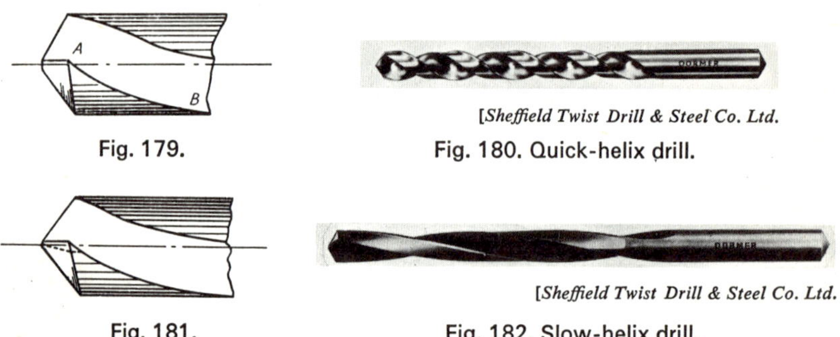

Fig. 179.

[*Sheffield Twist Drill & Steel Co. Ltd.*

Fig. 180. Quick-helix drill.

Fig. 181.

[*Sheffield Twist Drill & Steel Co. Ltd.*

Fig. 182. Slow-helix drill.

Preparation of drills   Maximum efficiency can only be expected from drills if they are correctly ground. The grinding of drills is dealt with in Chapter 14, but Fig. 183 illustrates the correct drill shapes. Twist drills are designed so that

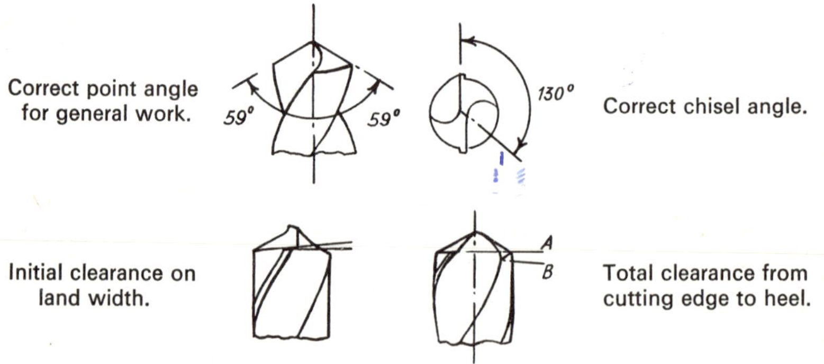

[*Sheffield Twist Drill & Steel Co. Ltd.*

Fig. 183. Point grinding of drills.

the thickness of the web gradually increases from the point to the run-out of the flutes. This provides added strength and rigidity. It is not usually necessary to thin the chisel edge of a new drill, but when about one third of the useful length has been ground away, the chisel has widened to such an extent that it needs to be thinned. If this is not done, the drilling thrust is considerably increased, and out of round and oversize holes may result, due to the inability of the drill to centralize itself properly.

Web or chisel thinning must be carefully carried out, Fig. 184, and is best effected by a shaped grinding wheel which is half the width of the flute. Equal amounts of material must be ground from either side of the chisel, which should not be thinned to a width less than the chisel edge of a new drill of equal diameter, i.e. approximately $12\frac{1}{2}\%$ of the drill diameter. The thinning should be gradually blended into the flutes and not terminated abruptly.

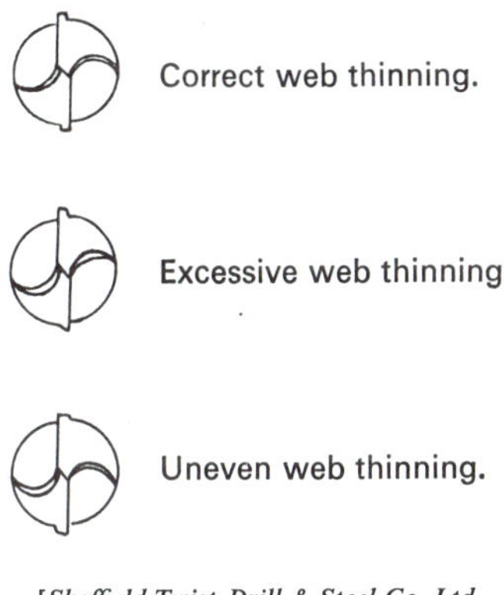

[*Sheffield Twist Drill & Steel Co. Ltd.*
Fig. 184. Web thinning of drills.

Use of drills Keep drills sharp; as soon as any dullness is suspected stop work and sharpen the drill. It is bad practice to force a dull drill, because much more grinding will be necessary when it is eventually ground. Use the correct cutting fluid for the material being drilled, soluble oil for steels and paraffin for aluminium. Cast iron, brass and phosphor bronze are drilled dry. Make sure that the fluid gets to the cutting edges of the drill. Avoid letting the flutes get choked with swarf, especially when drilling deep holes. If the whole flute is in the hole and it chokes, it will most certainly break; the drill must be lifted periodically to clear the flutes. Cast iron is more difficult to clear than steel because it breaks into small pieces; a thin piece of magnetized steel will do the trick, especially if the job must not be disturbed. All work must be held rigid; if it is in a vice then the vice must be bolted to the machine table. When using large drills a pilot hole must be made first and this must be larger than the web or core of the large drill. For a really accurate start a centre drill can be used with advantage. Multi-fluted drills, Fig. 185, are made for opening out cored holes. The ordinary two fluted drill must never be used for this purpose or it will be ruined on the hard sandy scale. When multi-fluted drills are not available it is good practice to first bore the cored hole to a depth of about 13 mm and to a diameter less than the drill to follow, and then drill. This is much kinder, the drill will not be damaged and a true hole will be obtained.

[Sheffield Twist Drill & Steel Co. Ltd.
Fig. 185. Multi-flute core drill.

Ease the pressure on the lever as the drill breaks through or the uneven cutting action will result in breakage. Avoid drilling through on to drill vices or machine tables, and arrange the work over a hole or on a parallel wooden block. If several drills are to be used on a job arrange the table so that the longest drill can be accommodated without disturbing the set-up. If a number of holes of the same depth are required use the depth gauge provided on the machine. Keep

Table 8. Peripheral speeds for high-speed twist drills

Material to be drilled	Cutting speed metre/min according to relative hardness of material
Aluminium and brass	30–60
Medium cast iron	24–30
Hard cast iron	15–21
Free cutting steels	18–30
Mild, structural, and tool steels	
(a) Up to 0·40% carbon content	24–30
(b) 0·45% to 0·70% carbon content	18–24
(c) 0·75% and up carbon content	12–18
Alloy steels	
(a) Up to 60T. tensile	15–21
(b) 60T. to 80T. tensile	9–15
(c) Over 80T. tensile	4·5– 9
Stainless steels	
(a) Magnetic	12–18
(b) Non-magnetic	6–12
Plastics	Up to 90

The speeds and feeds given in this table are approximate. In many instances due to good local conditions it will be practicable to increase them substantially.

Table 8(a). Metric size drills

m/min	Cutting speed				
	15	18	21	24	30
mm sizes	Revolutions per minute				
0·5	9695	11,634	13,573	15,512	19,390
1·0	4847	5817	6786	7756	9695
1·5	3237	3884	4532	5179	6474
2·0	2427	2912	3397	3883	4854
2·5	1941	2329	2717	3105	3882
3·0	1617	1940	2264	2587	3234
4·0	1213	1455	1698	1940	2425
5·0	970	1164	1359	1553	1941
6·0	808	970	1132	1294	1617
7·0	693	832	970	1109	1386
8·0	606	728	849	970	1213
9·0	539	647	755	862	1078
10·0	485	582	679	776	970
11·0	441	529	617	706	882
12·0	404	485	566	647	808
13·0	373	448	522	597	746
14·0	346	416	485	554	693
15·0	323	388	453	517	647
16·0	303	364	424	485	606
17·0	285	342	399	456	571
18·0	269	323	377	431	539
19·0	255	306	357	408	511
20·0	242	291	340	388	485
21·0	231	277	323	370	462
22·0	220	265	309	353	441
23·0	211	253	295	337	422
24·0	202	242	283	323	404

Rev/min for cutting speeds not given can be obtained by simple addition or subtraction, e.g.
45 m/min = 30 + 15 = 1455 rev/min (for 10 mm dia)
9 m/min = 24 − 15 = 5817 rev/min (for 0·5 mm dia)

the drill cutting, it must never be allowed to rub; on the other hand too much pressure will break a drill. Straight shank drills must be held tightly in the chuck; if they are allowed to slip they are quickly mutilated, the size cannot be read and they will cease to run true. For most school purposes a centre punch is sufficient to locate the drill and give it a start; the size of punch mark must be larger for larger drills. When marking out for accurate work a circle the size of the hole required is drawn and its periphery fixed by at least four dot punch marks, Fig. 186. If the drill is not started correctly the centre dots on the circumference will show up the inaccuracy, and if the drill is not allowed to go too deep it may be corrected by drawing over the centre with a small round nose chisel.

To drill a hole exactly on the diameter of a round bar set up as shown in Fig. 187. The disc is the same diameter as the bar to be drilled and the hole through its centre is the size of the drill to be used. This method is much easier than struggling with vee-blocks and clamps and is reliable.

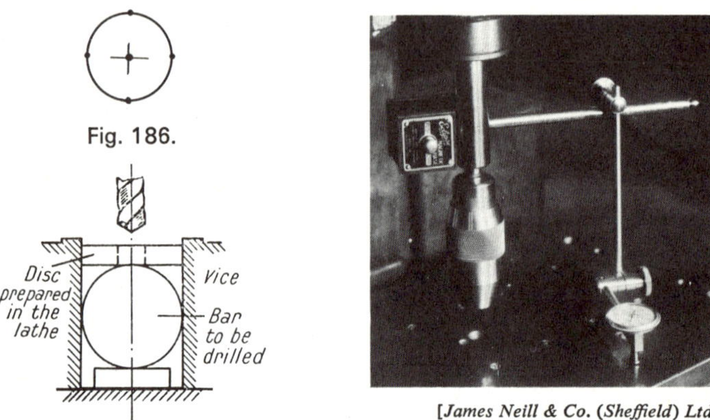

Fig. 186.

Fig. 187.

[*James Neill & Co. (Sheffield) Ltd.*

Fig. 188.

Work to be drilled may be held in a vice, supported in vee-blocks, bolted to an angle plate, box angle plate, tilting table or even between centres on a dividing head. The method will depend entirely upon the nature of the job in hand. If for any reason the machine table is tilted it must be levelled up afterwards most carefully. The use of a spirit level alone is not adequate. The most important thing is that the table must be square to the drill spindle. Illustrated in Fig. 188 is one very convenient testing method.

Drill sockets The size of shank on taper shank drills depends upon the size of the drill and normally increases with the drill. Drills with taper shanks other than standard may be obtained to order. If a taper shank is too small for the socket of the machine in which it is to be used the difference is made up with a taper sleeve, Fig. 189. These are available in single steps, e.g. 1 to 2, 2 to 3, etc., or maybe 1 to 3 or 1 to 4. They may also reduce as well as enlarge but their use

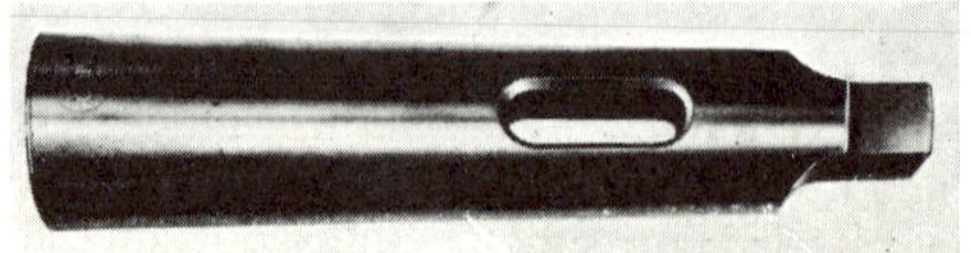

[*Samuel Osborn & Co. Ltd.*

Fig. 189. Taper sleeve for drills.

does tend to overload a machine by allowing the use of larger drills than the machine was designed for. It is more accurate to have one socket from say 1 to 4 than to build up with three single sockets. If it is necessary to drive a drill into its socket use a copper hammer. Make sure that the shank and socket are clean and free from swarf or hammer marks. Shanks must not be allowed to spin in sockets or irreparable damage will be done, e.g. tangs may be screwed off. Taper drills and sockets must be removed by means of a taper drift, Fig. 190, and copper hammer; hammering on the drill itself must never be allowed. Once a taper shank has been bruised it ceases to be an accurate, efficient tool. When removing a drill keep one hand on it; do not allow it to fall on to the drill table.

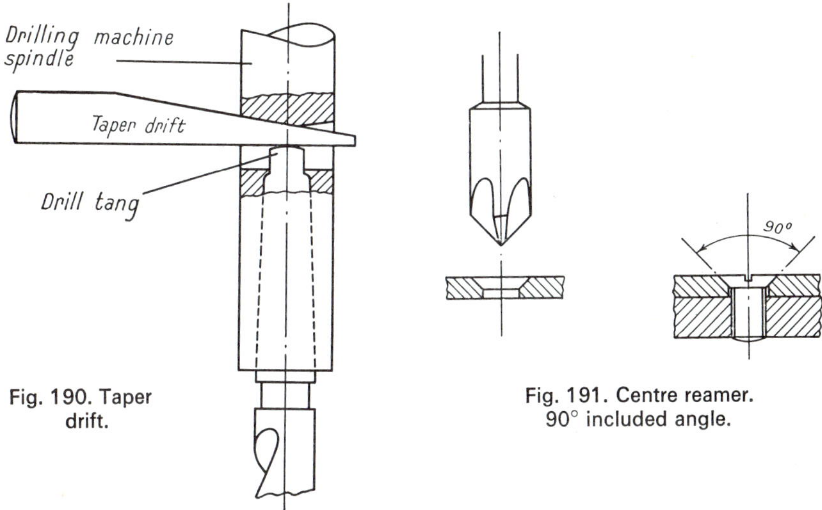

Fig. 190. Taper drift.

Fig. 191. Centre reamer. 90° included angle.

D-bits It is sometimes necessary to produce a more accurate hole, such as in a steam engine cylinder, than can be obtained by normal drills. The drawing in Fig. 192 is fairly self-explanatory, D being the size of the required hole. If this diameter can be ground then so much the better. Half the cylinder is cut

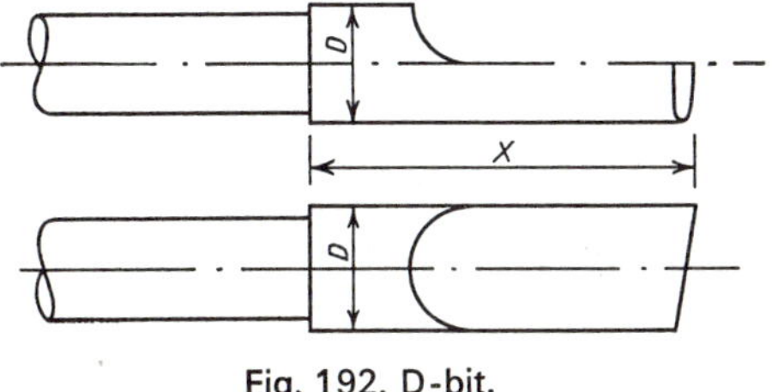

Fig. 192. D-bit.

away and its end ground to an angle less than 90°; rake is provided by giving relief to the end as indicated. The hole is started by drilling and boring to the length X and accurately to the diameter D. The longer X can be made the more accurate will be the result but this will, of course, depend upon the job. The drilling and boring gives the D-bit an accurate start from which it may proceed. Apply the appropriate cutting fluid (or use dry according to the material) but do withdraw periodically to clear the swarf or the bit will jam.

Countersinking, Fig. 191, may be done for a variety of reasons. If the countersink has to accommodate a screw or rivet head it must be done at 90°. If it is merely to be filled up with the tail of a rivet then the normal drill will be adequate.

Counterboring is usually done to accommodate the head of a cheese-headed or socket-headed screw. Cutters, Fig. 193, may be bought but in most workshops are made as shown in Fig. 194. The centre pin is better if removable so that pins

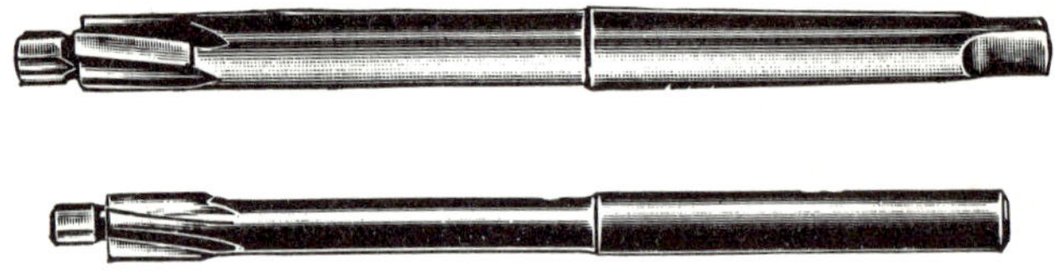

[*Buck & Hickman Ltd.*

Fig. 193. Counterboring cutters.

of different sizes may be used, increasing the range of the tool. Solid pins are easily broken off; to avoid this, drill the pilot hole and follow immediately with the counterbore without disturbing the job. If it gets out of line the pin will most certainly be broken off. The speed must be reduced for the counterboring operation.

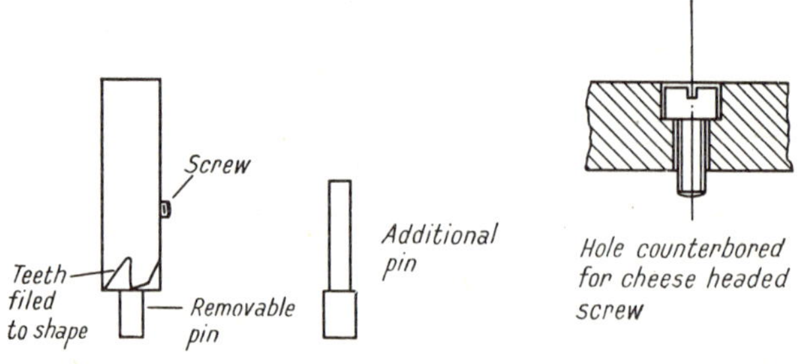

Fig. 194. Counterboring cutter.

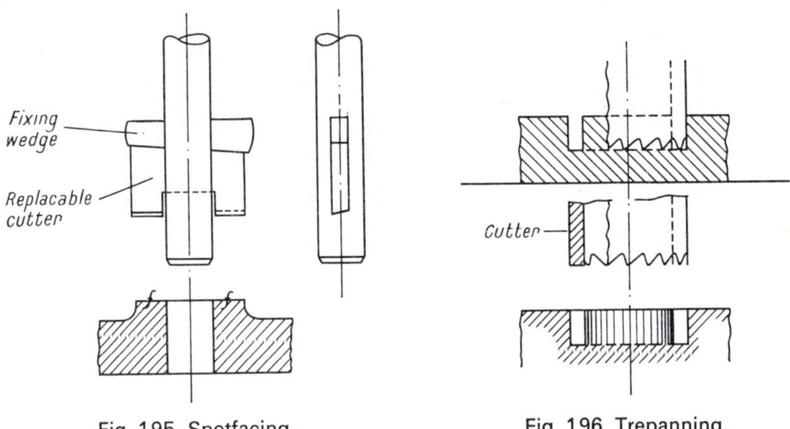

Fig. 195. Spotfacing.　　　　　Fig. 196. Trepanning.

Spotfacing, Fig. 195, is exactly the same operation as counterboring except that the surface is only levelled sufficiently to provide a square seating or facing for a bolt head or washer.

Trepanning, Fig. 196, may be done by specially made inserted tooth cutters or by a suitable shell-end mill. A shallow trepanning will provide a seating for a spring.

11 Lathes and Lathework

The lathe is possibly the oldest type of mechanical tool. From its early primitive form it has been developed into a variety of precision machines, which in one form or another, are responsible for much of the present-day engineering production and are the most widely used machine tools of modern industry. The capstan, turret, automatic and special purpose lathes are but adapted forms of the original centre lathe, which in its basic principles and construction is quite simple. The same centre lathe however, with the addition of various attachments, is capable of an almost limitless number of machining operations.

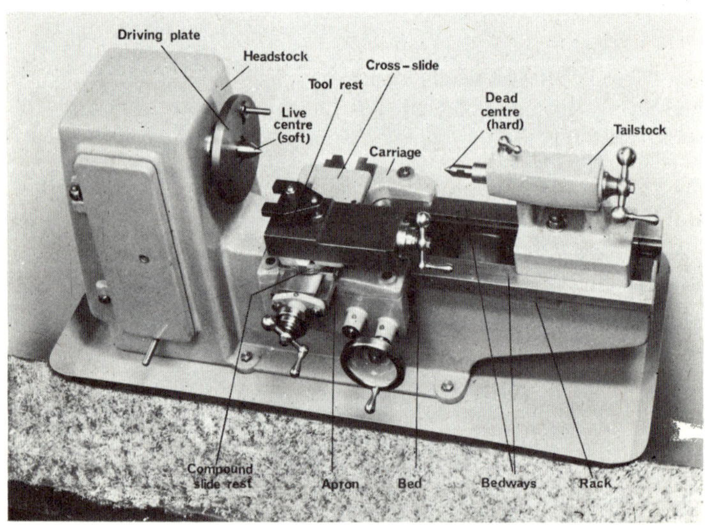

[*Myford Ltd*.]

Fig. 197. Basic training lathe.

The lathe consists essentially of a rigid bed, with its upper surfaces machined to form guides or bedways, incorporating a headstock in which the main spindle revolves, Fig. 197, *A carriage* and a *tailstock* slide along this bed parallel with the spindle axis. For the majority of basic turning operations the work is attached to, or is driven by, the *spindle* and a cutting tool is introduced to it by the carriage or tailstock. As the bed is aligned parallel in both planes to the axis of the spindle, a tool guided by the bedways will generate a true cylinder on

160

work revolved by the spindle and, with the tool operating at right-angles to the bed, a flat surface is produced. If the tool is actuated at an angle other than at 90° to the bed, a cone or portion of a cone will be generated, Fig. 198.

Basic training lathes The bed castings of lathes are of box form and are strengthened at intervals by webs or ribs to prevent their warping and to ensure that correct alignment is maintained. The ways themselves may be flat or have raised vee-guides. The headstock is also a heavy casting and is permanently attached to the bed. It contains the spindle bearings and the drive. The bearings are an important part of the lathe for it is upon their free running and lack of

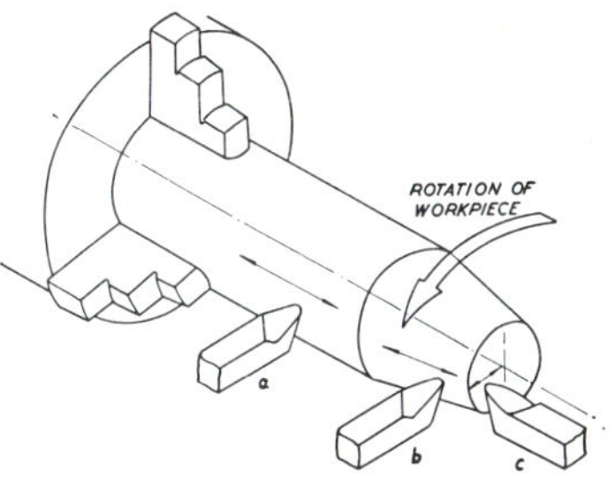

Fig 198. Basic turning operations.

(a) Tool moves in straight line parallel to axis—Cylinder generated.
(b) Tool moves in straight line at angle to axis—Conical form generated.
(c) Tool moves in straight line at 90° to axis—Flat surface generated.

'play' that the quality of the work produced depends. In the older and some smaller machines, plain bearings are fitted but it is more common for modern lathes to have taper roller bearings. The main spindle has a threaded nose to which work-holding devices are screwed, and also a tapered socket. It is driven by the machine's motor either through a belt drive over cone pulleys or through a gearbox. On some lathes a variable speed drive is incorporated and, as with the direct drive type, a further range of spindle speeds is made possible by means of a *back gear*, Fig. 199. The carriage is traversed along the bed by means of a pinion wheel which engages with a rack fitted beneath the front bedway. It may be operated by hand by a handwheel on the lathe *apron*. The carriage and apron together comprise the *saddle*. Between the tool and the bed, two further slides are situated. The lower of these, called the *cross slide*, operates at 90° to the bedway and is actuated by a handwheel above the apron. The third and upper slide is comparatively short and is located on a bush around which it may be revolved. This is the *top slide* which, with the revolving and locking mechanism, constitutes the *compound slide rest*. It is on the top slide that the tool is normally held in a toolpost or clamp. The tailstock, by which a further range of tools and work-holding devices may be held consists of a casting bored to take a sleeve or barrel with its axis in line with that of the headstock spindle. The tailstock can be moved along the bed and be locked to it in any position. The barrel of the tailstock is then advanced by a handwheel operating through a screw and nut and, as with the headstock spindle, it also possesses a tapered socket.

These, the fundamental parts of a lathe, are common to lathes of all types. The basic training lathes show these features to good advantage as the student is not confused by the numerous arms and levers of the more complicated machines; their simple and robust construction makes them suitable for school work. All slides are operated by hand feeds, for it is important that a beginner should learn to control the movement of a tool before automatic traverses are used. Lathes of this type will, moreover, perform a wide variety of operations and, apart from screwcutting, a large proportion of the turning undertaken in the metalwork room may be accomplished upon them.

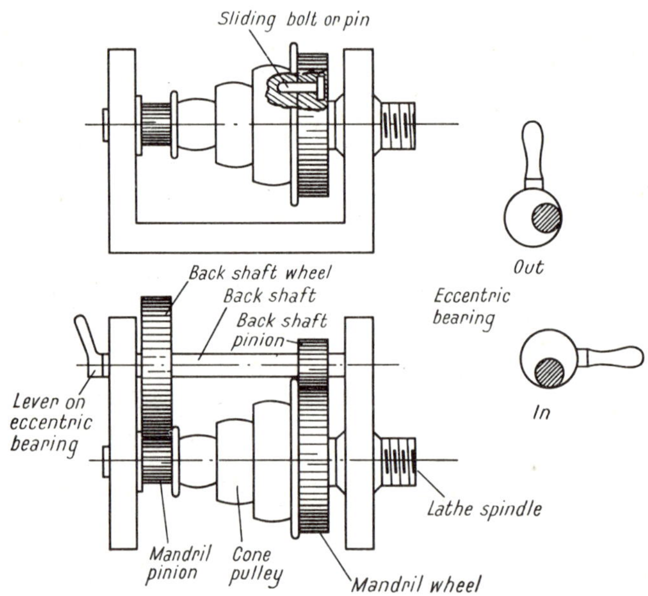

Fig. 199. Lathe back gear.

Screwcutting lathes   Screwcutting lathes, Figs. 200 and 202, have a *leadscrew* at the front of the bed which is driven by the main spindle through a positive gear drive on the end of the headstock. The leadscrew passes through the apron, and the saddle may be engaged with it by half nuts operated by a lever on the apron front. In this way motion may be transmitted to the tool in strict relationship to the revolutions of the spindle, Fig. 201a. Modern screwcutting lathes often incorporate a Norton gearbox, Fig. 219, whereby the ratio between spindle and leadscrew speeds may be set at will. Others have a partial gearbox which calls for only a few change wheels, whereas on the simpler types the leadscrew is driven directly by interchangeable gearwheels. Between the spindle and the first studwheel there is interposed a set of tumbler gears whereby the direction of rotation of the leadscrew in relation to that of the spindle can be reversed, Fig. 201b.

The leadscrew is used only when cutting screwthreads. The motion of the saddle, when engaged with the leadscrew, is normally too fast for plain turning. A feedshaft is therefore provided which, operating through worm and worm wheels in the apron, transmits a comparatively slow motion to the carriage or cross slide and provides means of automatic traverse both in line with, and

Fig. 200. Screwcutting lathe.

across the bed. The feed shaft is engaged by a lever or screw on the apron front. A further feature of the screwcutting lathe is the provision made whereby the tailstock may be moved laterally across the bed by small amounts and work be held between centres at an angle to the machine's axis. This facilitates the turning of slow tapers under automatic feed.

The size of a lathe is designated by the height of its spindle axis over the bedways. This gives the 'swing' of the lathe or half the largest diameter that the machine will accommodate. American lathes are designated by the full diameter of work that they will turn. Most lathes of this type have a gap in the bed at the headstock end, and a portion of the bed that may be removed to accommodate larger diameter work. If a number of machines are available in a workshop, it is advantageous to remove the bed section from one lathe only so that all work requiring extra swing is done on that machine. Misalignment of the bed on replacement of the section will cause inaccurate work to be produced; hence it should be disturbed as little as possible and, when replaced, the locating faces cleaned and the bed section well located before bolting down.

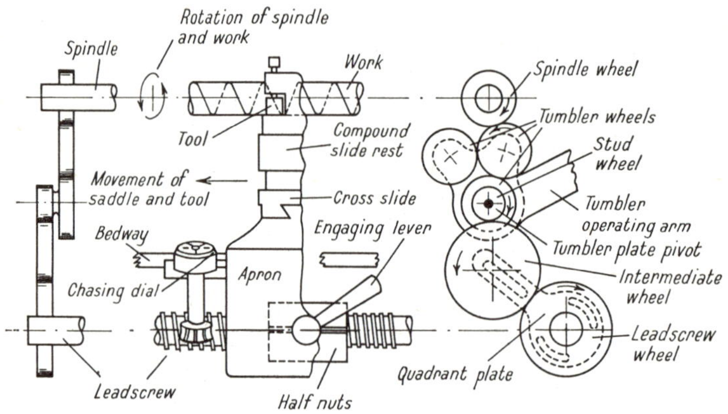

Fig. 201 (a). Screwcutting mechanism.

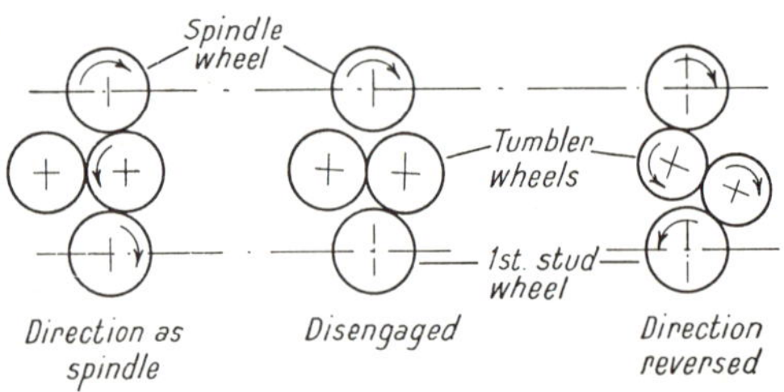

Fig. 201 (b). Tumbler wheel positions.

Modern lathes of all types have independent motors, usually situated in the base casting or stand. The method of starting and stopping, however, varies with the make of machine. On some lathes a clutch is provided and the motor may be left running during the short periods when work is being checked for size. Others have a combined clutch and switch, while on some of the smaller machines a switch only is fitted. If the latter type incorporate a reversing switch, care must be taken to ensure that the forward drive only is used.

164

The sudden switching on in reverse at high speeds could cause the chuck to become unscrewed from the spindle nose with disastrous results. Running in reverse has little application in the instructional workshop and is not required for the usual run of work. As a safety precaution it should be disconnected.

The larger lathes invariably incorporate an *all-gear head*, Fig. 202, enabling the spindle speed to be readily changed by the operation of external handles or levers. Not only does this enable rapid changes to be made but a larger and more evenly graduated range of spindle speeds is available. The gearwheels are located on splines on the spindle and layshafts, and are brought into mesh by the appropriate levers. They are so arranged that it is impossible to engage more

[*T. S. Harrison & Sons Ltd.*

Fig. 202. Screwcutting lathe
(all-geared head).

than is necessary for any one spindle speed. Lubrication is usually provided by splash from an oil bath in the boxed headstock. The oil level must be frequently checked, a dip stick or observation window being provided for the purpose.

When the headstock and bed of a lathe are separate castings, a means of slight adjustment is provided whereby the alignment of the spindle axis to the bedways might be effected. Though accurately positioned by the manufacturer and not normally requiring attention, spindle alignment should be checked at intervals by turning a test bar held in the chuck without engaging the tailstock centre. Under these conditions a true cylinder should be produced. If a taper results, the headstock must be re-aligned by slackening the locating bolts and moving the adjusting screws.

Holding work on the lathe Most of the elementary turning processes will be accomplished holding the work in a *chuck* located directly on the spindle nose.

A self-centring 3-jaw chuck, Fig. 203, will hold circular work true with the spindle axis. The jaws of self-centring chucks are actuated by a scroll in the chuck body and act in unison when an operating bevel gear is turned with a chuck key. A separate set of jaws are provided for holding large diameter work. When fitting the jaws it is essential to locate each jaw in its correct position with the scroll. The jaw marked with a number 1 is first inserted in its tee slot and made to engage with the scroll end and the procedure repeated with the other jaws in order. Only bright drawn and previously machined bars are held in self-centring chucks, for the rough surface and possible ovality of black bar and cast materials will soon strain the jaws and make them run out of truth. As the jaws are hardened they can only be trued by grinding with a toolpost grinder.

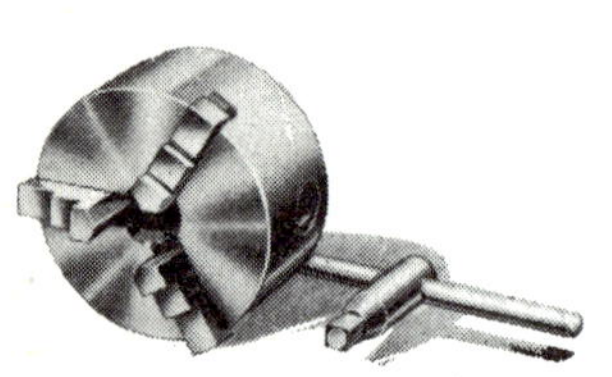

[*T. S. Harrison & Sons Ltd.*

Fig. 203. 3-jaw chuck.

[*T. S. Harrison & Sons Ltd.*

Fig. 204. 4-jaw chuck
with jaws reversed.

Black bar, square, rectangular and some irregularly shaped work may be held in a 4-jaw independent chuck, Fig. 204. The jaws of this type of chuck are reversible. As each jaw moves independently, work may be adjusted and brought to its required location by moving each jaw in turn. Metal of circular form is set true by holding chalk against the revolving surface or by rotating by hand against a surface gauge mounted on the machine ways. Square work is best tested by checking the corners in relation to a tool or scriber held in the toolpost. Eccentric work and pieces requiring to be set up in relation to a marked-out position for a bored hole, are tested by means of a bar held in a universal adapter in the toolpost or tailstock, or by pre-positioned toolmaker's buttons; and checked by reference to a test indicator, Fig. 205a.

Work requiring to be located on the lathe spindle, and not conveniently held in a chuck, may be bolted or clamped to a *faceplate*, either directly or in conjunction with an *angle plate*, Fig. 205. It is usually found more convenient to approximately position and bolt the work while the faceplate is on the bench, concentric rings on the plate acting as a guide, and then mount the plate with the work upon it to the machine. Its final position may then be checked as for work in the 4-jaw chuck. Balance weights are then mounted to ensure even running and lack of vibration caused by the centrifugal throw of eccentric loading.

166

When fitting a chuck or a faceplate to a lathe spindle, ensure that both external and internal screwthreads are clean and that positive engagement is made with the spindle shoulder. When removing chucks, place a board across the bedways. The bed of the lathe must be protected at all times, for any damage done to it will spoil all future work. Small tools and instruments should not be laid on the bedways but should be placed in an orderly manner on the machine cabinet or a bed-board placed to the right of the tailstock.

Working between centres　A further means of supporting work is between the lathe centres, Fig. 206a. The work is drilled at each end with a centre drill, and

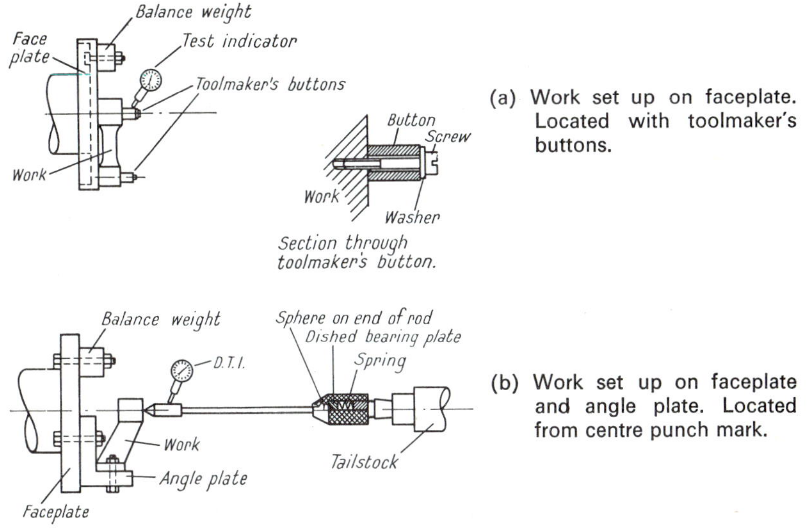

Fig. 205.

a *carrier* clamped to it. Carriers may be of the straight or bent tail types, Fig. 207. The work is driven by a *catch plate*, the bent tail carriers engaging with a slot in the plate face, and the straight types with a driving pin. When the latter are used the pin must be made to locate against the tail and not the clamping screw, otherwise the drive will be less positive and the screw may become bent. The lathe centre in the spindle, Fig. 208a, is made of soft steel so that it may be trued before work commences. To do so the compound slide rest is set to 30 degrees to the spindle axis and a light cut taken to ensure its true alignment. The centre in the tailstock is hardened as it has to withstand the friction of the revolving work. In setting up work between centres, the centre holes in the work are cleaned and a lubricant of tallow or Russian fat is applied at the tailstock end. The tailstock sleeve is locked while the work may be freely rotated yet with a complete absence of end play. During the cutting operation the location of this centre must be frequently checked, for the work will expand due to the heat generated by friction and cutting, and there is a possibility of the work seizing up on the centre with the eventual burning off of the tip. *Revolving centres*, Fig. 208c, eliminate this danger and are useful for holding tubular work. They are not to be recommended for precision work or when taking heavy cuts. Half centres, Fig. 208b, enable the ends of work so held to be faced and the turning of small diameters near the tailstock.

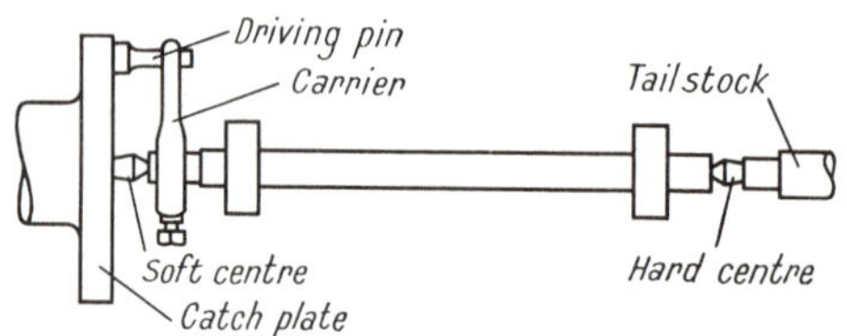

Fig. 206(a). Test bar between centres.

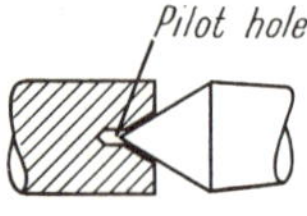

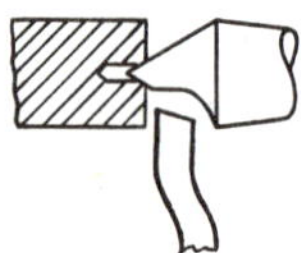

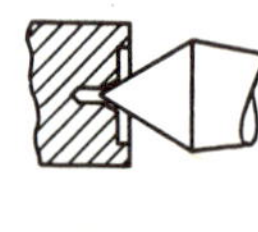

(a) Work located on centre.

(b) Effect of offsetting tailstock.

(c) Application of half centre.

(d) Protected centre.

Fig. 206(b). Centring work.

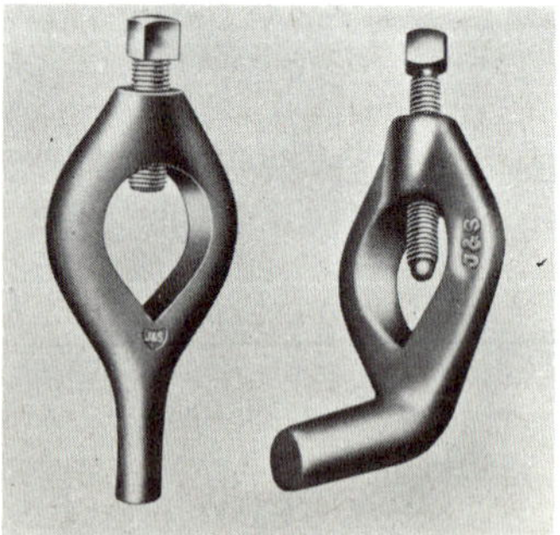

[*S. A. Jones & Shipman Ltd.*

Fig. 207.

The holding of work between centres enables it to be removed from the lathe and then set up again accurately and quickly. It also facilitates the setting up of the work on other machine tools and is widely used in industry where the various operations are often performed on different machines. In the metalwork room it is a great asset when only short periods are available for practical work and when work must be dismantled from a machine at the end of a lesson, often before completion. Work having cylindrical bores can be set up in this way on

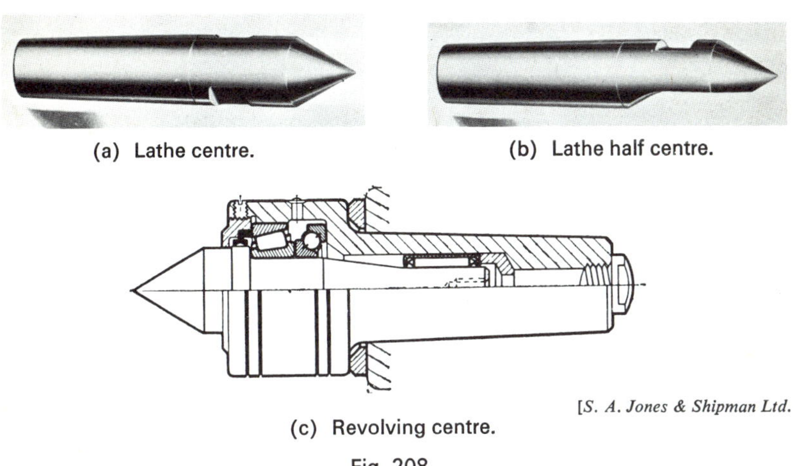

(a) Lathe centre.

(b) Lathe half centre.

(c) Revolving centre.

[S. A. Jones & Shipman Ltd.

Fig. 208.

mandrels, Fig. 209. Mandrels have a slight taper of a fraction of a mm over their length and are available in standard diameters. They are case-hardened and ground and the centres are recessed to protect them from damage if knocked or dropped.

When the end of an article is to be worked upon and it cannot be sufficiently well supported in a chuck or on a face plate, a fixed steady, clamped to the bed-ways, may be used, Fig. 210a. Similarly, long thin work that would bend or spring against the pressure of the tool is supported by a travelling steady fixed to the carriage, Fig. 210b. The steady bearing points are of phosphor bronze and they are positioned while the work is revolving. The lower bearing arm is first brought into contact with the work or, as with the fixed steady, until the

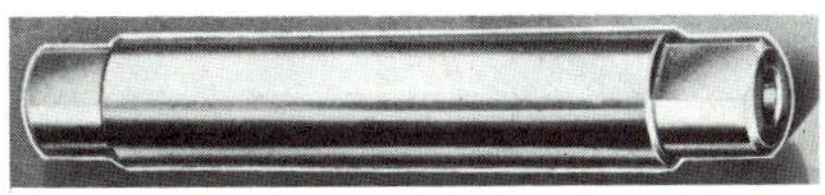

[S. A. Jones & Shipman Ltd.

Fig. 209. Mandrel.

169

work runs true; it is then locked. The other arms are then brought into light contact and also clamped. A liberal supply of lubricating oil must be kept on the work in the area of the steady bearings. The travelling steady is made to follow the tool when an initial cut is taken.

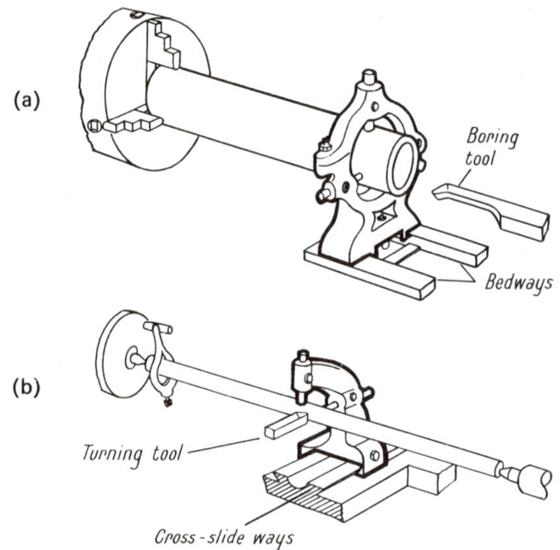

Fig. 210. (a) Use of fixed steady.
(b) Use of travelling steady.

Toolposts and clamps   The various patterns of tool-holding devices are shown in Fig. 211. The simple clamp is possibly the most suitable for use in the metal-work room as it will rigidly hold a variety of tools. Metal packing is used to bring the tool tip to centre height and the adjusting screw is then set to bring the clamp parallel with the surface of the base platform. The 4-way toolpost is employed mainly on production work when more than a single tool is repeatedly needed in quick succession. The American type toolpost is more generally used in conjunction with a tool-holder and has a *boat* located in a concave ring by means of which the tool may be rocked, hence raising or lowering the tool tip. This facilitates the setting of the tool to centre height but alters the cutting angle of the tool. The tool is less well supported than it is with the clamp and, as the slide rest is ahead of the tool, cutting close to the headstock is in many cases prevented and the rest is liable to damage by the chuck jaws.

   A further range of tools, notably drills and machine reamers, may be held in the tailstock. A drill chuck fits into the tailstock sleeve and grips drills and tools with plain shanks. The larger taper shank drills are located directly or by means of sleeves.

170

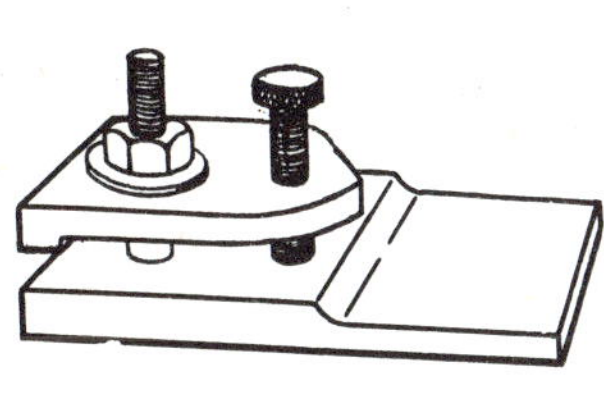

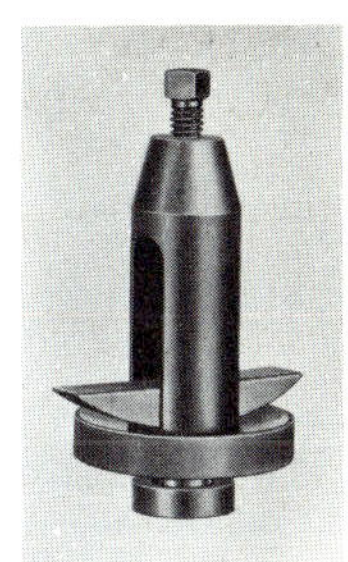

[*Raglan Engineering Co.* (1954) *Ltd.*

(a) Tool clamp.   (b) 4-way tool post.   (c) American type tool
                                                            post (ring and rocker).

Fig. 211. Tool holding devices.

Lathe tools   The type of lathe tool used for instructional work is a matter for the teacher to decide. There are three main types that might be considered: solid tools of a tool steel fashioned and heat-treated in the workshop; solid tools with a hardened tip brazed or butt-welded to a soft shank, which are manufactured and maintained in the standard shapes; or small tool bits held in a tool holder, Fig. 212. The forged tool, if made by the student, has the advantage of giving practice in the forging and heat treatment of tool steels. These processes, however, are difficult for a beginner to perform and the inexpert grinding of solid tools could prove wasteful of expensive material and time. Pre-formed tools with high speed steel tips will give good service and can be sharpened by grinding on the original faces, thus giving suitable practice in tool sharpening. The method of holding the tool against a grinding wheel, to preserve the original shape, is easily learnt. Cemented carbide-tipped tools are not normally used for

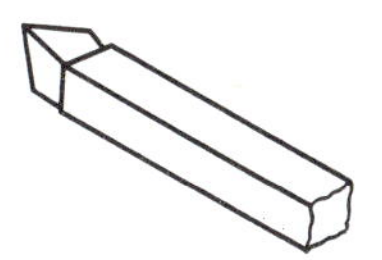

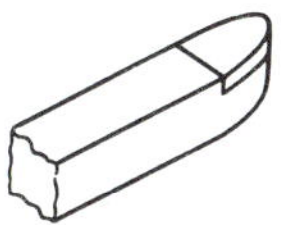

(a) Solid forged tool.   (b) Solid tipped tool.

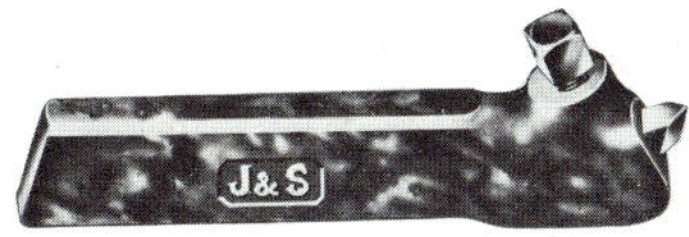

[*S. A. Jones & Shipman Ltd.*

(c) Tool holder and bit.

Fig. 212. Lathe tools.

basic instruction as special equipment is required to sharpen them, and the brittle nature of the material calls for cutting angles which differ from those of the steel tools. Small tool-bits of about 6 mm or 8 mm square held in a tool-holder may be considered to be the most suitable for the work done in the metalwork room. Though less strong than a solid tool they are adequate for most basic lathework operations. Students can shape the bits in cast or silver steel and perform the necessary hardening and tempering operations, and also grind hardened bits of H.S.S. or alloy steels. A student should, wherever possible, use a tool that he has prepared himself. The use of tool bits is an aid in this direction and it furthermore makes possible the comparison of the efficiency and life of the cutting edges of different materials under the same conditions. Two such bits with a cutting shape at either end will give four tool shapes covering a useful range of work in mild steel and the other common metals, Fig. 213.

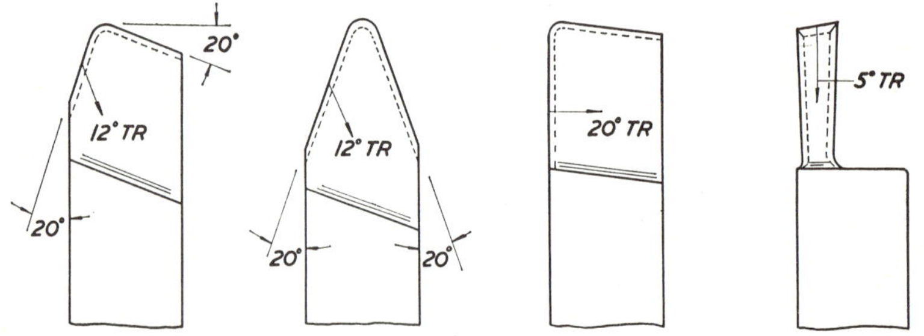

(a) Roughing.   (b) Round nose.   (c) Right hand knife.   (d) Parting off.
Fig. 213. Common lathe tool shapes (plan view). Arrows denote direction of top rake.

The *roughing tool* (a) has a straight cutting edge which forms an acute angle with the axis of the work—the tip of the tool trailing. With such an 'approach' angle, Fig. 214, heavy roughing cuts may be taken, because the forces acting on the tool under load are such that there is no danger of the tool 'digging in', and also swarf is directed away from the work.

A *round nose tool* (b) will take moderately deep cuts as it also presents a cutting edge at a suitable approach angle. The radiused tip gives a fine surface finish to work and, as it tends to wear less rapidly than a sharper pointed tool, it is suitable for machining cast iron and the tougher metals.

When a reduced diameter is to terminate at a 90 degree shoulder, a *knife tool* (c) is required. As only light finishing cuts are taken with this tool the approach angle is not important. To prevent undue wear and to produce a smooth surface, a knife tool should be given a slight radius at its tip with a slip stone after grinding to shape. Heavier cuts may be taken with a knife tool if it is set to give an appropriate approach angle, i.e. with the tool tip trailing.

A short *parting tool* (d) completes the main range of general purpose lathe tools for plain turning. The tool is ground leaving the parting blade to the left of the bit, because it is important to take parting cuts as near to the lathe head-stock as possible. Note the slight side clearances and also the angle at the tip. The former prevent 'binding' in the groove and the latter causes any remaining 'pip' to be left on the stock and gives a smooth surface to the parted workpiece. It is also advisable to grind a small groove behind the cutting edge to form a 'chip-breaker'. This prevents the formation of lengths of swarf which could become trapped between the sides of the tool and the walls of the groove—the main cause of parting tool breakage.

Tool shapes for cutting the various screwthreads and for special purposes can then be prepared as required. A student building up his own set of lathe tools in this way quickly comes to appreciate the essential features, and the quality

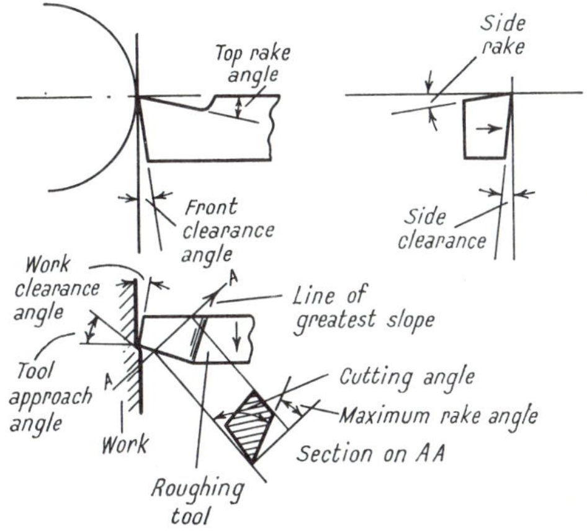

Fig. 214. Cutting angles—lathe tools.

of the work produced increases with the experience gained. The common tool-holders hold the bit at an angle to the horizontal providing a suitable degree of cutting rake for mild steel. Many of the tools therefore will require shaping on the clearance faces only and others only slightly on the top to provide side rake.

The cutting action of lathe tools consists of the edge forcing its way into the metal and cleaving away a chip or strip of metal by a wedge action. The main portion of the chip presses behind the cutting edge and the extreme tip cleans up the rough surface caused by the tearing away of the chip. The cutting angle of a tool is usually referred to as the angle between the upper surface and a line at 90° to the surface of the work. This is called the *rake angle*, Fig. 214. In turning, the surface of the work may be taken as the tangent at the point of contact. With too steep a cutting rake the tip is weak, though less power is absorbed in cutting, and there is a tendency for the tool to dig into the work. With insufficient rake chatter marks may occur and a good surface finish is not obtained.

The type of metal being cut determines the cutting rake. Generally a steeper angle is used on the softer and more ductile materials and little or no rake for the harder metals and those of a brittle nature. The ability of a metal to shear also has an effect and, for cast iron and brass, from which the chips come away in small particles, less power is required to cut them and no cutting rake is given. The common cutting rake and clearance angles are given in Table 9. Furthermore, as the angle at which the cutting edge meets the work in turning is effected by both the traverse of the tool and the rotation of the work, the cutting angle of the tool is a composite angle formed by front to back and side rake angles, Fig. 214. The grinding of the tool tip in this way also assists in directing the chip flow away from the work.

Other angles to be considered are the clearance angles at the front and side of the tool. To give maximum support to the cutting edge, they are as small as will allow contact between the edge and the work, and in most cases are about 6° to 8°.

Cutting action is assisted and surface finish improved by the use of a liquid coolant. Cutting fluids take much of the heat generated away from the work and the tool, and prevent a dulling of the edge that occurs when a tool's temper is drawn. They also lubricate the tool and aid the passage of the swarf over it. When turning steel a coolant composed of a solution of about 12 parts water to 1 part soluble oil is suitable. On the larger machines the fluid is fed to the work by a pump, while on the basic training lathes it may be applied by drip can or brush. When applied by brush, care must be taken to ensure that the brush does not foul the tool tip and continuous lengths of swarf be prevented from making contact with the can. The free graphite in cast iron makes the use of a lubricant unnecessary and it is always machined dry; so is brass which generates little heat when machined. Also the chips produced by these materials are small and if allowed to mix with a liquid, would form an abrasive sludge which, being carried to normally inaccessible parts of the machine, could cause wear in slides, screws, etc.

Speeds and feeds The speed at which a lathe should be run for a particular operation depends on many factors. In the early stages of training, speeds will be lower than the optimum and the cuts lighter while confidence in the machine is being built up. Students should, however, be encouraged to calculate the ideal spindle speed for the type and size of material being cut. Tables of surface speeds are given in Table 9; to convert to spindle speeds the following formula is used:

$$\text{Spindle rev/min} = \frac{\text{cutting speed in m/min} \times 1000}{\pi \times \text{dia of work in mm}}$$

This figure is then used as a guide only, because other factors such as the rigidity and condition of the machine; the amount of support provided for both workpiece and tool; and the type of tool and cut must be taken into account.

174

Table 9. Cutting speeds and tool angles (H.S.S.)

Material	Cutting speed m/min	Rake angles	Clearance angles
Cast iron	18– 24	0°	6°
High Carbon steel	12– 18	10°	6°
Mild steel	24– 30	20°	8°
Brass	60–120	0°	10°
Aluminium	180–300	30°	10°

These factors may only be determined by experience. In the facing of large diameters, the ideal cutting speed cannot be maintained over the whole of the cut, for the surface speed of the work passing the tool varies with the diameter. The average speed, or that suited to the mid-diameter, should be used for finishing cuts, though for heavy cuts on large work the lathe must be stopped and the speed changed at intervals. Machines fitted with a variable speed drive have an advantage here.

Depths of cut and rate of feed are also best determined by experience. Heavy roughing cuts are usually taken at a moderate speed and with as fast a rate of feed as is consistent with the set-up and condition of the machine. Finishing cuts are taken at an increased speed and with a slower rate of feed to give a good surface finish. It is kinder to both tool and machine to take heavy cuts at a reduced speed than light cuts at high revolutions. Such points will be appreciated and observed when hand-feeds are used on the basic training lathes. As with all machine tools the automatic feed must be disengaged before the lathe spindle is stopped. In practice it is also disengaged slightly before the end of the cut and taken to its final position by hand. The sudden stopping of a machine with the pressure on the tool will cause the tool to dig into the work and its edge to chip or shatter. Similarly the tool must always be fed to rotating work; the lathe must not be started with tool and work in contact. The capabilities of a machine tool must be realised if it is to be worked efficiently. It is important therefore that students should see a lathe, of a type on which they are to work, working to capacity. A demonstration of a really heavy cut gives an insight into a machine's potentialities and supplements personal experience. Though the time factor is not by itself all important in the metalwork room, it must be taken into account if machines are to be used efficiently; correct speeds and feeds should therefore be employed.

Care and maintenance The care and maintenance of a machine is the responsibility of the person operating it. This must be realized from the beginning of training. Respect the machine as if it were your private property. Work or tools should never be laid on the lathe bed, or the slides allowed to become marked or damaged in any way, and at the end of a period the machine should be thoroughly cleaned and the slides, ways and all moving parts lubricated. The importance of such attention is emphasized when it is realized that backlash and play in the slides are caused by wear due to abrasion. Small particles of swarf mixed with oil or coolant fluid form an abrasive compound which can find its way into vital parts of the machine. A well maintained lathe will give good service and require little adjustment.

Provision is made whereby side play in the slides may be taken up by adjusting *gib strips* or plates. When adjusting a slide ensure that the gib makes contact throughout its length and that all screws are given equal tension and are firmly locked. Unfortunately wear does not occur evenly and a compromise must often be made between the tight and slack spots.

The headstock bearings are possibly the most important part of the machine as far as effects on finish and quality of work is concerned. Solid bearings-must be provided with a constant supply of lubricant while the spindle is in motion. Other types of bearings should be lubricated to the maker's instructions. The appropriate lathe handbook will give the method of adjustment of the headstock bearings.

A shear pin is usually fitted to a part of the leadscrew drive; this should be located and its method of replacement ascertained.

Lathework operations The initial turning exercise might very well be the turning of an irregular workpiece to circular form as in the making of a pair of simple washers from sheet metal, Fig. 215a. The washers are marked out, drilled and then sawn and roughly filed to shape on the bench. They are then held on the lathe by means of a screwed mandrel or spigot held in the chuck. Small cuts are taken until the work is round. The work, being held by friction, will slip if too much pressure is applied. This provides a suitable safe holding device for the preliminary exercise when it is important to gain confidence in operating the machine. The production of a cylindrical form is more easily seen than when simply reducing a diameter, and with a suitably shaped tool the side chamfers could also be produced to illustrate the use of a simple form tool.

The second exercise, Fig. 215b, might include the production of a flat surface on the end of a bar by facing and incorporate the setting of the tool to centre height. The need for the tool tip to pass the centre of the work is readily seen when facing to the centre of a bar. A sharp pip denotes that the tool is too low, while if a rounded pip is left, the tool is too high. With the work revolving, the tip of the tool is brought to the work face by the carriage. It is then withdrawn by the cross slide, the carriage locked to the bed and the tool advanced by the top slide to provide a suitable depth of cut. The cut is then taken by operating the cross slide, a constant and even tool motion being given to provide a good finish on the work. Both top and cross slides are fitted with micrometer dials usually graduated with 0·02 or 0·05 mm divisions. The dials should be used to gauge the depth of cuts from the beginning of the course.

To reduce the diameter of a portion of a round bar, first measure the bar and calculate the amount of metal to be removed. With the work held firmly, and rotating at suitable speed, the tool is advanced to just make contact with the work. It is then removed by the saddle, the dial set to zero and the tool advanced by the depth of cut decided upon. Using the roughing tool, take a single or a number of cuts to bring the work to within a few millimetres of its finished size.

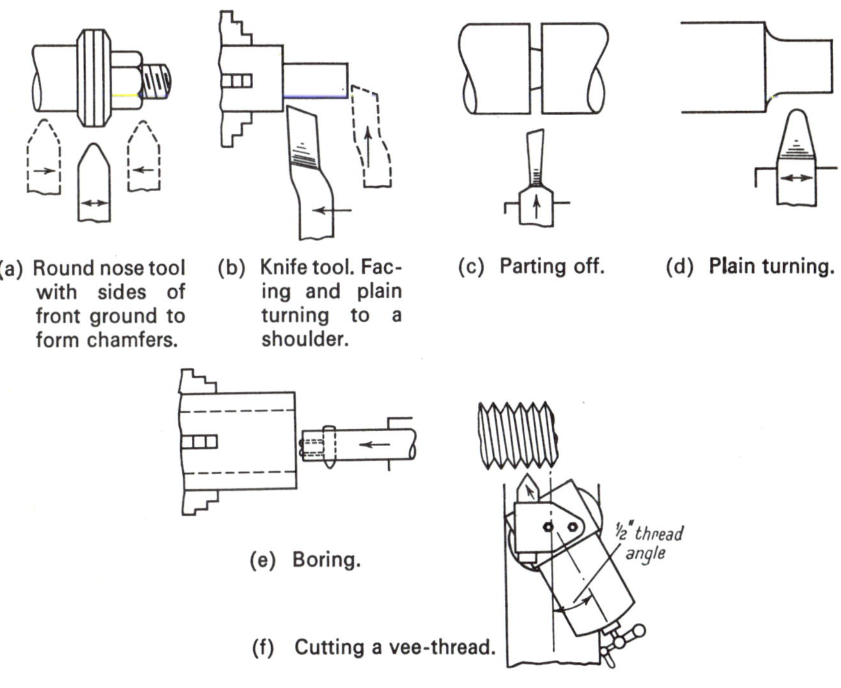

(a) Round nose tool with sides of front ground to form chamfers.

(b) Knife tool. Facing and plain turning to a shoulder.

(c) Parting off.

(d) Plain turning.

(e) Boring.

(f) Cutting a vee-thread.

Fig. 215. Turning operations.

In order to produce a square shoulder the finishing cut must be taken with a knife tool. At this stage, increase the spindle speed and traverse the tool slowly to produce a fine surface finish. Other basic turning operations are shown in Fig. 215 c–f.

The measurement of the work at this stage is done with calipers. As each cut is started so the work will be checked by stopping the lathe, adjusting the calipers and measuring from the end of the rule. An accuracy to within 0·1 mm is possible by these means, so the method is suitable for turning small spigots for riveting and screwthreads. For subsequent cuts, and particularly for the finishing cut, the tool will have to be adjusted to suit the readings obtained, though on a well maintained machine tool a student will learn to trust the dials and rapidly gain confidence in their use. Backlash does not enter into the calculations if the tool is moved only forwards and never back when readings are taken. The use of calipers in this way is a sounder method than setting them to the required diameter and frequently checking the work to see whether it conforms to what is, in effect, a set gauge. When so used there is a great temptation to test the work while it is revolving. This is dangerous practice and one that causes rapid wear of the caliper ends. The use of calipers to measure, rather than to test, is consistent with the method used with the micrometer at a later stage of the course. A good surface finish is to be demanded from the first turning exercises. No difficulty in this respect will arise if tools are correctly shaped and are sharp, and a free-cutting steel is used. A file is never used on cylindrical work and the use of emery cloth is to be discouraged.

Drilling operations are performed with the drill held in the tailstock. A centre drill is used to produce the centres in work that will later be located between the lathe centres and before drilling with a twist drill. The pilot portion of the smaller centre drill is rather delicate and care must be taken when introducing it to the work. The surface of the work must be flat, free from a pip at its centre and the drill frequently withdrawn and cleaned of its swarf. Similar withdrawing and cleaning is necessary when using twist drills. The shape of the drill point, cutting action and other drilling features are as for drilling in a drilling machine. With the work revolving and the drill stationary, however, there is less tendency for the drill to wander. Here accurate work is best drilled on a lathe whenever possible.

A further simple use of the tailstock is the location of a die or tap when starting a screwthread. The end of the tailstock sleeve is square with the axis of the lathe and a die held against it will be true with the work. A tap held in a drill chuck or located against the back centre will be square with a drilled or bored hole. The smaller dies may be held in a tailstock die-holder. When starting threads in this way the lathe motor is switched off and the chuck rotated by hand.

Tapers and conical forms may be produced on the lathe by four methods, Fig. 216. A straight edge of a tool may be set at the required angle and small chamfers and bevels formed by introducing it to the work. Short and steep tapers are generated by setting the compound slide rest at an angle to the bed and feeding the tool across the work with the top slide. Long and slow tapers may be cut under power feed by setting the tailstock out of line with the headstock, and positioning the work between centres. The use of a taper-turning attachment enables similar tapers to be cut without off-setting the tailstock. The attachment, Fig. 216d, is bolted to the rear of the bed and carries a slide which may be positioned at an angle to the bedways. The degree of the taper to be cut is shown by scales at either end. An extension arm is fitted to the cross slide and locates on a pivot above the slide. The cross slide is disengaged from its operating nut or, in some cases, the traverse screw is removed. Feed is given to the tool by the top slide which is set at 90° to the bedways. As the saddle is traversed so the cross slide and hence the tool is moved backwards or forwards and the tool tip traces a path parallel to that of the attachment slide. Preliminary checking of tapers may be made by measuring diameters at a set distance apart, but final determination of size demands the use of a gauge and testing with the aid of engineers' blue. In taper-turning the height of the tool must be at the dead centre height of the lathe or a true conical shape of the desired taper will not be generated.

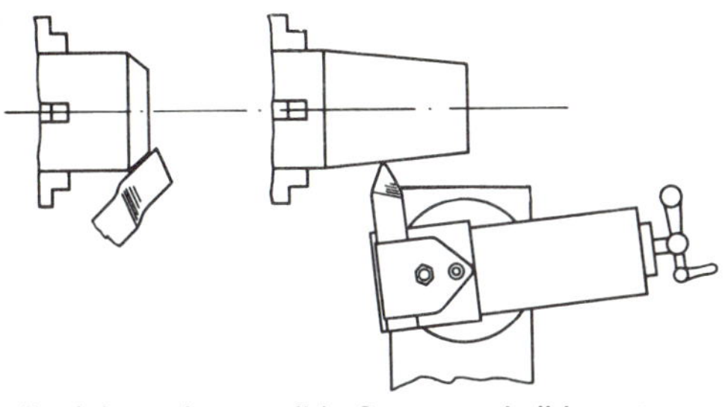

(a) Straight edge of tool forming a chamfer.

(b) Compound slide rest set at angle to bedways.

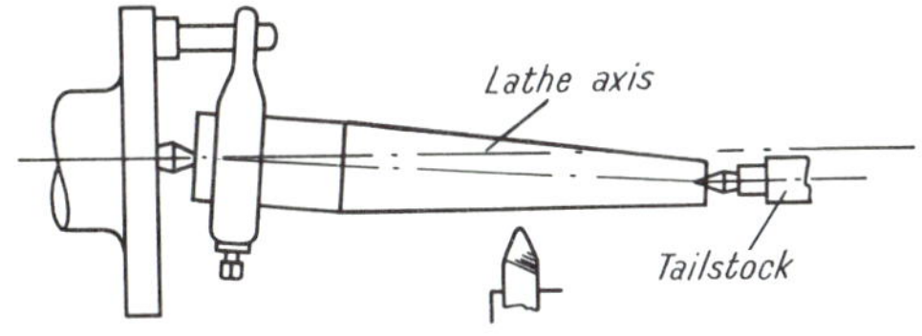

(c) Offset tailstock.

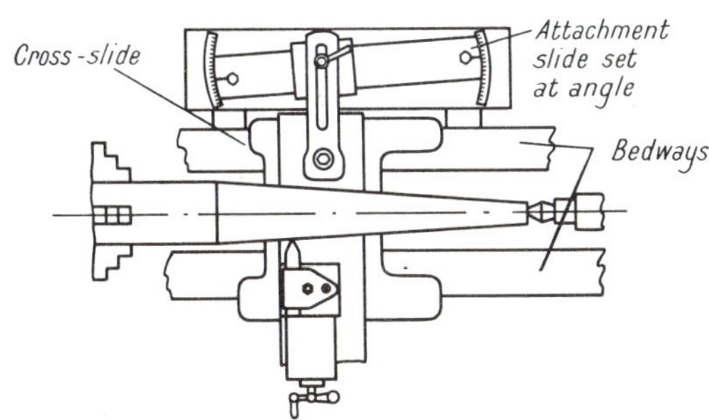

(d) Taper turning attachment.

Fig. 216. Methods of taper turning.

When the off-set tailstock method has been used, the tailstock must be re-positioned in order that parallel turning and accurate drilling operations may be resumed. This is best accomplished by the use of a test bar that has discs shrunk on to a mandrel, Fig. 206a. A light cut is taken over each disc, at the same setting of the cross slide, and the tailstock adjusted until both are of the same diameter.

Boring The turning of internal diameters, whether tapered or cylindrical, is undertaken by the use of a boring tool or small tool bit held in a boring bar, Fig. 217. The cutting angles are the same as for external turning except that a secondary clearance is necessary on the front of the tool. The bar is supported in a split square bar or on a vee block. As boring tools are more slender and their

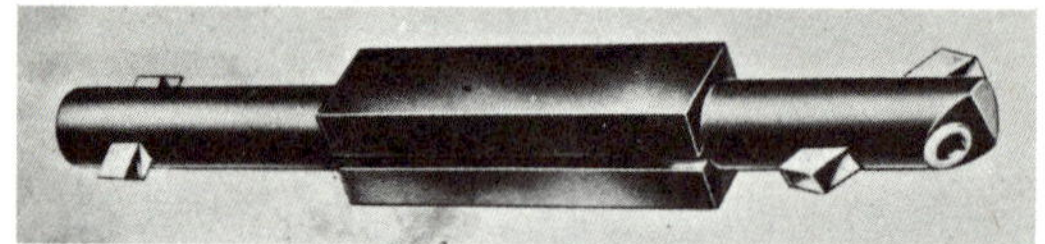

[*S. A. Jones & Shipman Ltd.*

Fig. 217. Boring bar.

tips less well supported than the external turning tools, lighter cuts must be taken, for there is danger of the tool springing and the bore becoming bell-mouthed. To alleviate this, final cuts are taken by passing the tool through the work a number of times at the same setting.

Knurling The raising of the surface of work and the forming of patterned grooves to provide finger grip may be performed by knurling. Two such patterns may be formed by the use of straight and diamond knurling tools, Fig. 218. Straight knurling tools have a single hardened-steel wheel with a milled edge, and those producing the diamond knurls have two wheels milled at opposing angles. In operation, the knurling tool is set at centre height and is then pressed

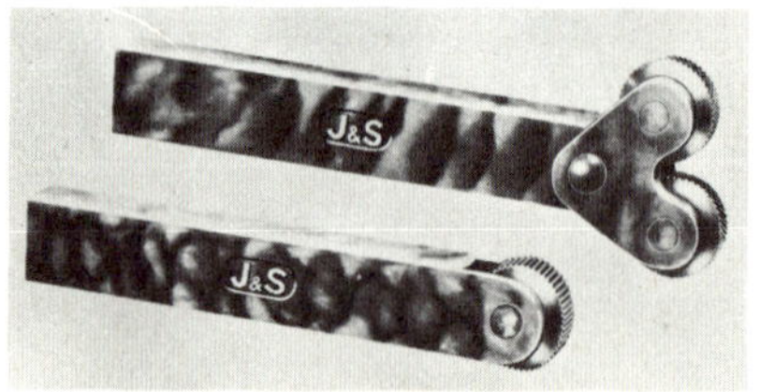

[*S. A. Jones & Shipman Ltd.*

Fig. 218. (*Above*) Diamond knurling tool.
(*Below*) Straight knurling tool.

into the revolving workpiece. If the wheels are not sharp and clean, considerable strain is put on the headstock bearings. Knurling tools having wheels that operate at opposite sides of the work are kinder to the machine in this respect. A common fault with diamond knurling is the tendency for the wheels to run out of synchronization, producing a pattern called 'cross knurling'. If this is seen to occur, check the tool for centre height, the alignment of the wheels with the work and then try a cut in a fresh spot. If cross knurling persists, remove the tool from the work and feed it in from the end, where the correct form is more easily achieved. The tool may then be traversed in both directions and pressure applied until a sharp peak is seen at the crest of each diamond. Knurling is performed at moderate speed and, as no cutting takes place, without lubricant.

Parting-off   Parting-off is an operation that can cause difficulty if there is play in the spindle bearings or the slides are slack and backlash is excessive. The tool used is comparatively thin and delicate, and care must be taken when feeding it into the work. The work should be parted as close to the headstock as possible and, as most parting tool breakages are caused by swarf becoming trapped between the tool and the sides of the groove, the operation is assisted if the tool is moved slightly from side to side as it is fed forward, hence cutting a groove a little wider than the tool. The front edge of the tool is bevelled in order that the work shall be cleanly parted and the remaining pip left on the piece in the chuck.

A good supply of coolant is necessary when parting steel to aid chip removal; also the speed of the work should be generally slower than for normal facing.

Form tools   The shaping of small radii may be accomplished by a synchronized hand movement of both saddle and cross feed. Accurate spherical shapes, however, demand the use of a form tool. As the area of the cut when using form tools is comparatively large, the speed of the work should be reduced and, in the later stages, fine scraping cuts should be taken. Form tools for the production of small radii on the ends of work can be incorporated with a parting tool, so parting off one piece and radiusing the next in one operation.

Screwcutting   In calculating the gear train to be used for the cutting of a particular screwthread, the pitch of the leadscrew must be taken into account. To cut a thread similar to that of the leadscrew, the spindle and leadscrew must turn in unison and the ratio between the stud wheel and the wheel on the leadscrew be 1:1. This may be expressed as

$$\frac{\text{pitch of thread to be cut}}{\text{pitch of leadscrew}} = \frac{1}{1} = \frac{\text{driving wheel}}{\text{driven wheel}}$$

being the formula used to determine the ratio and gear train for the cutting of all screwthreads on a lathe. In the chosen case any two similar wheels would do. If a thread of half the pitch of the leadscrew were to be cut the ratio would be 1:2 and a driving wheel of half the size of the leadscrew wheel would be used.

A set of about twelve changewheels are supplied with the average metric screwcutting lathe, ranging from wheels with 20 teeth to a wheel with 129 teeth. They proceed in steps of five or ten and there are some duplications. In the latter example a choice may be made from either 20:40; 40:80 or 60:120, since the ratio is not altered if both figures are multiplied by a common number. Such pairs of wheels will not engage when fitted to the fixed locations of the first stud and the leadscrew. Therefore a further intermediate wheel is fitted which may be of any size, because with simple trains, Fig. 219a, of this sort the ratio is not

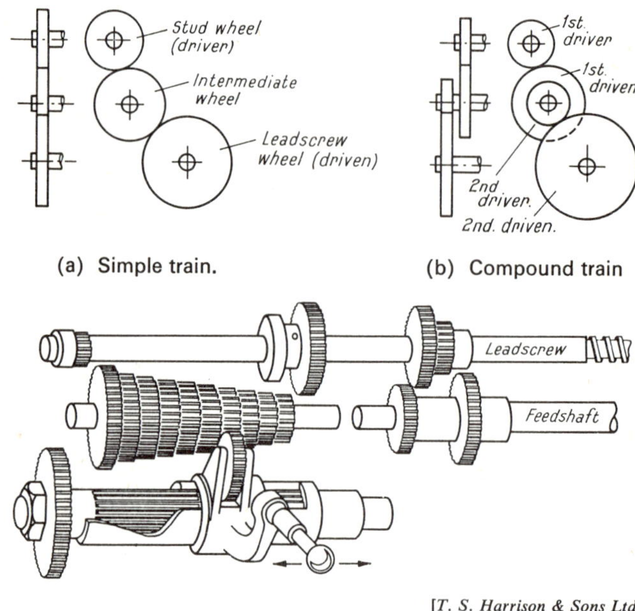

(a) Simple train.

(b) Compound train

(c) Norton gearbox.

Fig. 219.

altered thereby. The three wheels are then brought into mesh by means of the *quadrant plate*, Fig. 201a. Not all threads may be cut with simple trains, because of the limited space at the lathe end, and the need to restrict the number of change wheels supplied. For the cutting of such threads a compound train is used.

An example of a simple and a compound train is shown in Fig. 219. For compound trains the ratio is determined in the same way and then is divided into two ratios by factorizing. For example, to cut a screwthread of 0·45 mm pitch on a lathe with a 3 mm leadscrew the ratio will be 0·45:3. Multiplying by 20 to bring to whole numbers, 9:60 and again (as a nine-toothed wheel is not made) multiplying by 100, 900:6000. Expressing this ratio as a fraction and factorizing we obtain

$$\frac{\text{driving wheels}}{\text{driven wheels}} = \frac{900}{6000} = \frac{30 \times 30}{60 \times 100}$$

or, if two 30 wheels are not available,

$$\frac{20 \times 45}{60 \times 100}$$

A 20-toothed wheel as the first driver would be placed in mesh with a 60-toothed wheel, and a 45-toothed wheel as the second driver must engage with a 100-toothed second driven wheel, Fig. 219b.

Most modern screwcutting lathes incorporate a gearbox of the type shown in Fig. 219c which eliminates the necessity of setting-up changewheels. On lathes of this sort the various lever and arm positions for engaging the correct wheels are indicated on the machine.

Cutting metric screwthreads on an English lathe

The cutting of metric threads may be accomplished to a very close approximation on a lathe with an English leadscrew by employing a wheel of 127 teeth in the train. As there are approximately 25·4 mm in 1 in., there are 254 mm in 10 in. and hence 127 in a 5 in. length. The ratio 127:5 must therefore occur in the calculations of the gear train. The formula for finding the train for metric threads is:

$$\frac{5 \times \text{t.p.i. of leadscrew} \times \text{pitch to be cut in mm}}{127} = \frac{\text{Driving wheels}}{\text{Driven wheels}}$$

For example, to cut a screw having a pitch of 2·5 mm on a lathe with a leadscrew of 6 t.p.i., we have

$$\frac{5 \times 6 \times 2\cdot5}{127} = \frac{75}{127}$$

A simple train would be required with a 75 wheel driving a 127 wheel on the leadscrew through any intermediate wheel.

When fitting fresh change wheels, they must be clean, and those dismantled immediately covered or replaced in the cabinet. If swarf is allowed to get between the teeth, jamming and possible tooth breakage will result. After assembly, the chuck is pulled over by hand before the cover is replaced to ensure that the wheels revolve freely. During this checking they are lightly oiled. Play in the gears is automatically taken up when the leadscrew is engaged, hence the meshed gears should not be rigidly in contact. There should be a slight clearance between the teeth and also between the sides of adjacent gears. The saddle is made to engage with the leadscrew by the closing of the half nuts operated by the appropriate lever on the apron front. Successive cuts on a thread, however, must be made in line with each other and this is indicated by a rotating *chasing dial.* The chasing dial has a worm gear that engages with the leadscrew and has a pitch equal to, or a multiple of, the leadscrew pitch. Engagement can therefore be effected when both the spindle and the leadscrew have made a complete number of revolutions from the time of their last engagement. For the cutting of threads with the same pitch as the leadscrew, or multiples or sub-multiples of it, the saddle may be engaged in any position. For an even number of threads, engage the saddle when any dial graduation coincides with the datum line, and for any whole number of threads when any alternate line so registers. When cutting other threads the leadscrew may be engaged only when the original line on the dial is seen to be opposite the datum mark.

The shape of a screwcutting tool must correspond with the form of the thread being cut. The shape of the ISO metric and unified screwthreads is shown in Fig. 78a, p. 77. Side clearance must be provided on the leading edge at an angle greater than the helix angle of the thread being cut, and in order to strengthen the tip, less clearance is given on the trailing edge. The side edges of the top of square threading tools must be backed off slightly to prevent their becoming jammed in the groove. Although it is possible to grind the radius at the tip of a tool for cutting vee threads and hence give the correct form at the base of the thread, the crest radii cannot be shaped with a single point tool. Such threads are often left truncated, i.e. with flats at their peaks. In order to obtain true form throughout, they may be finished with a chasing tool. With the hand turning rest set up, or with a bar held in the toolpost, a chaser suited to the thread being cut is allowed to travel along the thread under slight hand pressure.

The setting up of tools for screwcutting demands more than the positioning of the tool at centre height. The shaped tool must also be square with the work. This is done with the aid of a thread angle gauge. In the cutting of deep vee-threads it is advantageous to set the compound slide rest in line with the trailing edge of the tool and to feed the tool in this direction. Cutting will therefore take place on one edge only and the swarf be readily cleared, leaving the work free from chatter marks.

The cutting of left-hand threads merely necessitates the reversing of the direction of rotation of the leadscrew by the tumbler gears and cutting from the headstock end of the bed towards the tailstock. To cut multistart threads, a single thread is first cut at the required lead and to the full depth. The tool position when the leadscrew is engaged, in relation to the work circumference, must then be altered to enable subsequent cuts to be taken. This may be accomplished in a number of ways. A simple method is to advance the tool parallel with the work by means of the compound slide rest, through an amount equal to the pitch of the thread. Some 2-start threads may be cut by engaging at different positions of the chasing dial. A more satisfactory method is possibly to rotate the work and spindle by half a revolution for a 2-start thread, 120° for a 3-start, etc., the leadscrew remaining stationary. This may be done by fitting a change wheel that has a number of teeth divisible by the number of thread starts, as the

184

first stud wheel of the gear train. Having cut the first thread, the wheel engaging with the stud wheel is removed, the contacting teeth of both being marked, and the spindle rotated the required amount by hand. The wheel is then replaced to engage with the next marked tooth of the stud wheel and the lathe is set for cutting the next thread, Fig. 220.

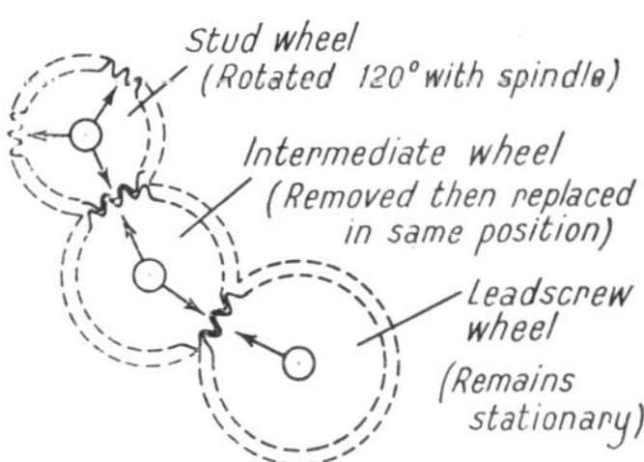

Fig. 220. Gear teeth marked for a 3-start thread.

Further lathework operations Work on the lathe can form a suitable introduction to the function of other workshop machines and in the absence of shaping and milling machines some operations normally carried out on them may, by the employment of attachments, be accomplished on the lathe. Small internal keyways may be cut by locking the headstock spindle and, with a boring tool placed on its side, traversing the saddle and taking cuts by hand, Fig. 221. Large castings that cannot be held on a face-plate may be bored by clamping them to the carriage or cross slide and passing a boring bar, held between centres, through them, Fig. 221b. With a fly cutter held in the headstock and the work passed across it by the cross slide, flat surfaces may be produced, Fig. 221c, and with end mills or woodruff cutters, similarly held, slots grooves and keyways may be cut, Fig. 221d.

Spinning Although metal spinning is best carried out on a special lathe capable of high speeds and with provision made to take the excessive end thrust imposed on the spindle bearings, light spinning in the softer metals, notably aluminium and copper, may be accomplished on the centre lathe. Spinning is the process employed for repeating shapes circular in plan by burnishing a disc of metal over a wooden former or chuck. The chuck is first turned from hardwood and screwed to the lathe spindle by means of a back plate. A wooden follower bears against the revolving centre in the tailstock and holds the disc in place. The disc is trued by slackening the follower a little while the work is revolving and pressing a strip of timber against the disc's rim. This operation can be rather dangerous and when spinning is done in schools it is better to indent the centre of the disc and locate it against a pip on the follower and a similar hollow in the chuck end. A tool of tempered and polished steel is then

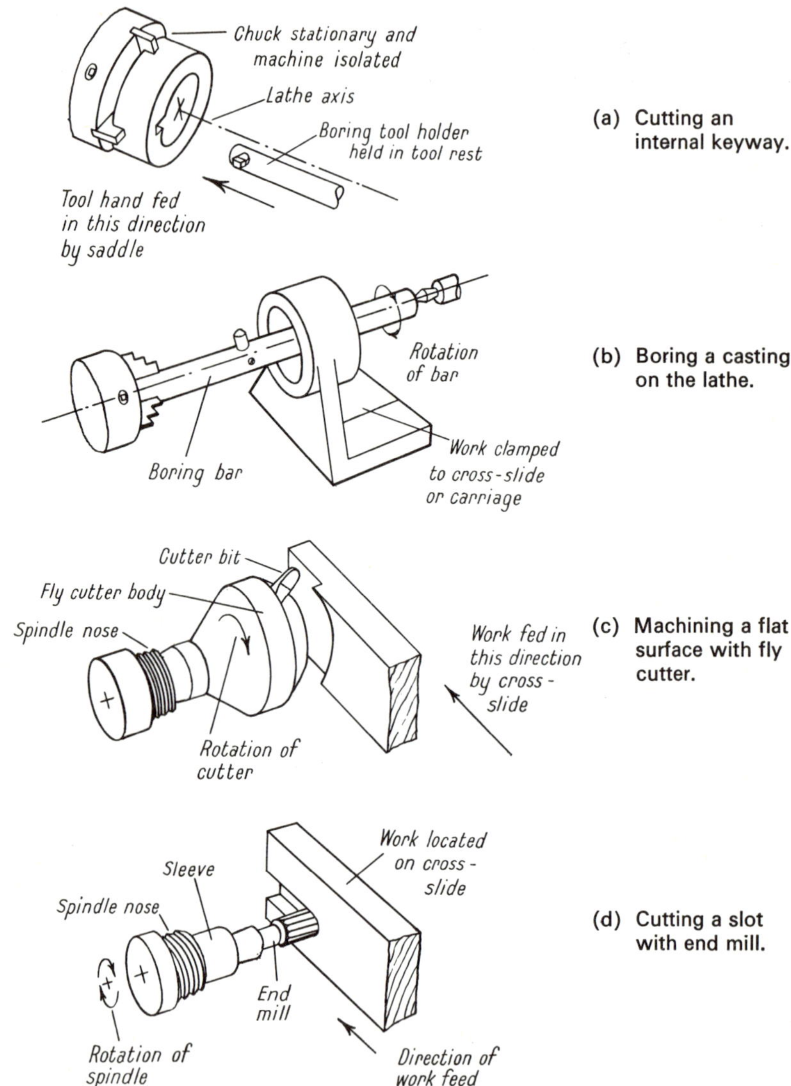

Fig. 221. Further lathework operations.

pressed against the surface of the metal to form the shape. The tool rests against a pin in the tool rest to give leverage for the considerable pressure required. A back stick is used in the early stages to prevent the edge buckling. The metal is annealed as required and the surface lubricated with tallow or grease. The edge of the final shape is trimmed by cutting away with a parting tool. Other tools may be used to decorate the surface with ribs, grooves or knurls.

12 Shaping

The shaping machine   The shaping machine is used mainly for the production of flat surfaces, vee-grooves, vee-slides and keyways. Machines are designated by the length of their stroke.

Illustrated in Fig. 222 is a shaping machine which is the common type of *crank shaper*. It has a solid massive body casting, the vertical face of which is machined to take the saddle. This saddle may be raised and lowered and is supported at its

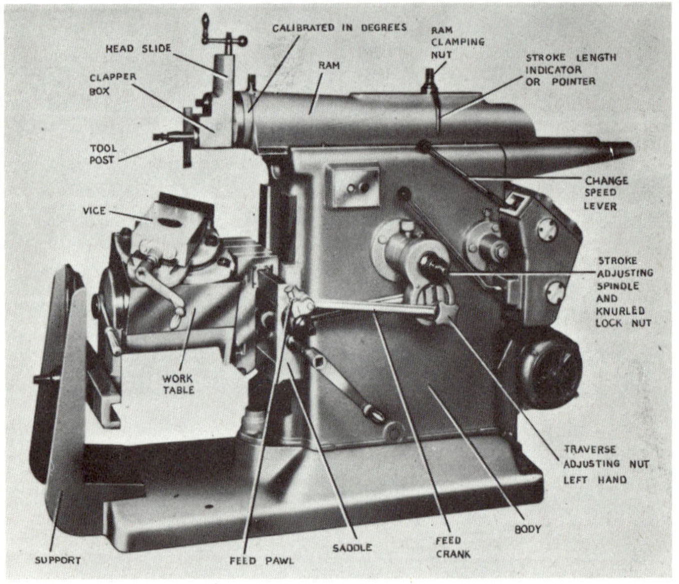

[*Newey Engineering Co. Ltd.*

Fig. 222. Shaping machine.

front end. Secured to the saddle by slideways is the worktable which carries the vice; this worktable may be traversed sideways automatically or by hand. On more expensive machines the worktable is compound, Fig. 223, and may be turned to angles other than the horizontal, and on some machines may also be tilted. The top surface of the body casting has slideways for the *ram*; these slideways are at right-angles to those for the worktable. To the front end of the ram

188

is fitted a toolpost, and the stroke of the ram may be adjusted to any length between zero and its maximum capacity. In addition to altering its length the position of the stroke may also be adjusted by releasing the nut on top of the ram. The tool-holder is fitted to a clapper-box which allows the tool to lift on the return stroke and to a certain extent reduces wear on the tool. The clapper-box may also be turned and set at angles other than the vertical. The whole tool-holder is fitted to a slide which may be set vertical or tilted accurately to any required angle. The travel of the slide is limited and usually operated manually although attachments for automatic downfeed may be fitted. The travel of the slide is used to set the amount of cut and the calibrated dial permits this to be done accurately.

[*Newey Engineering Co. Ltd.*
Fig. 223. Compound table shown turned.

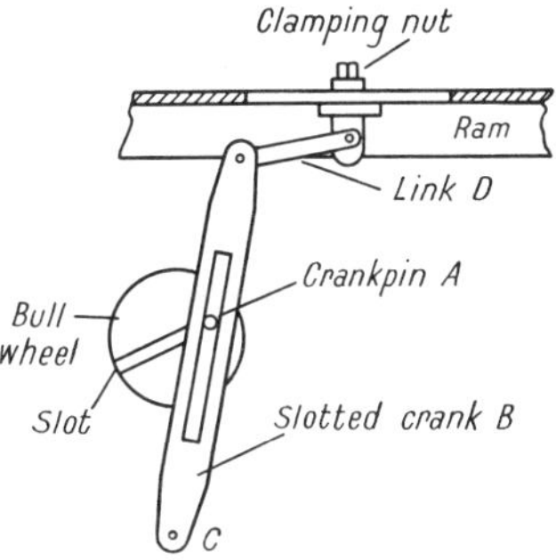

Fig. 224. Shaper driving mechanism.

Driving mechanism   The driving mechanism, Fig. 224, of the shaper is provided by a crank pin *A*, travelling in a circular path, secured at one end into a slot in the *bullwheel* and sliding in a slotted crank *B* at the other. The slotted crank oscillates about one end *C*, the other end being connected to the ram by an intermediate link *D*. The intermediate link is necessary to accommodate the rise and fall of the crank. On some shapers the intermediate link is dispensed with and the bottom end of the crank, Fig. 225 is slotted and slides up and down over its bearing. The position of the crank pin in the slot in the bullwheel decides the length of the stroke of the shaper. The further it is away from the centre the longer the stroke. This is shown diagrammatically in Fig. 226 and it will readily be seen from this that the idle return stroke is quicker than the forward cutting stroke.

Shaper speeds are usually given in strokes per minute and are arranged by means of a gearbox connected directly to a pinion which drives the bullwheel.

It must be appreciated that for each setting of the gearbox the cutting speed is increased as the stroke is increased, and that in order to arrive at the correct speed in metres per minute the stroke must be set first and the gearbox speed decided later. The experienced operator will not need to work this out mathematically; he will know when the speed is correct having regard to all the other factors—material, rigidity and security of the job.

The automatic cross-feed of the table is operated through the *crank*, Fig. 222. One end of the crank is fitted into the rotating slot and may be fixed at any point in the slot by means of the left-hand threaded nut. The further from the centre of the slot the crank is fixed, the longer will be its travel and the coarser the feed. At the other end, the crank operates a pawl in a toothed wheel which is keyed

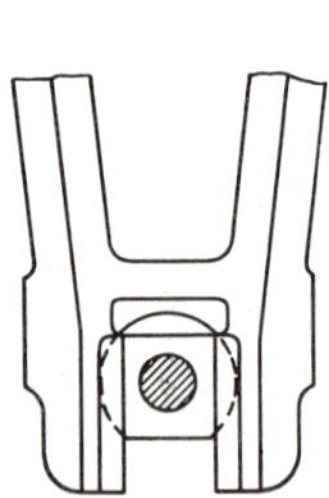

Fig. 225. Detail of crank bottom
when intermediate link is
dispensed with.

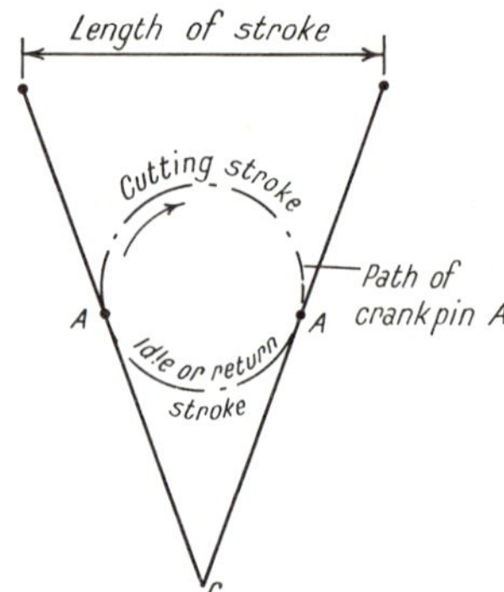

Fig. 226.

or pinned to the cross traverse shaft. The pawl may be lifted clear of the toothed wheel or engaged so that the shaft travels in either direction. These traverses usually operate more efficiently when the tool is cutting; if there is any end play in the shaft it merely rocks backwards and forwards. Any end play can usually be taken up by means of a nut and lock nut. Care must be taken not to let the traverse overrun or the nut may be stripped.

Tools used on the shaper are the same shape as lathe tools but are usually deeper and consequently stiffer. Special tool bit holders for shapers are made, Fig. 227, having a turret head for conveniently setting the tool at an angle.

Preparation of shaper for use When a new shaper is first used there are a number of preparations to make. Usually the calibration in degrees on the head slide needs to be 'zeroed'. This is done after the machine has been set level. An angle plate is bolted to the top of the worktable and a dial gauge fitted in the tool-holder. Adjust the head slide until the dial gauge reading is the same all the way up the angle plate, lock in position, check again, and then carefully mark across the zero mark on the slide to the machined portion of the casting on the end of the ram.

In the main body casting immediately below the ram is a large hollow. This is in the front and back of the casting and it is arranged to accommodate large shafts in which keyways have to be cut. Unfortunately this hollow leaves the bullwheel unprotected and it can collect a lot of swarf. If the bullwheel really gets loaded it rides on the pinion and if there is any play in the ram it vibrates vertically and the pattern of the bullwheel is transmitted to the work. To prevent this, a cover is fitted over the opening as shown in Fig. 228; this may readily be removed when the space is required to accommodate work.

The bevel wheels, which raise and lower the worktable, must also be protected against the swarf. Swarf can fall on to the bevel gears from the back of the worktable, and they can become so loaded that the movement is completely jammed. The simple cover, illustrated in Fig. 228, will prevent this without interfering with the operation of the gears.

Holding the work The methods of holding work are in many respects very similar to those employed on the milling machine. Shaper vices are usually larger in capacity than milling machine vices and are almost always of the swivelling type, and aligned by tenons or spigots on the underside. Use as large a vice as the worktable permits and if rough castings are to be held, protect the vice cheeks by means of suitable hardboard strips. Normally the vice jaws would be at right-angles to the ram, as this permits a safer grip, but on occasions they will have to be in line or indeed at any angle. If the vice is not adequate, then castings may be bolted direct to the worktable on its top face or sides, and box angle plates, angle plates and tilting tables may be used to assist when necessary. If the size of the table is inadequate then it may be enlarged by fitting angle plates to the sides as shown in Fig. 229. If a shaper is old and its accuracy suspect it is usual to fasten strips down to the worktable, machine these flat and then clamp on top of them. If the job is turned over and kept on these strips perfectly parallel faces will be the result. If the table is a long way out of truth, adjust carefully all slides and take as light a skim as possible off the top of the table. This of course must not be done too often, and indeed only when absolutely necessary.

Where time is limited work may be scrapped and time wasted by repeated setting and resetting. This can be avoided by using *auxiliary tables*, which are merely suitable slabs of cast iron spigoted and bolted to the worktable, and the work in turn bolted to the auxiliary table. Thus the job, complete with auxiliary table can be removed and replaced in a matter of minutes.

If the worktable is of the swivelling type, care must be taken to reset very carefully if, for any reason, it is disturbed from the horizontal.

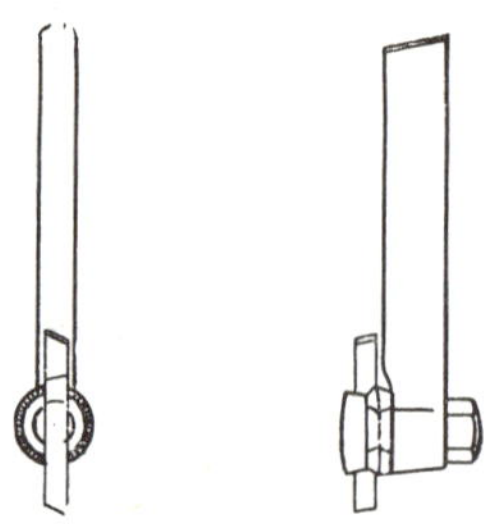

Fig. 227. Shaper tool holder with turret lead.

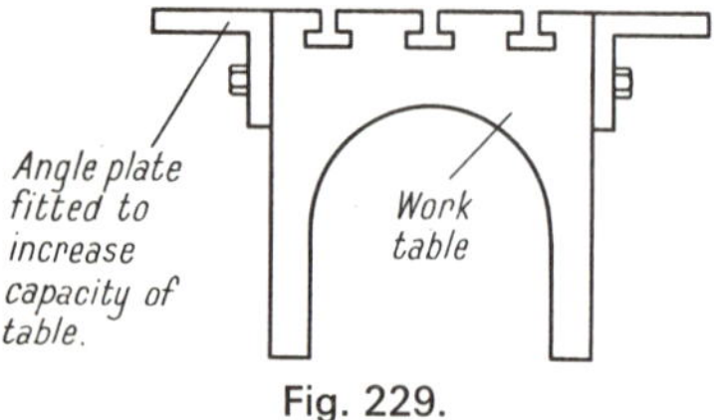

Fig. 229.

Fig. 228.

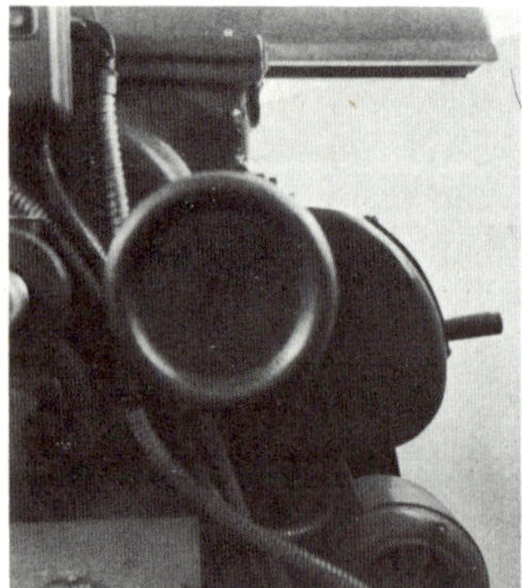

[Newey Engineering Co. Ltd.

Fig. 230. Shaper. Note handwheel for turning machine over by hand.

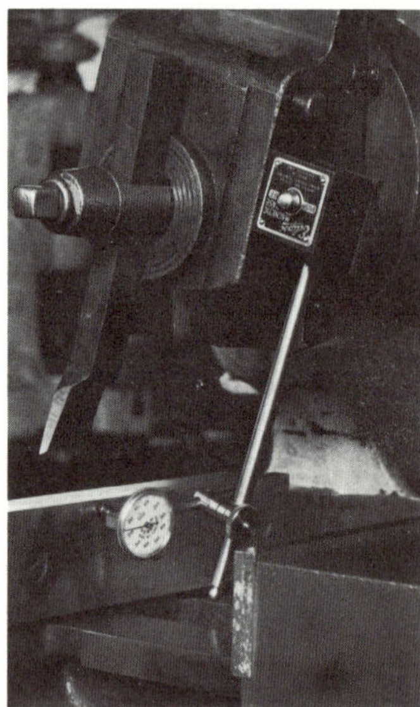

[James Neill & Co. (Sheffield) Ltd.

Fig. 231. Setting vice in line using dial gauge with magnetic base.

Precautions when using the machine   Once installed, machine tools have to last a long time so use them carefully. The shaper is no exception to this and there are a few simple precautions to be observed.

First, the top of the work must always be just below the bottom of the ram—avoid screwing down the tool head to reach the work. Before starting the machine, whether there is work in or not, bend down and sight over the vice to the ram, to make sure nothing is going to foul the main body casting. If the machine is fitted with a handwheel then turn it over by hand after each new setting. It is an excellent habit always to pull all machines round by hand before starting. When working down a deep vertical face pull round at the top and bottom of the job, to ensure that the tool slide will not foul in its extreme position. When working down a vertical face the tool and clapper-box is tilted towards the face to be cut, as shown in Fig. 232; this gives a clearance for the tool on the return stroke. When the clapper-box or the complete head slide is tilted, they will not pass between the ram slideways but will hit the main casting. This is most dangerous,

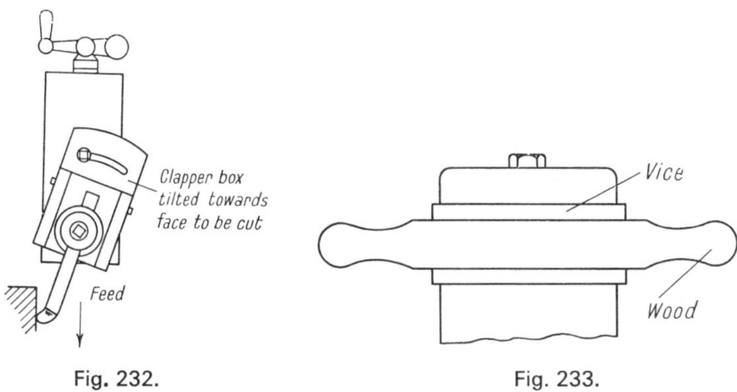

Fig. 232.   Fig. 233.

and if allowed to happen, the head slide will most certainly be broken off and the main casting damaged. The complete head slide needs to be tilted when cutting vee-slides, and the clapper-box tilted even further. If the toolpost is kept screwed up and the work kept as high as possible the danger of the toolpost fouling the main casting is considerably reduced, but the danger is always present and clearance must be carefully checked. When adjusting the height of the worktable, do slacken off the support at the front of the box or the lifting screw and bevel gears may be strained. When finally setting this support, the worktable must be central on its slides and fully over the support. If the table and the support are not in line the latter may be tilted, and when the traverse is started, the table will have to climb the knee slide and will eventually jam. Some part of the traverse mechanism will then be strained. Try to arrange the work in the centre of the table and not too near the front, so that the ram can operate as fully supported as possible.

One precaution operators must always take to avoid personal injury is to press down when tightening or slackening the tool-holder. It is dangerous to lift, as this lifts the clapper-box and the fingers may be trapped between the tool and the work.

Shaper vices are very heavy and awkward to lift and are usually greasy. To assist in lifting them, fix a substantial piece of wood, as shown in Fig. 233, tightly between the jaws; this provides a safe hand hold.

When machining mild steel, the swarf flies and is a nuisance when trodden underfoot. The tray illustrated, Fig. 234; is very useful for collecting swarf and keeps the area round the machine tidy.

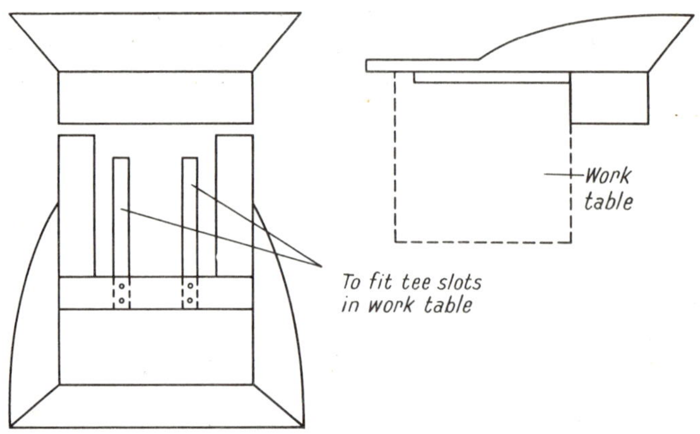

Fig. 234. Sheet metal shaper tray.

Setting the stroke   There is a definite routine for setting the stroke; it is not arrived at by hit-and miss methods. First measure the job and decide the length of stroke required; then turn the shaper, whatever its setting, to the back of the stroke. Next slacken the knurled lock nut, Fig. 222, and using the crank handle turn the spindle clockwise to increase, and anticlockwise to decrease, until the required stroke is obtained. The pointer will indicate on the scale when the desired length is arrived at. Finally set the position of the stroke. To do this, first bring the tool to the front or back of the job, whichever is more convenient, then slacken the clamping nut on top of the ram. Turn the handwheel until the pointer is at the back or front, in which ever position the tool was arranged, and finally tighten the nut on top. The stroke of the machine is always a little longer than the job and the majority of the spare length is arranged at the back of the stroke in order to give the clapper-box time to settle down before commencing the next stroke. A few shapers are so calibrated that the stroke is increased by turning anticlockwise and decreased by turning clockwise. If a shaper is so arranged it will be obvious by the direction in which the stroke-length indicating scale is calibrated, to the back or to the front of the shaper.

13 Milling and Milling Machines

The process of milling consists of passing the work against a revolving cutter, and we saw, in Chapter 11, how simple operations of this sort may be accomplished on the lathe. There are some machining operations, however, that cannot be done on the lathe, versatile though it is, and others, which though within the scope of the lathe and its attachments, are more conveniently performed on a separate machine tool.

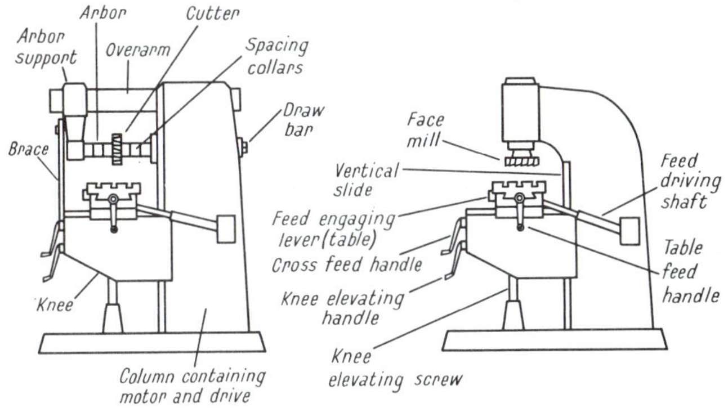

(a) Plain horizontal milling machine.

(b) Plain vertical milling machine.

Fig. 235. Knee type milling machines.

The milling machine of a century ago was adapted directly from the lathe and milling machines with a bed similar to that of a lathe, known as Lincoln Type milling machines, are still used for some specific types of milling operations and make possible the rapid production of identical parts. The milling machines found in the metalwork room, however, are usually of the *knee type*, in which a heavy column, with a vertical slide, carries a knee which may be raised or lowered against a cutter revolving above it. There are two basic types: the *horizontal milling machine*, in which the cutter is located on a horizontal *arbor*, and the *vertical milling machine*, in which the cutter is located at the end of a vertical spindle (Fig. 235). The two types differ only with respect to their drive and spindle positions, the column, knee, slides and table being similar in each case. Where one milling machine only is to be installed, a plain horizontal machine with a separate vertical head attachment will enable the range of work discussed to be covered. Separate machines would possibly make the machining of larger work possible and save time in setting up the head for vertical milling.

The knee may be raised or lowered by means of a handwheel working through a shaft, bevel wheel and screw. The upper surface of the knee carries a slide operated by a handwheel at the front of the machine and upon this is the table, given longitudinal movement by further handwheels at either end. In this way work fastened to the table may be moved in all three directions and, as the operating screws carry micrometer dials reading usually to 0·02 mm, work may be positioned accurately in relation to the cutter. On the plain milling machines, power feed is available in the longitudinal direction only, for most cutting operations are performed in this way. The automatic feed operating lever is positioned on the front of the table and can be disengaged at the end of a cut by positioning the knock-off screw in its slot on the table side.

Horizontal milling machines   On the horizontal milling machine, the cutter is held on an arbor, which receives its drive from the spindle located in the column at 90° to the vertical slide. The main spindle is driven by the motor through a belt driven over cone pulleys or through a gearbox. The front of the spindle has a tapered socket into which the arbor fits, motion being transmitted through driving dogs, and the arbor being retained by a drawbolt through the spindle. The front end of the arbor is supported by the bearing of a support located on the overarm. The cutter itself is positioned on the arbor, and clamped firmly to it by spacing collars and a nut. In most cases the friction of the collars against the side of the cutter is sufficient to prevent it slipping, though for heavy loading, and when using thin slitting saws, the drive may be transmitted to the cutter by a key, acting in keyways on the arbor and in the cutter bore.

The efficiency of milling operations depends very much on the accuracy and alignment of the arbor and care must be taken to ensure its correct location in the spindle. Before fitting, the arbor shank and spindle socket are cleaned, and the arbor driven in sharply with the driving dogs in the correct position. Most milling machines have an arbor-ejecting device, which usually consists of a nut acting against an arbor or draw bar shoulder, and may be positioned at the front or rear of the machine. This nut must be in its inoperative position before the draw bar is finally tightened.

In fitting cutters to the arbor, certain precautions should be adopted. At no time should a spanner be placed on the arbor nut when the support is not in position, for if the arbor is pulled only slightly out of line, the cutter will run eccentrically and the efficiency of the machine be seriously reduced. Cutters are positioned as near the column of the machine as is consistent with the work being done, and a suitable set of spacing collars is fitted to cover the first two or three threads of the arbor. Both bores and faces of cutter and collars must be clean. Dirt trapped between the faces will reduce the clamping friction by which the cutter is driven and could cause the cutter to run out of line or, in the case

196

of a slotting cutter, to cut a groove greater than its nominal width. The procedure is to fit cutter and spacing collars, and then replace the nut, finger-tight only. The arbor support is then located and locked, and the nut finally tightened with the key or spanner.

Work on the horizontal milling machine is not restricted to the use of cutters positioned on the arbor. Face mills may be located directly in the spindle socket and end mills also by the use of suitable sleeves or adapters, Fig. 236. Holes may be drilled in work, and boring be accomplished, if a boring bar is made to replace the arbor.

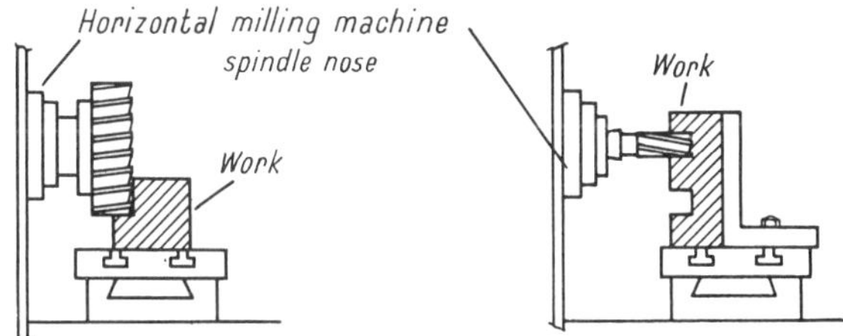

Fig. 236. Face and end mills on horizontal milling machine.

Vertical milling machines In the vertical milling machine, or the plain horizontal type fitted with a vertical head, the spindle rotates about a vertical axis, through a drive and spindle mounted above the table. The cutter is located in the end of the spindle either directly by means of its tapered shank and a draw bar, or it is held in a special chuck. In this respect the vertical milling machine resembles a drilling machine, but with the slides below the cutter, enabling work to be brought to and moved against the cutter while it rotates in its fixed location. The head may also be set at an angle to the vertical to enable faces to be machined at an angle to the table. Work done on the vertical milling machine is normally of a lighter and more delicate nature, for, with the exception of the face and some shell end mills, the cutters used are smaller and less rigidly held than their counterparts on the horizontal machine. However, a great variety of work not conveniently performed on the horizontal machine may be undertaken, and in the metalwork room recessing, the cutting of keyways, grooves, tee and dovetail slots and slides will be performed on milling machines of the vertical type.

Milling cutters Milling cutters may for convenience be divided into three main types. *Plain cutters* are used on the horizontal milling machine for the production of flat surfaces and may include those that cut on their sides as well as on their periphery. *Face mills* cut mainly on their face and would include end mills and those normally used on the vertical machine. *Form cutters* do not generate flat surfaces; they include radiusing and gear cutters and the like.

Cylindrical slab cutters Of the plain milling cutters, the *slab cutter* is used to machine wide areas of metal to flat plain surfaces, Fig. 237. The *helical* or *spiral mill* is the more common, for the helix of the cutter tooth distributes the load evenly during the whole of the cutting operation and ensures a good finish and an absence of chatter marks that would otherwise result from the uneven loading given by straight teeth. Helical teeth have a slicing action that is conducive to

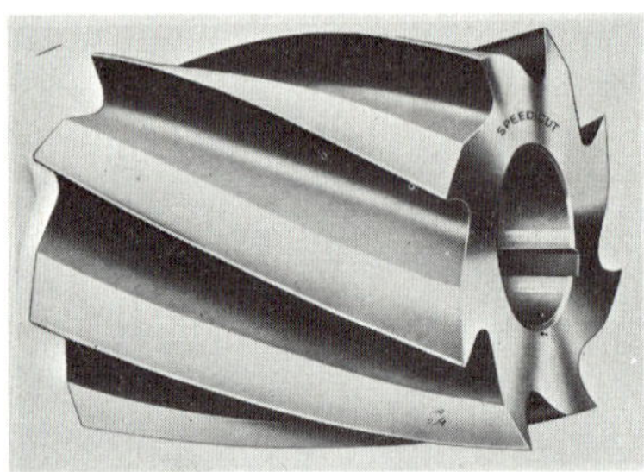

[*Firth Brown Tools Ltd.*

Fig. 237. Plain cylindrical slab cutter.

smooth cutting. The long chips so produced tend to be carried around with the cutter. To break them into smaller pieces, so aiding their removal, such cutters are frequently gashed, the gashes being staggered so as not to affect the surface finish of the work.

Side and face cutters, as their name implies, have cutting edges both on their sides and on their periphery, Fig. 238. They are used for surfacing narrow work

(a) Straight teeth.

[*Firth Brown Tools Ltd.*

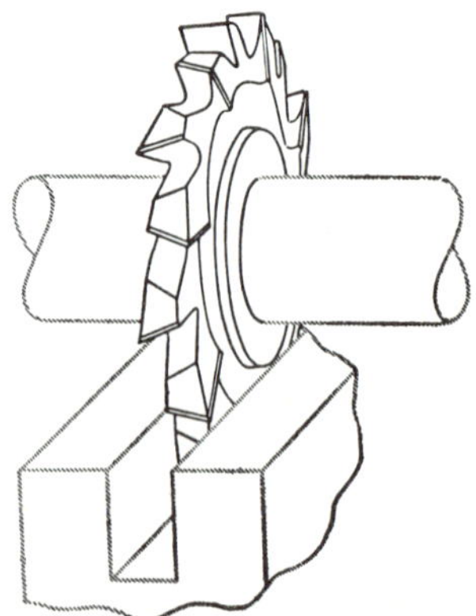

(b) Staggered tooth.

[*S. A. Jones & Shipman Ltd.*

Fig. 238. Side and face cutters.

and for machining vertical and horizontal faces at one time. They can usefully be employed in cutting grooves of greater width than the cutter but, as the side teeth are ground during sharpening, they cannot be relied upon to machine an accurate slot. Two side and face cutters, separated by spacing collars of the required dimensions, may be used to produce parallel work in one cut. Such an operation is called *straddle milling*, Fig. 239a. When more cutters are used and work is machined on a number of faces, the operation is termed *gang milling*, Fig. 239b.

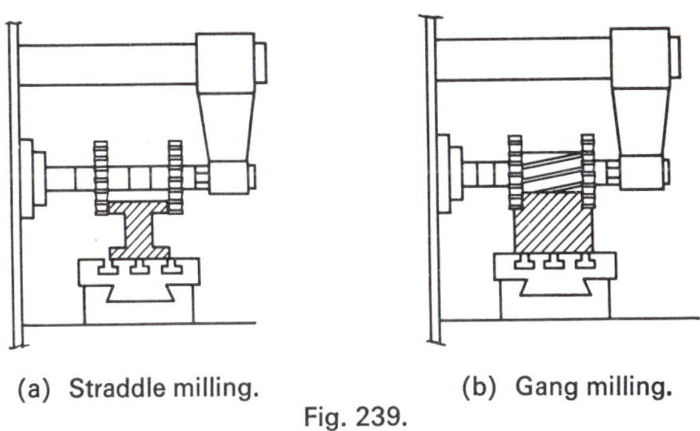

(a) Straddle milling.   (b) Gang milling.

Fig. 239.

It will be appreciated that side and face cutters having straight teeth on the face will have no cutting rake on the side teeth. To improve their cutting action, many such cutters have their face teeth cut at an angle. This produces a positive rake on one side and a negative rake on the other. Cutters for general purpose work therefore are best if of the staggered tooth type, Fig. 238b, having positive rake on both sides on alternate teeth.

Slotting cutters are used to produce accurate slots in work. Having teeth only on their external diameters, the sides are slightly concave, or dished, above the tooth depth, so that sharpening will not affect the width, Fig. 240a.

Slitting saws, similar in form to the slotting cutters, are larger in diameter in relation to their width, Fig. 240b. They may be used for the narrower slots, although their main function is in the sawing or slitting of metal, and, as they are frequently used on thin material, they have teeth of small pitch. In the selection of slitting saws, the pitch of the tooth in relation to the gauge of metal being cut can be considered to be similar to that of the choice of hacksaw blade when cutting sheet metal, i.e. two or more teeth should be in contact with the work at any one time. The thinner slitting saws are rather delicate and, in parting heavy stock, a wider and more robust cutter will be found to be more economical than a very fine one.

Angle cutters provide a convenient way of machining small vee-grooves and faces at the common angles without complicated setting up of the work. They may be single- or double-angled, Fig. 241. Single-angle cutters are measured by

(a) Slotting cutter.

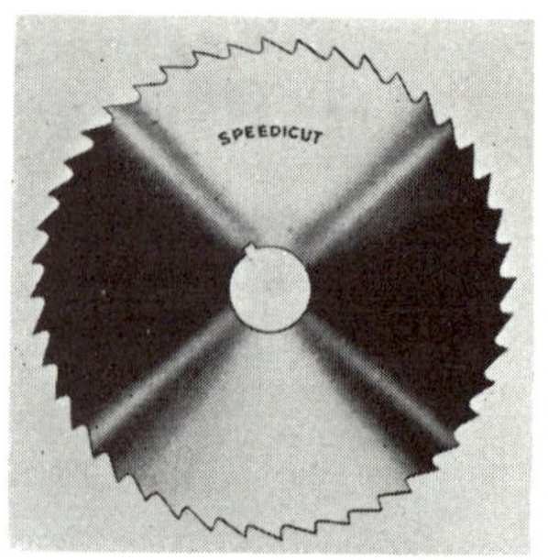

(b) Slitting saw.

[*Firth Brown Tools Ltd.*

Fig. 240.

(a) Single-angle cutter.

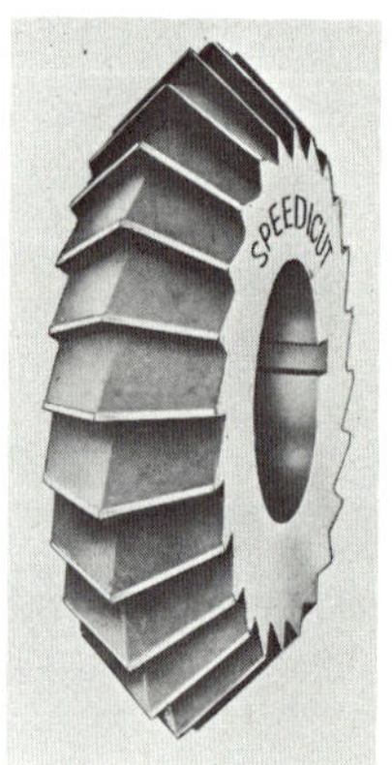

(b) Double-angle cutter.

[*Firth Brown Tools Ltd.*

Fig. 241.

the angle between the cutting faces and may be right- or left-handed. Double-angle cutters that are symmetrical are similarly designated, and those of unequal angles are measured separately from a line perpendicular to the bore to the point of greatest circumference. The unequal double-angle cutters are normally used for special production work but 45° single-angle and 90° double-angle cutters have many applications in the metalwork room.

The point at which the cutting faces meet is weak and will dull and wear rapidly unless care is taken. When cutting a vee-groove, a preliminary cut to the near depth of the groove should first be made with a slotting cutter before introducing an angle cutter to the work.

Face mills The simple *fly cutter* may be considered as an elementary form of face mill. A plane surface is generated by the sweep of the tool through an arc over the surface of work, moving in a straight line against it. The larger face mills are usually of the inserted tooth type, with cutting bits of tool steel or cemented carbide located in a mild or medium carbon steel body. The bits are held in position by tapered pins or wedges or some similar device. This arrangement is not only initially more economical but facilitates maintenance and the replacement of teeth.

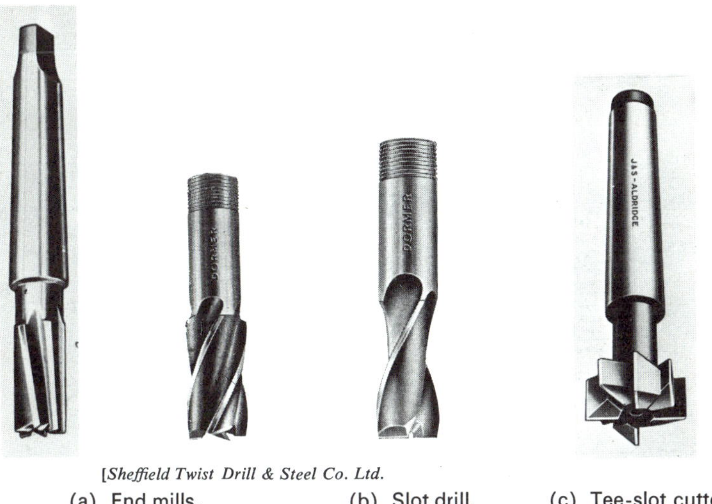

[*Sheffield Twist Drill & Steel Co. Ltd.*

(a) End mills.   (b) Slot drill.   (c) Tee-slot cutter.

Fig. 242.

Face mills may be located directly in the spindle of a horizontal milling machine and cut a vertical plane surface, Fig. 236. More usually they are used on a vertical machine and cut in the horizontal plane.

End mills are similar in action to face mills although on a much smaller scale, Fig. 242a. The shank is integral with the cutting body and may be tapered, plain or threaded to fit a special chuck. The teeth on the sides may be parallel with the cutter axis or have a right- or left-hand helix. The normal range of end mills have right-hand helices and give a positive rake when cutting in the normal 'up-cut' manner. Side rake is also provided on the side teeth.

Shell end mills The larger end mills are usually of the shell type, Fig. 243a. The cutter is bored and recessed and is held on a stub arbor, Fig. 243b, of less expensive material. The rear face of the cutter contains a groove or key-slot by which it is driven, and the stub arbor has an internal thread which takes the fixing screw.

Slot drills   End mills can be used only from the edge of work or from previously prepared holes. Slot drills, on the other hand, have but two cutting teeth on their ends and side. The end teeth, reaching to the centre of the cutter, enable it to be sunk directly into the metal. The large flutes of the slot drill also aid swarf disposal. Slot drills will produce an accurate groove equal to the drill diameter, Fig. 242b.

(a) Shell end mill.

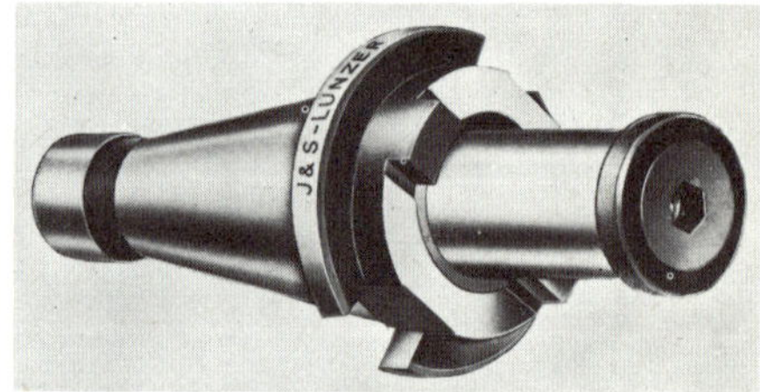

(b) Stub arbor.

[*S. A. Jones & Shipman Ltd.*

Fig. 243.

Tee-slot cutters, Fig. 242c, are used to undercut tee-slots after the central groove has been made with a slotting cutter or slot drill. Similarly shaped cutters are used to cut the ways for woodruff keys.

Many other specially shaped end mills are available and of these the *dovetail cutter* will be found useful for the shaping of machine slides, Fig. 244. Being rather fragile, cutters of this type should not be required to remove large amounts of material. In general, the more delicate end mills should be used for finishing cuts after the majority of the metal has been removed by more robust cutters or on other machine tools. The life of milling cutters and the amount of useful work they will do between regrinds depends very much on the way they are used. The choice of cutter for a particular job depends on many factors, but by careful planning of the whole job cutters will be used only for those operations to which they are most suited, and will then give excellent service.

Form cutters are made in a great variety of shapes for specific purposes, but those in common use in the metalwork room would normally be restricted to concave and possibly convex cutters and to the involute form cutters used for cutting gear teeth, Fig. 245. The clearance to the cutting edges of form cutters

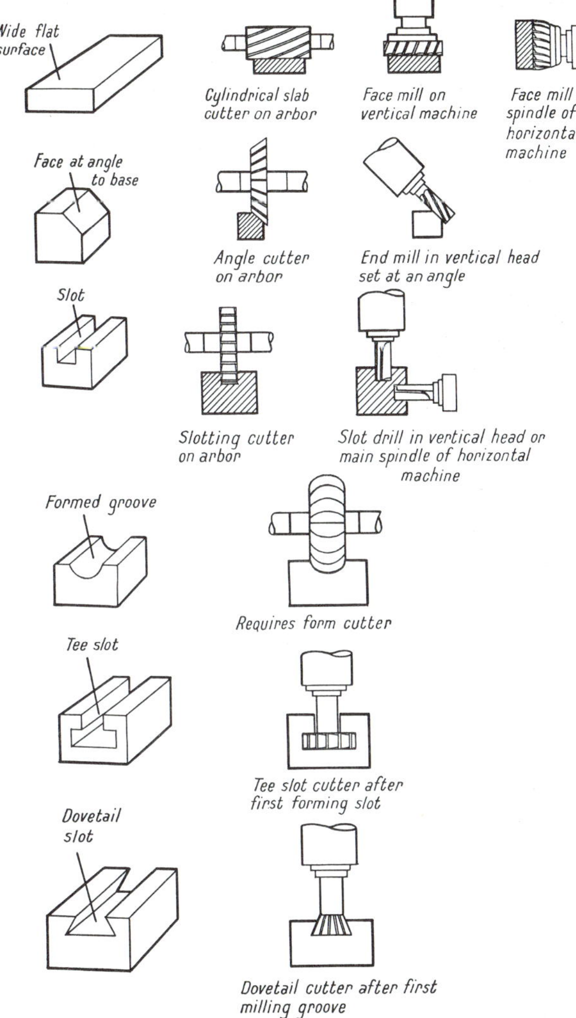

Fig. 244. Basic milling operations.

is produced by *relieving*. This operation is performed on a special lathe by the reciprocating action of the cross slide, which advances over each tooth in turn. A special forming tool is used or a single point tool is actuated by a template and stylus. In order to preserve the correct shape and size during sharpening, form cutters are ground on their faces only.

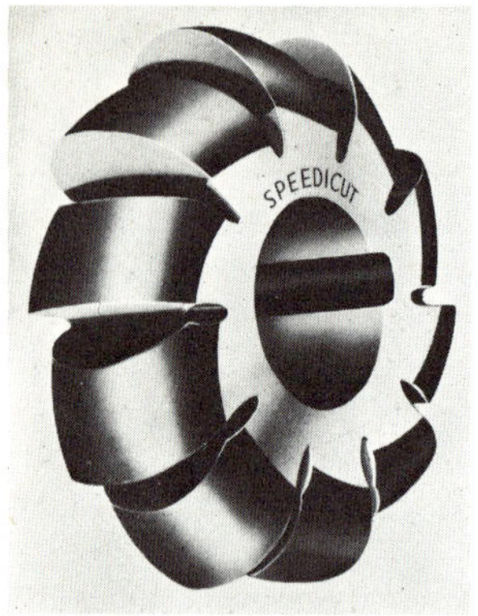

(a) Radiusing cutter.   (b) Involute form gear cutter.

[*Firth Brown Tools Ltd.*

Fig. 245. Form cutters.

Cutting action The cutting angles on a milling cutter tooth may be considered to be similar to that of a single-point tool used on the lathe or shaping machine, Fig. 246. The cutting rake is formed by the angle the tooth face makes with a radial line drawn from the centre of the cutter bore. General purpose milling cutters have a tooth rake angle of about 10° to 15° and are hence suitable for

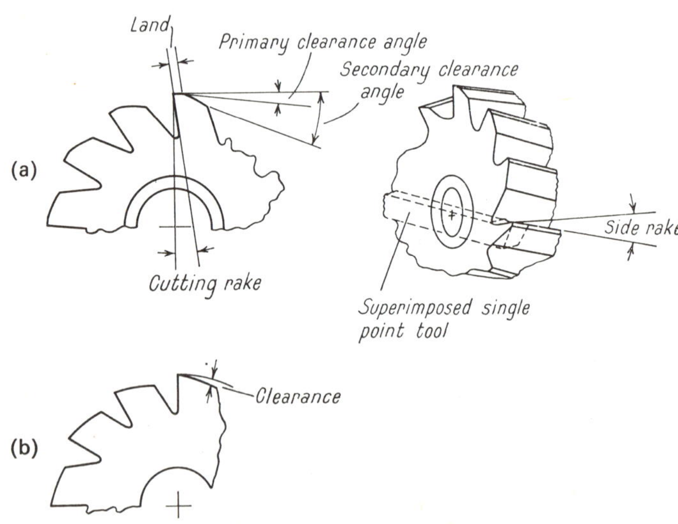

Fig. 246. (a) Fluted tooth milling cutter.
          (b) Relieved tooth milling cutter.

cutting most metals. Side rake is provided on some cutters by the angle of the milled gash and on others by forming the teeth on a helix. This is kept small, as excessive side rake imposes an end thrust on the spindle bearings and is not conducive to swarf clearance. Clearance must be given to cutter teeth to enable the edge to bite into the metal and also to provide means of chip disposal. Primary and secondary clearance angles are therefore given as in a lathe boring tool. The number of teeth on a cutter is determined in relation to the work it will have to do. The size of the gash behind the tooth must be large enough to clear the swarf, yet in order to prevent vibration and chatter, a cutter should contain a sufficient number of teeth to keep two or more in contact with the work at all times. Hence a slitting saw used to cut thin sections will have a greater number of teeth than a slab mill used for removing heavy quantities of metal and forming large chips in roughing operations.

When viewed from the front of the machine, the spindle and arbor of the plain horizontal milling machine rotate in an anti-clockwise direction and the power feed to the table is from right to left. When work is fed in this direction to a cutter so rotating, the process is called *up-milling*, Fig. 247a. *Down-* or *climb-milling*, in which either the cutter or the feed is in the other direction, Fig. 247b, allows heavier cuts at speed to be taken because the work is forced against the table through the action of the cut, the force passing through it to

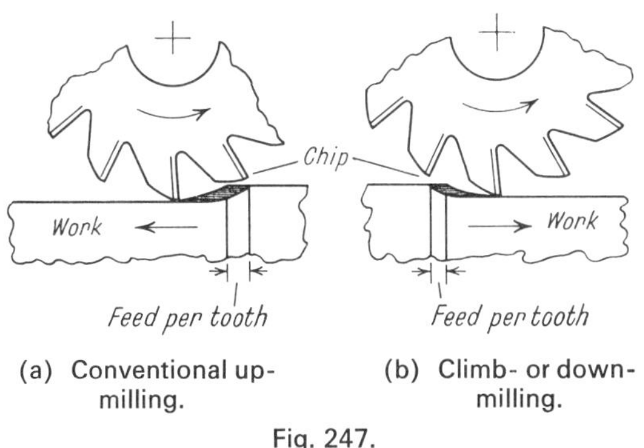

(a) Conventional up-milling.   (b) Climb- or down-milling.

Fig. 247.

the more rigid parts of the machine. This method is not normally used in the toolroom or instructional workshop. Machines employed on this type of work are specially designed or are fitted with a backlash eliminator.

The application of a cutting fluid when machining steel improves the efficiency of the cutting action and gives a better surface finish. The function of coolants in milling is similar to that in other machining operations (see p. 174). If pump or drip feed is not available coolant can be fed to the top of the cutter by brush, from where it will be carried to the cutting edge by rotation of the cutter. It must not be applied by brush to the work, or the brush may be drawn into the cutter. A sulphurized cutting oil is used for heavy milling operations with good results. Cast iron and brass are machined dry; paraffin is used on aluminium.

Because of the expense of milling cutters and the time and labour involved in their sharpening, students should carefully calculate the cutter speed and rate of feed needed for the type of operation and material. Although in the training of craftsmen the time factor and costing of the job are not all important, yet a machine tool, as with the hand tools, should be used to its greatest efficiency. Problems of available power will not normally arise, for most machining jobs done in the metalwork room will be well within the capacity of the machine. Students should, however, realize just what is happening at the cutting edge of a tool and learn to decide upon the depth of cut, and the speeds and feeds to use. It is only by a study of the machine tool, and the effects of its operation, that work of quality can be produced and the operator attain the status of the craftsman. Although the approach to milling machine work is mainly by calculation, there are variables in each operation that make experience and skill a distinct part of milling technique.

Speeds and feeds Table 9 on p. 175 gives the surface speed in metres per minute at which it is best to cut the various metals, and the values, of course, apply to all machine tools. A range is given for each type of material and it is within this range, depending on the rigidity with which the work is held, the state of the machine and the spindle speeds possible, that the cutter speed is set. The following formula is used to convert surface speed to cutter revolutions.

$$\text{Rev/min} = \frac{\text{surface speed in m/min} \times 1000}{\pi \times \text{dia of cutter in mm}}$$

For the average metalwork room, where sharpening facilities are limited, it is essential to use cutters of high-speed steel. Cast steel cutters are not normally available but if they are used they must be run at slower speeds and be provided with a constant and liberal supply of coolant.

When up-milling, a wedge-shaped chip is removed by each tooth, Fig. 247a. The thickness of this chip will depend on the rate of feed of the work into the cutter in relation to the number of teeth on the cutter, and its speed. As the cutting edge meets the tip of the chip wedge first, it has to force its way into the metal. A positive feed is therefore required to prevent the edge becoming dulled through *slip* when entering the work. The feed is best determined by calculating the thickness of the wedge to be removed by each tooth. A conservative estimate of the amount each tooth should remove would be from about 0·05 mm for a delicate slitting saw or small end mill, to about 0·2 mm for a helical slab cutter. The rate of feed on the automatic traverse is usually stated in terms of mm per revolution of the cutter. To find the rate of feed per tooth, therefore, divide the stated figure by the number of teeth on the cutter. For milling operations generally, it is better to run at a lower spindle speed, take lighter cuts and give a fairly fast feed, than to take heavy cuts at high speed and with a slow rate of feed. A lighter feed is required when starting a cut over the corners of work. This is done by hand, the power feed not being engaged until the cutter is working uniformly at its full depth.

Location and fastening of work   The location and fastening of work to the table of the machine will depend on the shape of the work and the type of operation to be carried out, Fig. 248. There are, however, common principles that are applicable to the fastening of work on all machine tools. Firstly, it is essential that the work be rigidly held and be supported against the thrust of the cut. If possible the work should be clamped firmly to the table by clamps held by bolts located in the table tee-slots. The clamp is positioned parallel to the table surface by packing at its outer end, and the bolt is placed nearer the work than the packing strip or block, Fig. 248b. Students will recognize in this the application of elementary principles of moments, for the force exerted on the work depends on the tension of the nut and the distance of the point of contact from its application. Clamps are therefore provided with elongated holes. A clamp must grip a portion of the work that is in direct contact with the table, or packing strips must be placed beneath the point of contact. If clamps are placed over projecting or unsupported sections, there is a danger of the work fracturing under pressure or working loose through vibration.

Tee-bolts suited to the table slots are used in order to distribute the load over the underside of the slots. Standard hexagonal bolt heads are not suitable as the pressure is concentrated over a small area and the table may fracture in their vicinity. Tee-bolt heads should be made for, and kept near, each machine tool, and various lengths of steel studding should be available together with the washers, nuts and clamps. In this way, not only will work be rigidly held, but much time will be saved searching for suitable clamping material. Before clamping work, both the underside of the work and the table surface must be wiped clean. Even very small pieces of material trapped between the contacting faces will cause misalignment of the work, insufficient grip and possible fracture of castings. A sheet of timber or similar soft material should be placed beneath the rough surface of castings to enable them to bed down firmly.

Much light work may be held in a machine vice bolted to the table. When work is so held, the fixed jaw is made to take the thrust. Rough castings are not normally held in a vice, but when they are, sheets of soft material such as lead or aluminium should be placed against the jaws to take up the irregularities of the cast surfaces in contact with them. Under the varying pressures exerted on the work by a milling cutter or shaping tool, parallel work has a tendency to ride up the jaws of a vice if the movable jaw is at all loose in its location against the base slide. To counteract this, a circular bar may be held between the moving jaw and the work. With the bar towards the upper edge of the vice jaw, greater

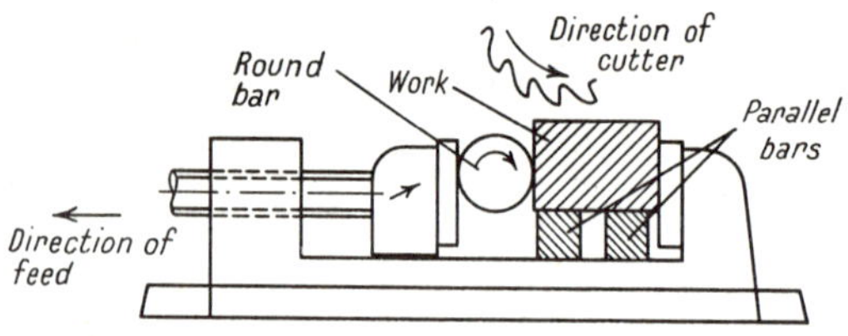

(a) Use of round bar in machine vice.

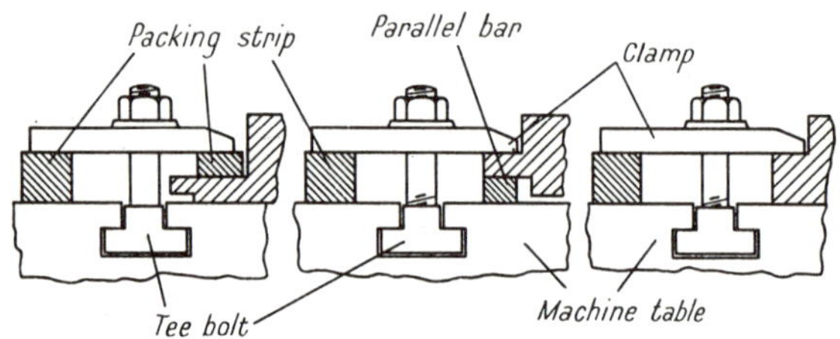

(b) Clamping to machine table.

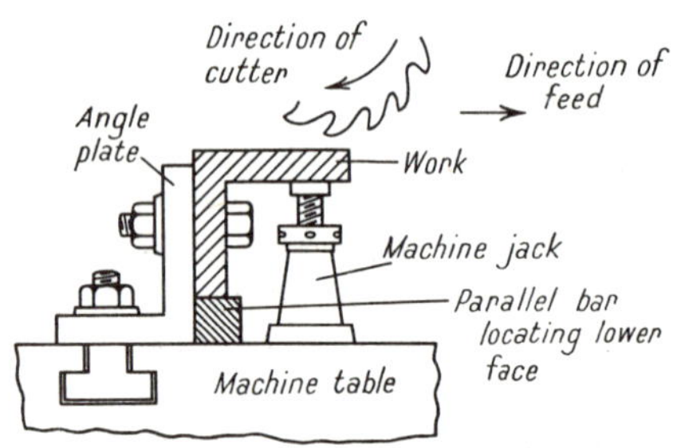

(c) Work bolted to angle plate.

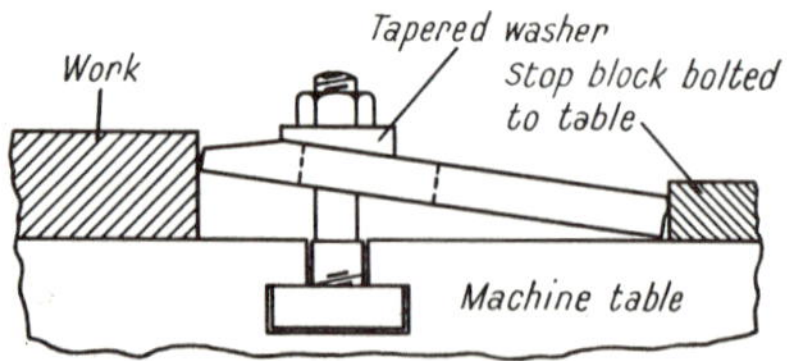

(d) Clamping narrow work to a machine table.

Fig. 248. Methods of holding work.

pressure is exerted on the front of the work, while with the bar in a lower position, work will bed down at the rear, Fig. 248a. By adjustment in this way, work is settled down on the vice base or on the locating parallel strips. When fitting work to a vice, it is tapped lightly with a copper hammer as the vice jaw is tightened. When parallel bars are used, they should be gripped firmly between the base of the work and the vice slide.

Work that cannot be conveniently clamped directly to the table or be held in a vice, may be bolted to an angle plate, Fig. 248c. Here again, the plate should be positioned so that the force of the cut is transmitted through the plate to the table. Overhanging parts must not be left unsupported. Machine jacks or tapered packings are used to take the downward thrust. The location of thin-section work requires particular attention. Stresses in the metal are relieved when material is removed, causing thin work to spring out of shape when clamps are removed after a cutting operation. When dealing with work of this nature, first clamp it down and then take roughing cuts. Then release the work and reposition it; it should be lightly held for the finishing cut, which removes any irregularities in the surface caused by the relieving of internal stresses.

The alignment of the work on the table is accomplished by locating a test indicator on a rigid part of the machine and traversing a face of the work against it. On a horizontal machine the indicator can be held at the end of a bar gripped lightly between the collars of the arbor, while on a vertical machine an adapter can be made to enable the indicator to be held in the spindle or chuck. A more convenient method is provided by the use of a magnetic base which may be positioned on the main vertical slide or on the arbor, as shown in Fig. 249. One end of the surface to be tested is moved gently against the indicator plunger until movement of the needle takes place; the dial is then set to zero. When the table is traversed and the face is moved along the plunger, any variation of alignment between the work and the operating slide screw can readily be seen by deflection of the needle. The work is then moved clear of the indicator, tapped lightly to alter its position and the process repeated until the face can be traversed without needle deflection. When setting up a vice in this way, it is the fixed jaw that is checked. If the vice jaws are in a bad condition and irregularities of the jaw surfaces make such testing difficult, a parallel bar should be lightly gripped in the vice and register made from the side of the bar.

The preliminary setting-up of work, when a first cut is to be made to produce a surface from which other measurements will be taken, can be made by testing with a try-square against the vertical slide or side of the table. The vice can also be set in this way when the jaws are in line with the arbor. With the vice jaws parallel to the table screw, a straight bar may be gripped and the distance of the ends of the bar from the side of the table tested with a surface gauge. A strip of metal that will comfortably fit into the table slots and protrude a short way above the surface of the table is often used as a rapid method of setting work, for with the strip in position a straight edge of the work is simply pushed against it and bolted down. A square with dowel pins that will locate in the table grooves is used for setting work in line with the arbor axis. However, where accurate location is demanded, a test indicator must be used.

Each individual job represents its own problem of setting-up but generally work should be as low as possible on the machine table, held rigidly in the area in which the cut is to take place and supported against thrust. The location should be tested with reference to the machine slides and all contacting faces clean and free from burrs. The slides not required to feed the work to the cutter, normally the vertical and cross slides, are locked once the position of the work and the depth of cut have been set. To further increase the rigidity and enable heavy cuts to be taken, braces may be fitted which lock the knee and overarm together.

[*James Neill & Co. (Sheffield) Ltd.*

Fig. 249. Checking alignment of work with test indicator.

Operation and safety When setting up work on a machine tool the work is set up first. Not only does the absence of the cutter give more room for setting up at a convenient height, but the cutter is not liable to damage, nor are the operator's hands. Tools are placed conveniently to hand on a machine cabinet, not on the machine table. The spanners and tools commonly required for work on a particular machine should be kept adjacent to it. If the correct spanners are available, nuts will not become damaged and accidents are less likely to occur. Loose objects must not be left on the table while cutting is taking place and operating handles should be removed or disengaged before a cut is started. When fitting or dismantling a cutter the machine motor is switched off and the cutter gripped firmly. Cutter edges are sharp and will break the skin if allowed to slip. Before switching on, make a final check to see that the work is rigidly held and that all holding-down bolts are tight. Any movements of the work while the cutter is in motion could have disastrous results, not only to the work but to the operator and others in the workshop. A cutter guard must be in position when a milling machine is in use and, apart from the application of cutting fluid to the top of the cutter, hands must be kept well away. When cutters are being set up it is better to withdraw the whole overarm rather than to remove the arbor end bearing support, for being heavy it may fall and damage the machine bed.

The arbor bearings should be lubricated frequently while running, as should all machine slides and screws. The accuracy of the work produced depends very much on the state of the machine and its care and upkeep is as much a part of the operator's task as the operation itself. In this respect the maintenance of the holding-down equipment should not be overlooked. Clamps must be kept free from burrs and bolts and nuts given an occasional oiling.

In operation, much use is made of the micrometer dials adjacent to the slide-operating handwheels. With the work firmly clamped to the table and the cutter revolving at the correct speed, the knee is elevated until the work just makes contact with the cutter. The work is then withdrawn, the dial set to zero and the knee raised to give the required depth of cut. In no case is work brought into contact with a stationary cutter. The setting of work with feeler gauges is not only inaccurate but dangerous. When using a face mill, or side and face cutter, the cutter position is similarly located by 'zeroing' the cross slide dial and traversing the work with reference to its readings. Slots and grooves may be accurately positioned in relation to a face. The cutter width must, of course, be taken into consideration in operations of this sort.

The depth of cut will vary with the type of work being done, and as with other metal cutting operations the majority of the metal is removed by heavy roughing cuts; a final light finishing cut is then taken. Too light a cut on any material will cause the cutter edges to become dulled as slip occurs as the teeth enter the work when up-milling, Fig. 247a. Sufficient depth of cut to enable the cutter to bite readily into the work should be given, but not enough to cause chatter or excessive vibration.

The skin of castings should be removed with a single-point tool in the lathe or shaper. If it has to be done on a milling machine the initial cut should penetrate well below the skin to prevent dulling of the cutter by abrasion.

Dividing head Work may also be held on the milling machine between the centres of a dividing head and its tailstock, Fig. 250, or directly in the dividing head chuck. Plain dividing heads are rotated by a crank arm operating through a worm and worm gear and the operating handle may be locked in position on an index plate provided with rows of holes of different numbers in concentric circles. By this means work can be rotated through an angle or circular work be divided into an equal number of parts. Such operations are called *simple indexing*. The dividing head is used to cut splines, tangs, spur and bevel gears, as well as flats on circular work. Some dividing heads have provision for holding work at an angle or vertical to the table, and rotating it while in these positions.

[*Midgley & Sutcliffe Ltd.*

Fig. 250. Plain dividing head.

The cutting of helical gears and cutters and the flutes of twist drills and spiral reamers is accomplished by compound or *differential indexing*. Such operations can only be performed on a universal milling machine having a table that may be set at an angle to the cross slide and having provision whereby the dividing head may be geared to the table feed screw. By these means work is automatically rotated as it is fed to the cutter at an angle.

On most standard models the crank and head are geared in the ratio 40:1, hence 40 turns on the handle will cause the spindle and the work to make a complete revolution. One complete turn of the handle therefore gives an angular movement of $\frac{1}{40}$th of a turn or 9°. By the use of index plates containing a varying number of equidistant holes, predetermined amounts of angular rotation may be made. The rotation of the crank arm required when dividing work into a number of parts is considered in relation to the number of holes the plunger must pass on a circle containing a suitable number of holes. The number of parts

212

is first divided into 40, which will, for all numbers except 40 itself, produce a fraction. The denominator of the fraction, or multiple or sub-multiple of it, determines the number of holes required in the plate, and the numerator the number of holes to pass. Whole numbers that occur when the divisions are less than 40 refer to complete revolutions of the crank arm. For example, to divide work into 16 divisions, $\frac{40}{16} = 2\frac{8}{16} = 2\frac{1}{2}$, hence the crank handle must take $2\frac{1}{2}$ turns each time. Any even number of holes will do and the sector arms should be set at 180°. Similarly, to cut 54 teeth, we have $\frac{40}{54}$ and 40 holes must be passed on a 54 hole circle, or 20 holes on one containing 27.

In operation, the sector arms are set to enclose the number of holes it is required to pass each time. The work is positioned for the first cut with the plunger in contact with the face of one arm. The arms, which are locked together, are then rotated to bring the trailing arm in contact with the plunger, in which position it is set for the next cut. When setting the dividing head for angular rotation, as distinct from the division of a circle into a number of parts, the required angle is divided by 9, since a complete revolution of the crank handle will rotate the work through 9°. The resulting fraction is then treated in the same way as in the previous examples.

14 The Sharpening of Metal-cutting Tools

The efficiency of any metal-cutting tool depends on the maintenance of the correct rake and clearance angles and the keenness of the cutting edge. Only by using a tool that is sharp can a good surface finish be obtained and work of good quality be produced. It is important to have sharp tools from the beginning of a course, so as to appreciate correct and efficient cutting action. Also, much frustration and faulty learning are saved and the breakages of the smaller drills and taps avoided, if tools are adequately maintained. Much of the tool sharpening will, in the first instance, fall on the craft master, but from an early stage of

Fig. 251. Off-hand grinding.

their training students should learn tool-sharpening techniques and be encouraged to shape and maintain their own tools. The ability to fashion, heat-treat and sharpen metal-cutting tools is fundamental to the metalworker's craft.

Off-hand grinding Many of the small tools in use in the craftroom may be sharpened by off-hand grinding on a bench or pedestal grinding machine. Two wheels are provided, one with a coarse grit and the other with a fine grit. With a wheel revolving towards the work the tool is introduced with the cutting edge to the top. Burrs that are likely to form will then be at the trailing edge and not at the cutting edge itself, and the lines formed by the abrasive grains will run in a line taken by the tool passing the metal when cutting. To grind in line with a thin cutting edge, or radially around a point, causes a weak tip which readily breaks off and the tool soon becomes blunt. In order to preserve the shape of the wheel, work must be moved laterally across the face of the wheel giving equal wear to all parts. If the work is held in one place a groove soon appears making the future production of straight edges difficult.

In holding work for off-hand grinding, the hand is held behind the tool rest with the fingers located against it, Fig. 251. The tool is then held quite close to the tip and to the wheel.

Small tool bits are held in this way and not in a tool-holder. This is so that suitable pressure is applied, for if the pressure is too great, excessive heat is produced at the tip and the temper of carbon steel tools will be drawn. Dipping the tool in water, to cool it, is not to be encouraged. Minute cracks may be set up through frequent heating and quenching causing a consequent weakening of the cutting edge. As the more frequent use of the pedestal grinder is in the

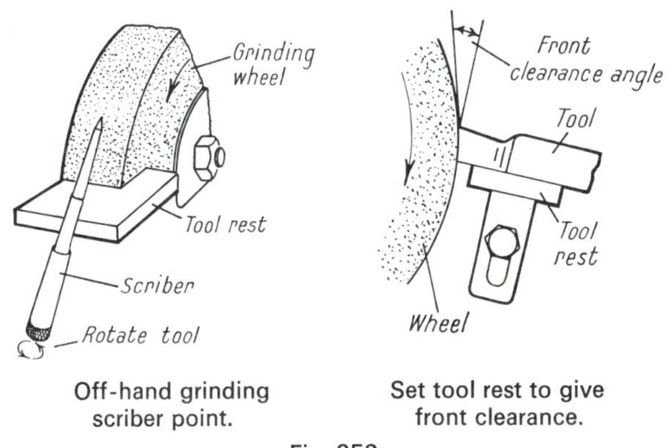

Off-hand grinding
scriber point.

Set tool rest to give
front clearance.

Fig. 252.

grinding of lathe and shaper tools, it is advantageous to have the rest set at an angle suited to their clearance angles, Fig. 252. The rest must also be positioned close to the wheel, or work may be carried down the gap between the rest and the face of the wheel, causing damage to the tool and the wheel and possibly injury to the operator.

As much of the grinding as possible is done on the face (or circumference) of the wheel, for, as well as being more easily dressed on the face, grinding wheels are less able to withstand side forces. The slightly concave face given to the clearance angles of tools when ground on a wheel's face is not usually detrimental. When grinding shaper tools on a small wheel, however, the curvature produced should be rectified by a final grinding on the side of the wheel. To provide flat surfaces, and hence true and consistent angles, off-hand grinding machines fitted with cup wheels are often used, particularly when tools of cemented carbide are being ground. In practice, the top and sides of single-point tools are ground on the sides of the wheel, these faces normally requiring but little metal to be removed from them. When much metal is to be removed they should first be ground on the wheel face, using the coarse wheel first and then the fine, and then finally finished off on the side. Tipped tools are ground on the front clearance face only.

At first, practice tool-sharpening on the simple tools such as scribers, centre punches and chisels. Possibly the best way for a beginner to acquire the technique of grinding lathe tools is to practice holding the faces in turn against any vertical surface, and then repeating the hold on the machine. To begin with, only the front clearance face of a standard shaped tool should be ground. As an aid to off-hand tool grinding, templates cut to the required angles can be hung from the machine and the work compared to them to assess the accuracy. The sharp edges formed at the junction of adjacent straight faces, as with knife and vee-forming tools, are weak and will break away or soon wear if not removed. Such tools should therefore be slightly radiused with a slip stone after grinding.

Sharpening twist drills Gauges and templates are particularly useful in the checking of twist drills sharpened by off-hand grinding. This technique is difficult to acquire but is nevertheless most important, for, although in industry drills are ground in the toolroom on a machine specially designed for the purpose, in schools drills are mostly ground by hand. The best way to learn is to get a drill of reasonable size, say 12 mm diameter, and practice the action against a vertical surface. If this is of a transparent material the contacting portions of the drill faces may be seen. So that the grinding lines may be perpendicular to the lip edges, the drill is held against the side of the wheel with the lip horizontal and the axis making an angle of 59° with it. The drill is then rotated with the right hand while at the same time the shank is rocked through an arc downwards and forwards to give the necessary clearance on the lip face, Fig. 253a. The left hand resting lightly on the rest guides the drill and ensures even treatment to both faces. On inspection after grinding, the web should be central, the lips of equal length and at the correct angle, and when viewed from the side adequate clearance should be seen, Fig. 253d. Gauges for checking the angle are supplied by most twist drill manufacturers. The length of the point corners are checked in the larger drills by the use of a gauge fastened to the wall near the machine, Fig. 253c. The centre hole in the end of the drill fits on to the gauge point, and lines are scribed on the chalked surface from the point corners. The two lines should coincide.

Attachments to the pedestal grinder include a jig for the purpose of grinding twist drills accurately. Such attachments are useful particularly for the grinding of the larger drills. Care must be taken to ensure that excessive pressure does not cause the lip to become burnt, for the drill is advanced to the wheel by a screw and pressure is more difficult to judge than when grinding by hand.

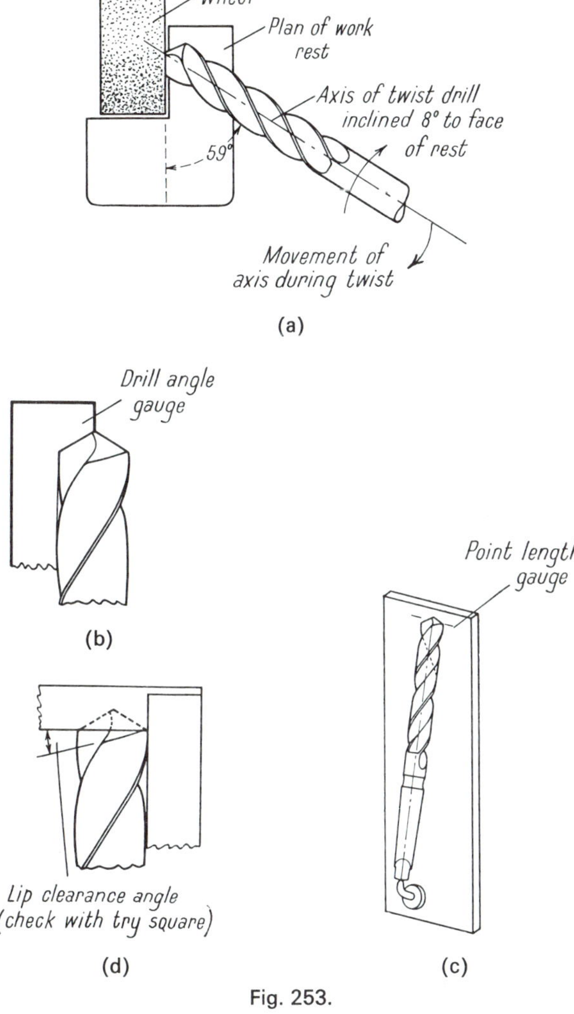

Fig. 253.

It is important to note that the pedestal grinding machine is provided solely for the grinding of hardened steel and metal-cutting material and no other work should ever be done upon it. If it is desired to grind soft metal or to fettle castings, a suitable wheel should be provided. Soft metal rapidly loads the wheel which subsequently causes tools to burn. Because of the abrasive dust produced when grinding, the machine should be situated well away from other machine tools.

The surface speed of wheels for tool grinding is about 25m/s; grinding machine spindles therefore run at high speeds and the need for frequent lubrication of the bearings should not be overlooked.

Fitting grinding wheels Grinding wheels are supplied with a lead bush at their centres by which they are located on the spindle of the machine. When fitting a wheel, this bush should be of a size enabling it to fit snugly but loosely on its spindle. If it is felt to be too tight a fit, it must be scraped out with a bearing scraper (and not forced on) for any strain exerted on the wheel may cause it to crack. The soundness of the wheel must be tested before fitting. If tapped lightly with a small metal bar, held loosely between finger and thumb, flaws that may be present are indicated by the dull note emitted. The wheel is held in position between two flanges which should be of between $\frac{1}{3}$ and $\frac{1}{2}$ the diameter of the wheel. The inner flange is keyed to the shaft and the outer flange clamps the wheel by transmitting the pressure of the locking nut, Fig. 254. The flanges are recessed

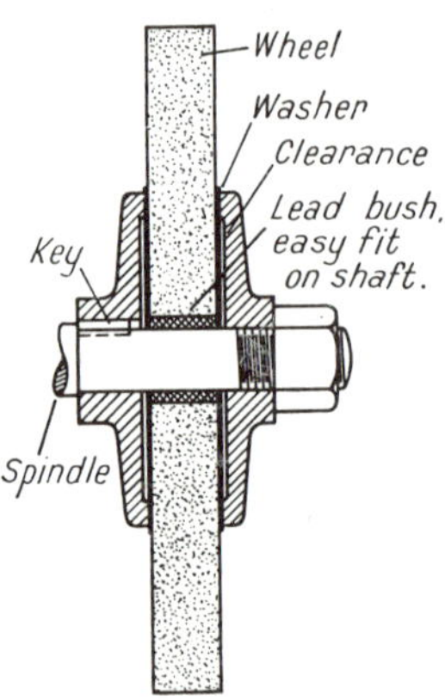

Fig. 254. Location of grinding wheel on spindle.

at their centres and make contact with the wheel for only a small distance along its sides. Wheels are usually supplied with paper washers attached to their sides. If not, rubber, leather or paper washers should be used to bed down the wheel in the areas in contact with the flanges. This will distribute the load and ensure a rigid grip. The clamping nut is tightened sufficiently to hold the wheel in place but must not be over-tightened, for to do so would put undue strain on the wheel.

Modern wheels are manufactured to a high degree of uniformity and accuracy and do not normally require balancing before fitting. To correct the balance, the wheels are secured on a mandrel supported by knife edges, and either some of the lead is scraped from the sides of the central bush, or small lead weights are attached to the sides of the wheel. Although wheels are tested for flaws before dispatch it is advisable to run a newly fitted wheel for a few minutes without load and with cover guards in position. If there is an undetected flaw or crack in the wheel, it will disintegrate in the early stages of its running. Hence while this is done the operator should stand well clear.

All wheels will require truing to ensure that they revolve without vibration and are concentric with the axis of the machine spindle. To do this the wheel dresser is fitted with an adjustable bush that locates against the tool rest. From time to time wheels must be trued in this way, not only to ensure their concentricity but in order to remove the surface when it has become loaded or

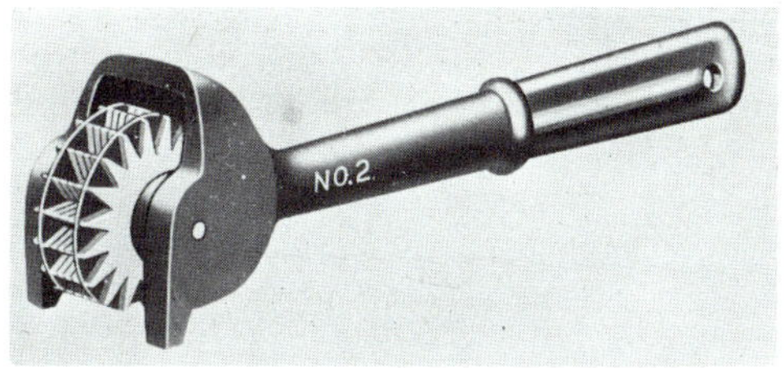

[*S. A. Jones & Shipman Ltd.*

Fig. 255. Huntingdon wheel dresser.

glazed and also to return a worn wheel to its original shape. Wheels used for off-hand grinding are dressed with a lump of abrasive crystal or with a star emery dresser, Fig. 255, which digs below the surface of the wheel and releases the outer layer of abrasive grains from the bond.

Cutter grinding The grinding of cutters and the sharpening of taps and reamers demands the use of a machine in which both the abrasive wheel and the work is rigidly located and held. Cutter grinding machines, Fig. 256, carry the wheel at the end of a spindle that may be raised or lowered and be locked in position. The table, on which the work is held, may be traversed past the wheel and fed towards it. Either the table or the wheel may be positioned so that the work is presented to the face or the side of the wheel. Much work can be done with plain wheels on the cutter grinder, although the varying shapes of cutters necessitate a further selection of wheel shapes. The more common of these are the cup wheels, for sharpening the normal range of general purpose tools. Shapes of cup wheels include both straight and flaring, the dish wheel and a fine disc wheel for gashing. The wheels are positioned and held on the spindle in the same way as for the pedestal machine.

A diamond, bedded in a holder, is used for dressing the finer wheels. It is clamped to the table and slowly advanced towards the revolving wheel until it can be heard to just make contact. It is then made to pass the wheel until contact is lost, and then advanced by a very small amount, usually about 0·025 mm and the process repeated. The diamond, being harder than the abrasive grains, cuts the grit rather than just tearing grains from the bond as the hand dressing tool does. The diamond must be made to pass steadily across the wheel or a coarse texture will be given to the wheel which will in turn produce a rough finish on the work.

[Clarkson (Engineers) Ltd.
Fig. 256. Cutter grinding machine.

The setting-up of work on the cutter grinder demands the use of suitable attachments. Milling cutters used on the horizontal milling machine are first mounted on a mandrel and then set up between centres on the table. Taps and reamers and some end mills may be located directly on the centres, while slot drills and tools that cannot be conveniently held by these means are held in a collet on a universal head. The location of the individual tooth to be ground is facilitated by an adjustable tooth rest or finger, and the tooth is held against this during sharpening by hand pressure. When straight teeth are being ground, the rest may be positioned on the machine table and allowed to travel past the wheel with the tool. Cutters with helical teeth and those whose teeth cannot be set parallel to the table face must be rotated while being traversed. When cutters of this type are being set up, the tooth rest is located on the body of the machine. Milling cutters may be sharpened by two methods. In Fig. 257b, the wheel rotates away from the cutting edge and the burr will form on the trailing edge, consistent

220

with good grinding practice. To support the work against the pressure of the revolving wheel the rest is mounted above the work. The normal method of cutter grinding is shown in Fig. 257a, where the rest is in its more rigid position below the tooth, and where the work is kept in contact with it by the action of the wheel. As only light cuts are taken, the burr produced on the cutting edge is not large and is removed after grinding with a slip stone. As the wheel is normally of a much larger diameter than that of the cutter and the tooth land is comparatively small, the amount of curvature produced by grinding on the face of the wheel is not excessive and sharpening is satisfactorily accomplished in this way. The use of a cup wheel, however, will give a straight and true

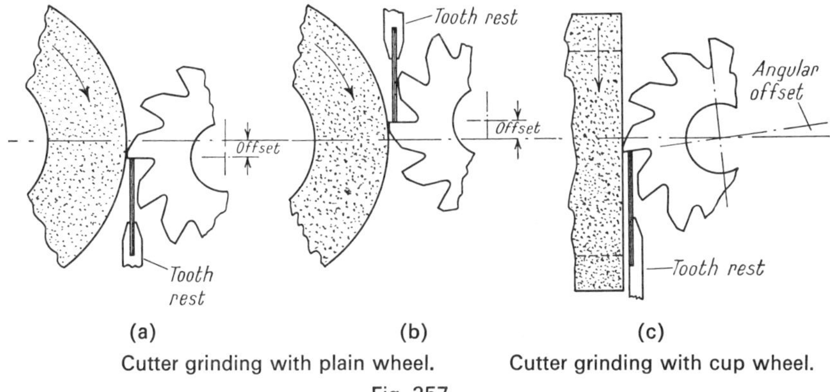

(a)	(b)	(c)

Cutter grinding with plain wheel.   Cutter grinding with cup wheel.

Fig. 257.

cutting face, and the method illustrated in Fig. 257c should be used where the land is large or the available plain wheel is small in diameter. Care must be taken when using a cup wheel to see that the wheel clears the next tooth above, for it will be seen that the off-set required to give the correct clearance angle is angular rather than parallel as for plain wheels. This requires the adjustment of the tooth rest instead of the relation between wheel and work heights.

In practice, the work is set up with the tooth rest in position and the work, wheel and tooth rest are adjusted to give the approximate angle. The wheel is then revolved by hand and the tooth fed to it. On inspection the points in contact are readily seen and adjustment is made until the machine is set to give a cut corresponding to the original (maker's) angle. With the wheel revolving, the first tooth is advanced until contact is made. All edges of the cutter are then made to pass the wheel at this setting in turn, each tooth being taken across until contact is lost. The process is repeated and light feeds given until all teeth have been sharpened. A final very light cut is then taken, starting from the opposite side of the cutter. This is to compensate for possible error caused by wear in the wheel.

The teeth of relieved form cutters are sharpened on their front faces only. This is accomplished by the use of a dished wheel, Fig. 258a. By a similar method, a plain wheel radiused on its face is used to grind the flutes of taps, Fig. 258b. Only plug taps should require this treatment as the taper and second taps can more conveniently be ground on their tapered ends. Although it is possible to sharpen these taps by off-hand grinding, the process calls for some skill and can be more accurately accomplished by mounting between centres or in a collet on the cutter grinder, and then setting-up to give the required clearance to the lead.

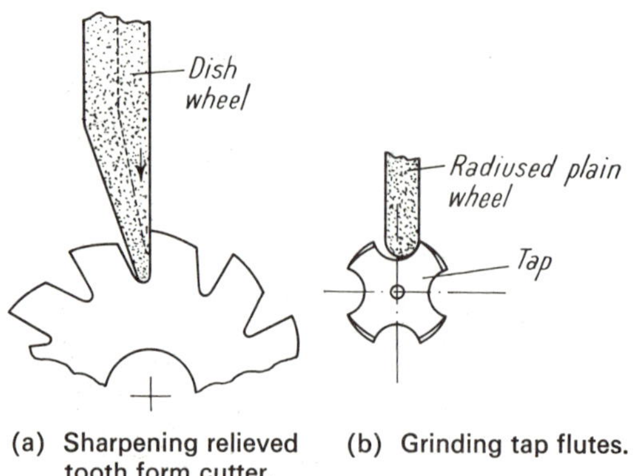

(a) Sharpening relieved tooth form cutter.

(b) Grinding tap flutes.

Fig. 258.

Toolpost grinder   Cylindrical grinding is not normally undertaken on the simple forms of cutter grinder, as provision must be made for the work to revolve at speed. Lathe centres, however, may be ground successfully if a hand wheel is fitted to the universal head. Centres are frequently ground in the metalwork room by using a toolpost grinder on the lathe, Fig. 259. With the compound rest set at 30° to the axis of the spindle and the grinder mounted upon it, the wheel is advanced over the centre positioned in the lathe spindle. When grinding on the lathe, care must be taken to ensure that no abrasive dust falls on to the lathe bed. A tray placed below the centre will catch most of the waste material but the lathe should also be cleaned thoroughly, when the operation is completed.

Grinding wheels   Grinding wheels are composed of fine grains of abrasive material or grit held together in a matrix or *bond*. They therefore provide many hundreds of small cutting edges which remove minute chips of metal from the work and throw them away from the wheel in the form of red hot sparks. These abrasive grains become dulled in the course of their cutting and it is a feature of grinding wheels that, when blunted, the grains break away from the wheel and so present fresh sharp edges. To ensure this process the correct type of wheel must be used and the selection of a grinding wheel for a particular job depends on a number of factors. First of these must be the composition of the abrasive material. Since the early days of the development of grinding when natural sandstone, emery and corundum were used, great advances have been made in the production of wheels using manufactured materials. Modern grinding wheels contain abrasives of either aluminium oxide or silicon carbide, although for some special operations wheels impregnated with diamond dust are used. Wheels of aluminium oxide are normally employed for tool and cutter grinding.

[*T. S. Harrison & Sons Ltd.*

Fig. 259. Grinding a 60°-centre in the lathe.

The grains are produced by heating bauxite in an electric-arc furnace and crushing the resulting crystalline material. This is then passed through sieves, the particle size determining the grain size number. The grades range from a very coarse grit (No. 8) to a very fine grit (No. 600).

The second factor is the hardness or softness of the wheel as determined by the strength of the bond. This denotes the grade of the wheel. Soft wheels are those from which the abrasive grains readily break away, and hard wheels those that retain their grains under pressure and cutting. Hard wheels are used to cut soft metals and soft wheels to cut hard. The function of the bond is to give support to the grains and also to release them when their cutting edges have become dulled. Bonds are made from a number of different substances according to the grain size and the type of work being done. They may be of the vitrified, silicate, resin or rubber types. The more common of these for the grinding of hardened steel and the sharpening of tools is the *vitrified wheel*. It is so called because the wheel is manufactured by mixing the abrasive grains with a clay and baking in a mould until the clay becomes vitrified. This process produces a porous texture, for the density and structure of wheels must be a further factor in their selection.

Grinding wheels are not solid masses of grit and bond but contain numerous small air pockets which provide clearance to the grains and enable the metal chips and dulled grains to be thrown clear of the wheel, Fig. 260.

Other factors affecting the choice of grinding wheel are the amount of stock to be removed, the surface finish required, the area of the work in contact with the wheel during the cutting operation and whether or not a liquid coolant is to be used. To maintain tools in good condition they are sharpened as soon as the edges become dulled, hence the total amount of metal to be removed in the

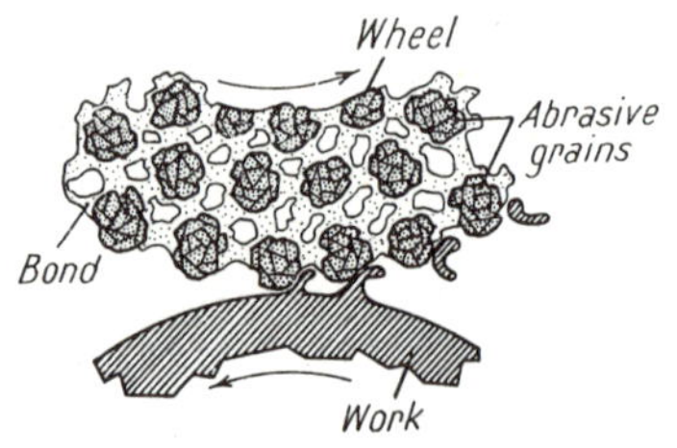

[*Carborundum Co. Ltd.*
Fig. 260. Structure and cutting action of grinding wheel.

sharpening of tools and cutters is small. Similarly, as only the cutting edge of a tool receives treatment, only a small portion of the wheel is in contact with the work at any one time. Surface finish, of course, requires to be as fine as possible and it is more convenient to grind tools dry than under a flood of coolant. For the general type of work a satisfactory result can be obtained with a wheel with an aluminium oxide abrasive of medium to fine grain size, in a vitrified bond giving a normal structure and a soft to medium grade. Wheel classification symbols are given in Table 10. When ordering grinding wheels, the symbol of the old wheel should be quoted or the type of machine and its spindle speed be stated.

The sharpening of the cemented carbide tools demands the use of a special wheel usually referred to as a *green wheel* as the grit is of silicon carbide and of that colour. As considerable heat is generated by the process, tools of this type are usually ground under a flood of liquid coolant demanding a special machine employing a cup wheel.

Table 10. Grinding wheel symbols

Abrasive		Grain size		Grade		Structure		Bond	
Aluminium oxide	A	coarse	8– 24	soft	E–I	dense	0– 2	vitrified	V
		medium	30– 60	medium	J–P	normal	3– 8	silicate	S
Silicon carbide	C	fine	80–180	hard	Q–U	open	9–12	shellac	E
		very fine	260–600					rubber	R
								resinoid	B

15 Metal Finishing

Metals are finished or polished to improve their appearance and as a protection against oxidation. A well finished tool or article has a psychological effect upon the user, it is treated with greater care and respect, and in consequence better work is done with it. Hand finishing of metal surfaces can be a tedious business. In the handicraft room the usual procedure is to file, drawfile and then polish with emery cloth, finishing off with double O and on steels adding a little oil. Endeavour to carry out these processes in the same direction to obtain quicker results, keeping flat surfaces flat. Edges should be straight and square, and any chamfers or bevels should be flat and not rounded. Nothing looks worse than carelessly rounded edges. Emery cloth should always be used with a flat tool and never on the fingers.

Engine turning has legitimate uses but should not be employed to cover up a poor finish. In the craft room it is done by fixing a piece of dowel or cork of suitable diameter in a drill chuck, charging the end with carborundum paste and then working over the surface of the work to produce an even pattern.

Polishing and buffing   This process is usually confined to the non-ferrous metals. Separate wheels or mops should be kept for work on steel. Do not expect too much from the buff; it will not remove scratches but will rather show them up. All work from the pickle bath must first have all superfluous hard solder removed by filing and scraping. Always scrape along a scratch or at an angle to it, never across. Use next fine emery cloth or pumice and water; and Water-of-Ayr stone if any small scratches persist. Finish off and finally on the polishing machine, Fig. 261. This machine is similar to the grinding machine except in the arrangement of the spindle ends. The buffing machine has a tapered screw at each end, a right-hand thread on the right-hand end and a left-hand thread on the left-hand end. This arrangement ensures that both mops tend to tighten on when in use. Keep two mops of similar size on the spindle to preserve the balance of the machine and never run a spindle bare; screw on a smooth protecting piece. There is no tool-rest or guard but a leather receptacle can be fitted below and behind the mop with advantage. If work is pressed too hard into the mop it may grab the work, tearing it out of the hands. The work should be held firmly against its periphery at a point on its front underside. Work being buffed gets hot and there is a great temptation to hold it by means of a rag or apron. This practice is highly dangerous since if the mop picks up the rag or apron the consequences could be most serious. Instead put the job down and wait for it to cool.

A wide variety of mops are available for different uses and materials. They are usually made of calico and are charged periodically with polishing compounds or carborundum stick. So far as possible, keep separate mops for the different compounds. When using felt bobs and fingers for internal use, take care that they fit easily into the vessel being polished. After buffing, complete the polishing with a clean rag and a little metal polish.

Colouring of metals For successful colouring the metal surfaces must be perfectly clean; any oxide, dirt or grease will cause uneven action of the solutions. To degrease, boil in a solution of caustic soda, but this has the disadvantage of etching any scratches left on a surface. Carbon tetrachloride may also be used and sand blasting, if available, is most effective. Bath brick and pumice powder are often used in the school workshop. After rinsing and thoroughly cleaning the work must not be touched by the hands or exposed to the atmosphere any longer than is necessary. Scratches or blemishes left on a surface will not be covered up by colouring or oxidizing or plating processes; if anything they will be accentuated. Before colouring, the metal must be treated to give the kind of surface required. If a bright finish is required, it must be bright dipped or polished, but if a dull finish is required it must be sandblasted, scoured with pumice powder and finished with a scratch brush. For better results and a more even colouring, remove the metal from the solution as soon as it begins to take effect and give a good scratch brushing. Rinse in clean water and replace in colouring solution. As final washing and polishing operations tend to lighten the colours, leave the work in the solution until a little darker than required. Colours may be finally fixed by rubbing with lanoline. Generally all acid solutions work quicker and more effectively when hot, and the density of colour will increase with the period of immersion. Remember that a number of these solutions are poisonous. The colouring processes should be carried out in a fume cupboard, or an efficient extractor fan should be fitted in the room. A rubber apron and gloves should be worn, to give minimum protection, and a plentiful supply of hot and cold running water should also be available.

The following Tables give a colouring guide:

Colouring of copper and brass Many alloys of copper and zinc are known as brass and, as their exact composition may not be known, it is difficult to assess their exact reaction to acid solutions.

Colour	Composition		Procedure
Dark antique	Cover with butter of antimony (antimony chloride)		Allow to dry
Light brown	Copper sulphate	1 part	Use in hot solution
	Water	2 parts	

Colour	Composition		Procedure
Brown	Ferrous nitrate (nitrate of iron)	115 g	Use cold
	Sodium thiosulphate	115 g	
	Water	1·15 litre	
Brown	Barium sulphide		Use in hot solution
Brown	Hydrochloric acid	12 parts	Apply with a brush.
	Arsenic	1 part	Stop action by washing
	Iron oxide	1 part	in water
Brown	Ammonium sulphide	1 g	Use in hot solution
	Water	200 g	
Dark brown	Potassium sulphide	1 g	Use in hot solution
	Water	200 g	
Bronze	Copper acetate	12 g	Use hot
	Iron oxide	12 g	
	Ammonium chloride	5 g	
Antique bronze	Copper nitrate	1 g	Paint solution on the
	Ammonium chloride	1 g	work
	Calcium chloride	1 g	
	Water	20 g	
Green	Ammonium chloride	0·5 g	Use cold
	Cream of tartar	1·5 g	
	Common salt	3 g	
	Copper nitrate	28 g	
	Water	142 g	
Sage Green	Copper nitrate	1·5 g	Use in hot solution
	Water	170 g	
Olive green	Iron perchloride	1 part	
	Water	2 parts	
Olive green	Ammonium chloride	1 part	
	Water	2 parts	
Dark green	Copper sulphate	1 part	Apply paste to work
	Zinc chloride	1 part	allow to dry, wash off
	Water	1 part	and expose to light
Flemish grey	Hydrochloric acid	7 g	Mix arsenic with acid
	White arsenic	7 g	add water, then potas-
	Potassium sulphate	0·3 g	sium sulphate
	Water	4·5 litre	Use cold
Steel blue	Sodium thiosulphate	115 g	Use solution fairly hot
	Acetate of lead	56 g	
	Water	1 litre	
Black	Concentrated solution of barium sulphide or ammonium sulphide		Use hot
Black	Copper nitrate	1 part	Add ammonia cau-
	Water	2 parts	tiously until the preci-
			pitate which first forms
			is just re-dissolved
Black	Copper sulphate	60 g	Add ammonia cau-
	And sufficient water to dissolve it		tiously until the preci-
			pitate which first forms
			is just re-dissolved

Colouring of iron and steel

Colour	Composition		Procedure
Light brown to black through purple and blue	Lead acetate Sodium thiosulphate Water	0·7 g 0·7 g 28 g	Use hot for 30 min at a temp. of 94°C
Blue black	Sodium thiosulphate Water	0·7 g 28 g	Use hot for 10 min
Black	Canning's black oxidising salts Water	5 kg 2·3 litre	Use in hot solution 10 to 15 min

Colouring zinc

Colour	Composition		Procedure
Brownish black	Copper nitrate Water	30 g 142 g	Dip in solution, wash in running water
Grey black	Copper acetate Ammonium chloride Water	15 g 15 g 142 cm³	Immerse in solution, rub off 5 or 6 times
Ebony black	Canning's zinc blacking salts Water	114 g 4·5 litre	Use hot 60°C–70°C
Ebony black	Copper nitrate Ammonium chloride Copper chloride Hydrochloric acid Water	30 g 30 g 30 g 30 g 30 g	

Gun barrel colouring

Colour	Composition		Procedure
Brown or Black	Industrial alcohol Spirit of nitrous ether Tincture of steel (B.P. strength) Nitric acid Copper sulphate Mercuric chloride Water	115 cm³ 115 cm³ 450 cm³ 85 cm³ 85 cm³ 30 g 4·5 litre	Swab with pad of cotton wool, then put in steam chest or oven for 3 hrs — repeat until colour is deep enough. The rub with boiled linseed oil

Frosting aluminium First wash the metal in warm water containing a pinch of potash, and then immerse in a 5% solution of caustic soda and water almost at boiling point. When the metal turns black it must be taken out and washed in cold water. Next dip in a 10% solution of nitric acid and finally wash in hot water.

Colouring tinplate

Colour	Composition		Procedure
To produce a crystalline surface	Nitric acid	30 g	Heat tinplate until tin is just up to melting point, then cool by immersing in solution
	Sulphuric acid	284 g	
	Water	3·5 litre	

Also apply hot dilute nitro-muriatic acid for a few seconds, wash in water, dry and coat with lacquer.

Ready prepared proprietary brands of solutions may be obtained in powder and liquid form, complete with instructions for use.

Lacquering This consists of applying a coating of lacquer or varnish to metallic surfaces which have been polished or coloured, to preserve their finish. Lacquer may be applied by brushing, dipping and spraying, and may be used hot or cold. Spraying gives the best results but is outside the scope of most school workshops. The article, first cleaned and free from grease, is warmed in an oven or over a stove, given an even coating of lacquer and then allowed to cool slowly, preferably in the oven where it was heated, the gas flame being turned off. Proprietary brands of lacquer are obtainable and should be applied with a best quality soft hair brush. An inferior brush which deposits bristles on the

Colour and composition of lacquers

Colour	Composition		Procedure
Colourless	Methylated spirit	1 litre	Mix well, allow to stand for a week, strain and bottle for use
	Fine shellac	42 g	
	Gum sandarac	28 g	
Green	Methylated spirit	1 litre	As above
	Fine shellac	42 g	
	Turmeric	42 g	
Fine gold	Methylated spirit	1 litre	Grind the shellac and sanders in a mortar, dissolve in spirit, strain before using
	Fine shellac	70 g	
	Red sanders	3·5 g	
Deep gold	Methylated spirit	1 litre	Dissolve shellac in spirit, add other ingredients, mix well, allow to stand for two days, strain and bottle for use
	Shellac	115 g	
	Trurmeric	14 g	
	Gamboge	14 g	
	Dragons-blood	3·5 g	
Bronze	Methylated spirit	1 litre	Mix well and expose to a gentle heat for a few hours. When cold, strain and bottle for use
	Shellac	14 g	
	Sandarac	7 g	
	Gum acaroides	3·5 g	
	Gamboge	3·5 g	

work can be most exasperating. The process should be carried out in the metal-finishing room or in a lacquering cabinet or under warm, dry, dust-free conditions. If a proprietary brand of lacquer is bought then the appropriate solvent must be obtained with it for cleaning the brush. If a lacquer with methylated spirit as a base is prepared in the workshop then the methylated spirit can be used as the solvent. To get really good results by brushing, considerable practice is necessary. The brush must not be overloaded and must be used with a slow, steady stroke and very light pressure. Too much pressure will give a streaky film and if the stroke is too quick air bubbles are left in the film. On the other hand, if the stroke is too slow the lacquer becomes tacky before the next stroke is applied and will not flow out evenly. The aim must be to produce a perfect film in one stroke only. A wash of methylated spirits before beginning the process helps the lacquer to spread evenly. Normally lacquers are colourless but they may be tinted, either to give a definite colour or merely to impart an added richness to the finish of the article.

Dips   Sometimes, prior to lacquering, metals are dipped in acid mixtures and washed in hot running water.

Colour	Composition		Procedure
Bright dip for brass	Sulphuric acid	10 parts	
	Nitric acid	5 parts	
	Water	5 parts	
Matt or dead dip for brass	Sulphuric acid	1 litre	Dissolve the zinc in the nitric acid first
	Nitric acid	1 litre	
	Metallic zinc	42 g	
Steel bronze for brass	Oxide of iron	1 part	
	White arsenic	1 part	
	Hydrochloric acid	12 parts	
Optical or dead black	Lamp black mixed with gold size to a paste		Add turpentine to the thinness required

To silver brass for barometer dials and scales   Dissolve fine silver in HNO_3 and boil. Then put in fine table salt and 56 g of cream of tartar together and well mix with a little water to make a sloppy mess. Add the dissolved silver ($AgNO_3$). Rub the sloshy precipitate on to the well-cleaned brass and wash off when silver is deposited.

Burnishing   This method of polishing, using a burnisher, is the most expeditious and gives the greatest lustre to a polished surface. The action of burnishing is to close the pores of the metal, flattening and levelling small irregularities to increase the brilliancy. It removes the marks left by the emery or other polishing materials and gives the burnished surface a black lustre resembling that of a mirror. The action is quite distinct from that of polishing which achieves results by cutting away irregularities with abrasives without an appreciable flow of the metal. Burnishing is an important operation for electro-deposits which consist of a multitude of small crystals with intervals between them and with facets reflecting the light in every direction. The deposited metal is hardened and forced into the pores of the underlying metal and the durability is thus increased.

Burnishers must be very hard (they must of course be of a harder substance than the work) and have a perfect polish. They are made of hardened cast steel, or agate, flint or blood stone, and are of a shape to suit the curves or projections of the job.

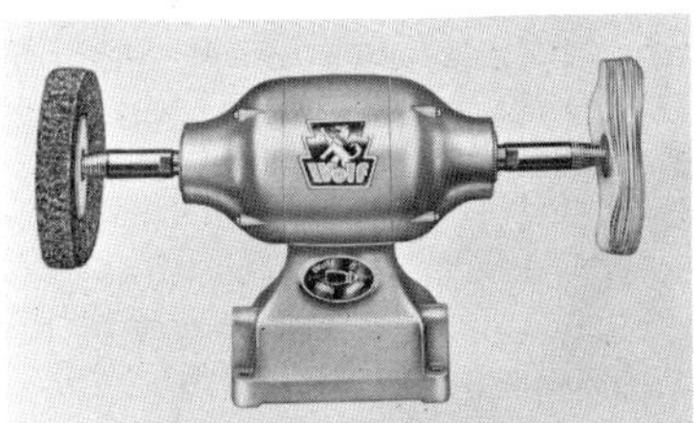

[*Wolf Electric Tools Ltd.*
Fig. 261. Electric polisher.

Burnishing is divided into two distinct operations, the first is roughing and the second is finishing. Tools for roughing have a sharp edge and those for finishing a rounded surface. The job to be burnished is placed on a bench and held firmly by the left hand or if more convenient may be gripped in a vice. The surface is wetted with argol solution and the burnishing tool dipped in vinegar It is then moved to and fro over the surface, using a gentle but steady pressure, great care being taken to see that the tool does not drag or scratch. The tool is kept in contact with the work the whole time and not lifted between strokes. At intervals the work should be sprinkled with vinegar and occasionally rinsed in the argol solution.

A cold solution of argol is made in a stoneware jar by dissolving cream of tartar in water using 7 to 14 grammes per litre. As the burnishing proceeds, the tool tends to lose its bite and slips over the surface. To restore the action of the burnisher it is rubbed periodically on a peice of leather fixed to the bench top or to a piece of wood. The leather is covered with polishing rouge or Venetian tripoli or rotten-stone or tin putty or emery.

Painting A well applied coat of paint enhances the appearance of a job immensely. Simple as it may appear, if success is to be achieved there are a few simple rules to be observed. It is best to have a cabinet for the purpose, and keep in this cabinet the paints, brushes and turpentine. Paint tin lids should be replaced properly and paint brushes kept in good condition, thoroughly cleaning them before and after use, and suspending them in turpentine when not in use. Do this by drilling a hole through the handle and pushing through a pin to rest on the top of the vessel used for this purpose. Articles to be painted must be thoroughly cleaned, degreased and any scale removed. Some provision must be made for hanging or supporting the job when painted, and all arrangements made before painting is started. Spraying, of course, gives better results than brushing, but arrangements should be made to confine the paint to a definite area. Thoroughly clean the spray after each period of use. Castings should not be painted unless filled, the nature of the filling depending on the kind of paint to be used. Time spent in filling is well worthwhile and considerably improves the appearance of the finished job. Several coats will be necessary and rubbing down must be done, using wet and dry cloth.

Hammer and crackle paints give an excellent finish to metalwork but should not be used indiscriminately; there are occasions when flat paint is more appropriate. They are available in attractive colours so do avoid too much use of black. The stoving is quite simple. An oven can be made from steel plates and stood over a tinman's stove or an old gas oven may be used. Again better results will be obtained if the paint is sprayed on, but if applied with a brush stipple it on generously. The paint does not keep very long and should be obtained as required and in small quantities. Hammer paints which do not require stoving are also available.

Stove enamelling is perhaps outside the scope of the handicraft room but if it is done, and especially if in conjunction with spraying, then precautions must be taken to see that there is adequate ventilation and that it is not in a part of the shop where there would be any danger of fire. In industry of course there are definite regulations regarding the use of paints and lacquers and these should be borne in mind.

Anodizing and dyeing   Anodic oxidation, or anodizing, is an electrolytic process for thickening the oxide film present on aluminium surfaces. It is done for several reasons: to provide a key for painting, to provide an insulation coating for an electrical conductor, for decorative purposes, or to increase the resistance of an aluminium surface to corrosion. All aluminium which is to be exposed to the atmosphere should be anodized. The oxide film formed by anodizing may be dyed to any desired colour. Pure aluminium anodizes more consistently than alloy, and if a job is to be anodized metal must be purchased accordingly. It is economic practice to purchase pure aluminium sheet for spinning and subsequent anodizing and keep the snippings and melt for producing pure aluminium castings; these will anodize much better than alloy castings. Like most other metal finishes, anodizing does not cover up scratches and irregularities but emphasizes them. The finishing or pre-treatment of aluminium articles for anodizing is most important. Sand castings present most difficulties because of their coarse grain structure, and the position of gates and risers is sometimes to be seen when the process is completed; if they can be arranged at the back of a job when moulding, so much the better. On small jobs, scratch vents can be used instead of risers. The mechanical treatment before anodizing will depend on the nature of the article. Spun work in pure aluminium may need treatment with a little emery cloth, followed by polishing on a polishing machine. Castings will have to be filed, draw-filed and carefully treated with emery cloth before polishing on the machine. Sand blasting and wire brushing may help with castings before filing. The use of good clean facing sand and some form of mould coat will help to get a clean smooth casting and eliminate some of the laborious filing. Highly polished surfaces produce a bright glasslike sheen, whilst sand blasting and scratch brushing give varying degrees of the matt finishes desired on some classes of work. Next, and highly important, is degreasing, either by the use of petrol or trichlorethylene, or by immersion for 10 to 20 seconds in a caustic soda solution at about 80°C. After this wash in running water, neutralize by a dip in a 10% nitric acid bath and again wash. If the work is at all scratched and the caustic soda solution is too strong there is a tendency to etch. Whatever the method of degreasing, the article must not be touched by hand before anodizing.

There are a number of electrolytes for anodic oxidation of aluminium, the three main ones being: (a) sulphuric acid; (b) chromic acid; and (c) oxalic acid. The first-named is the most common and is used in concentrations of 10 to 25% by weight. Chloride-free water must be used.

The anodic film is produced in the electrolyte by the passage of direct or alternating current. The articles are coupled to both anode and cathode bars in equal numbers. If a.c. is used, the current is passed for twice the time used in the d.c. process. The d.c. supply should be 1 to 2 volts and 1·5 to 2·5 amperes per 100 square centimetres of aluminium in the tank. The thickness of the anodic film produced depends on the time of immersion; 40 to 60 minutes gives a good thick film.

The bath is usually made of wood or metal, with a lead lining which forms the cathode, the anode bar being of copper. Heating with portable immersion heaters is advisable in smaller tanks. A temperature of 18°C to 27°C is required, the higher temperature yielding coarser-grained films most suitable for production of deep shades.

All materials to be anodized should be tightly and efficiently coupled to the anode bar, and all connected materials below the electrolyte surface should be of aluminium. Contacts being used regularly should be stripped and washed thoroughly in caustic soda after each anodizing cycle, otherwise a resistant non-conductive layer of aluminium will form and poor anodic film will result. When making connections, the area of contact should be as small as possible and in positions not easily seen on the finished article. Very small parts for anodizing should be held in an aluminium basket. After anodizing, thoroughly remove all electrolyte immediately and dye the articles as soon as possible.

All dyestuffs have some affinity for anodic film, but better results will be obtained by using those with a maximum affinity.

Concentration of the dyebath will depend upon the intensity of colour required, but increased dyeing time in dilute solution gives better results than short periods in concentrated dyebaths. The bath may be cold or hot, but better results are obtained with a hot bath, temperatures of 70°C to 80°C giving best results. After dyeing, the articles are washed in cold water and then sealed. The sealing operation closes the pores of the anodic film and is done in several ways:

(*a*) By immersion in boiling water for 5 to 10 minutes.

(*b*) By drying in an oven with hot air and then applying a wax finish such as lanolin, paraffin wax or linseed oil.

(*c*) By chemical treatment with cobalt acetate and sodium silicate and acid, thoroughly washing off afterwards.

If an article is not dyed, the sealing process is carried out immediately after anodizing.

Electroplating   Electroplating or electro-deposition is the depositing of metals by means of an electric current. If an electric current is passed through a solution of metallic salts the solution is decomposed and the pure metal precipitated. The metals commonly deposited in this way are copper, nickel, chrome, cadmium and silver. On most jobs a deposit of copper prior to the nickel or chrome etc. is an advantage. As with anodizing, the article must be cleaned, degreased and thoroughly washed, and not touched by hand between each vat and process. Solutions are available in which the metal is cleaned, degreased and coppered at the same time. The salts are mixed in a plain iron vat of cold water; lead-lined vats are not suitable. Anodes are of steel and copper in the proportion of four steel anodes to one copper. A supply of 4 to 6 volts is suitable and the current is regulated by a rheostat according to the quantity of articles in the vat. The average current should be 0·012 amperes per square centimetre of surface. The articles are suspended by copper wire from the middle (cathode) rod and immersed in the solution with the current switched on. Articles which are to be nickel-plated are removed after about 3 minutes, then swilled in cold water, put through a 10% sulphuric acid dip and again swilled before placing in the nickel vat.

Copper baths   If the articles to be coppered are cleaned and then copper-plated, a separate copper-plating solution may be made up as follows. Dissolve 200 g of copper sulphate in 1 litre of distilled water, and add to it, drop by drop, liquid ammonia at full strength. A green precipitate will appear and sink to the bottom. Continue to add ammonia until this precipitate is dissolved and the solution becomes a clear blue colour. Dilute this solution with half its volume of distilled water. Next make a solution of 300 g of potassium cyanide to 1 litre of water, and add to the first solution until it becomes a rich amber colour. Expose to the air for a few hours, then filter and dilute with double its volume of water. The solution is now ready for use.

Nickel-plating This may be done in stoneware or lead-lined wooden tanks, which are available in a wide range of sizes.

Proprietary brands of salts are also available and should be made into a solution by dissolving in water as directed. The correct density of the solution is stated and may be tested by means of a hydrometer. The pH value may be tested by using comparator paper, similar to litmus paper, taking care to obtain the correct comparator paper for the bath being used. The paper is immersed in the solution and undergoes a colour change, the final colour being checked by comparison with the chart supplied on the box containing the papers. If solutions have to stand for a long time between periods of use, the density and pH values must be tested, and corrected if necessary, before further use. Anodes are of rolled nickel and their area should be approximately equal to the cathode area, i.e. the area to be plated. The electric supply should be 0·1 to 0·2 volts d.c. and 0·3 to 0·6 amperes per square centimetre of the area to be plated. The current is switched on before the vat is loaded and the current supply increased as the load increases. The positive leads of the electric supply are connected to the anode, and the negative leads to the work to be plated, which then becomes the cathode. After leaving the plating bath, the article is washed and may also be lightly buffed or polished. When not in use all vats should be kept covered and free from dust and dirt, and if possible locked up in a separate room, as some of the solutions used are poisonous. Plating work should be done in a fume cupboard or a room with adequate means of extracting fumes. Fumes from silver and chrome plating are dangerous, and this should not be attempted in school workshops unless special provisions for extracting the fumes are present.

Faults in plated work

(a) *Stripping of the coat* is sometimes caused by faulty cleaning—when the work is not thoroughly degreased, the article enters the bath with an alkaline surface. It should be neutralized in dilute H_2SO_4. If a nickel solution is out of balance (another cause) add H_2SO_4 to produce an alkaline solution with a pH value of 6·0 or more.

(b) *Pitting* is caused when hydrogen bubbles are not released from the surface of the article. The bath requires agitating. For possible organic contamination, add small quantities of hydrogen peroxide.

(c) *Rough deposits* are due to solid particles settling on the surface during plating. To prevent this filter the solution.

(d) *Streaky or black deposits* are caused by metallic contamination. To prevent this, work the solution at a low voltage, with agitation, for a long period, (*e*) *Rough and dark corners.* If corners appear grey and rough, or black and powdery, the current is too high.

(*f*) *Thin deposits* occur when the insertion time is too short. Density of the solution should also be checked.

(*g*) *No deposit.* This results from reversed current or a contaminated solution.

Standard Tables

1. ISO screwthread tables

ISO Metric Coarse

Size	Pitch (mm)	Minor diameter (mm)	Tapping size drill (mm)	Clearance size drill (mm)
M 2·5	0·45	1·97	2·1	2·55
M 3	0·50	2·3	2·5	3·05
M 4	0·7	3·01	3·3	4·1
M 5	0·8	3·87	4·2	5·1
M 6	1·0	4·77	5·0	6·2
M 8	1·25	6·47	6·6	8·2
M10	1·5	8·16	8·5	10·2
M12	1·75	9·85	10·25	12·2
M14	2·0	11·55	12·0	14·25
M16	2·0	13·55	14·0	16·25
M20	2·5	16·93	17·5	20·25
M22	2·5	18·93	19·5	22·25
M24	3·0	20·32	21·0	24·25

ISO Metric Fine

Size	Pitch (mm)	Minor dia (mm)	Tapping drill (mm)	Clearance drill (mm)
M 8	1·00	6·74	6·8	8·2
M10	1·25	8·47	8·6	10·2
M12	1·25	10·47	10·8	12·2
M14	1·50	12·16	12·3	14·25
M16	1·50	14·16	14·25	16·25
M20	1·50	18·16	18·25	20·25
M22	1·50	20·16	20·25	22·25
M24	2·00	21·55	21·75	24·25

Unified Coarse (UNC)

Size	t.p.i.	Major dia (in)	Minor dia (in)	Tapping drill (mm)	Clearance drill (mm)
No. 4	40	0·112	0·085	2·25	2·95
No. 6	32	0·138	0·104	2·80	3·60
No. 8	32	0·164	0·130	3·50	4·30
No. 10	24	0·190	0·150	3·90	4·90
$\frac{1}{4}$ in	20	0·250	0·189	5·20	6·50
$\frac{5}{16}$ in	18	0·3125	0·244	6·50	8·20
$\frac{3}{8}$ in	16	0·375	0·298	8·00	9·80
$\frac{7}{16}$ in	14	0·4375	0·350	9·30	11·30
$\frac{1}{2}$ in	13	0·500	0·406	10·80	13·00
$\frac{9}{16}$ in	12	0·5625	0·460	12·25	14·75
$\frac{5}{8}$ in	11	0·625	0·514	13·50	16·50
$\frac{3}{4}$ in	10	0·750	0·627	16·50	19·50
$\frac{7}{8}$ in	9	0·875	0·739	19·25	22·75
1 in	8	1·000	0·847	22·25	25·75

Unified Fine (UNF)

Size (in)	t.p.i.	Major dia (in)	Minor dia (in)	Tapping drill (mm)	Clearance drill (mm)
$\frac{1}{4}$	28	0·250	0·206	5·5	6·5
$\frac{5}{16}$	24	0·3125	0·261	7·0	8·2
$\frac{3}{8}$	24	0·375	0·324	8·5	9·8
$\frac{7}{16}$	20	0·4375	0·376	9·8	11·3
$\frac{1}{2}$	20	0·500	0·439	11·5	13·0
$\frac{9}{16}$	18	0·5625	0·494	13·0	14·75
$\frac{5}{8}$	18	0·625	0·565	14·5	16·5
$\frac{3}{4}$	16	0·750	0·673	17·5	19·5
$\frac{7}{8}$	14	0·875	0·787	20·5	22·75
1	12	1·000	0·898	23·5	25·75

2. Old British standard screwthread tables

British Association (BA)

No.	Pitch (mm)	Major dia (mm)	Minor dia (mm)	Tapping drill (mm)	Clearance drill (mm)
0	1·00	6·0	4·80	5·00	6·10
1	0·90	5·3	4·24	4·50	5·50
2	0·81	4·7	3·73	4·00	4·85
3	0·73	4·1	3·24	3·45	4·25
4	0·66	3·6	2·82	3·00	3·75
5	0·59	3·2	2·40	2·65	3·30
6	0·53	2·8	2·16	2·30	2·90
7	0·48	2·5	1·91	2·00	2·60
8	0·43	2·2	1·68	1·80	2·25
9	0·39	1·9	1·42	1·55	1·95
10	0·35	1·7	1·27	1·40	1·75

The unit of size is the millimetre, 0·9 mm is the base, and by raising it to the power corresponding to any BA number the approximate pitch of that number is obtained thus:

$$\text{Pitch of No. } 2 = 0·9^2 = 0·81 \text{ mm}$$

English Standard Threads for Model Engineering (Whitworth form of thread)

Outside dia (in)	Core dia (in)	Threads per inch (t.p.i.)	Tapping drill	Clearance drill
$\frac{1}{8}$	0·0930	40	No. 40	No. 30
$\frac{5}{32}$	0·1252	40	No. 30	4 mm
$\frac{3}{16}$	0·1555	40	$\frac{5}{32}$ in	No. 12
$\frac{7}{32}$	0·1867	40	$\frac{3}{16}$ in	No. 2
$\frac{1}{4}$	0·2187	40	$\frac{7}{32}$ in	$6\frac{1}{2}$ mm
$\frac{5}{16}$	0·2725	32	7 mm	Letter O
$\frac{3}{8}$	0·3350	32	Letter R	Letter W
$\frac{7}{16}$	0·3883	26	10 mm	$11\frac{1}{2}$ mm
$\frac{1}{2}$	0·4508	26	$\frac{29}{64}$ in	$\frac{33}{64}$ in

British Standard Whitworth (BSW)

Outside diam (in)	Core diam (in)	Threads per inch (t.p.i.)	Tapping drill	Clearance drill
$\frac{1}{16}$	0·0412	60	No. 56	No. 52
$\frac{3}{32}$	0·0671	48	No. 50	No. 41
$\frac{1}{8}$	0·0930	40	No. 40	No. 30
$\frac{5}{32}$	0·1162	32	No. 31	4 mm
$\frac{3}{16}$	0·1342	24	$\frac{9}{64}$ in	No. 12
$\frac{7}{32}$	0·1654	24	No. 18	No. 2
$\frac{1}{4}$	0·1860	20	No. 11	$6\frac{1}{2}$ mm
$\frac{5}{16}$	0·2414	18	Letter D	Letter O
$\frac{3}{8}$	0·2950	16	Letter N	Letter W
$\frac{7}{16}$	0·3461	14	Letter S	$11\frac{1}{2}$ mm
$\frac{1}{2}$	0·3933	12	Letter X	$\frac{33}{64}$ in
$\frac{5}{8}$	0·5086	11	$\frac{33}{64}$ in	$\frac{41}{64}$ in
$\frac{3}{4}$	0·6220	10	$\frac{5}{8}$ in	$\frac{49}{64}$ in
$\frac{7}{8}$	0·7328	9	$\frac{47}{64}$ in	$\frac{57}{64}$ in
1	0·8400	8	$\frac{27}{32}$ in	$1\frac{1}{64}$ in

British Standard Fine (BSF)

Outside dia (in)	Core dia (in)	Threads per inch (t.p.i.)	Tapping drill	Clearance drill
$\frac{7}{32}$	0·1731	28	No. 16m	No. 2m
$\frac{1}{4}$	0·2007	26	No. 4m	Letter F
$\frac{9}{32}$	0·2320	26	Letter B	Letter L
$\frac{5}{16}$	0·2543	22	$\frac{17}{64}$ in	Letter O
$\frac{3}{8}$	0·3110	20	$\frac{21}{64}$ in	Letter W
$\frac{7}{16}$	0·3664	18	$\frac{3}{8}$ in	11·1 mm
$\frac{1}{2}$	0·4200	16	$\frac{7}{16}$ in	13·0 mm
$\frac{9}{16}$	0·4825	16	$\frac{1}{2}$ in	$\frac{37}{64}$ in
$\frac{5}{8}$	0·5335	14	$\frac{35}{64}$ in	$\frac{41}{64}$ in
$\frac{11}{16}$	0·5960	14	$\frac{39}{64}$ in	$\frac{45}{64}$ in
$\frac{3}{4}$	0·6433	12	$\frac{21}{32}$ in	$\frac{49}{64}$ in
$\frac{13}{16}$	0·7058	12	$\frac{23}{32}$ in	$\frac{53}{64}$ in
$\frac{7}{8}$	0·7586	11	$\frac{25}{32}$ in	$\frac{57}{64}$ in
1	0·8719	10	$\frac{57}{64}$ in	$1\frac{1}{64}$ in

British Standard Brass Screwthreads

Outside dia (in)	Core dia (in)	Threads per inch (t.p.i.)	Tapping drill (in)	Tapping drill (mm)	Clearance drill (in)	Clearance drill (mm)
$\frac{1}{8}$	0·0758	26	No. 47	1.90	No. 30	3.30
$\frac{1}{4}$	0·2008	26	No. 6	5·10	Letter F	6·50
$\frac{3}{8}$	0·3258	26	Letter Q	8·30	Letter W	9·80
$\frac{1}{2}$	0·4508	26	$\frac{29}{64}$	11·50	$\frac{33}{64}$	13·00
$\frac{5}{8}$	0·5758	26	$\frac{37}{64}$	14·75	$\frac{41}{64}$	16·25
$\frac{3}{4}$	0·7008	26	$\frac{45}{64}$	18·00	$\frac{49}{64}$	19·50
$\frac{7}{8}$	0·8258	26	$\frac{53}{64}$	21·00	$\frac{57}{64}$	22·50
1	0·9508	26	$\frac{61}{64}$	24·25	$1\frac{1}{64}$	25·75
$1\frac{1}{8}$	1·0758	26	$1\frac{5}{64}$	27·50	$1\frac{7}{64}$	29·00
$1\frac{1}{4}$	1·2008	26	$1\frac{13}{64}$	28·50	$1\frac{17}{64}$	32·50
$1\frac{1}{2}$	1·4508	26	$1\frac{29}{64}$	37·00	$1\frac{33}{64}$	38·50

Depth of thread = 0·0246 in.

3. Old British drill, wire and sheet metal tables
Morse Twist Drills Letter and Number Sizes

Description	Size (in)	Description	Size (in)	Description	Size (in)
Letter Z	0·4130	No. 11	0.1910	No. 46	0·0810
Letter Y	0·4040	No. 12	0·1890	No. 47	0·0785
Letter X	0·3970	No. 13	0·1850	No. 48	0·0760
Letter W	0·3860	No. 14	0·1820	No. 49	0·0730
Letter V	0·3770	No. 15	0·1800	No. 50	0·0700
Letter U	0·3680	No. 16	0·1770	No. 51	0·0670
Letter T	0·3580	No. 17	0·1730	No. 52	0·0635
Letter S	0·3480	No. 18	0·1695	No. 53	0·0595
Letter R	0·3390	No. 19	0·1660	No. 54	0·0550
Letter Q	0·3320	No. 20	0·1610	No. 55	0·0520
Letter P	0·3230	No. 21	0·1590	No. 56	0·0465
Letter O	0·3160	No. 22	0·1570	No. 57	0·0430
Letter N	0·3020	No. 23	0·1540	No. 58	0·0420
Letter M	0·2950	No. 24	0·1520	No. 59	0·0410
Letter L	0·2900	No. 25	0·1495	No. 60	0·0400
Letter K	0·2810	No. 26	0·1470	No. 61	0·0390
Letter J	0·2770	No. 27	0·1440	No. 62	0·0380
Letter I	0·2720	No. 28	0 1405	No. 63	0·0370
Letter H	0·2660	No. 29	0·1360	No. 64	0 ·0360
Letter G	0·2610	No. 30	0·1285	No. 65	0·0350
Letter F	0·2570	No. 31	0·1200	No. 66	0·0330
Letter E	0·2500	No. 32	0·1160	No. 67	0·0320
Letter D	0·2460	No. 33	0·1130	No. 68	0·0310
Letter C	0·2420	No. 34	0·1110	No. 69	0·0292
Letter B	0·2380	No. 35	0·1100	No. 70	0·0280
Letter A	0·2340	No. 36	0·1065	No. 71	0·0260
No. 1	0·2280	No. 37	0·1040	No. 72	0·0250
No. 2	0·2210	No. 38	0·1015	No. 73	0·0240
No. 3	0·2130	No. 39	0·0995	No. 74	0·0225
No. 4	0·2090	No. 40	0·0980	No. 75	0·0210
No. 5	0·2055	No. 41	0·0960	No. 76	0·0200
No. 6	0·2040	No. 42	0·0935	No. 77	0·0180
No. 7	0·2010	No. 43	0·0890	No. 78	0·0160
No. 8	0·1990	No. 44	0·0860	No. 79	0·0145
No. 9	0·1960	No. 45	0·0820	No. 80	0·0135
No. 10	0·1935				

Imperial Standard Wire Gauge

No	Dia (mm)	Dia (in)	No.	Dia (mm)	Dia (in)	No.	Dia (mm)	Dia (in)
0000	10·160	0·400	11	2·946	0·116	26	0·457	0·018
000	9·449	0·372	12	2·642	0·104	27	0·4166	0·0164
00	8·839	0·348	13	2·337	0·092	28	0·3759	0·0148
0	8·230	0·324	14	2·032	0·080	29	0·3454	0·0136
			15	1·829	0·072	30	0·3150	0·0124
1	7·620	0·300	16	1·626	0·064	31	0·2946	0·0116
2	7·010	0·276	17	1·422	0·056	32	0·2743	0·0108
3	6·401	0·252	18	1·219	0·048	33	0·2540	0·0100
4	5·893	0·232	19	1·016	0·040	34	0·2337	0·0092
5	5·385	0·212	20	0·914	0·036	35	0·2134	0·0084
6	4·877	0·192	21	0·813	0·032	36	0·1930	0·0076
7	4·470	0·176	22	0·711	0·028	37	0·1727	0·0068
8	4·064	0·160	23	0·610	0·024	38	0·1524	0·0060
9	3·658	0·144	24	0·559	0·022	39	0·1321	0·0052
10	3·251	0·128	25	0·508	0·020	40	0·1219	0·0048

4. Conversion tables
Millimetres into Inches

mm	in	mm	in	mm	in
1	0·0394	18	0·7087	35	1·3779
2	0·0787	19	0·7480	36	1·4173
3	0·1181	20	0·7874	37	1·4567
4	0·1575	21	0·8268	38	1·4961
5	0·1968	22	0·8661	39	1·5354
6	0·2362	23	0·9055	40	1·5748
7	0·2756	24	0·9449	41	1·6142
8	0·3150	25	0·9842	42	1·6535
9	0·3543	26	1·0236	43	1·6929
10	0·3937	27	1·0630	44	1·7323
11	0·4331	28	1·1024	45	1·7716
12	0·4724	29	1·1417	46	1·8110
13	0·5118	30	1·1811	47	1·8504
14	0·5512	31	1·2205	48	1·8898
15	0·5905	32	1·2598	49	1·9291
16	0·6299	33	1·2992	50	1·9685
17	0·6693	34	1·3386		

Comparison of Screwthread Sizes

ISO metric	BA	BSW	BSFine	UNC	UNF
2·5	8			3	3
	7				
	6			4	4
3	5	$\frac{1}{8}$		5	5
	4			6	6
4	3			8	8
5	2	$\frac{3}{16}$	$\frac{3}{16}$	10	10
	1			12	12
6	0	$\frac{1}{4}$	$\frac{1}{4}$	$\frac{1}{4}$	$\frac{1}{4}$
8		$\frac{5}{16}$	$\frac{5}{16}$	$\frac{5}{16}$	$\frac{5}{16}$
10		$\frac{3}{8}$	$\frac{3}{8}$	$\frac{3}{8}$	$\frac{3}{8}$
		$\frac{7}{16}$	$\frac{7}{16}$	$\frac{7}{16}$	$\frac{7}{16}$
12		$\frac{1}{2}$	$\frac{1}{2}$	$\frac{1}{2}$	$\frac{1}{2}$

8 metric sizes replace: 9 BA; 7 BSW and 6 BSFine sizes.

Relation of sheet metal thicknesses: SI metric and old standard wire gauge

Sheet metal thicknesses	SI metric (mm)		Old standard wire gauge		
	First choice	Second choice	SWG No.	mm	in
		3·5	10	3·3	0·128
	3·0		11	3·0	0·116
		2·8	12	2·7	0·104
	2·5				
		2·2	13	2·3	0·092
	2·0		14	2·0	0·080
		1·8	15	1·8	0·072
	1·6		16	1·6	0·064
		1·4	17	1·4	0·056
	1·2		18	1·2	0·048
		1·1			
	1·0		19	1·0	0·040
		0·9	20	0·9	0·036
	0·8		21	0·8	0·032
		0·7	22	0·7	0·028
	0·6		23	0·61	0·024
		0·55	24	0·56	0·022
	0·5		25	0·51	0·020
		0·45	26	0·46	0·018
	0·4		27	0·42	0·0164
			28	0·38	0·0148
		0·35	29	0·35	0·0136
	0·3		30	0·32	0·0124

Density of Metals and Approximate Melting Temperatures

Metal				Melting temperature °C	Specific gravity
Aluminium (casting)				575– 630	2·76
Brass (casting)				985	8·1
Copper				1100	8·79
Iron (cast)				1000–1200	7·5
Iron (wrought)				1500–1600	7·74
Lead				330	11·35
Silver				960	10·48
Steel				1400	7·8
Tin				235	7·29
Zinc				400	7·19
Spelters	Copper	Zinc			
Soft	50	50		870	
Medium	54	46		885·	
Hard	60	40		894	
Silver solders					
Ternary alloys of silver, copper and zinc					
Extra Easy				680– 700	
Easy				605– 723	
Medium				720– 765	
Hard				745– 778	
Enamelling				730– 800	
Soft solders	Tin	Lead	Bismuth		
Plumber's	1	2	—	225	
Tinman's	1	1	—	170	
Tinman's Fine	2	1	—	160	
Pewterer's	1	1	1	112	

Examination Questions

The following abbreviations for the various Examining Boards have been used at the ends of questions:

AEB   Associated Examining Board
ALSEB   Associated Lancashire Schools Examining Board
EMREB   East Midland Regional Examinations Board
NWSSEB   North Western Secondary School Examinations Board
OCSEB   Oxford and Cambridge Schools Examination Board
OLE   Oxford Local Examinations
SUJB   Southern Universities Joint Board
UCLES   University of Cambridge Local Examinations Syndicate
WJEC   Welsh Joint Education Committee
YREB   Yorkshire Regional Examinations Board

In the examination questions which follow, approximate metric values equivalent to the original values in British units have been inserted in brackets.

Metalwork (Ordinary Level)

Materials and Heat-treatment

1. (i) How does the composition of mild steel differ from that of cast steel?
   (ii) If you were given a specimen of each of these, what **two** tests would you apply, and what reactions would you look for in order to identify them?   (AEB 1966)

2. (*a*) Complete each of the following sentences. The first one has been done for you.

   (i) Copper can be annealed by heating it to a dull red and either quenching or allowing it to cool.
   (ii) Copper can be hardened by...
   (iii) Tool steel can be annealed by ....
   (iv) Tool steel can be hardened by ....
   (v) Mild steel can be surface hardened by ....
   (vi) Brass can be annealed by ....

   (*b*) Write down each of the following metals in order of hardness, putting the hardest first; Aluminium, Steel, Lead, Brass.   (ALSEB 1967)

3. Mild steel can be treated to produce a wear-resistant skin. Give an example where this treatment would be required.
   Describe in detail how the wear-resistant skin would be obtained in the school workshop.
   Give **two** reasons why the industrial method is not suitable for use in school workshops.   (NWSSEB 1967)

4. A piece of high carbon steel is subjected to the heat treatments named in the order shown. Select *three* of the treatments and state how they are carried out, and the effect on the metal in each case.
(1) Annealing   (2) Normalizing   (3) Hardening   (4) Tempering   (YREB 1967)

5. What is meant by 'chemical cleanliness' when related to work in brass, copper, etc.? How is the process of cleaning carried out and what are the materials used in cleaning the metal? What precautions should be taken in the use and storage of the materials involved?   (OLE 1967)

6. The jaws of a pin vice are made from high carbon steel. Describe how this type of steel is manufactured, and explain how you would treat the jaws to prevent wear in use.   (WJEC 1967)

7. (*a*) Explain how you would identify the following materials, (i) by inspecting fractured samples, and (ii) by another simple workshop test: (1) cast iron, (2) wrought iron, (3) mild steel, (4) high carbon steel, (5) high speed steel.
   (*b*) From your own experience suggest a use for each of **three** of the above metals. Include in your answer the reasons for its suitability for the purpose you have chosen.   (UCLES 1967)

8. Write an account of the manufacture of **either** pig iron **or** mild steel **or** copper. Mention in your account the main sources of supply of the materials used in conjunction with the manufacturing process, and the market forms of the finished product.   (OLE 1967)

9. Three centre punches have been made. Describe how you would harden and temper them. When used, one is found to have the point flattened, the second breaks off and the third stands up to hard use. Give the reasons for these differences.   (SUJB 1967)

   (*a*) Describe (i) the case hardening of mild steel; (ii) the hardening and tempering of tool steel, mentioning the colours and temperature range involved.
   (*b*) What is the essential difference between iron and steel?   (OCSEB 1967)

11. If you were given five specimens of different metals to identify, each 1 in. (25 mm) diameter and 6 in. (150 mm) long, and were told that they were brass, aluminium, mild steel, copper and tool steel, describe:

   (*a*) the simple tests you could apply to them in the school workshop to identify them,
   (*b*) the result of each test on each specimen.   (AEB 1968)

12. What materials would you use for **four** of the following, briefly mentioning the important properties of the material which make it suitable for each particular purpose:
   (*a*) Centre punch.
   (*b*) Toast rack.
   (*c*) Cylinder of a steam engine.
   (*d*) Decorative bracket for a hanging flower basket.
   (*e*) Bed of a lathe.   (OCSEB 1968)

13. When metal is heated in air, oxidation takes place. Write about its effect for good or ill when (i) forging, (ii) soldering, (iii) annealing, (iv) tempering. Your considerations should cover a wide range of metals.   (OLE 1968)

14. When testing the blade of a screwdriver you have made, the end becomes distorted —it has bent but not broken. Give the reason for this and describe how you would remedy the fault.   (WJEC 1968)

15. What is an 'alloy' and how is it made? Choose **three** alloys. Name the metals used to produce each alloy and in **each** case give **one** example of its use in engineering. (NWSSEB 1968)

16. Name **four** alloys you have used in the workshop and opposite **one** of these state the metals that it is made from?   (WJEC 1969)

17. (i) Complete the following sentences. Write the missing words on your answer paper:

(a)   (a) The blast furnace converts .... into ....
       (b) The open-hearth furnace is used to produce ....
       (c) 'Duralumin' is principally an alloy of .... and ....
       (d) Brass is an alloy of .... and ....
       (e) Silver solder is an alloy of ...., ... and ....
       (f) Hacksaw blades are made of .... or ....

(ii) Draw a simple sectional elevation of a blast furnace and include the following features (hatching is not required):

The 'skip'. Name the contents making up the 'charge' (or burden).
Charging bells.
Exit for waste gases.
Blast or bustle pipe.
Tuyeres.
Tapping notches for slag and iron.
The hearth.   (UCLES 1969)

18. When grinding a scriber, colours appear at the tip of the tool on the grindstone. (a) Why do the colours appear? (b) What effect does this have on the scriber? (c) State in detail, how you would make the scriber fit for use.   (WJEC 1969)

Benchwork

1. Given a piece of 4 in. (100 mm) × 4 in. (100 mm) × 20 s.w.g. (0·9 mm) copper, describe how you would make a shallow circular dish: e.g. sweet dish.   (AEB 1966)

2. You are given a 4 in. (100 mm) diameter ring which has been forged from ¾ in. (20 mm) × 3/16 in. (5 mm) mild steel bar. An unsuccessful attempt has been made to braze the joint on it.
    Describe the steps you would now take to ensure that this ring is successfully brazed. (AEB 1961)

3. For the production of high quality work, tools and equipment must be regularly maintained.

Describe how you would keep the following tools and pieces of equipment in first-class condition: (*a*) a bench vice; (*b*) a wheel brace; (*c*) a grindstone; (*d*) a forge. (WJEC 1967)

4. Using notes and sketches, show how you would set each of the following tools to a dimension of ¾ in. (20 mm). In each case explain why you consider the method you have given to be the best.

Inside calipers   Odd-leg calipers   Spring dividers.   (AEB 1967)

5. Make sketches of the following tools used in tinplate work: a hatchet stake; a bick iron; a creasing iron; a pair of folding bars; a rawhide mallet. From these tools, choose any **three** and illustrate one use for each.   (WJEC 1967)

6.   (i) What are the advantages and disadvantages of cutting metal with a lever bench shear?
  (ii) If the shear is not cutting well, in what **two** ways could you improve its efficiency?
  (iii) What **two** precautions would you recommend to the operator to ensure his own safety and that of others?   (AEB 1967)

7. (*a*) (i) Give **three** reasons why copper is used for the 'bit' of a soldering iron.
  (ii) What damage to the tinned 'bit' can be expected if it is allowed to reach red heat?
(*b*) (iii) Zinc chloride solution ('killed spirits') and resin fluxes are commonly used in soft soldering processes.
  (1) Explain what function flux performs in the soldering process.
  (2) When and why would you use a resin flux in preference to zinc chloride? (UCLES 1967)

8. Name the tool(s) you would use for each of the following processes:
  (i) tightening a nut sunk below the surface;
  (ii) cutting a hot mild steel bar ½ in. (12 mm) × ½ in. (12 mm);
  (iii) making a ½ in. (12 mm) diameter hole in thin sheet metal;
  (iv) marking an arc of 1 in. (25 mm) radius;
  (v) 'finishing' a cup-head rivet;
  (vi) starting to spread a rivet;
  (vii) cutting off metal which is rotating in a lathe;
  (viii) sinking a copper dish;
  (ix) filing a 3/16 in. (5 mm) wide slot;
  (x) threading a rod.   (AEB 1967)

9. Describe **four** of the following operations, using freehand sketches: riveting; tinning; screwing a thread; tapping a hole; sinking a bowl or tray.   (SUJB 1967)

10. Make a drawing of a pistol-grip adjustable hacksaw and show in an enlarged drawing how the tension is put on the blade. When replacing a blade what precautions should be taken?

For what particular types of work are blades made with 18, 24 and 32 teeth per inch (25 mm) respectively?   (OCSEB 1967)

11. The following are usually used together: surface plate, scribing block, vee block and clamps. Make a sketch showing these being used in unison on some casting or piece of work. (SUJB 1967)

12. Make sketches of the following rivets: the snaphead, the countersunk head, the flat head, and the tubular, and give a practical example of a use for each.
   Illustrate clearly the stages in forming the head on a snaphead rivet. (WJEC 1968)

13. (*a*) Why is it frequently necessary to planish work in copper and gilding metal? Explain how you would planish a small circular bowl.
   (*b*) Describe in detail how you would silver solder a circular base ring on to this bowl. (OCSEB 1967)

14. State very briefly what is meant by each of the following metalworking terms: quench, fettle, jump up, temper, raise, ream, bore, sweat, tap, seam, anneal, swarf, suds, part off. (WJEC 1968)

15. Describe three permanent and two semi-permanent ways of joining metal together. Draw the objects to which these methods could be applied. One joint should be applied to one object. (SUJB 1968)

16. Name **two** safety precautions you would observe when performing each of the following operations:
   (*a*) facing $\frac{1}{4}$ in. (6 mm) diameter brass rod in the lathe;
   (*b*) pickling a copper dish after annealing;
   (*c*) using a 3-jaw chuck open to its fullest extent;
   (*d*) using a hammer and cold chisel;
   · (*e*) drilling a $\frac{1}{4}$ in. (6 mm) hole in 22 s.w.g. (0·7 mm) sheet brass on a drilling machine.
   (AEB 1968)

17. With the aid of drawings describe how you would make a wire edge on the top edge of a seamed cylinder of 3 in. (75 mm) diameter and 5 in. (130 mm) long made of tinplate. (SUJB 1968)

18. Sketch and describe **four** devices for locking nuts, other than locknuts. When a locknut is used the locknut should be put on **before** the main nut. Why is this? (OLE 1968)

19. (*a*) Explain how you would control the depth of an external screw thread using a circular split die and stock so that there would be a tight fit between the rod you have threaded and a standard hexagonal nut.
   (*b*) Outline two faults which can arise when cutting an external thread by hand and state how they may be avoided. (UCLES 1968)

20. (*a*) Draw a section of: (i) a safe edge, and (ii) a wired edge, in tin plate.
   (*b*) When would you use each method in preference to the other? Give an example in each case. (AEB 1968)

21. (*a*) Choose a practical example, preferably from your own experience, to assist in explaining the processes involved in either snap head or countersunk head riveting.
    (*b*) What factors were considered when:

        (i) deciding where the rivets should be placed,
        (ii) calculating the rivet length?

    (*c*) Faced with the possibility of having to use bright drawn mild steel rod for making a double countersunk-head riveted joint state one difficulty you would expect to encounter and explain how you would overcome it.   (UCLES 1968)

22. (*a*) What is a spring washer used for?
    (*b*) Name **two** other devices which can be used for the same purpose as a spring washer.
    (*c*) Where is a tee bolt used?
    (*d*) Give **two** occasions where you would wear goggles in the workshop.   (WJEC 1969)

23. (*a*) Give **one** use you have made of:

        (i) a round file;
        (ii) a three square file;
        (iii) a warding file;
        (iv) a needle file.

    (*b*) How would you clean a file after filing an aluminium casting?
    (*c*) Why should you ensure that a file does not come into contact with oil?
(WJEC 1969)

24. (*a*) Show by sketches a set of three taps that would be used for cutting internal threads in a blind hole. Indicate the main difference between each of the taps.
    (*b*) Explain how you would tap a blind hole in a piece of mild steel, and what precautions you would take.
    (*c*) State the name of a material that (i) requires no lubrication when being tapped, (ii) requires lubrication when being tapped.   (EMREB 1969)

25. Describe in detail **two** methods, other than using the tank cutter, to cut a 2 in. (50 mm) diameter hole into a piece of 18 s.w.g. (1·2 mm) mild steel plate 6 in. square (150 mm). Illustrate your answer fully and list all the tools you would use for the purpose.   (WJEC 1969)

26. Explain briefly, or illustrate by means of a sketch, the meaning of the following technical terms: planish, face off, strickle, scribe, swage, ductile, normalize, case harden, datum, safe-edge, counterbore, knurl, set, calibrate.   (WJEC 1969)

Forgework and Casting

1. Sketch a pair of fullers and show what provision is made for one to be held in the anvil and the other in the hand. Give an example of the use of fullers.   (YREB 1966)

2. Which part of the anvil is used when 'drawing down'?
  The chopping area   The hardie   The bick   The punch hole
Which is the correct heat colour to use when forging mild steel?
  Black   Yellow   Dull red   Bright red
What is the name of the hollow end which may be caused through careless drawing down of mild steel rod?
  Scaling   Burning   Piping   Chipping
Which tongs arc used for gripping round stock?
  Open mouth   Pick up   Round nose   Hollow bit
Which hammer face is used to rough form the head of a round-headed rivet?
  Cross pein   Ball pein   Straight pein   Flat pein
What is the correct name for the air hole of a forge hearth?
  Tuyère   Bosh   Nozzle   Inlet
Which tools are used to finish circular-section forged work?
  Fullers   Swages   Flatters   Hardies
Name the process for joining together two pieces of almost melting wrought iron.
  Fire welding   Riveting   Brazing   Sweating
Which impurity causes 'hot shortness' in steel?
  Carbon   Sulphur   Phosphorus   Manganese
Which punch is used to start a round hole forged in mild steel?
  Oval   Round   Square   Hexagonal   (YREB 1967)

3. Make a neat dimensioned freehand pictorial sketch of a forged hook and staple mounted on a vertical back board. The overall size of your hook and staple should be approximately $5\frac{1}{2}$ in. (140 mm). Describe in detail exactly how you would make the staple.   (OLE 1967)

4. (*a*) Explain (i) how you would assess the suitability of foundry sand for moulding, and (ii) what steps you would take to restore it to condition if found unsatisfactory.
  (*b*) Why and when is parting sand (or powder) used?
  (*c*) Sketch and identify **three** moulding tools and explain how they are used. (UCLES 1967)

5. Explain clearly, with the aid of labelled drawings, the moulding procedure when using a split pattern.
  State the precautions necessary when casting in the school workshop.   (OCSEB 1967)

6. With the aid of sketches describe how you would weld together two pieces of $\frac{5}{8}$ in. (15 mm) diameter mild steel end to end, using the blacksmith's weld.   (SUJB 1967)

7. Show how you would form, by forging, a $\frac{1}{2}$ in. (12 mm) square hole in a piece of wrought iron $\frac{5}{8}$ in. (16 mm) square in cross section   (WJEC 1968)

8. Choose **three** of the following pairs and explain what they mean to you in connection with casting. Illustrate with sketches where appropriate.
  (*a*) Runner and Riser.
  (*b*) Cores and Core Prints.
  (*c*) Degassing and Fluxing.
  (*d*) Cope and Drag.
  (*e*) Rammer and Strickler.   (NWSSEB 1968)

9. Name and sketch **four** tools or pieces of equipment used in casting, and give their uses.   (WJEC 1968)

10. (*a*) Make sketches of **five** tools used for moulding, and state their names.
    (**d**) Complete these sentences:
      (i) The lower moulding box (or flask) is called the ....
      (ii) The upper moulding box (or flask) is called the ....
      (iii) Parting powder is used for ....   (ALSEB 1968)

11. The blacksmith uses a vice known as a leg vice. Sketch this vice, name the materials from which it is made and note the special features that make it suitable for a blacksmith. With notes and sketches explain why a leg vice is not such an efficient holding device, for square and rectangular stock, as the engineer's bench vice.   (YREB 1969)

12. Draw a section through a 'rammed up' moulding flask, showing the pattern cavity and the arrangements to ensure that the molten metal can be poured in to produce a satisfactory casting. Label the various parts and passages. How is provision made for the escape of gases from the flask?   (NWSSEB 1969)

13. With the aid of sketches, describe how you would forge a $2\frac{1}{2}$ in. (65 mm) diameter ring at the end of a length of mild steel $\frac{1}{2}$ in. (12 mm) in diameter.   (SUJB 1969)

14. You are making a gate which requires a number of 'S' scrolls all of which are the same size. The ends of the scrolls are to be tapered.
    Describe how you would make these scrolls from $\frac{1}{2}$ in. (15 mm) $\times$ $\frac{5}{16}$ in (8 mm) black mild steel naming four of the tools you would use. Sketches may be used to illustrate your answer. The lengths of stock are cut to size reading for forging.
(EMREB 1969)

Machine Work

1. Show how you could use a lathe to put a screwthread on a rod of metal, using hand dies. Sketch a tail-stock die holder. What advantages has the use of a tail-stock die holder over the normal hand die stock method?   (YREB 1966)

2. If, when you are turning bright drawn mild steel on the lathe, the metal tears and leaves a rough surface, what **five** steps could you take in an attempt to remedy this?
(AEB 1966)

3. (*a*) Show by means of labelled drawings the important rake and clearance angles on a typical lathe tool.
    Give a table of the rake and clearance angles you would use when turning (i) mild steel, (ii) aluminium, (iii) brass.
    (*b*) What is the function of a lathe back gear? How is this gear engaged?   (OCSEB 1967)

4. Make a freehand sketch of two views of a lathe tool-post holder, showing clearly how the tool is adjusted to cut on centre. Why is it important that the tool be adjusted to its correct height?
    Describe in detail how you would set up a lathe and prepare a piece of mild steel bar for turning between centres.   (OLE 1967)

5. A 1 in. (25 mm) diameter by 12 in. (300 mm) long bar of bright mild steel is faced at both ends and centre drilled ready for turning to a diameter of $\frac{7}{8}$ in. (20 mm). Describe with the aid of sketches how you would:

(*a*) select and correctly insert the lathe centres;
(*b*) mount the work between centres;
(*c*) test that the lathe is turning parallel;
(*d*) correct any tendency to produce a taper.   (UCLES 1967)

6. A lathe dead centre is found to be blunt and deeply scored.

(*a*) What could have caused this damage?

(*b*) Describe in note form how this centre could be made fit for use again in the school workshop without the use of grinding facilities.   (AEB 1968)

7. (*a*) What are the causes of the following faults on a lathe:

(i) the cross-slide feed is very slack,
(ii) the tailstock centre burns out?

(*b*) State **three** reasons why chatter marks occur on a workpiece and discuss suitable remedies.   (UCLES 1968).

8. Make freehand drawings of (*a*) two types of lathe-steadies and (*b*) the clapper-box on the shaping machine.   (SUJB 1968)

9. (*a*) Using the cylinder and piston of a model steam engine as your example name and describe a method of achieving a close fit between the two components and identify the materials you would use.

(*b*) After machining a small cast iron surface plate in the workshop it is necessary to further true the top surface by hand so that on presentation to a master surface plate, not less than ten spots per square inch (per 650 sq. mm) of engineers blue will be visible. Describe and use sketches to show how you would achieve this accuracy.   (UCLES 1968)

10. A single-throw crankshaft with two end journals for a model steam engine is to be machined from a solid bar. With the aid of sketches and a brief description, show how the crankshaft can be produced.   (NWSSEB 1968)

11. (*a*) (i) Two sets of jaws are provided with a 3-jaw self-centring chuck. From your experience, describe a typical use for each set. Use sketches to illustrate your answers.

(ii) How do you fit the jaws of a self-centring chuck?
(iii) Why cannot the jaws be reversed?   (UCLES 1968)

12. Describe the principles and purpose of lubricating moving machinery parts. With the aid of drawings, show **two** different methods of employing oil as a lubricant to moving parts.   (SUJB 1968)

13. (*a*) State three necessary qualities of good coolant and give two different examples of the use of coolants in the school workshop.

(*b*) State three necessary qualities of a good lubricant and give two examples of the use of different lubricants in the school workshop.   (AEB 1969)

14. Sketch, describe briefly, and state the uses of the following tools:
  (*a*) A centre drill.
  (*b*) A parting tool.
  (*c*) A lathe carrier.
  (*d*) A centre.
  (*e*) A knurling tool. (EMREB 1969)

15. A 12 in. (300 mm) length of 2 in. (50 mm) diameter mild steel bar, which is too large to pass into the headstock spindle, has to have both of its ends faced. Using notes and sketches show how this operation may be **safely** carried out on a school lathe.
  Sketch the method by which the centre of one of the faced ends may be found using odd leg calipers, a rule and a scriber only. (YREB 1969)

16. (*a*) Sketch a tool you have used in the shaping machine.
  (*b*) What was the tool used for?
  (*c*) What is the purpose of the clapper box on the shaping machine? (WJEC 1969)

Metalwork (Advanced Level)

Materials and Heat-treatment

1. The percentage of the alloying elements determines the quality of brass.
  Explain the differences between the three main categories of brass, and give examples of particular uses to which the brass in each category is put.
  Relate your examples wherever possible to uses in the school workshop (WJEC 1967)

2. Write an account of the manufacture and properties of **two** of the following metals and their common alloys, aluminium, copper, zinc, lead. Give an account of the uses of these two metals and their alloys, in industry and in school workshops. (UCLES 1967)

3. (*a*) State what you understand by the following metallurgical terms:
      (i) hardness,
      (ii) ductility,
      (iii) malleability,
      (iv) tensile strength,
      (v) toughness.

  (*b*) Describe in some detail how you would be able to identify the following metals by using a series of simple workshop tests:
      (i) cast iron,
      (ii) cast steel,
      (iii) wrought iron,
      (iv) high speed steel,
      (v) mild steel.

  (*c*) What is meant by a spark test and how is it possible to identify ferrous metals by this method? (SUJB 1968)

4. (*a*) Describe the composition, manufacture and uses of (i) cast iron, (ii) stainless steel, (iii) high speed steel.

(*b*) Describe a modern method of steel making.   (WJEC 1968)

5. (*a*) Describe the properties of two alloys used in the school workshop and compare these with the properties of the parent metals.

(*b*) Describe the constitution and properties of two other alloys which are used extensively in engineering.   (AEB 1968)

6. Describe briefly the production of aluminium. State its properties and give examples of the ways in which these properties have been utilized to the advantage of:

(*a*) mechanical engineers,
(*b*) builders,
(*c*) electrical engineers,
(*d*) the housewife.   (OLE 1968)

7. Modern methods of steel making have made it possible to control the introduction of alloying elements with great accuracy. Discuss the effect these advances have made in modern industry, illustrating your answer with practical examples.   (WJEC 1969)

8. (*a*) Name two alloys used as bearing metals. State their constituents and explain the precise properties they must possess in order to fulfil their function.

(*b*) Sketch and describe a thrust and a journal bearing and give a practical example where each would be used. Explain the function of the bearings in each case.   (UCLES 1969)

9. What specific advantages are achieved by using alloy steels instead of straight carbon steels? Develop your answer by referring to the constituents, properties, and uses of four alloy steels.   (UCLES 1969)

10. (*a*) Describe the changes which take place when steel is heated to a temperature exceeding 700° Centigrade (Celsius) and explain the meaning of the following terms: lower critical point, upper critical point, critical range, pearlite and austenite.

(*b*) Write a detailed account of hardening and tempering a piece of high carbon steel noting all the changes which occur during these processes.

(*c*) Give your reasons why whale oil, brine or caustic soda are sometimes preferred as quenching media when hardening steel.   (SUJB 1969)

11. Steels may be classified as 'low carbon', 'mild', 'medium carbon' and 'high carbon'. Distinguish between these various kinds of steel, and describe one method of producing a steel.

What are **alloy steels**? Give a short description of three of them.   (OLE 1969)

Benchwork

1. A copper vase is to be raised and its rim requires stiffening. This is done by the addition of a decorative wire.

(*a*) Using sketches and notes, describe how you would (i) make a decorative wire using 16 s.w.g. (1·6 mm) copper wire as the basic material, and (ii) apply it to the raised vase.

(*b*) Describe an alternative method whereby the rim may be stiffened during the raising of the vase.   (AEB 1967)

2. Give brief descriptions of each of the following technical terms, and relate them to metalworking practice: (*a*) caulking; (*b*) planishing; (*c*) parting; (*d*) chilling; (*e*) swaging; (*f*) anodizing; (*g*) sweating; (*h*) forming. Illustrate your answer wherever possible. (WJEC 1967)

3. Relating your answer to personal experience, describe how you would make a silversmith's hinge or joint. Include details and sketches of all tools used and the problems encountered in making and assembling the chenier and bearers.

NOTE: The fitting and silver soldering of the hinge to the object for which it has been made are not to be included in the answer.   (UCLES 1967)

4. The two methods used in the workshop to make a cylindrical container from sheet metal are (*a*) by raising, (*b*) by seaming.

Describe in detail how you make a container 6 in. (150 mm) high and 3 in. (75 mm) in diameter from 18 s.w.g. (1·2 mm) copper sheet, by each of the above methods.

Set out your answer in the form of a process sheet with suitable illustrations of the basic stages of manufacture.   (WJEC 1967)

5. Certain problems and types of work in engineering require the use of scrapers. Discuss the technique and appropriate use of scraping by describing situations you have experienced or seen. Draw sketches to illustrate your answer and include in them clear views of the tools mentioned.   (UCLES 1967)

6. In what condition should hammers and stakes be kept that are used for beaten metalwork? How is this condition maintained?

Sketch full size a 5 in. (130 mm) well-proportioned vase. Sketch the hammer and the stakes you would use in the raising of the vase from a sheet of gilding metal.

Describe and sketch the stages of making the vase.   (OLE 1967)

7. Explain the following processes, giving typical situations preferably from your own experience, where they would be used: snarling, caulking, stitching, chasing.   (UCLES 1967)

8. By means of sketches, show the difference between the following pairs of tools and articles of equipment, and explain briefly a use for each:

(*a*) a pin vice and a hand vice;
(*b*) a castellated nut and a captive nut;
(*c*) a plug gauge and a feeler gauge;
(*d*) a screw pitch gauge and a screw cutting gauge.   (WJEC 1968)

9. Discuss the considerations to be taken into account when deciding whether a vessel is to be made by seaming or raising. Illustrate your answer by sketching and describing appropriate practical examples.   (UCLES 1968)

10. Define **brazing**. Describe and illustrate various ways in which parts may be held together during brazing operations. State and describe briefly the scientific principles involved in a single brazing operation. Discuss, giving examples, the categories of brazing alloys in common use.   (OLE 1968)

11. Engineer's, machine, hand, pin, and leg vices are to be found in most school work-shops. Explain the reasons for such variety and describe **one** different use of each type.

Illustrate with three-dimensional sketches **three** of these vices and list, with reasons, the materials used in the construction of each.   (WJEC 1969)

12. Distinguish between the process of hollowing and that of raising, making reference to the metal flow in each case.

Give the names of the hammers and mallets which are the most suitable for these operations and sketch sections of their working faces.

Draw the outline of one article you would raise and one which you would hollow. Explain why these processes are the most suitable for the examples you have chosen. (AEB 1969)

Machinework

1. Write an essay on the effects of rakes and clearances in the cutting action of the hand and machine tools commonly found in the school workshop.   (AEB 1967)

2. Make sketches to show the difference between and the specific uses of each of the following lathe centres:

    (*a*) the revolving centre;
    (*b*) the half centre;
    (*c*) the ball-ended centre;
    (*d*) the dead centre.

Explain in each case the reason for your choice.   (WJEC 1967)

3. Make sketch diagrams to show clearly how (*a*) the tail-stock may be offset for taper turning, (*b*) how short tapers may be turned by using the top slide.

What effect on taper turning has a tool that is not set at centre height?

Explain in detail the checks you would make to ensure that the resetting of a tail-stock after taper turning was accurate for parallel turning.   (OLE 1967)

4. Make sketches to show clearly the rake and clearance angles on each of the following cutting tools:

    (*a*) twist drill;
    (*b*) lathe tool;
    (*c*) reamer.

State with reasons what variation, if any, is required to the rake and clearance angles of a roughing tool when used to cut (i) mild steel, (ii) brass, (iii) aluminium, on a lathe. (WJEC 1967)

5. A prerequisite of metalwork is accuracy. Write an essay on measuring to fine limits as carried out in your school workshop.   (OLE 1967)

6. Explain in detail how you would utilize the centre lathe to cut an $\frac{1}{8}$ in. (4 mm) square keyway along a bar of mild steel 5 in. (130 mm) long and 1 in. (25 mm) in diameter.

Illustrate clearly how you would set up the work in the machine, and make a sketch of the cutting end of the tool you would use.   (WJEC 1968)

7. Using sketches and notes describe four different types of metal cutting drill. State for what purpose each is used and how they are maintained in good condition.   (AEB 1968)

8. Friction, which may be defined as resistance to motion, is the greatest single cause of machine wear. Lubricants, coolants and cutting oils reduce friction to a minimum Write an essay on the principles and practice of lubrication and cooling.   (OLE 1968)

9. (a) Name and describe the special uses of **three** different types of cutters used in a horizontal milling machine.
   (b) Make a simple diagram showing the direction of feed and the direction of rotation on a horizontal milling machine. State the reason why the work is fed in the direction you have shown.
   (c) Describe briefly one operation which could be done on a vertical milling machine but not on a horizontal milling machine.   (AEB 1968)

10. (a) By means of a cross-sectional orthographic sketch, show how a grinding wheel is mounted on to the spindle of a pedestal grinding machine.
   (b) Name some of the abrasive materials which are used to manufacture grinding wheels.
   (c) Explain how you would 'true' a wheel that had been badly worn.
   (d) What type of grinding wheel would you use to sharpen a cemented carbide tool?   (SUJB 1968)

11. (a) Draw up a list of rules designed to prevent danger to the operator of a bench or pedestal-grinder and which will also ensure that abrasive wheels are maintained in good condition.
   (b) Write short notes on the use of abrasives in the school workshop.   (AEB 1968)

12. (a) Make a well proportioned drawing of a twist drill naming the different features and showing the correct cutting angles.
   (b) What do you understand by the term 'web thinning' and why is it done?
   (c) Give your reasons for using a quick-helix drill when drilling aluminium.
   (d) State the causes of the following common faults in drilling and explain how they may be overcome:

> (i) The corners of the drill wear away rapidly.
> (ii) The finished hole is oversize.
> (iii) The cutting edges chip.
> (iv) The drill will not start cutting when pressure is applied.   (SUJB 1968)

13. What considerations would govern your choice of materials if asked to make a small machine vice, of base size 6 in. (150 mm) × 3 in. (75 mm), in your school workshop?
   Outline your method of approach and prepare a sequence-of-operations chart, including a three-dimensional sketch of the proposed vice.   (WJEC 1969)

14. Explain the principles that underlie metal cutting as exemplified in the following:
   a lathe tool,   cold chisel,   twist drill,   tinsnips.
In each case show the way in which the general principles apply to the individual tool actions.   (UCLES 1969)

15. Write an essay on cutting speeds and feeds. Make reference to the different materials used in the school workshop as well as to the different methods of machining these. (AEB 1969)

16. Name the material you would use to make a new No. 2 morse taper dead centre. How would you ensure that the taper was an accurate fit in the tailstock?

Describe, in the form of a process sheet, the stages in its manufacture, from rod to setting up in position in the tailstock. Illustrate your answer fully. (WJEC 1969)

17. The lathe tool posts in general use on school lathes are the American type, the English type and the four-way. Sketch each of these and discuss their advantages and disadvantages. (OLE 1969)

18. (a) Explain in detail, the basic functions of cutting lubricants which are used when machining certain types of metal.

(b) Name the cutting lubricants you would use when turning (i) mild steel, (ii) copper, (iii) aluminium, (iv) stainless steel.

(c) Name two metals which do not require cutting lubricants and give your reasons why they are unnecessary.

(d) Describe, using diagrams where necessary, two methods of applying cutting lubricants on a lathe. (SUJB 1969)

19. Fixed rates for cutting speeds when milling cannot be exactly stated owing to the variations in conditions which are encountered. Discuss the variations encountered in plain milling. Give a simple formula to find the number of revolutions required for a given cutting speed in ft per min (m/min) and discuss the chip shape produced by a feed motion against the cutter and that known as down-cut or climb milling. (OLE 1969)

Forgework and Casting

1. The upsetting or jumping up of a length of metal may be achieved in a number of ways. Describe these processes and sketch three examples of work which require up-setting for their making.

C scrolls and S scrolls, with or without flared ends, form an important motif in wrought iron work. Sketch these scrolls and describe the making of an S scroll with flared ends. (OLE 1967)

2. What imperfections occur most commonly in castings produced in aluminium alloy?

Using the headings (a) pattern, (b) moulding, and (c) melt, explain the reasons for these faults and say how they could be avoided. (UCLES 1968)

3. Describe with suitable illustrations the processes of (a) jumping up, (b) drawing down, (c) swaging, (d) forge welding. Explain briefly a purpose to which each of these processes could be put. (WJEC 1968)

4. In choosing his method of producing a forged article the blacksmith is often guided by factors other than the final shape. Use examples, from your own experience if possible, to illustrate how these factors affect the design and manufacture of the finished work. (UCLES 1968)

5. Use a typical example from your own experience to describe the fire welding process giving particular attention to problems that may arise when this is carried out. Explain how the welding process differs from other similar methods of joining metals. (UCLES 1969)

6. Draw a cross-section through a Smith's Hearth to show:
  (*a*) the hearth bed,
  (*b*) the water-cooled tuyère.
  (*c*) the position of the fire in relation to the tuyère, and
  (*d*) the position in the fire at which you would place the metal to be heated.
  What checks would you make before lighting the forge fire?
  What is an oxidizing fire? Explain why an oxidizing fire is undesirable and the precautions you would take to prevent this developing.   (AEB 1969)

7. (*a*) Discuss the factors to be taken into account when deciding whether a casting requires:

      (i) a one or two-part pattern,
      (ii) a cored pattern.

  (*b*) When is it advisable to employ the odd-side method of moulding? Use examples from your own experience if possible to illustrate your answer.   (UCLES 1969)

Index